T0260275

Medical Data Analysis and Processing using Explainable Artificial Intelligence

The text presents concepts of explainable artificial intelligence (XAI) in solving real world biomedical and healthcare problems. It will serve as an ideal reference text for graduate students and academic researchers in diverse fields of engineering including electrical, electronics and communication, computer, and biomedical.

- Presents explainable artificial intelligence (XAI) based machine analytics and deep learning in medical science.
- Discusses explainable artificial intelligence (XA)I with the Internet of Medical Things (IoMT) for healthcare applications.
- Covers algorithms, tools, and frameworks for explainable artificial intelligence on medical data.
- Explores the concepts of natural language processing and explainable artificial intelligence (XAI) on medical data processing.
- Discusses machine learning and deep learning scalability models in healthcare systems.

This text focuses on data driven analysis and processing of advanced methods and techniques with the help of explainable artificial intelligence (XAI) algorithms. It covers machine learning, Internet of Things (IoT), and deep learning algorithms based on XAI techniques for medical data analysis and processing. The text will present different dimensions of XAI based computational intelligence applications. It will serve as an ideal reference text for graduate students and academic researchers in the fields of electrical engineering, electronics and communication engineering, computer engineering, and biomedical engineering.

Explainable AI (XAI) for Engineering Applications

Series Editors: Aditya Khamparia and Deepak Gupta

Explainable AI (XAI) has developed as a subfield of Artificial Inteligence, focussing on exposing complex AI models to humans in a systematic and interpretable manner. This area explores, discusses the steps and models involved in making intelligent decisions. This series will cover the working behavior and explains the ability of powerful algorithms such as neural networks, ensemble methods including random forests, and other similar algorithms to sacrifice transparency and explainability for power, performance, and accuracy in different engineering applications relates to the real world. Aimed at graduate students, academic researchers and professionals, the proposed series will focus key topics including XAI techniques for engineering applications, Explainable AI for Deep Neural Network Predictions, Explainable AI for Machine learning Predictions, XAI driven recommendation systems for Automobile and Manufacturing Industries, and Explainable AI for Autonomous Vehicles.

Deep Learning in Gaming and Animations: Principles and Applications
Vikas Chaudhary, Moolchand Sharma, Prerna Sharma, and Deevyankar Agarwal

Artificial Intelligence for Solar Photovoltaic Systems: Approaches, Methodologies and Technologies
Bhavnesh Kumar, Bhanu Pratap, and Vivek Shrivastava

Smart Distributed Embedded Systems for Healthcare Applications
Preeti Nagrath, Jafar A. Alzubi, Bhawna Singla, Joel J. P. C. Rodrigues, and A.K. Verma

Medical Data Analysis and Processing using Explainable Artificial Intelligence
Edited by Om Prakash Jena, Mrutyunjaya Panda, and Utku Kose

For more information about this series, please visit: https://www.routledge.com/Explainable-AI-XAI-for-Engineering-Applications/book-series/CRCEAIFEA

Medical Data Analysis and Processing using Explainable Artificial Intelligence

Edited by
Om Prakash Jena
Mrutyunjaya Panda
Utku Kose

CRC Press
Taylor & Francis Group
Boca Raton London New York

CRC Press is an imprint of the
Taylor & Francis Group, an **informa** business

Front cover image: Yurchanka Siarhei/Shutterstock

First edition published 2024
by CRC Press
2385 NW Executive Center Drive, Suite 320, Boca Raton. FL 33431

and by CRC Press
4 Park Square, Milton Park, Abingdon, Oxon, OX14 4RN

CRC Press is an imprint of Taylor & Francis Group, LLC

© 2024 selection and editorial matter, [Om Prakash Jena, Mrutyunjaya Panda and Utku Kose]; individual chapters, the contributors

ISBN: 978-1-032-19112-6 (hbk)
ISBN: 978-1-032-19113-3 (pbk)
ISBN: 978-1-003-25772-1 (ebk)

DOI: 10.1201/9781003257721

Typeset in Times
by codeMantra

Contents

Preface

For the widespread introduction of AI models into clinical practice, transparency and explainability are an absolute necessity because an incorrect prediction can have serious consequences. Researcher must be able to understand the underlying reasoning of AI models so that they can trust the predictions and be able to identify individual cases in which an AI model may give incorrect predictions. It is most likely that an interpretation that is too complex to interpret and understand would not have any practical impact.

When it relates to the application of artificial intelligence (AI) in healthcare, Explainability is among the most highly debated issues. While in some computational tasks, AI-driven systems have been shown to outshine humans, the absence of Explainability continues to spark criticism. Explainability, however is not a strictly technical challenge, but instead refers to a variety of medical, legal, ethical and social issues requiring thorough exploration. This book provides a detailed assessment of the role of explainability in medical AI and provides an ethical assessment of what explainability means for clinical practice to implement AI-driven tools.

This book highlights the latest developments in health care and medicine in the application of Explainable artificial intelligence and data science. It provides, along with the latest research results, a summary of the problems, threats, and opportunities in the field. It makes the evolving issues of digital health and explainable AI in health care and medicine available to a broad readership by addressing a wide variety of practical applications. A first step in creating a culture of openness and accountability in health care is the availability of explainable and interpretable models. As such, this book offers details on the theory and practice of computational models of public and personalized health knowledge for scientists, researchers, students, business practitioners, public health organizations, and NGOs.

There is a need to sensitize developers, healthcare professionals and policymakers to the complexities and limitations of ambiguous algorithms in medical AI and to promote multidisciplinary cooperation to move forward in order to ensure that medical AI lives up to its promises. Explainability needs to be approached from a technical point of view, both in terms of how it can be done and what is useful from a growth perspective. We defined informed consent, certification and acceptance as medical devices and accountability as key touchpoints for explainability when looking at the legal perspective. The value of understanding the interplay between human actors and medical AI is highlighted from both medical and patient viewpoints.

This integrate several aspects of Explainable AI based Computational Intelligence like Machine Learning and Deep Learning from diversified perspectives which describe the recent research trends and advanced topic in the field. The purpose of the book is to endow to different communities with their innovative advances in theory, analytical approaches, numerical simulation, statistical analysis, modelling, advanced deployment, case studies, analytical results, computational structuring and significance progress in the field of Machine learning and Deep Learning in Healthcare applications.

About the Editors

Dr. Om Prakash Jena is currently working as an Assistant Professor in the Department of Computer Science, Ravenshaw University, Cuttack, and Odisha, India. He has 11 years of teaching and research experience in the undergraduate and post-graduate levels. He has published several technical papers in international journals/conferences/edited book chapters of reputed publications. He is a member of IEEE, IETA, IAAC, IRED, IAENG, and WACAMLDS. His current research interest includes Database, Pattern Recognition, Cryptography, Network Security, Artificial Intelligence, Machine Learning, Soft Computing, Natural Language Processing, Data Science, Compiler Design, Data Analytics, and Machine Automation. He has many edited books, published by Wiley, CRC press, Taylor & Francis Bentham Publication into his credit and also the author of four textbooks under Kalyani Publisher. He also serve as a reviewer committee member and editor of many international journals.

Dr. Mrutyunjaya Panda holds a Ph.D degree in Computer Science from Berhampur University. He obtained his Master in Engineering from Sambalpur University, MBA in HRM from IGNOU, New Delhi, and Bachelor in Engineering from Utkal University in 2002, 2009, 1997 respectively. He is having more than 20 years of teaching and research experience. He is presently working as Reader in P.G. Department of Computer Science and Applications, Utkal University, Bhubaneswar, Odisha, India. He is a member of MIR Labs (USA), KES (Australia), IAENG (Hong Kong), ACEEE(I), IETE(I), CSI(I), ISTE(I). He has published about 70 papers in International and national journals and conferences. He has also published 7 book chapters to his credit. He has 2 text books and 3 edited books to his credit. He is a program committee member of various international conferences. He is acting as a reviewer of various international journals and conferences of repute. He is an Associate Editor of IJCINI Journal, IGI Global, USA and an Editorial board member of IJKESDP Journal of Inderscience, UK. He is also a Special issue Editor of International Journal of Computational Intelligence Studies (IJCIStudies), Inderscience, UK. His active area of research includes Data Mining, Image processing, Intrusion detection and prevention. Social networking, Mobile

Communication, wireless sensor networks, Natural language processing, Internet of Things, Text Mining etc.

Dr. Utku Kose received the B.S. degree in 2008 from computer education of Gazi University, Turkey as a faculty valedictorian. He received M.S. degree in 2010 from Afyon Kocatepe University, Turkey in the field of computer and D.S. / Ph. D. degree in 2017 from Selcuk University, Turkey in the field of computer engineering. Between 2009 and 2011, he has worked as a Research Assistant in Afyon Kocatepe University. Following, he has also worked as a Lecturer and Vocational School - Vice Director in Afyon Kocatepe University between 2011 and 2012, as a Lecturer and Research Center Director in Usak University between 2012 and 2017, and as an Assistant Professor in Suleyman Demirel University between 2017 and 2019. Currently, he is an Associate Professor in Suleyman Demirel University, Turkey. He has more than 100 publications including articles, authored and edited books, proceedings, and reports. He is also in editorial boards of many scientific journals and serves as one of the editors of the Biomedical and Robotics Healthcare book series by CRC Press. His research interest includes artificial intelligence, machine ethics, artificial intelligence safety, optimization, the chaos theory, distance education, e-learning, computer education, and computer science.

List of Contributors

Rudrajit Choudhuri
Department of CSE
St. Thomas College of Engineering and
    Technology
Kolkata, India

Sunanda Das
Department of Computer Science
    Engineering
Jain University
Bangalore, India

M. Durgadevi
Department of Computer Science and
    Engineering
College of Engineering and Technology,
    SRM Institute of Science and
    Technology, Vadapalani Campus
Chennai, India

Arkaprovo Ghosal
Department of Chemical Engineering
Birla Institute of Technology & Science
Pilani, India

Gousia Habib
Department of Computer Science
    Engineering
National Institute of Technology
    Srinagar
Srinagar, India

Amiya Halder
Department of CSE
St. Thomas College of Engineering and
    Technology
Kolkata, India

S. Karthika
Department of Computer Science and
    Engineering
College of Engineering and Technology,
    SRM Institute of Science and
    Technology, Vadapalani Campus
Chennai, India

D. Klyushin
Department of Cybernetics
Taras Shevchenko National University
    of Kyiv
Kyiv, Ukraine

Sumalatha Lingamgunta
School of Computer Science and
    Engineering
University College of Engineering,
    JNTUK
Kakinada, India

Tanmaya Mahapatra
Department of Computer Science and
    Information Systems
Birla Institute of Technology & Science
Pilani, India

Swathi Jamjala Narayanan
School of Computer Science and
    Engineering
School of Computer Science and
    Engineering, Vellore Institute of
    Technology
Vellore, India

Bishwajeet Kumar Pandey
Department of Computer Science
    Engineering
Jain University
Bangalore, India

Smruti Sudha Pattnaik
Department of Gynae Oncology
AHPGIC, Cuttack, Odisha

Boominathan Perumal
School of Computer Science and
    Engineering
School of Computer Science and
    Engineering, Vellore Institute of
    Technology
Vellore, India

Shaima Qureshi
School of Computer Science and
    Engineering
National Institute of Technology
    Srinagar
Srinagar, India

Sangeetha Saman
School of Computer Science and
    Engineering, Vellore Institute of
    Technology
Vellore, India

Tanvir Habib Sardar
Department of Computer Science
    Engineering
GITAM University
Bangalore, India

Apurba Sarkar
Department of CST
Indian Institute of Engineering Science
    and Technology
Howrah, India

Pravat Kumar Sarangi
Department of Statistics,
    Ravenshaw University
Cuttack, Odisha

S. Siva Sathya
Department of Computer Science
Pondicherry University
Kalapet, Pondicherry

Priyanka Sharma
Department of Computer Science
Swami Keshvanand Institute of
    Technology, Management &
    Gramothan
Jaipur, India

Rohan Singh
Department of Chemical Engineering
Birla Institute of Technology & Science
Pilani, India

Sarthak Singh
Department of Electrical & Electronics
    Engineering & Department of
    Physics
Birla Institute of Technology & Science
Pilani, India

S. Lourdumarie Sophie
Department of Computer Science
Pondicherry University
Kalapet, Pondicherry

Prafulla Kumar Swain
Department of Statistics
Utkal University,
Bhubaneswar, Odisha

Manas Ranjan Tripathy
Department of Statistics, Ravenshaw
    University
Cuttack, Odisha

A. Urazovskyi
Department of Cybernetics
Taras Shevchenko National University
    of Kyiv
Kyiv, Ukraine

Manjula Devarakonda Venkata
Department of CSE
Pragati Engineering College
Surampalem, India

1 Explainable AI (XAI) Concepts and Theory

Tanvir Habib Sardar
GITAM University

Sunanda Das and Bishwajeet Kumar Pandey
Jain University

1.1 INTRODUCTION

The recent development of cutting-edge technologies, paradigms, and architectures enables access and processing of different types and volumes of data [1]. This makes the datasets consist of hundreds and thousands of inputs that map to a few probabilistic decisions. As the human mind can work on only a few inputs and their interrelation analysis to contribute to a set of probabilistic decisions, a new automated model was required to deal efficiently with the countless inputs with complex interrelation capacity to derive proper decisions [2]. Artificial intelligence (AI) is the technology that provides this automated job by modeling the decision-making process using suitable techniques. AI is an emerging and impactful technology domain that is designed to solve problems and help humans by enabling human-intelligence-emulated machines to execute automated jobs. The usage of AI in the research and IT industry comes with incentives as the AI generates the opportunity for decreased production cost while lessening the risk factors, quality decision-making process, enhancing productivity quantity, and even production of new services and products.

AI is heavily built-up on machine learning (ML) techniques and algorithms as well as ML-specific domains, especially deep learning (DL). However, the non-ML techniques such as logical reasoning, behavior-based methods, statistical derivations, and searching methods are also provided enough support in the development of the AI domain. ML is a broad technology domain and is considered the forthcoming algorithmic and automated solution generator for fields such as recommender systems for users of a commodity [3], diagnosis of diseases by implicit data-driven model, self-governing transportation model provider, etc. The DL techniques have enabled ML further by efficient support in fields where ML algorithms without DL perform poorly such as image recognition and speech processing. ML and DL, being subset of broad AI techniques, enable AI in achieving success in efficiently dealing with real-world high-dimensional datasets in a nonlinear space and a hierarchically nested style to settle down between probabilistic decision sets. Along with DL, other complex techniques of AI like support vector machine (SVM), random forests (RF), and complex classifiers, such as regressions, kernel machines, decision trees, etc., generated a quite high dividend for successful AI applications.

DOI: 10.1201/9781003257721-1

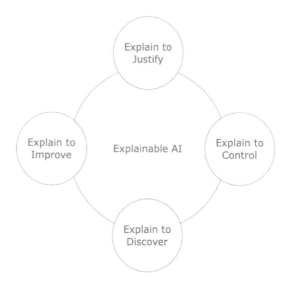

FIGURE 1.1   The explanations provided by XAI systems.

However, these complex techniques of AI which deal successfully with high-dimensional data come with the trade-off of transparency issues and create a "black box" model [4]. These "black box" models don't provide suitable reasoning for a particular decision answered by the AI system. It is left to the user either to take the decision or to leave it. This lack of explainability of "black box" AI models becomes non-deployable to many domains such as financial sectors, public judgment government offices, and health sectors until the decisions are properly explainable [5,6]. This is because the risk of lying to a wrong decision of a non-transparent "black box" AI model would harm more than the benefits obtained by it [7]. To address this non-transparency issue, the explainable AI (XAI) field has emerged [8]. The XAI System provides an explanation to a novice user for an AI system regarding the justification of the working mechanism, the control techniques, and explainability to discover and improve the decision-making process of an AI system. Figure 1.1 shows the explainability offered by an XAI for an AI model. Figure 1.2 is a self-descriptive depiction that differentiates the major reasons behind the separation of XAI and AI.

1.2   FORMAL DEFINITIONS OF EXPLAINABLE ARTIFICIAL INTELLIGENCE

In simple terms, we can define the EAI as a technique to evaluate the final decision of an AI system based on the decisions of the internal parts. The mapping of the final decision with the decision made by internal parts of an AI system provides logical rationality to trust the outcome of the AI system [9]. In general, the AI community is agreed that the XAI should not be a "black box." An AI system is interpretable if the system inputs are mathematically mapped to the output [9]. The "interpretability"

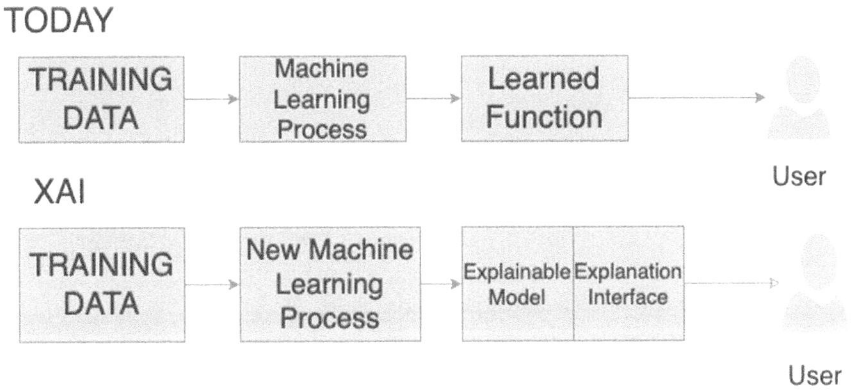

TODAY

TRAINING DATA → Machine Learning Process → Learned Function → User

XAI

TRAINING DATA → New Machine Learning Process → Explainable Model | Explanation Interface → User

FIGURE 1.2 AI vs. explainable AI (Source: DARPA).

term is mostly used by the ML community, and the "exchangeability" term is used by AI. However, these two terms are used often interchangeably [10].

The XAI focus on the following [11]:

- Transparency: The output decisions should be clearly explained in the format and language known to the users.
- Causality: A model derived from data should provide the understanding of not only inferences but also the basic phenomena.
- Bias: The training data or objective function-related shortcomings should not provide the model with a biased view of the world.
- Fairness: The decisions made by the AI system should be validated with fairness constraints.
- Safety: It is related to obtaining confidence in the reliability of an AI system, without deriving explanatory conclusions.

1.3 THE WORKING MECHANISM OF EXPLAINABLE ARTIFICIAL INTELLIGENCE: HOW EXPLAINABLE ARTIFICIAL INTELLIGENCE GENERATES EXPLANATIONS

AI models provide explanations using the (1) human brain-like facilities such as logical reasoning and, (2) scientific techniques of inquiry such as modeling based on feature similarity, Bayesian probabilistic methods, and queries. However, it is also challenging to choose a particular technique for visualization of the derived AI model's explanation. Human reasoning processes are usually copied to different AI and XAI systems. Modern XAIs usually are created by a constructive accumulation of interpretable data structures, using logical reasoning and easily comprehensible visualization techniques. A coherent and collaborative solution of a suitable explanation of an XAI model is achieved using many of such logical reasoning-based approaches and their interrelations. A basic explainable model for AI and its working mechanism is shown in Figure 1.3.

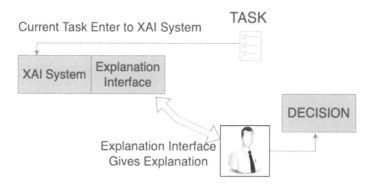

FIGURE 1.3   The explainable model of AI: XAI.

The following are the concepts in the logical reasoning used intensively in AI techniques:

- **Inductive reasoning**: Opposite to deductive reasoning, it is a bottom-up reasoning technique where logical conclusions are derived from the specific evidence to the general. The Bayes theorem-based models are used by XAI to infer prior and posterior probabilistic decisions of an AI model based on previously observed data [12].
- **Analogical reasoning**: The human brain performs analogical reasoning, which provides us with similarity modeling to provide an understanding of why a few objects are similar/dissimilar to each other. Likewise, many AI techniques use similarity modeling using unsupervised grouping (like clustering [13]), supervised probabilistic decisive outcome modeling (like classification [14], nearest neighbor [15]), and reduction of data by removing irrelevant dimensions (like principal component analysis [16].
- **Causal attribution**: It is a method to decide the reasons behind the behavior of an entity. Attributions are prepared for reasons which are analyzed by the human brain. In AI, the use of causal attribution assists developers to discover the possible reasons for the similarity deduction of objects and their subsequent grouping.
- **Contrastive explanations and counterfactual reasoning**: Human brain can comprehend a data model or even visualize up to some extent as per its capacity for remembrance and interpretation using contrast and differences in data. Counterfactual reasoning enables the human brain to analyze or visualize data by flipping among different suitable options it learned earlier. AI systems, on the other hand, use plain charts to display raw data, line charts to depict temporal data, trees, and graphs for the depiction of structured and hierarchical data, etc.

1.4   HOW HUMANS REASON (WITH ERRORS)

The last section has explained how humans think with logical reasoning and how AI and XAI emulate it. However, humans also employ heuristic reasoning to come to a decision quickly but with a quite higher rate of decision errors. The dual-process model [17] of cognitive psychology best describes this.

1.4.1 DUAL-PROCESS MODEL

This model provides an effective way for diagnostic reasoning. This model groups two systems into the fast and slow learning process, respectively [17].

System 1: It heuristically thinks to come to a decision, making this process fast and low in effort. Generally, inductive reasoning is employed in heuristically learning where the decision is taken based on the comparative similarity of prior observations. This model is good for experienced users as the prior knowledge facilitates pattern matching. However, novice users get into a cognitive bias toward this system.

The main reason for errors in system 1 is due to heuristic biases of oversimplification and overconfidence of the user [18].

System 2: The decision is evaluated based on logical reasoning, making this process slow and high in the effort. This model requires experienced users to design mathematical reasoning with logic and semantics. System 1 thinking can interfere with system 2 as system 2 users as an alternative to logical reasoning, may use bounded rationality [19] or prospect theory [20].

The dual-process model not only describes the process of good decisions and their rationality but also describes the reason behind wrong or suboptimal decisions [21].

The main reason for errors in system 2 is due to the use of a wrongly calibrated tool or poor understanding of the domain [22, 23].

1.4.2 FORWARD AND BACKWARD REASONING

The system 1 process can interfere with system 2 processes and end up with a wrong decision [24]. Patel et al. [23–25] have observed that expert doctors use a data-driven (e.g. lab tests) and forward-oriented reasoning strategy which leads to a decisive diagnosis. On the other hand, the novice doctor's hypothesis-driven and backward-oriented reasoning strategy leads to a wrong diagnosis. This happens due to little experience and validation bias of novice doctors [26]. A properly designed XAI-based system can mitigate this problem.

1.5 HOW EXPLAINABLE ARTIFICIAL INTELLIGENCE SUPPORT REASON AND SOLVE HUMAN ERROR ISSUE

As mentioned above, the human thinking process leads to error. Human cognitive biases are addressed and solved by XAI systems.

1.5.1 MITIGATE REPRESENTATIVENESS BIAS

The occurrence of representative bias is the result of the wrong classification of a prior case as the present case. Lack of experience and poor observation of salient features are the key cause of it. This bias is mitigated by keeping a prototype set that represents similarity (and dissimilarity) ranked order and its subsequent decision value. Each case goes through a similarity checking using the prototype stack and gets to a correct decision.

1.5.2 MITIGATE AVAILABILITY BIAS

The availability bias happens to a lack of knowledge regarding the rate of occurrence of a particular outcome. The solution is achieved by keeping track of prior probability taken from the training datasets [27].

1.5.3 MITIGATE ANCHORING BIAS

This bias occurs from a skewed perception of the user on a decision for a certain anchor. This skewed perception is a barrier to discovering another decision. This problem can be mitigated by showing how the findings of input features can be mapped to multiple decisions [18].

1.5.4 MITIGATE CONFIRMATION BIAS

This bias is early confirmation of a decision that happens due to overconfidence or ignoring some evidence. The backward-driven reasoning should be avoided to prevent this bias. The evidence-based findings are properly analyzed by XAI before building a hypothesis to prevent and mitigate confirmation bias.

1.6 APPLICATIONS AND IMPACT AREAS OF EXPLAINABLE ARTIFICIAL INTELLIGENCE

Although XAI is a comparatively new area of research and development, it has already provided many techniques and been applied to many domain areas. These different domain areas generated a wide range of impacts on technology, business, and research [28]. In these domain-based applications, a companion technique is used to generate the explanation from the so-called black box AI models. These companion techniques generate syntax and semantics in human comprehensible format by extracting the correlational features from complex and multi-staged learning-based AI systems. One of the initial applications of the XAI was focused on obtaining the explanations of DL image classification. The explanation is provided in terms of heat maps. These heat maps represent the gaps in different probability distributions among the AI model and a wrong decision [29]. Nevertheless, this field of image recognition is very dynamic in terms of the employment of different techniques, and sometimes resolute with issues and features specific to the field. This makes it very difficult to obtain a fully fledged and clear understanding of this domain.

One major issue with the XAI is that the literature on XAI has mainly focused on problems of non-explained solutions of AI models. While these non-explained AI models can be reviewed in-depth, in this discussion, we focus on the advantages which can be taken out from explainability. Simply put, we will not discuss inadequate or deficient natures of the applications, but rather focus on novel solutions presented by the XAI.

1.6.1 THREAT DETECTION

One of the major focuses of the information technology security domain is to detect the threat and triage it effectively. The subdomains of this domain such as antivirus tools, automated code analysis, and network traffic monitoring for intrusion detection and prevention are also vastly researched. Although many relevant techniques are developed, an all-weather fully automated system of threat detection and triage is still not developed due to the issue of non-prevention of false-positive cases. Some techniques filter out all legit network traffic while ignoring the actual threats and in turn significantly reducing the amount of information-requiring analysis [30]. A major issue still lies in the opaque model of these threat detectors. An XAI model that explains the user behaviors, network traffic sources, and anomalies of these threat detectors would massively improve the quality of the true positives and employ trust in these threat detector AI models.

1.6.2 OBJECT DETECTION

AI technique of Artificial Neural Networks (ANNs)-based architectures such as YOLO trained on voluminous big data is used to generate a portfolio. This portfolio is then used for object detection. A large number of parameters of ANN such as the number of inner layers, loss function characteristics, features of optimizers and regularizers, filters, etc. make the explainability of the mechanism behind object detection AI difficult. Thus, the making of the explainability is limited to the data feature feeding-based descriptions, saliency map model [31], prototype generation [32], or example-based modeling [33]. For sensitive industry-specific object detection, AIs (e.g. object detection in railway tracks) require a human-rational founded explanation to achieve certified trust in the AI system [34].

1.6.3 ADVERSARIAL ML PREVENTION

A ML learning algorithm is built based on the learning data. In adversarial ML, this learning process is intentionally manipulated by providing erroneous data in the learning phase, such that the ML process generates error outcomes [35]. In case no prior AI learning model exists, such for cases of big data domains, it becomes difficult to detect such manipulations. The techniques to solve these manipulations are proposed in some recent works [36]. Many of these proposed works employ a neural sub-network to detect malicious data [37]. XAI has a great scope in this domain as effective detection or prevention of malicious training phase would enhance the trust in ML systems [38].

1.6.4 OPEN SOURCE INTELLIGENCE

In the field of Open Source Intelligence (OSI), an AI system is used only for information retrieval from the open-source data repositories [39]. The issues reported concerning OSI are regarding the amount and availability of open-source data, the genuineness of the data, the aggregation of open source data and the consequences, and the background of the data and language, etc. These issues are specially considered for the adversarial attack on OSI-based AI [40]. An XAI system can deliver a detailed description of detecting these adversarial attacks. XAI can also feed other OSI systems the adversarial attack launch-related information, making them give them prior knowledge in dealing with them. Although all OSI false data is not generated due to adversarial effects. Sometimes during event reporting and generating OSI, some data items become inaccurate, misleading, or unknown or the facts deviations happen very frequently. This makes the data generated false in the OSI-based AI systems as well. An XAI can provide estimated values of false information inputted by the system and their effect on the outcome, making the AI system more trustable.

1.6.5 AUTOMATED MEDICAL DIAGNOSIS

In recent years, many works are reported that deal with designing ML-based AI models to provide an automated medical diagnosis. In these AI systems, doctors act as an input provider to the system. The inputs are generally data from different tests and health symptoms. The AI system provides the output in terms of diagnosis of a disease or treatment for the disease or both. These outputs are reviewed by the doctors and then the doctors provide feedback to the system so the AI system can be more accurate in diagnosis and treatment suggestions [41]. An XAI system can provide an in-depth analysis of each part of these medical diagnosis AI systems so that the outcome predictions of diseases are perfect and trustworthy.

1.6.6 AUTONOMOUS VEHICLES

DL-based AI models are being designed and tested globally for driverless autonomous vehicle design. An XAI system can explain the working of these cars in detail and can be very useful for certain situations. For example, when an accident happens, an XAI can provide the reasons behind the sensor and learning errors caused by the accident. This will further enhance the driving quality and make the automated vehicles safer [42].

1.7 BENEFITS OF EXPLAINABLE ARTIFICIAL INTELLIGENCE

- **Error Reduction:** The domains which are sensitive to decisions and their implications such as Medicine, Finance, Legal, etc., are extremely pretentious for erroneous calculations.
- **Model biasing Reduction:** Many research pieces of evidence suggest that AI models are biased toward certain processes or features. An XAI model can decrease the influence of these unfair forecasts reason by explanation-based decision-making.
- **Accountability and Answerability:** |||As AI systems usually generate some percentage of error, allowing an individual who can be accountable and answerable for AI errors can mark the whole arrangement additional competence.

Reducing Impact of Model Biasing Responsibility and Accountability Governance Code Confidence Code Compliance

FIGURE 1.4 Benefits of XAI.

- **Confidence in Model:** A successful AI model boosts the confidence of its users. Critical designs such as autonomous vehicles, diagnosis of medical diseases, the finance decisions by banks and insurance agencies, etc., requires high confidence in the AI system to obtain the optimal solution.
- **Code Compliance:** The authorities who develop AI systems are now under pressure to explain their AI model for better understanding for their clients.

The pictorial depiction of the benefits of XAI systems is provided in Figure 1.4.

1.8 RESEARCH CHALLENGES OF EXPLAINABLE ARTIFICIAL INTELLIGENCE

The AI in the beginning was re-traceable, interpretable, and understandable by humans. XAI interpretation and XAI systems evaluation are technical challenges faced by the XAI research community. The right to be forgotten is another legal challenge of XAI because every individual wants certain data to be deleted so that third parties cannot trace them. Demand for identical human understanding and machine explanation is another practical challenge in front of XAI [43]. There is a high volume of current activity going on in the research areas of XAI either on the research side or in the application of XAI in industrial development. It is a widely accepted truth that scientists should not only keep the facts but also appropriately describe them [43].

Inside an explanation framework, the system takes input from the current task and a recommendation, decision, or action created by an explainable model and that goes to an explainable interface. Humans make decisions based on the explanation they get from the interface [44]. To create an explainable model, researchers used a technique called model induction. Model induction is a methodology used to infer an explainable model from any model as a black box [44].

1.9 USE CASES OF EXPLAINABLE ARTIFICIAL INTELLIGENCE

Most of the XAI solutions that exist in the market are crafted by the existing organization. Although some open-source solutions have existed in the market such as Lime, DeepSHAP, and SHAP. The use cases of XAI are slowly penetrating slowing in many sectors. Some of the examples of XAI use cases are provided below:

- E-commerce customer retention: With the AI reasoning technique, an XAI can deliberately predict the group of customers who would retain in an E-commerce website.
- Insurance claim management: Poor customer feedback is generated if a claim is made based on poor reasoning. Thus, using XAI if the system explains the claim result to the customer then it would improve the satisfaction of the customers.
- Pricing of products: The XAI can be used to forecast a logical reasoning-based explanation of certain product pricing. For example, an XAI can explain to customers why certain health insurance costs a certain amount.
- Banking sector: A good design XAI can provide a detailed description of fraud detection, customer engagement, pricing, quality improvement of Robo-advisors, payment exceptions, etc.

The following two use case domains of XAI impact areas: Social media and health-care are elaborated in the following subsections. These two areas would provide us with a good understanding of XAI's usefulness and importance.

1.9.1   USE CASE OF EXPLAINABLE ARTIFICIAL INTELLIGENCE: SOCIAL MEDIA

COVID-19 creates new trends for people dependent on restaurants for their food. Earlier, people wanted to spend more time at the dining table of the restaurant. Now, they prefer to eat at home so they are expecting food delivery on their doorsteps. The XAI method is in use to predict clients' sentiments in the Food Delivery Service (FDS) areas [45]. Customer sentiment must be observed in social media sources such as blog posts, feedback, surveys, comments, reviews, or tweets that refer to the food quality, service providers, waiting time, and other information [46]. FDS organizations must know their customers and always differentiate positive comments as compliments and negative comments as complaints [47]. The negative sentiments are further classified into various complaint categories using topic modeling [48]. In [49], research data was sampled for their proposed experiment from the Foody.vn and diadiemanuong.com websites. At the stage of the beginning application of ML, the sampled information is preprocessed, classified, and labeled as shown in Figure 1.5. Training, validation, and test data are the three ways of sampling data. The training dataset is taken under consideration during the ML processing and is used to manage the parameters. The validation dataset is a dataset of illustration used as a hyper parameter of a classifier.

1.9.2   USE CASE OF EXPLAINABLE ARTIFICIAL INTELLIGENCE: HEALTHCARE

The term XAI was found for the first time in a paper [50]. Nowadays, embedded human-AI-based technology in the medical domain is now becoming more concern for research. Though the embedding of computer systems with AI systems is still complex, research is still going on for finding the best use with simpler complexity.

Advancement in the field of artificial intelligence [51] makes human beings more prone to adopt intelligent systems in their daily life to the healthcare system.

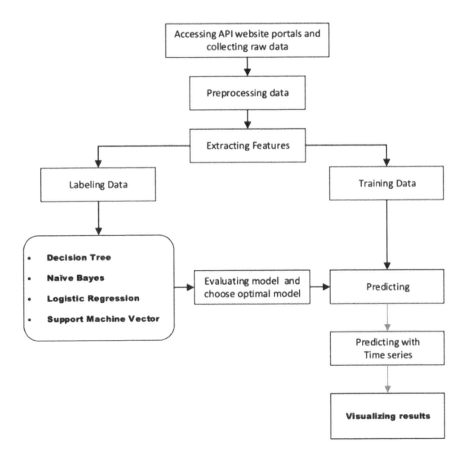

FIGURE 1.5   An overview of the research model in [49].

Recently, based on massive demands, a new field is introduced EAI, to fulfill all the requirements. EAI follows more transparency and ethical [52] principles in AI which becomes more trustworthy to adopt. Already many subdomains of the medical field such as neuro-science, critical disease identification like COVID-19, cancer prediction, and genomic studies are taking the advantage of proper use of EAI [53–56].

The use of AI and machine learning-based techniques in healthcare are practically trying to be implemented in many developed countries to enhance the intensive care and monitoring activities in hospitals. This advancement is not only economical but also can be a better-qualified solution in medical diagnosis for accurate prediction and disease detection. Implementation of AI technologies in the healthcare system is to convert the traditional healthcare systems to automated AI-based healthcare systems with reducing the risk of diseases or threats. Now AI-based technologies are being implemented in the medical industry like surveys of drug discovery, decision-making for proper medication, investigations for proper clinical diagnosis, AI-based surgery, and radiology.

1.9.2.1 Explainable Artificial Intelligence in Healthcare for Decision-Making

The aim of XAI systems in health care is to give more explanations to medical experts for the AI decision-making system in understandable terms. Explanations of a system not only give clear ideas but also help the users to make the correct decisions ethically [57]. The ML-based system with XAI in healthcare takes a major role in making decisions among pneumonia and asthma patients who are admitted to the hospital based on lower risk while there are limitations of beds in hospitals. A novel XAI approach [58] in addition to an incremental decision support system has shown the novelty of XAI for medical diagnosis based on decision trees. This helps medical experts each inform the other and come to a decision together. Their system can guide physicians in determining which test results are most useful given existing data.

1.9.2.2 Explainable Artificial Intelligence in Healthcare for Medicine

The application of AI has proven a major impact in all areas of healthcare from diagnostics to treatment. The use of XAI in medicine is to help medical professionals to understand the machine-based decisions for several disease cases of patients. The explainability of AI tools has already taken the position in many sectors based on the trust of medical professionals due to its transparency, trustworthiness, and explainable behavior. Sometimes some medical terms can't be understood by patients because of their complexity. Then the use of XAI makes this possible more simply and easily.

It is being observed that practically some systems based on AI which are designed with high expectations, make us wrong by producing false results for studying medicine in healthcare [59]. Then the demand automatically comes to design such a system with proper information to justify correctly the applicability of medicines and diagnosis rather than a simple prediction [60]. Thus, explainability and transparency of XAI in medicine have become the new research area to give more concerns [61].

In paper [62], an XAI-based novel method is proposed to explain the classification of cardiac pathology to understand the heart condition. HistoMapr-Breast, an XAI-based software, shows its effectiveness for the biopsies of breast cancer [63]. Some researchers have introduced [64] a model which is capable of intermediate learning during processing and able to give an explainable correct report where the input data is a combination of text and images.

1.9.2.3 Explainable Artificial Intelligence in Healthcare for Diagnosis

The potentiality of XAI in medical AI applications has been explored in a few research papers. It is observed that the XAI outperforms well for the diagnosis of patient disease, whereas the black-box nature of DL methods becomes a failure. When the DL models having millions of parameters in them are unable to give proper explanations to the medical experts, then XAI models are the only options to choose. In a research paper [65], an XAI model is proposed for allergy diagnosis. Some ML techniques are applied by using k-fold cross-validation. An IF-THEN rule-based explanation is extracted based on a random forest. A clear explanation of the perspective view for the medical expert is mentioned for the diagnostic predictions. Paper [66] shows an XAI framework with detailed information on cluster results for treating breast cancer therapies. An XAI-based framework using logistic regression (LR), decision tree (DT), and KNN for hepatitis patients is presented in [67] to help medical practitioners. A research paper [68] introduces us to a CNN-based model with the XAI method for chronic wound classification. In [69], the authors have proposed an AI model for glioblastoma multiform (GBM) classification. In addition to explainability, they use LIME XAI methods to compute the local feature relevance to samples in the test set. An ensemble clustering method extended with the XAI model for brain injury diagnostic analysis is presented in [70] to give proper knowledge to medical experts. In [71], researchers proposed a CNN-based model for analyzing chest X-ray (CXR) images of COVID patients. Till now many researchers have shown the uses of XAI along with AI-based models in practical domains with high accuracy.

1.9.2.4 Future Opportunities for Explainable Artificial Intelligence in Healthcare

The use of ML and AI has become highly potential in the application of a variety of tasks in medicine. In some cases, it has been seen that in some applications fewer explanations and improper information are problematic to deal with in real life. The demand and use of AI systems provide the base of XAI as Clinical Decision Support Systems (CDSSs). These systems can lead to medical practitioners for clinical decision-making and in some cases life-saving decisions. In the future, XAI can play a major role in healthcare where providing diagnosis and treatment suggestions is itself a big challenge. The rapid advancement of AI for image analysis can be the future of auto of several radiology or pathology images. Speech recognition is already being applied to patient communication and XAI in near future can take major areas in healthcare for diagnosis as well as surgery. DL involves lots of dramatic changes in healthcare, including diagnosis and surgery. The accuracy of deep-learning-based diagnosis is surprisingly helpful to human medical experts. Though there are certain limits to deep-learning-based techniques for practical deployment in medicine. In the interdisciplinary health care system, the success depends not only on the AI-based techniques but also on the explainability of the AI model. Before acceptance and implementation of XAI, a detailed explanation is required from the medical experts. Thus, the research on XAI is the motivation to survey XAI in healthcare.

1.10 LIMITATIONS OF EXPLAINABLE ARTIFICIAL INTELLIGENCE

The most prominent limitation of XAI methods is that these XAI methods deal with the estimates of black-box models and that makes it very challenging to comprehend the internal working of those models. For example, an AI with ML implementation of a global DT where each tree can be used to explain the mechanism of a random forest. A random forest algorithmic model consists of dozens of separate DTs. Every decision tree is trained with many of the features and data obtained from the dataset. This is quite a difficult explanation for this AI black box. Along with that, to make the explanation more interpretable some more techniques can be employed. For example, the above DT's interpretability can be enhanced by generating a smaller version of the DT and keeping only a few variables into consideration. But, this would in turn provide just an approximation for the model's functioning making a large part of the complexity not attained or accounted for in the explanation. This phenomenon of limited explainability is termed an AI black box as "ersatz understanding" by [72–77].

Another problem with explainability lies with the fact that most XAI techniques are developed using linear models which can misrepresent black box AI models built with highly nonlinearity [6]. Although many nonlinear explainability methods are already developed (e.g., decision trees), the explanations are usually quite simple and sometimes considered oversimplification as compared to the nonlinear black-box models of AI. These explanations, thus, required to be interpreted with care and caution.

1.11 CONCLUSION

The XAI is an approach to explain the AI's internal working mechanism in a layman's language and terms. An AI model's merit and demerits are explained by XAI. The theory and concepts behind the XAI model are explained in this chapter. This chapter first summarizes the definitions of XAI in formal terms followed by the working mechanism of XAI used for AI model's explanation deduction. The reasoning process of a human brain is briefed and then the XAI's capacity in solving human error in thinking process is explained. The applications and benefits of using XAI are then provided. This chapter also provides the research challenges in XAI and in detailed use cases of XAIs in different domains. This chapter also provided the limitations of XAIs.

REFERENCES

[1] Sardar, T.H. and Ansari, Z.. 2022. "Distributed Big Data Clustering using MapReduce-based Fuzzy C-Medoids,"*Journal of the Institution of Engineers (India) Series* B103: 73–82. 10.1007/s40031-021-00647-w.

[2] Hagras, Hani. 2018. "Toward human-understandable, explainable AI." *Computer* 51(9): 28–36.

[3] Makridakis, S. 2017. "The forthcoming artificial intelligence (AI) revolution: Its impact on society and firms," *Futures* 90: 46–60.

[4] Nott, G. (2017). "Explainable artificial intelligence: Cracking Open the Black Box of AI," Computerworld. www.computerworld.com.au/article/617359/explainable-artificial-intelligence-cracking-open-black-box-ai.

[5] Andreas, H., Chris, B., Constantinos, S.P., and Douglas, B.K. 2017. "What do we need to build explainable ai systems for the medical domain," arXiv preprint arXiv:1712.09923.

[6] Cynthia, R. 2019. "Stop explaining black box machine learning models for high stakes decisions and use interpretable models instead," *Nature Machine Intelligence* 1(5): 206–215.

[7] "Artificial Intelligence and Machine Learning in Financial Services," report, Financial Stability Board, 1 November 2017; www.fsb.org/wp-content /uploads/P011117.pdf.

[8] Xu, F., Uszkoreit, H., Du, Y., Fan, W., Zhao, D., and Zhu, J. 2019. "Explainable AI: A brief survey on history, research areas, approaches and challenges." In *CCF International Conference on Natural Language Processing and Chinese Computing*, Springer, 563–574.

[9] Derek, D., Sarah, S., and Tarek, R.B. 2017. "What does explainable AI really mean? A new conceptualization of perspectives," arXiv preprint arXiv:1710.00794, 2017.

[10] Amina, A. and Mohammed, B. 2018. "Peeking inside the black-box: A survey on Explainable Artificial Intelligence (XAI)," *IEEE Access* 6: 52138–52160.

[11] Wierzynski, C. 2018. "The Challenges and Opportunities of Explainable AI," Intel. com. https://ai.intel.com/the-challenges-and-opportunities-of-explainable-ai/.

[12] Abdul, A., Vermeulen, J., Wang, D., Lim, B. Y., and Kankanhalli, M. 2018. "Trends and trajectories for explainable, accountable and intelligible systems: An HCI Research Agenda." In *Proceedings of the SIGCHI Conference on Human Factors in Computing Systems. CHI'18*, Montreal.

[13] MacQueen, J. 1967. "Some methods for classification and analysis of multivariate observations," *Proceedings of the Fifth Berkeley Symposium on Mathematical Statistics and Probability* 1(14): 281–297.

[14] Cortes, C. and Vapnik, V. 1995. "Support-vector networks," *Machine Learning* 20(3): 273–297.

[15] Altman, N.S. 1992. "An introduction to kernel and nearest-neighbor nonparametric regression," *The American Statistician* 46(3): 175–185.

[16] Hotelling, H. 1933. "Analysis of a complex of statistical variables into principal components," *Journal of Educational Psychology* 24(6): 417.

[17] Kahneman, D. and Egan, P. 2011. *Thinking, Fast and Slow.* New York: Farrar, Straus and Giroux.

[18] Lighthall, G.K. and Vazquez-Guillamet, C. 2015. "Understanding decision-making in critical care," *Clinical Medicine & Research* 13(3–4): 156–168. doi: 10.3121/ cmr.2015.1289.

[19] Silveira, M.S., de Souza, C.S., and Barbosa, S.D.J. 2001. "Semiotic engineering contributions for designing online help systems," In *Proceedings of the* 19th *Annual International Conference on Computer Documentation (SIGDOC'01).* ACM, New York, NY, USA, 31–38.

[20] Tversky, A. and Kahneman, D. 1992. "Advances in prospect theory: Cumulative representation of uncertainty," *Journal of Risk and Uncertainty* 5(4): 297–323.

[21] Baron, J. 2000. *Thinking and Deciding.* New York: Cambridge University Press.

[22] Croskerry, P. 2009. "Clinical cognition and diagnostic error: Applications of a dual process model of reasoning," *Advances in Health Sciences Education* 14(1): 27–35.

[23] Patel, V.L., Arocha, J.F., and Zhang, J. 2005. "Thinking and reasoning in medicine," *The Cambridge Handbook of Thinking and Reasoning* 14: 727–750.

[24] Croskerry, P. 2009. "A universal model of diagnostic reasoning." *Academic Medicine* 84(8): 1022–1028.

[25] Arocha, J.F., Wang, D., and Patel, V.L. 2005. "Identifying reasoning strategies in medical decision making: A methodological guide," *Journal of Biomedical Informatics* 38(2): 154–171.

[26] Crowley, R.S., Legowski, E., Medvedeva, O., Reitmeyer, K., Tseytlin, E., Castine, M., and Mello-Thoms, C. 2013. "Automated detection of heuristics and biases among pathologists in a computer-based system," *Advances in Health Sciences Education* 18(3): 343–363.

[27] Lundberg, S.M. and Lee, S.I. 2017. "A unified approach to interpreting model predictions," In *Advances in Neural Information Processing Systems (NIPS 2017)*, 4765–4774.

[28] Hempel, C.G. and Oppenheim, P. 1948. "Studies in the logic of explanation," *Philosophical Science* 15(2): 135–175.

[29] Babiker, H.K.B. and Goebel, R. 2017. "An introduction to deep visual explanation," In NIPS 2017- Workshop Interpreting, Explaining and Visualizing Deep Learning, Long Beach, CA, 1–9.

[30] Pohn, B., Kargl, M., Reihs, R., Holzinger, A., Zatloukal, K., and Muler, H. 2019. "Towards a deeper understanding of how a pathologist makes a diagnosis: Visualization of the diagnostic process in histopathology," In *IEEE Symposium on Computers and Communications (ISCC 2019)*, Barcelona City, 1081–1086, doi: 10.1109/ISCC47284.2019.8969598.

[31] Chang, C.H., Creager, E., Goldenberg, A., and Duvenaud, D. 2017. "Interpreting neural network classifications with variational dropout saliency maps. *Proceedings of NIPS* 1(2): 1–9.

[32] Kim, B., Koyejo, O., and Khanna, R. 2016. "Examples are not enough, learn to criticize! Criticism for interpretability," In *Advances in Neural Information Processing Systems 29: Annual Conference on Neural Information Processing Systems 2016*, 5–10 December, Barcelona, Spain, 2280–2288.

[33] Li, O., Liu, H., Chen, C., and Rudin, C. 2018. "Deep learning for case-based reasoning through prototypes: A neural network that explains its predictions," In *Proceedings of the Thirty-Second AAAI Conference on Artificial Intelligence, (AAAI–18)*, 2–7 February 2018, New Orleans, LA, 3530–3537.

[34] Lecue, F. and Pommellet, T. 2019. "Feeding machine learning with knowledge graphs for explainable object detection," In Suarez-Figueroa, M. C., Cheng, G., Gentile, A. L., Gu´eret, C., Keet, C. M., Bernstein, A., (eds.) *Proceedings of the ISWC 2019 Satellite Tracks (Posters & Demonstrations, Industry, and Outrageous Ideas) co-located with 18th International Semantic Web Conference (ISWC 2019)*, 26–30 October 2019, Auckland, volume 2456 of CEUR Workshop Proceedings, 277–280. CEUR-WS.org (2019).

[35] Huang, L., Joseph, A.D., Nelson, B., Rubinstein, B.I., and Tygar, J. D. 2011. "Adversarial machine learning," In *Proceedings of the 4th ACM Workshop on Security and Artificial Intelligence*, 2011: 43–58.

[36] Feinman, R., Curtin, R.R., Shintre, S., and Gardner, A.B. 2017. "Detecting adversarial samples from artifacts." arXiv preprint, arXiv:1703.00410.

[37] Metzen, J.H., Genewein, T., Fischer, V., and Bischoff, B. 2017. "On detecting adversarial perturbations." arXiv preprint, arXiv:1702.04267.

[38] Holzinger, K., Mak, K., Kieseberg, P., and Holzinger, A. 2018. "Can we trust machine learning results?." Artificial intelligence in safety-critical decision support. *ERCIM NEWS* 112: 42–43.

[39] Glassman, M. and Kang, M.J. 2012. "Intelligence in the internet age: The emergence and evolution of open source intelligence (OSINT)," *Computer Human Behaviour* 28(2): 673–682.

[40] Devine, S.M. and Bastian, N.D. 2019. "Intelligent systems design for malware classification under adversarial conditions." arXiv preprint, arXiv:1907.03149.

[41] Kieseberg, P., Malle, B., Fr¨uhwirt, P., Weippl, E., and Holzinger, A. 2016. "A tamper-proof audit and control system for the doctor in the loop," *Brain Information* 3(4): 269–279. 10.1007/s40708-016-0046-2

[42] Glomsrud, J.A., Ødeg°ardstuen, A., Clair, A.L.S., and Smogeli, Ø. 2020. "Trustworthy versus explainable AI in autonomous vessels," In: *Proceedings of the International Seminar on Safety and Security of Autonomous Vessels (ISSAV) and European STAMP Workshop and Conference (ESWC) 2019*, Sciendo, 37–47.

[43] Longo, L., Goebel, R., Lecue, F., Kieseberg, P., and Holzinger, A. 2020. "Explainable artificial intelligence: Concepts, applications, research challenges and visions," In *International Cross-Domain Conference for Machine Learning and Knowledge Extraction*, Springer, Cham, 1–16.

[44] Hagras, Hani. 2018. "Toward human-understandable, explainable AI." *Computer* 51(9): 28–36.

[45] Adak, Anirban, Pradhan, B., and Shukla, N. 2022. "Sentiment analysis of customer reviews of food delivery services using deep learning and explainable artificial intelligence: Systematic review," *Foods* 11(10): 1500.

[46] Lokeshkumar, R., Sabnis, O.V., and Bhattacharyya, S. 2020. "A novel approach to extract and analyse trending cuisines on social media," In *Lecture Notes on Data Engineering and Communications Technologies*, Springer, Cham, Switzerland, 645–656.

[47] Singh, R.K. and Verma, H.K. 2020. "Influence of social media analytics on online food delivery systems," *International Journal of Information System Modelling Design* 11: 1–21.

[48] Yu, C.-E. and Zhang, X. 2020. "The embedded feelings in local gastronomy: A sentiment analysis of online reviews," *Journal of Hospital and Tourism Technology* 11: 461–478.

[49] Nguyen, Bang, Nguyen, V.H., and Ho, T. 2021. "Sentiment analysis of customer feedbacks in online food ordering services," *Business Systems Research: International journal of the Society for Advancing Innovation and Research in Economy* 12(2): 46–59.

[50] Shortliffe, E.H. and Buchanan, B.G. 1975. "A model of inexact reasoning in medicine," *Mathematical Biosciences* 23(3): 351–379. 10.1016/0025-5564(75)90047-4.

[51] Shi, W., Tong, L., Zhu, Y., and Wang, M. D. 2021. "COVID-19 automatic diagnosis with radiographic imaging: Explainable attentiontransfer deep neural networks" *IEEE Journal of Biomedical Health Information*, 25(7), 2376–2387. Doi: 10.1109/JBHI.2021.3074893

[52] FATE: Fairness, accountability, transparency, and ethics in AI. Microsoft Research. July 2021. [Online]. Available: https://www.microsoft.com/enus/ research/theme/fate/

[53] Lauritsen, S.M. et al. 2020. "Explainable artificial intelligence model to predict acute critical illness from electronic health records," *Nature Communication* 11(1): Art. no. 3852.

[54] Goh, K.H. et al. 2021. "Artificial intelligence in sepsis early prediction and diagnosis using unstructured data in healthcare," *Nature Communication* 12(1), Art. no. 711.

[55] Binder, A. et al. 2021. "Morphological and molecular breast cancer profiling through explainable machine learning," *Nature Machine Intelligence* 3: 355–366. [Online]. Available: 10.1038/s42256-021-00303-4

[56] Anguita-Ruiz, A., Segura-Delgado, A., Alcalá, R., and Aguilera, C.M. 2020. "eXplainable artificial intelligence (XAI) for the identification of biologically relevant gene expression patterns in longitudinal human studies, insights from obesity research," *PLoS Computational Biology* 16(4), Art. no. e1007792.

[57] Gilpin, L.H., Bau, D., Yuan, B.Z., Bajwa, A., Specter, M., and Kagal, L. 2018. "Explaining explanations: An overview of interpretability of machine learning," In *Proceedings of the 2018 IEEE 5th International Conference on Data Science and Advanced Analytics (DSAA)*, 1–3 October 2018, Turin, Italy, 80–89.

[58] Monteath, I. and Sheh, R. 2018. "Assisted and incremental medical diagnosis using explainable artificial intelligence," In *Proceedings of the 2nd Workshop on Explainable Artificial Intelligence*, 13–19 July 2018, Stockholm, Sweden, 104–108.

[59] Topol, E.J. 2019. "High-performance medicine: The convergence of human and artificial intelligence." *Nature Medicine* 25: 44–56.

[60] Arrieta, A.B., Díaz-Rodríguez, N., Del Ser, J., Bennetot, A., Tabik, S., Barbado, A., García, S., Gil-López, S., Molina, D., and Benjamins, R. 2020. "Explainable Artificial Intelligence (XAI): Concepts, taxonomies, opportunities and challenges toward responsible AI," *Information Fusion* 58: 82–115.

[61] Vellido, A. 2019. "The importance of interpretability and visualization in machine learning for applications in medicine and health care," *Neural Computing Applications* 32: 18069–18083.

[62] Zheng, Q., Delingette, H., and Ayache, N. 2019. "Explainable cardiac pathology classification on cine MRI with motion characterization by semi-supervised learning of apparent flow," *Medical Image Analysing* 56: 80–95. [CrossRef]

[63] Tosun, A.B., Pullara, F., Becich, M.J., Taylor, D., Fine, J.L., and Chennubhotla, S.C. 2020. "Explainable AI (xAI) for anatomic pathology," *Advances in Anatimic Pathology* 27: 241–250. [CrossRef]

[64] Hicks, S.A., Eskeland, S., Lux, M., de Lange, T., Randel, K.R., Jeppsson, M., Pogorelov, K., Halvorsen, P., and Riegler, M. 2018. "Mimir: An automatic reporting and reasoning system for deep learning based analysis in the medical domain," In *Proceedings of the 9th ACM Multimedia Systems Conference*, Amsterdam, The Netherlands, 369–374.

[65] Kavya, R., Christopher, J., Panda, S., and Lazarus, Y.B. 2021. "Machine learning and XAI approaches for allergy diagnosis," *Biomedical Signal Processing Control*, 69: 102681.

[66] Amoroso, N., Pomarico, D., Fanizzi, A., Didonna, V., Giotta, F., La Forgia, D., Latorre, A., Monaco, A., Pantaleo, E., and Petruzzellis, N. 2021. "A roadmap towards breast cancer therapies supported by explainable artificial intelligence," *Applied Science* 11: 4881.

[67] Peng, J., Zou, K., Zhou, M., Teng, Y., Zhu, X., Zhang, F., and Xu, J. 2021. "An explainable artificial intelligence framework for the deterioration risk prediction of hepatitis patients," *Journal of Medical System* 45: 1–9.

[68] Sarp, S., Kuzlu, M., Wilson, E., Cali, U., and Guler, O. 2021. "The enlightening role of explainable artificial intelligence in chronic wound classification," *Electronics*, 10: 1406.

[69] Rucco, M., Viticchi, G., and Falsetti, L. 2020. "Towards personalized diagnosis of glioblastoma in fluid-attenuated inversion recovery (FLAIR) by topological interpretable machine learning," *Mathematics* 8: 770.

[70] Yeboah, D., Steinmeister, L., Hier, D.B., Hadi, B., Wunsch, D.C., Olbricht, G.R., and Obafemi-Ajayi, T. 2020. "An explainable and statistically validated ensemble clustering model applied to the identification of traumatic brain injury subgroups," *IEEE Access* 8: 180690–180705.

[71] Wang, L., Lin, Z.Q., and Wong, A. 2020. "COVID-Net: A tailored deep convolutional neural network design for detection of COVID-19 cases from chest X-ray images," *Scientific Reports* 10: 19549.

[72] Babic, Boris, Gerke, S., Evgeniou, T., and Cohen, I.G. 2021. "Beware explanations from AI in health care," *Science* 373(6552): 284–286.

[73] Jena, Om and Pattnayak, Parthasarathi. 2021. "Innovation on Machine Learning in Healthcare Services: An Introduction." 10.1002/9781119792611.ch1.

[74] Patra, Sudhansu, Jena, Om, Kumar, Gaurav, Pramanik, Sreyashi, Misra, Chinmaya and Singh, Kamakhya. 2021. "Random Forest Algorithm in Imbalance Genomics Classification." 10.1002/9781119785620.ch7.

[75] Chatterjee, R., Ray, R., Dash, S.R., and Jena, O.P. 2021. "Conceptualizing Tomorrow Healthcare Through Digitization." 10.1002/9781119818717.ch19

[76] Patra, Sudhansu, Mittal, Mamta, and Jena, Om. 2022. "Multiobjective evolutionary algorithm based on decomposition for feature selection in medical diagnosis. 10.1016/B978-0-323-99864-2.00005-6.

[77] Abed, Amira, Shaaban, Essam, Jena, Om, and Elngar, Ahmed. 2022. "A Comprehensive Survey on Breast Cancer Thermography Classification Using Deep Neural Network." 10.1201/9781003226147-9.

2 Utilizing Explainable Artificial Intelligence to Address Deep Learning in Biomedical Domain

Priyanka Sharma
Swami Keshvanand Institute of Technology,
Management & Gramothan

2.1 INTRODUCTION: BACKGROUND AND DRIVING FORCES

The study of computer systems carrying out activities that need human intelligence is known as artificial intelligence (AI). AI systems strive to perform intelligent activities that are correlated with the cognitive processes of the human minds, such as perception, knowledge representation, experience learning, problem solving, natural language processing, reasoning, etc. Nowadays, there are several uses in a wide range of industries of AI systems, including: education, healthcare, law, manufacturing, entertainment, finance, autonomous driving, cellphones, agriculture, social media, and a number of other fields.

ML and AI have shown they have the power to transform business, government, and society. They are capable of performing as accurately as humans over a variety of duties, including speech and image recognition, language translation, etc. However, deep learning (DL) – their most accurate product to date, is sometimes referred to as a "black box" and opaque [1]. Indeed, these models feature an enormous number of weights and parameters (millions or billions), all of which are meant to represent the knowledge gained through training sets. These weights are not only many, but it is also quite difficult to determine how they relate to the problem's physical settings. This makes it extremely difficult to explain such forms of AI to users (Figure 2.1).

Machine learning algorithms' output and outcomes can now be understood and trusted by human users through a set of methods, termed as explainable artificial intelligence (XAI). An AI model, its anticipated effects, and potential biases are all described in terms of explainable AI. It contributes to defining model correctness, transparency, outcomes, fairness, and in decision-making supported by AI. When putting AI models into production, a business must first establish trust and confidence. A company can adopt a reasonable strategy for developing AI with the help of AI explainability. Humans find it difficult to understand and trace the steps taken by the algorithm as AI develops. The process is converted a black box – very tough to comprehend. Data are used to generate these black box models. Furthermore,

DOI: 10.1201/9781003257721-2

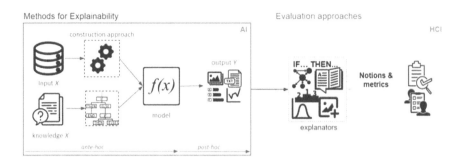

FIGURE 2.1   Explainable artificial intelligence.

nobody, not even the engineers or data scientists who developed the algorithm, is able to comprehend or describe what exactly is going on inside of them, let AI alone decide how the algorithm came to a particular conclusion [2] (Figure 2.2).

This article is organized as: The introduction of EAI and the importance of these systems, especially in biomedical domain, are discussed in Section 2.1. In Section 2.2, XAI taxonomy is described. The focus of study narrows down on the state of art in Section 2.3, where several logics based and human-centered methods are demonstrated. Nowadays, the diagnosis/testing processes are carried out by a significant role of DL algorithms, thereby making the AI decisions more trustworthy for physicians and patients, so in Section 2.4, we have demonstrated the role and significance of DL using XAI along with its several techniques and applications in healthcare domain. Section 2.5 discusses some of the pros and cons of XAI with DL.

2.2 XAI TAXONOMY

There are many words used in the literature to describe the opposite of "black box" aspect of some AI, ML, and DL models particularly [3]. The following terms are distinguished:

- **Transparency:** If a model has the ability to be comprehensible on its own then that is deemed transparent. Transparency is the antithesis of "black-box."
- **Interpretability:** Ability to deliver interpretations in human-understandable words is known as "interpretability."
- **Explainability:** This concept relates to the idea of explanation serving as a conduit between people and AI systems. It includes human-comprehensible and accurate artificial intelligence (AI) systems. Although the semantic implications of these phrases are identical, they confer distinct levels of AI that humans can accept [4]. The XAI ontology and taxonomy are summarized below in greater detail for your reference:
  - **Transparent models:** Common transparent models include Bayesian networks, rule-based learning, decision trees, and k-nearest neighbors (kNN). These models frequently produce transparent decisions,

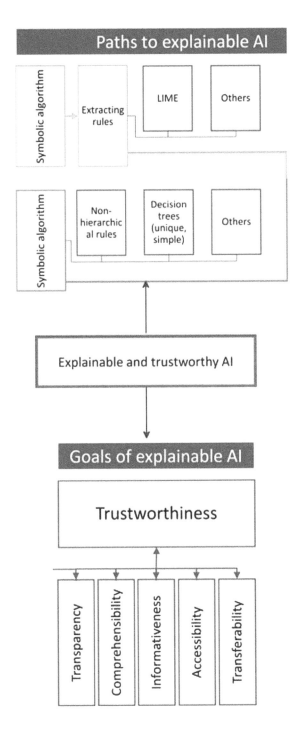

FIGURE 2.2 Securing AI for clinical decision-making, biomedicine, and other XAI environments.

but openness by itself does not ensure that the model will be simple to understand.

- **Opaque model:** Random forests, SVMs, neural networks, and are included in typical opaque models. These models are opaque even though they frequently reach high accuracy.
- **Model-agnostic:** XAI techniques are created with the intention of being broadly applicable. They must therefore be adaptable enough to operate merely on the basis of connecting a model's input to its outputs, independent of the model's inherent design.
- **Model-specific:** Model-specific XAI techniques frequently make use of model knowledge and seek to make a specific type of one or more models more transparent.
- **Explanation by simplification:** Alternatives to the original models can be identified to explain the forecasting by using a simplification model by approximation. To explain a more sophisticated model, we may, for instance, create a linear model or decision tree based on a model's predictions.

Relevance of the explanation for each feature: This concept is related to simplicity. After all potential combinations have been taken into account, this kind of XAI technique seeks to assess a characteristic according to its typical expected marginal influence on the model's decision (Figure 2.3).

- Visualization is the foundation of this kind of XAI method. In light of this, it is possible to use the family of data visualization techniques to interpret the prediction or choice made based on the input data.
- The model's behavior under similar input conditions to the one we are interested in describing is revealed through local explanations. They reproduce the model in a limited area, close to an important occurrence.

The term "interpretability" rather than "explainability" is more commonly used in the ML literature; however, Burkart and Huber (2020) argued that this phrase is insufficient because it does not encompass all potential issues with comprehending "black-box" models. Explainability, not just interpretability, is necessary to win users' trust and get significant insights into the causes, motivations, and decisions behind "black-box" techniques [5] (Figure 2.4).

2.3   REVIEW OF STATE OF ART

The majority of XAI research currently being conducted is still focused on sensitivity analysis, local pseudo explanations attribution, feature propagation and game-theoretic Shapley additive explanations (SHAP). Grad-CAM and gradient-based localization and some of the more popular techniques are described in this section.

2.3.1   Methods Focused on Features

Game theory is used in the SHAP method to explain machine learning predictions. By presenting the features as participants in a coalition game, SHAP aims to

XAI Methods   ML Methods

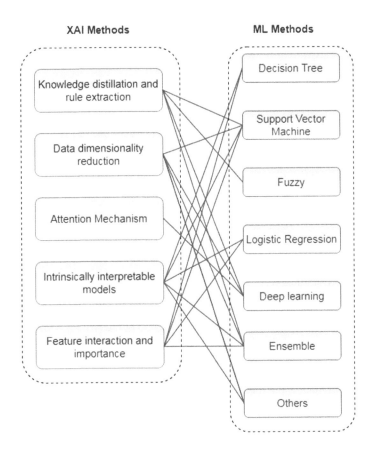

FIGURE 2.3 XAI methods mapped with machine learning methods.

determine how much each feature contributed to a certain choice [6]. The prize in the game is a measure of importance that is additive in nature, familiar as Shapley value, and it represents the weighted average contribution of a certain feature within all possible feature combinations.

The explanation of Shapley values, however, is not every time clear if the model is not additive, since predictive models can have non-independent pay-off splits [7]. Although SHAP can be regarded as model-neutral, it is not always easy or efficient to apply optimal SHAP implementations to all types of model.

Pre-trained networks and networks that do not follow the defined fully convolutional network design are not eligible for the use of CAMs. In addition, the completely connected layer and map scaling may cause spatial information to be lost [8]. Grad-CAM and Grad-CAM++ are two expansions of the fundamental CAM model aim to significantly improve the explainability of CNNs.

Grad-CAM generalizes class activation mapping (CAM) to any arbitrary convolutional neural network architecture with no retraining. The last convolutional layer receives the gradients for any target class, and a significance rating is produced in relation to the gradients. The parts of the input image that the CNN prioritized in

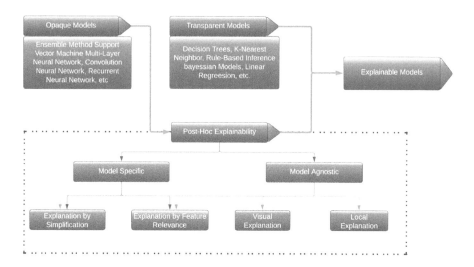

FIGURE 2.4   XAI framework.

making judgments are shown in a heatmap depiction of the Grad-CAM, just like with other techniques. Grad-CAM, however, only creates coarse-grained visualizations and is unable to explain why the same object appears more than once in a picture [9].

When it comes to the input, feature-oriented methods can shed light on where a decision is being made, but they can't fully explain how and why the model arrived at those judgments. As a result, a person could not precisely duplicate the justifications provided by the model.

2.3.2   GLOBAL METHODS

A neural network's explanations on a global level can be explained through global attribution mappings, side-to-side subpopulations, by framing attributions as weighted conjoined ranks for features with exact semantic descriptions. The benefits include the ability to capture various subpopulations using granularity parameters [10].

A clustering approach K-medoids approach is used to organize similar local feature importance into clusters after GAMs identify a pair-wise rank distance matrix between features. The medoid of each cluster then provides a global attribution for the pattern found in each cluster [11]. This method is thus applicable to feature exploration among various sample subpopulations.

Deep attribute maps are a mechanism for expressing the explainability of gradient-based algorithms, according to Ancona et al. (2018). The framework compares and contrasts various saliency-based explanation models. To create a heatmap that explains a model's forecast, the gradient of the output is simply multiplied by the corresponding input. Negative and positive contributions are indicated, respectively to the output decision by the colors red and blue. Explanations are susceptible to input fluctuations and noisy gradients. Deep evolutionary maps alone are unable to explain whether two models yield results that are similar or dissimilar [12].

2.3.3 CONCEPT METHODS

Concept activation vector is a method to explain a neural network's internal states worldwide by mapping human-understandable properties to the high-level latent data that is collected by the neural network. As a result, CAVs show how much these abstract properties converge on a user-selected set of ideas that are easily understood by humans. Human bias is there, of course, but by defining the idea, it is easy to identify any flaws in the model's learnt decision-making process. Consequently, human bias is eliminated by automatic concept-based explanations, which automatically extract CAVs without human oversight. The human-understandable concepts are segregated from in-class photos at different spatial resolutions rather than being selected [13].

2.3.4 SURROGATE METHODS

A model-agnostic technique – LIME – is used to create locally optimized explanations of ML models. In order to understand the local behavior of a global "black box" model's prediction, LIME trains an interpretable surrogate model [14]. A local weighted model is taught on a set of variations of the original picture after dividing the input image into patches.

2.3.5 LOCAL, PIXEL-BASED TECHNIQUES

Layer-wise relevance propagation makes use of predetermined propagation rules to explain the relationship between the output and input of a multilayered neural network. The technique generates a heatmap, giving information on which pixels and to what extent they contributed to the model's prediction. LRP thus highlights helpful input that helped a network make a choice [15]. Although LRP can be applied to a network that has already been trained, this method is post hoc and so only applies if the network uses backpropagation.

2.3.6 HUMAN-CENTERED METHODS

Despite their benefits, the aforementioned techniques do not offer clear and human-understandable explanations. With post hoc suggestions regarding the characteristics or places inside an image, they "just scratch the surface" of the "black box" and seek to "minimize harm." This is fundamentally different from how individuals typically make decisions, create analogies that may be explained in court or to another expert, analyze similarities, and make correlations [16]. The aforementioned approaches utterly disregard logic while failing to address essential problems about model parameters and structure related to the nature of the problem. Recently, a fundamentally different approach to explainability was put forth in Angelov and Soares (2020), which examines it as an anthropomorphic (human-centered) phenomenon rather than reducing it to statistics. Humans evaluate objects (such as pictures, music, and movies) holistically rather than feature- or pixel-by-feature.

2.4   DEEP LEARNING – RESHAPING HEALTHCARE

In recent years, Artificial Intelligence and Machine Learning have grown significantly in acceptance. The situation changed even further with the start of the COVID-19 pandemic. We observed a swift digital transition and the adoption of disruptive technology throughout various industries throughout the crisis. One prospective industry that benefited greatly from the introduction of disruptive technologies was healthcare. DL, machine learning, and AI have become the industry's constituent parts [17]. DL has a significant impact on the healthcare industry and has made it possible to enhance diagnosis and patient monitoring.

DL has greatly advanced automated picture analysis. Prior to that, systems completely created by human domain specialists were frequently used to perform picture analysis. Such a system for image analysis might, for instance, include a statistical classifier that uses specially created picture features to carry out any specific task. The included characteristics are low-level image features like corners or edges as well as higher-level image characteristics like the hypothetical cancer border. In DL, the mentioned characteristics are educated by a neural network rather than being created in order to produce the best possible output. A DL system might produce the word "cancer" after receiving an image of cancer as input.

2.4.1   DEEP LEARNING METHODS

The primary objective of a DL model is to discover a concept hierarchy so that a continuous vector representation encodes a distinct degree of abstraction in each of the model's layers. Conventional ML algorithms were unable to process natural data in its raw form, such as image and language [18]. Designing feature extractors that can efficiently convert raw data into internal representations or feature vectors that can be analyzed by pattern recognition and machine learning algorithms has required a lot of engineering work and domain knowledge for a long time. Modern machine learning systems can learn internal representations as well as feature vectors that can be employed to identify and classify complex nonlinear correlations in a dataset. The credit goes to powerful DL techniques. A deep neural network's processing units in its various layers train to represent its inputs so that the model can accurately anticipate the desired output [19]. DL methods are implemented using a variety of neural network designs for various applications. The following list includes some most popular deep neural network architectures:

2.4.1.1   Multi-layer Perceptron or Deep Feed-Forward Neural Network

This is the most straightforward architecture of any DL model. There are various hidden layers, an input and an output layer. Nodes at the input layer merely transmit input data to the hidden nodes without performing any computation. The input data is subjected to nonlinear modifications through hidden layers. Final output probabilities for potential outcomes are estimated by the output layer [20]. The gradient descent approach is employed to teach the network and identify the ideal set of weights after it is initialized with random weights. Deep neural network training typically involves the following three steps:

1. The data is fed to the network during the forward pass. Training samples move through hidden layers starting at the input layer before being calculated as an output probability by the output layer.
2. Loss function calculates the error by contrasting the output of the network with the desired output.
3. The weights/ parameters are modified in the backward pass in the reverse direction of gradient vector. This shows, for each weight, how much the network's error would rise or reduce if the weight were altered slightly (Figure 2.5).

2.4.1.2 Restricted Boltzmann Machine

It is a variant of neural networks with bi-directionally coupled stochastic processing units. A RBM contains two types of neurons: visible neurons and hidden neurons. These neurons must organize into a bipartite graph with no connections between nodes inside a set of neurons but symmetric connections between visible and hidden units. Because of this characteristic, RBMs can be trained using more effective algorithms than unrestricted Boltzmann machines.

The Gibbs sampler is used to create data from the RBM after training it with a random state in the first layer. Until the equilibrium distribution is reached, all the units in the subsequent layers are iteratively updated based on the states of the units in the top layer. Finally, by maximizing the RBM's likelihood, the weights within the RBM are calculated. RBMs can be stacked on top of one another to create a deep RBM [21]. RBMs are typically employed in classification tasks for feature extraction. In addition, they have found use in collaborative filtering, topic modeling, and dimension.

In Restricted Boltzmann Machine schematic diagram, there is no connection between units that are located on the same layer. Symmetric connections exist between visible and hidden units (Figure 2.6).

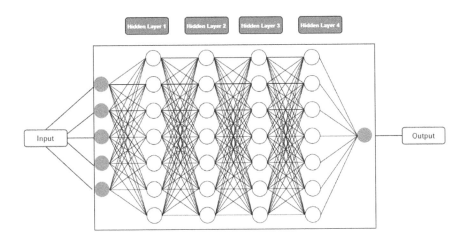

FIGURE 2.5 An entirely coupled deep feed-forward neural network.

Visible Units   Hidden Units

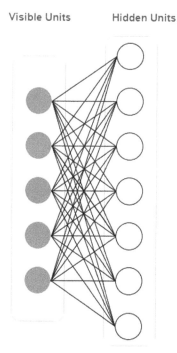

FIGURE 2.6   A Restricted Boltzmann Machine (RBM).

2.4.1.3   Deep Belief Network

A Deep Belief Network (DBN) is a probabilistic generative graphical model made up of many layers of latent variables that are hidden from view, with connections only existing between the layers as a whole. Although DBNs are unique varieties of RBMs, there are some distinctions. The major distinction is that an RBM's network is undirected since hidden and visible variables are not completely independent of one another [22]. On the other hand, a DBN's directed topology makes it possible to investigate variable dependencies. A DBN with one visible layer and three hidden layers is represented here, where top two layers are connected by undirected connections, which are shown as dashed lines. Directed connections are made between the lower layers.

2.4.1.4   Autoencoder

It is an unsupervised neural network that compresses data and reduces dimensionality. Autoencoders have the capacity to learn generative data models. During the encoding step, an autoencoder uses recognition weights to transform the input data into an abstract form. The input is then recreated by employing a generative set of weights during the decoding step to transform the abstract representation back into the original data. Multilayer perceptrons and autoencoders both use comparable training and propagation mechanisms and have a similar architectural design (Figure 2.7).

Visible layer   Hidden layer 1   Hidden layer 2   Hidden layer 3

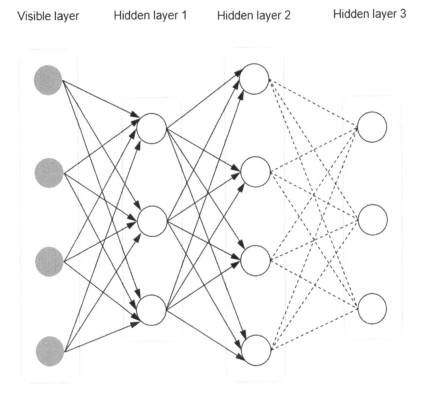

FIGURE 2.7 A Deep Belief Network (DBN).

An autoencoder's objective is to reconstruct the input, whereas a multi-layer perceptron's objective is to forecast the target value in relation to the input. An autoencoder can be trained in two stages: the first involves learning features through unsupervised training, and the second involves fine-tuning the network through supervised training [23]. A deep autoencoder neural network's schematic topology is depicted in Figure 2.8.

2.4.1.5 Convolutional Neural Network

A CNN is a type of artificial neural network that takes its cues from how the visual cortex of animals is organized. CNNs have proven to be the best models for working upon 2-D data with a grid-like topology such as photos and videos.

A CNN has two different kinds of layers: convolutional layers and subsampling layers. A CNN's schematic structure is shown in Figure 2.9. Local feature maps are created after the input picture has been convolved with trainable filters at all feasible offsets in the first convolution layer. The size of the feature maps decreases in the following subsampling layer after the feature maps have been subsampled using a pooling process [24]. As successive convolution and subsampling layers are applied to feature maps, higher-level alterations of the input are created.

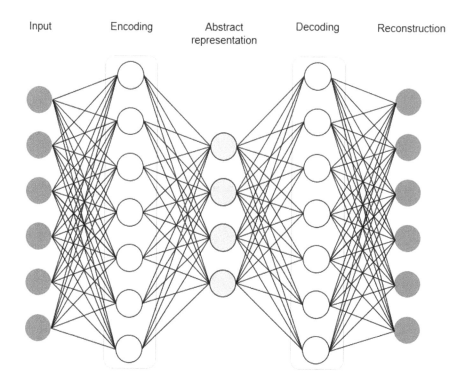

FIGURE 2.8   A deep Autoencoder neural network.

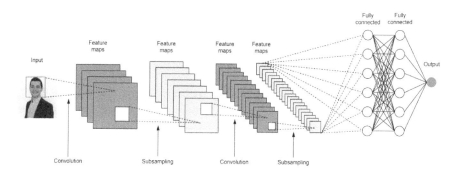

FIGURE 2.9   A Convolutional Neural Network (CNN).

2.4.1.6   Recurrent Neural Network

When processing sequential data (time series or texts), RNN can capture the sequential aspects of the data and employ the temporal patterns to anticipate the following likely event. Figure 2.10 shows the conceptual layout of an RNN and how it develops over time. As can be seen, each layer has a state vector that subtly stores the processor unit's context that has been exposed to that point in time. Then this vector is sent

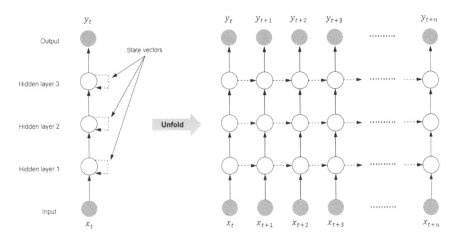

FIGURE 2.10 A recurrent neural network.

to the same processing unit, where it is updated in light of the input from that time step and an output is created that will serve as the next layer's input.

It has been demonstrated that RNNs are more suitable than typical feed-forward neural networks for natural language processing (NLP) applications since they can process samples with varying input and output lengths [25]. The vanishing gradient problem causes the inability to accurately represent long-term dependencies in lengthy input texts of the fundamental RNN model.

2.4.1.7 Long Short- Term Memory and Gated Recurrent Unit

By utilizing gating mechanisms and memory cells that regulate how long prior knowledge should be stored in order to be used to process future words as well as when prior knowledge should be updated or forgotten, gated recurrent unit (GRU) and long short-term memory (LSTM) networks have successfully addressed the vanishing gradient problem. Since a GRU is an LSTM that has been simplified, less computation is required. So, compared to LSTMs, GRUs are more scalable. But LSTMs are more robust and adaptable than GRUs.

DL techniques have demonstrated a significant capacity for identifying complicated structures in high-dimensional data, and as a result, they have found extensive use in a variety of scientific, educational, commercial, medical, transportation, and other disciplines [26].

2.4.2 Deep Learning Applications in Healthcare

2.4.2.1 Improved Patient Monitoring and Health Records

Both organized and unstructured data from the worlds of medicine and healthcare can be processed and analyzed using DL and machine learning models. Maintaining accuracy while classifying medical records may become challenging. In order to keep smart health records, machine learning and its subset DL can be applied [27].

2.4.2.2 Drug Research

DL is essential for figuring out how to combine medications. DL has the potential to simplify, accelerate, and reduce the complexity of the difficult work of drug discovery. Disruptive technologies like AI, machine learning, and DL supported the development of vaccines and medications during the epidemic. DL algorithms can generate a molecule with the desired qualities and anticipate pharmacological properties and drug-target interactions. Genomic, clinical, and population data may be processed by DL algorithms with ease, and we can use numerous toolkits to look for patterns in the data [28]. Researchers can now define protein structures more quickly by molecular modeling and predictive analytics using ML and DL.

Diagnostics and Imaging in Medicine: To make a diagnosis, DL models can decipher medical pictures like CT scans, MRI scans, X-rays, etc. The algorithms can identify any risk and highlight irregularities in the medical photos. The detection of cancer makes heavy use of DL. Machine learning and DL were key enablers of the recent advancement in computer vision. Diseases are more quickly diagnosed by medical imaging, making treatment simpler.

2.4.2.3 Detecting Fraud and Health Insurance

DL is effective at identifying insurance fraud and foreseeing potential problems. DL provides health insurance businesses another benefit because the models can forecast behaviors and future trends and recommend intelligent policies to their customers.

2.4.2.4 Making Clinical Trials Simpler

Clinical studies are difficult and costly. Scientists can pool participants from many data points and sources using DL and ML to do predictive analytics to find possible candidates for clinical trials [29]. DL will also make it possible to continuously monitor these trials while minimizing human mistake and interference.

2.4.2.5 Individualized Care

DL models make it simpler to examine health information of a patient's medical record, critical symptom, test findings, and other data. As a result, this makes it possible for medical professionals to comprehend each patient and offer them a customized course of treatment. These innovative technologies make it possible to identify numerous, effective therapy alternatives for various patients. ML models can employ deep neural networks to identify impending hazards or health issues and deliver particular medications or treatments.

2.4.2.6 NLP and Deep Learning

DL methods are used in NLP for classification and identification. These two technologies can be used to categorize and identify health data, as well as to create voice and chatbots. Chatbots are essential in the present telemedicine context. It facilitates quicker and simpler communication with patients [30]. In addition, these chatbots were utilized to promote COVID-19 and respond to important questions [31].

2.5 RESULTS

Artificial Neural Network performed a series of embedded transformations can be seen as:

$$y_i = f_n(\Sigma\ (w_{ij}f_{n-1}\left(\ldots f_2\left(\Sigma\ \left(w_{kl}\ f_1\left(\ \Sigma\left(\ w_{mn}p_n\right)\ \right)\ \right)\ \right)\ \right)\ )$$

where y_i represents the ith output; w shows corresponding weight; m is the number of inputs/features and l depicts number of neurons at a hidden layer; f_1, f_2 and f_n denote activation function of the input layer, hidden layer and output layer respectively.

The study done here includes aresearch on XAI and medical XAI publications every year starting from 2010 to July 2022. The analytical study is shown in the graph demonstrated in Figures 2.11 and 2.12.

Various DL techniques are applied on the Caltech dataset, taken from Kaggle. com. A performance comparison of these techniques is shown in Table 2.1.

2.6 BENEFITS AND DRAWBACKS OF XAI METHODS

2.6.1 VALIDITY

Validity is determined by whether or not the explanation is accurate and matches with what the end user anticipates. Having a radiologist determine whether the answer fits the pathology that the neural network was designed to classify, for instance, can be used to determine whether a visual explanation is valid in the case of visual explanation.

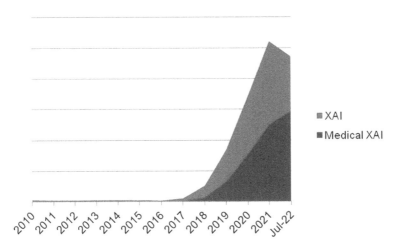

FIGURE 2.11   XAI v/s medical XAI publications per year.

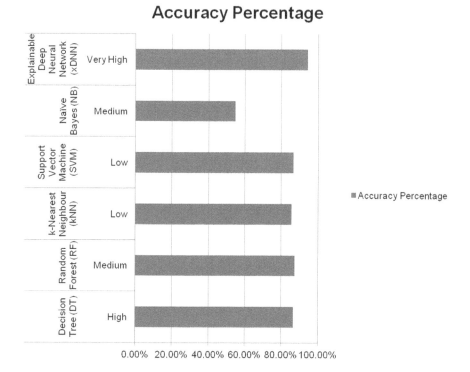

FIGURE 2.12   % of accuracy in various techniques.

TABLE 2.1

Performance Comparison of Various Deep Learning Methods for the Caltech Dataset

S. No.	Method	Level of Interpretability	Accuracy Percentage (%)
1.	Decision Tree (DT)	High	86.73
2.	Random Forest (RF)	Medium	87.53
3.	k-Nearest Neighbor (kNN)	Low	85.69
4.	Support Vector Machine (SVM)	Low	86.65
5.	Naive Bayes (NB)	Medium	54.83
6.	Explainable Deep Neural Network (xDNN)	Very High	94.27

2.6.2 USABILITY

We define usability as the ability of XAI methods to be "plug-and-play." The most user-friendly strategies are post hoc model independent ones. Typically, these techniques use perturbation-based visual explanation strategies like occlusion sensitivity. Any trained neural network can be used with these approaches to produce a visual explanation.

2.6.3 COST OF COMPUTATION

While rarely mentioned in studies, the computational cost of XAI can be evaluated by contrasting how these explanatory strategies operate. It is clear that these explanations are relatively expensive to write because model-based techniques incorporate the explanation into the neural network's construction.

2.6.4 ROBUSTNESS

By purposefully modifying a few parts of DL framework and observing how these changes affect the provided explanation, it is possible to evaluate how robust XAI techniques are. With the help of two tests: (1) The parameter randomization test contrasts the visual explanation provided by a trained CNN with the visual explanation provided by an untrained CNN of the same design that was randomly started. (2) The visual explanation from a trained CNN is compared to that from a CNN trained with arbitrarily imputed labels on the same dataset in the data randomization test.

2.6.5 FINE-TUNING

Fine-tuning is necessary for some explanation procedures, while it is not necessary for others to fine-tune the parameters related to the XAI technique. Given that model-based techniques incorporate the explanation into the neural network's construction, it follows that optimizing the network will have an impact on the explanation.

The majority of backpropagation algorithms only provide a small set of tuning parameters for visual explanation. For instance, in Grad-CAM, the user must select the layer at which to examine the activation, and in Deep SHAP, samples from the training set must be selected in order to calculate the background signal.

The perturbation must frequently be chosen when using visual explanation techniques based on perturbations. For instance, the user must specify the size and form of the occluded areas for occlusion sensitivity and LIME, respectively. The user must decide which type of perturbation strategy is best in meaningful perturbation.

2.6.6 OPEN SOURCE

The majority of XAI techniques are accessible through open source. Frequently, the original paper authors will provide the source code. Additionally, many strategies are used in XAI packages like captum.ai.

2.7 CONCLUSION

This article surveyed several research papers using XAI in DL domain. XAI framework is discussed along its methods. Many of machine learning methods like decision tree, SVM, Regression, ensemble learning are mapped with XAI techniques. The emergence of DL has revolutionized the medical sector that has vast coverage in the field of XAI. DL's various methods such as convolutional neural network, multi perception neural network, recurrent neural network, DBN, autoencoder, etc. are demonstrated along with the applications of DL in healthcare. In addition to these, a review of state of art is also described that involves diverse methods to work upon. Machine learning algorithms: Decision Tree, Random Forest, Naïve Bays, k-Nearest Neighbor, SVM and Explainable Deep Neural Network (xDNN) are applied on Caltech-256 dataset in which xDNN performed the best by providing highest level of interpretability along with highest accuracy percentage. Several pros and cons of XAI are also mentioned in detail at the end of the article.

REFERENCES

[1] Shevskaya, N. V., Akhrymuk, E. S., and Popov, N. V. (2022). "Causal relationships in explainable artificial intelligence," *2022 XXV International Conference on Soft Computing and Measurements (SCM)*, Saint Petersburg, pp. 138–141, doi: 10.1109/SCM55405.2022.9794848.

[2] Angelov, P. P., Soares, E. A., Jiang, R., Arnold, N. I., and Atkinson, P. M. (2021). "Explainable artificial intelligence: An analytical review." *Wiley Interdisciplinary Reviews: Data Mining and Knowledge Discovery*, 11(5), e1424.

[3] Ancona, M., Ceolini, E., Öztireli, C., and Gross, M. (2018). Towards better understanding of gradient-based attribution methods for deep neural networks.

[4] Angelov, P. and Soares, E. (2020). "Towards explainable deep neural networks (xDNN)." *Neural Networks*, 130, 185–194.

[5] Angelov, P. P. and Gu, X. (2018). "Toward anthropomorphic machine learning." *Computer*, 51, 18–27.

[6] Arrieta, A. B., Díaz-Rodríguez, N., Del Ser, J., Bennetot, A., Tabik, S., Barbado, A., García, S., Gil-Lo´pez, S., Molina, D., Benjamins, R., Chatila, R., and Herrera, F. (2020). "Explainable artificial intelligence (XAI): Concepts, taxonomies, opportunities and challenges toward responsible AI." *Information Fusion*, 58, 82–115.

[7] Byrne, R. M. (2019). "Counterfactuals in explainable artificial intelligence (XAI): Evidence from human reasoning." *Proceedings of the Twenty-eighth International Joint Conference on Artificial Intelligence (IJCAI-19)*, Macao, Vol. 1, pp. 6276–6282.

[8] Prentzas, N., Pitsiali, M., Kyriacou, E., Nicolaides, A., Kakas, A., and Pattichis, C. S. (2021). "Model agnostic explainability techniques in ultrasound image analysis," *2021 IEEE 21st International Conference on Bioinformatics and Bioengineering (BIBE)* Kragujevac, pp. 1–6, doi: 10.1109/BIBE52308.2021.9635199.

[9] Couteaux, V., Nempont, O., Pizaine, G., and Bloch, I. (2019). "Towards interpretability of segmentation networks by analyzing DeepDreams." *Interpretability of Machine Intelligence in Medical Image Computing and Multimodal Learning for Clinical Decision Support*, Shenzhen pp. 56–63. Springer.

[10] Gilpin, L. H., Bau, D., Yuan, B. Z., Bajwa, A., Specter, M., and Kagal, L. (2018). "Explaining explanations: An overview of interpretability of machine learning." *2018 IEEE 5th International Conference on Data Science and Advanced Analytics (DSAA)*, Turin, pp. 80–89. IEEE.

[11] Nazar, M., Alam, M. M., Yafi, E., and Su'ud, M. M. (2021). "A systematic review of human-computer interaction and explainable artificial intelligence in healthcare with artificial intelligence techniques," *IEEE Access*, 9, 153316–153348, doi: 10.1109/ACCESS.2021.3127881.

[12] Lotsch, Jorn, Kringel, Dario, and Ultsch, Alfred. (2022). "Explainable Artificial Intelligence (XAI) in biomedicine: Making AI decisions trustworthy for physicians and patients," *BioMedInformatics* 2, 1–17, ISSN: 2673-7426.

[13] Mathews, S.M. (2019). "Explainable artificial intelligence applications in NLP, biomedical, and malware classification: A literature review," In: Arai, K., Bhatia, R., Kapoor, S. (eds) *Intelligent Computing. CompCom 2019. Advances in Intelligent Systems and Computing*, Vol 998. Springer, Cham, 10.1007/978-3-030-22868-2_90.

[14] Pesquita, C. (2021). Towards Semantic Integration for Explainable Artificial Intelligence in the Biomedical Domain, HEALTHINF.

[15] Payrovnaziri, S. N., Chen, Z., Rengifo-Moreno, P., Miller, T., Bian, J., Chen, J. H., Liu, X., and He, Z. (2020). "Explainable artificial intelligence models using real-world electronic health record data: A systematic scoping review," *Journal of the American Medical Informatics Association*, 27(7), 1173–1185.

[16] Moradi, Milad and Samwald, Matthias. (2022). Deep Learning, Natural Language Processing, and Explainable Artificial Intelligence in the Biomedical Domain, Artificial Intelligence (cs.AI), Computation and Language (cs.CL), Machine Learning (cs.LG), FOS: Computer and information sciences, FOS: Computer and information sciences, arXiv 2022.

[17] Sharma, P. and Rathi, Y. (2016). "Efficient Density Based Clustering Using Automatic Parameter Detection", S. C. Satapathy et al. (eds.), *Proceedings of the International Congress on Information and Communication Technology, Advances in Intelligent Systems and Computing*, Udaipur, pp. 433-441, ISBN 978-981-10-0766-8, Springer.

[18] Arrieta, A. B., Díaz-Rodríguez, N., Del Ser, J., Bennetot, A., Tabik, S., Barbado, A., García, S., Gil-Lopez, S., Molina, D., Benjamins, R., Chatila, R., and Herrera, F. (2020). "Explainable artificial intelligence (XAI): Concepts, taxonomies, opportunities and challenges toward responsible AI," *Information Fusion* 58, 82–115.

[19] Byrne, R. M. (2019). "Counterfactuals in explainable artificial intelligence (XAI): Evidence from human reasoning," In *Proceedings of the Twenty-eighth International Joint Conference on Artificial Intelligence (IJCAI-19)*, Macao, Vol. 1, pp. 6276–6282.

[20] Sharma, P. and Rathi, Y. (2016). "Efficient densitybased clustering using automatic parameter detection", S. C. Satapathy et al. (eds.), *Proceedings of the International Congress on Information and Communication Technology, Advances in Intelligent Systems and Computing*, Udaipur, pp. 433–441, ISBN 978-981-10-0766-8, Springer.

[21] Adadi, A. and Berrada, M. (2018). "Peeking inside the black-box: A survey on explainable artificial intelligence (XAI)," *IEEE Access* 6, 52138–52160.

[22] Chattopadhay, A., Sarkar, A., Howlader, P., and Balasubramanian, V. N. (2018). "Grad-CAM++: Generalized gradient-based visual explanations for deep convolutional networks," In *2018 IEEE Winter Conference on Applications of Computer Vision (WACV)*, Lake Tahoe, NV, pp. 839–847.

[23] Vilone, Giulia and Longo, Luca. (2020). "Explainable artificial intelligence: A systematic review," *Artificial Intelligence (cs.AI), Machine Learning (cs.LG), FOS: Computer and Information Sciences*, FOS: Computer and information sciences, I.2.0; I.2.6; I.2.m, arXiv, 2020.

[24] Pawar, U., O'Shea, D., Rea, S., and O'Reilly, R. (2020). "Incorporating Explainable Artificial Intelligence (XAI) to aid the Understanding of Machine Learning in the Healthcare Domain", AICS.

[25] Joshi, G., Walambe, R., and Kotecha, K. (2021). "A review on explainability in multimodal deep neural nets," *IEEE Access*, 9, 59800–59821, doi: 10.1109/ACCESS.2021.3070212.

[26] Tjoa, E. and Guan, C. (Nov. 2021). "A survey on explainable artificial intelligence (XAI): Toward Medical XAI," In *IEEE Transactions on Neural Networks and Learning Systems*, 32(11), 4793–4813, doi: 10.1109/TNNLS.2020.3027314.

[27] Abeyagunasekera, S. H. P., Perera, Y., Chamara, K., Kaushalya, U., Sumathipala, P., and Senaweera, O. (2022). "LISA: Enhance the explainability of medical images unifying current XAI techniques," *2022 IEEE 7th International conference for Convergence in Technology (I2CT)* Mumbai, pp. 1–9, doi: 10.1109/I2CT54291.2022.9824840.

[28] Giuste, F. et al. (2022). "Explainable artificial intelligence methods in combating pandemics: A systematic review," *IEEE Reviews in Biomedical Engineering*, doi: 10.1109/RBME.2022.3185953.

[29] Marvin, G. and Alam, M. G. R. (2022). "Explainable augmented intelligence and deep transfer learning for pediatric pulmonary health evaluation," *2022 International Conference on Innovations in Science, Engineering and Technology (ICISET)*, Chittagong, pp. 272–277, doi: 10.1109/ICISET54810.2022.9775845.

[30] Jia, Yan, McDermid, John A., Lawton, Tom, and Habli, Ibrahim. (2022). "The role of explainability in assuring safety of machine learning in healthcare." arxiv abs/2109.00520, doi: 10.1109/tetc.2022.3171314.

[31] Kim, B., Wattenberg, M., Gilmer, J., Cai, C., Wexler, J., Viegas, F., and Sayres, R. (2021). Interpretability beyond feature attribution: Quantitative testing with concept activation vectors (TCAV), doi: 10.48550/arXiv.1711.11279.

3 Explainable Fuzzy Decision Tree for Medical Data Classification

Swathi Jamjala Narayanan, Boominathan Perumal, and Sangeetha Saman
Vellore Institute of Technology

3.1 INTRODUCTION

Explainable artificial intelligence (XAI) helps in decision-making by displaying and interpreting the results of predictions (Islam et al., 2021). Based on the findings from Chatterjee et al. (2021) numerous health data sources and the advancement of technology, we conclude that public health services are still enduring transformation and innovation on parallel with other public service sectors, such as education. Paramesha et al. (2021) presented the some of the AI-driven applications such as clinical trial management, drug research, healthcare decision support systems, virtual aid, and genome sequencing. In the health care domain, XAI plays a major role in allowing doctors to diagnose patients and treat them instantaneously. Several proofs of concept have confirmed that this is feasible for urgent reading of patient test results generate by AI. Though there are several articles presenting how well machine learning (ML) algorithms work in health care domain (Pattnayak and Amiya Ranjan, 2021), only a few of those ML models have been widely used in clinical settings. The black-box method used in ML is the main cause of this significant obstacle. To overcome this setback in deploying the ML algorithms widely in clinical practice, it is high time to understand why and how the algorithms make decisions. This is further an obstacle even when deep learning strategies (Sahu et al., 2022) are applied for medical problem-solving. In such cases, the black-box model of decision-making is not helpful in many scenarios to explore and understand the reason behind a particular prediction. Hence, XAI has been used extensively in recent years to overcome the drawbacks mentioned. The XAI technique makes it possible for users to understand how the AI system performed to achieve the desired result. This helps in confirming why a decision was made by the system, and tree experts can understand the reason behind the decision made and confirm to its correctness to proceed further for patient diagnosis.

Traditional methods such as sparse linear models, support vector machines, and neural networks are easier to understand and use but they lack explanation. Recently, ML and related fields such as expert systems (Panigrahi et al., 2021) and deep learning techniques have been used successfully in detecting COVID-19 and other disorders.

DOI: 10.1201/9781003257721-3

Deep approaches like CNN influence several layers like convolution and pooling to check the regions that influence the result before deciding on classification. However, for a variety of reasons, the aforementioned explainable procedures cannot directly facilitate healthcare physicians in understanding the decision. In such cases, it is preferred to utilize rule-based strategies for achieving better interpretation. Rule sets are more understandable and useful for deriving explanations. As decision trees are widely used for generating rules, it is also observed that the traditional way of decision trees cannot deal with ambiguity or inconsistencies that remain in real-world data. The possible solution for this is the application of fuzzy decision trees (FDT) (Narayanan et al., 2014, 2015, 2016a, b, 2021). The fuzzy logic framework helps in both managing the input data inaccuracy and the ambiguity in the vocabulary used to explain results. In the process of FDT generation, choosing the best attributes as the root node and its corresponding childnodes is the crucial step, here a few techniques are augmented in this process to make FDT more explainable. Having known that FDT possess the characteristics of interpretability and comprehensibility, here we propose a few procedures to further explore on the decisions that are made in the intermediate procedures of FDT generation. In practice, each data input can lead to many different decision paths. It is important to analyze every decision path to understand better on how a final prediction is made.

In this chapter, the contribution is presented in terms of an explainable fuzzy decision tree model for a classification task. The process of choosing the best node and its partitions are explained in detail. The purpose of cluster validity indices is shown considering eight cluster validity indices and the impact of those indices in the results is also presented. The generation of fuzzy rules and its interpretation is presented over a medical data for classification task.

3.2   LITERATURE SURVEY

Over the last decade, ML models with difficult processes and architectures, such as deep learning, have been successfully utilized to handle a variety of ML and AI hard challenges on medical data. Though several approaches proved to best models for classification or prediction, the current need to understand the decision made is still considered a cumbersome task. Especially, in the health care domain, understanding a decision made based on the patient vitals is important in any stage of diagnosis and treatment. To demonstrate how XAI might be used in medical XAI applications, Zhang et al. (2022) conducted a survey of current developments in medical diagnosis and surgical applications employing XAI. Firstly, we present the different AI models and XAI models that were widely used in medical applications. Ieracitano et al. (2021) investigated the interpretability and explainability of the deep CNN-based system to gain a better understanding of the mechanism of cortical source activity when the brain gets ready to either open or close the hand. Using occlusion sensitivity analysis, the researchers were able to determine which parts of the brain are more crucial for classification. The saliency maps are then segmented using the K-means clustering technique, which automatically detects the cortical source locations most important to task prediction. An XAI framework was bring forward by Peng et al. (2021) to help physicians predict the prognostic value of hepatitis patients.

In this study, the authors evaluated simple models RF, XGBoost, and SVM with intrinsic XAI methods like decision tree (DT), logistic regression (LR), and kNN. Furthermore, the authors applied the post hoc methods partial dependence plots (PDPs), LIME, and SHAP, LIME.

To detect brain hemorrhages in CT images, Kim et al. (2021) created an explainable CNN model. The Grad-CAM is a method for analyzing deep learning algorithms that shows the region of interest (ROI) that can be recognized in a task of image classification as a heatmap of feature values. Stenwing et al. (2022) built four different ML models (Random Forest, Adaptive Boost Classifier, LR, and Naive Bayes.) with equal discriminative abilities. The SHAP values demonstrated how various models interpret various features. By examining the discrepancies between several ML models trained and evaluated on the same datasets, this study contributed to the emerging field of explainable ML. In comparison to medical theory, the study conducted indicates variations among the four ML models considered along with the critical factors for mortality. Hu et al. (2022) proved the promise of ML algorithms for earlier stage prognostic prediction in sepsis patients. XGBoost proved to be the best performing model. To get the best predictability and interpretability, the researchers first employed SHAP in the XGBoost model. Doctors may also benefit from the detailed justifications developed by SHAP force analysis to explain why the model suggests particular high-risk actions. Bloch et al. (2021) used Data Shapley to value the data to find the Alzheimer's subjects with the most relevant information. The leave-one-out (LOO) data valuations were employed as a comparison technique. The Random Forest, eXtreme Gradient Boosting, and Kernel SHapley Additive exPlanations values were utilized for model training and model interpretation, respectively. The random forest classifier has already been used successfully in genomics (Patra et al., 2021) yielding profitable results even on imbalanced data. The objective was to avoid ML models from overfitting and thereby improve generalization. Ibrahim et al. (2020) used deep neural networks, recurrent neural networks, CNNsto predict acute myocardial infarctions, as well as the decision-tree-based model, XGBoost, to broaden the range of cardiovascular diseases (CVD) diagnoses. Shapley value, a game theory concept, is used in the testing dataset to acquire a deeper understanding of the model prediction and find features that contribute more to the prediction. For the diagnosis of knee osteoarthritis, Kokkotis et al. (2022) developed a unique fuzzy logic-based feature selection method, learning algorithms, and post hoc explainability studies. To analyze the behavioral and risk factor contributions to KOA diagnosis, SHAP was employed to rank features according to their influence on the final Random Forest outputs and to establish a mini-explanatory model. Having seen such different models that are proven to be applicable for achieving XAI, it is strongly observed that the comprehensibility and interpretability power of decision trees are advantageous in understanding why a decision is made. Suzuki et al. (2022) proposed the Explainable local correction tree (LCT), a combination of decision trees used on the CTG and 7-point medical datasets. This strategy identifies the information the previous model missed and appropriately incorporates that information into the new data to correct the model.

Further literature focuses on decision trees especially FDT as XAI. Alonso et al. (2020) employed 15 datasets to test the efficacy of employing a pool of gray-box classifier models (such as decision trees and fuzzy rule-based classifiers) to automatically describe the black-box classifier. Li et al. (2022) combined a CNN model with a fuzzy decision tree regularization and demonstrate the interpretability of learning models in respiratory sound analysis. Each lung sound prediction was then explained by a sequence of fuzzy logic in this method. In this work, FDT were used to handle the uncertainty in the decision-making operation, which improves the model's interpretability. FDT that provide decision rules in this way are more likely to be accepted by doctors. To make decisions regarding the scheduling of tracheostomies for COVID-19 patients, Rabcan et al. (2021) created the Fuzzy Decision Tree and Fuzzy Random Forest fuzzy classifiers (FRF). Due to the good interpretability of results, the proposed classifiers have evolved as decision tree-based classifiers. With uncertain data, FDT outperforms crisp classifiers in both classification and prediction. FDT and decision trees enable the analysis of each outcome's underlying causes and the tracing of the path from the end state to the point of start in time and relation to events. The FDT exhibits the best interpretation and converts easily into decision rules for the advancement of decision-making about the timing of tracheostomy in COVID-19 patients, which is another key fact to highlight. Chen et al. (2021) suggested a neuro-fuzzy method for acquiring precise and intelligible fuzzy rule bases to enhance clinical decision support on popular medical data. The first step in the process is to establish a concise rule base by employing a decision tree-based learning mechanism that can identify basic rule structures. The obtained concise rules are then transformed into their corresponding fuzzy rules by replacing the categorical values with Gaussian membership functions. Fernandez et al. (2022) employed FDT-based classifiers, with each instance firing several rules. The authors presented many factual explanations within the framework of FDT, which can take into account multiple rules to provide more comprehensive explanations. The experiments were conducted on five different datasets. El-Sappagh et al. (2021) presented an Fuzzy rule based and RF model for detecting Alzheimer's disease (AD) progression and diagnosis. Furthermore, the authors first used SHAP to choose the key features for the classifier. The authors then employed a system with fuzzy rules. Progression prediction interpretations about feature impacts may have a local explanation according to SHAP. Additionally, the fuzzy rule-based approach might provide forms in natural language to assist patients and doctors in interpreting the AI model. Ultsch et al. (2021) presented an ALPODS-Algorithmic Population Descriptions-based symbolic ML method that generates user-understandable knowledge for its decisions in biomedical data. Fuzzy reasoning rules stated in the ordinary language of domain experts are created for the identified subpopulations (diagnose cases based on clusters). Being motivated by the approaches proposed by the experts, we propose an approach to consider FDT as explainable FDT by incorporating strategies to understand why a particular decision is made in the intermediate procedures like clustering and inference during FDT generation. Chen et al. (2022) developed a novel approach for learning an interpretable fuzzy rule-based system for clinical decision support in dementia diagnosis. The diagnosis of dementia is formulated as a pairwise clustering problem using an adaptation of the graph theory idea of dominating sets. Then, a peeling-off approach was employed to iteratively extract a dominating set from the created edge-weighted graph, allowing it to automatically find a predetermined set of clusters. Then, for each dominant set, a parameterized fuzzy rule is created and further refined in a framework for trained adaptive network-based fuzzy inference.

This chapter is organized as follows. Section 3.3 describes the fuzzy classification problem. Section 3.4 presents the process of induction of a fuzzy decision tree. Section 3.5 presents the case study of FDT over HCV medical data for classification purposes. Section 3.6 concludes the chapter with possible work followed by references.

3.3 FUZZY CLASSIFICATION PROBLEM

The first and most crucial step in implementing FDT is to divide each attribute in the input space into corresponding fuzzy partitions (or clusters). As objects in one group become more similar to those in other groups, clustering is the tool for organizing patterns into groupings. (Jain and Dubes, 1988). For various applications, a huge number of clustering methods have been developed in the literature. They are broadly classified as partitional, hierarchical, and overlapping. K-means and other partitional clustering methods, the data is hard (crisply) divided. The clusters in hard partitions are therefore disjoint because it simply indicates that a pattern often can relate to a particular partition's clusters. Agglomerative, divisive, and other hierarchical clustering algorithms, among others, separate the input space into a number of embedded partitional clusters that, whether in top-down or bottom-up, generate a tree-like structure. Partitions may slightly overlap since most real-world data sets cannot be properly separated into a large number of non-overlapping groups. All these partitional and hierarchical clustering techniques fail miserably in this situation in terms of producing partitions that accurately reflect the underlying structure of the data. By applying a membership function with a value ranging from zero to one to relate each pattern with each cluster, fuzzy clustering algorithms may analyze these data sets effectively.

The following is an example of a simple fuzzy classification problem. A set of learning patterns is referred to as $U = \{x^1,....,x^n\}$, in which each pattern x^i is a collection of values $x_t; t = 1,....., p$ within the p elements attribute vector set x. There are many conditional attributes and one decision attribute in the classification problem. Each conditional attribute x_t specifies some prominent feature (or property or condition) of the system under consideration. A conditional property x_t might be either discrete or continuous. For the case of a discrete attribute, the attribute x_t is fuzzified into fuzzy singletons. Regarding continuous attributes, the attribute x_t is fuzzified toward a defined number of m_t fuzzy sets, $F_{tq}; t = 1,...., p, q = 1,....,m_t$, i.e., any data point x_t^i refers to more than one cluster having varying degrees of membership rather than simply one cluster. The degree of membership $\mu_{F_{tq}}(x_t^i)$ for the ith value of the attribute x_t in the fuzzy set F_{tq}. A membership degree $\mu_{F_{tq}}(x_t^i)$ which provides values between zero and one, describes how well the data object x_t^i interacts with the cluster qth.

$$0 \le \mu_{F_{tq}}(x_t^i) \le 1, \quad 1 \le i \le n, \quad 1 \le q \le m_t \qquad (3.1)$$

A data point in a cluster's center has a higher membership degree than an object on its edges. When the data point x_t^i is beyond from qth cluster, its membership value $\mu_{F_{tq}}(x_t^i)$ approaches zero. Likewise, the nearer the data point x_t^i to the cluster center of the cluster q; the nearer the membership value $\mu_{F_{tq}}(x_t^i)$ to one. The membership degree is closer to $1/m_t$, the data point x_t^i is so far away from the among all cluster centers, where m_t is the number of clusters of attributes x_t. In fuzzy clustering, the sum of the membership values showing how effectively one data point belongs to each cluster is always equal to 1. That is,

$$\sum_{q=1}^{m_t} \mu_{F_{tq}}(x_t^i) = 1, \quad 1 \le i \le n \tag{3.2}$$

The Decision attribute y assigns each pattern to one of the s classes of considerations. Each class l ($l =1$, s) has been represented as a crisp set with membership degree of y^i, ith pattern's decision attribute value to lth class is written in the following form:

$$\mu_l(y^i) = \begin{cases} 1; & \text{if } y^i \text{ belongs to } l\text{th class,} \\ 0; & \text{otherwise.} \end{cases} \tag{3.3}$$

A simple fuzzy classification rule is expressed as follows:

$$f(x_1 \text{ is } F_{1q}) \text{ and } ....(x_p \text{ is } F_{pq}) \text{ then } (y \text{ is } l) \tag{3.4}$$

The performance of an FDT developed with the use of the Fuzzy ID3 technique will be investigated in this chapter. The FDT induction makes use of the ideal number of clusters c to every node of the tree. Our focus is on cluster validity rather than clustering techniques, thus we use classic FCM and multiple fuzzy cluster validity indices to obtain optimal fuzzy partitions which capture the basic structure of the attribute values.

3.4   INDUCTION OF FUZZY DECISION TREE

Three fundamental steps constitute the induction of the fuzzy decision tree: fuzzy clustering, induction of the fuzzy decision tree, and inference of the fuzzy rule for classification. Using the FCM technique, the optimal number of fuzzy clusters were created for each continuous attribute in the input space. The optimal cluster number validates the cluster indices explaining why a particular cluster number of c is chosen based on a particular attribute. Section 3.4.1 presents the pseudo-code of the FCM algorithm for creating fuzzy partitions for each attribute in the input space. The fuzzy cluster validity indices used to find out the optimal number of clusters for each attribute are represented in Section 3.4.2.

Figure 3.1 depicts the architecture for developing FDT with the optimal number of fuzzy clusters. The popular fuzzy ID3 technique is used for FDT induction, as

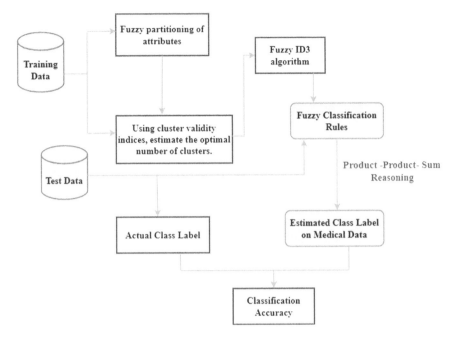

FIGURE 3.1 FDT architecture with optimal fuzzy partitions.

described in Section 3.4.3. The fuzzy rule inference is accomplished by the Product-Product-Sum reasoning mechanism.

With the classification purpose in mind, the fuzzy partitions for discrete (or categorical) characteristics in the input space are produced as fuzzy singletons, and FCM is used to obtain fuzzy partitions spanning from 2 to 9 clusters for each continuous attribute. The fuzzy cluster validity metrics are used to validate the resulting fuzzy partitions for each cluster number. The optimal number of clusters is chosen, and the fuzzy partitions are created based on the optimality criterion of fuzzy cluster validity indices. In this instance, we will probably obtain various optimal partitions for every continuous attribute in the input space.

Table 3.1 shows the notations used to denote the fuzzy clustering and cluster validity indices.

3.4.1 Fuzzy c-means Clustering

The continuous attribute values are partitioned into c fuzzy sets using the Fuzzy c-means (FCM) algorithm by minimizing the following objective function:

$$J_r(U,V) = \sum_{q=1}^{m}\sum_{i=1}^{n}\mu_{qi}^r \left\| x_t^i - v_{tq}\right\|^2, \quad V = \{v_{t1}, v_{t2}, ..., v_{tm}\}, \quad U = [\mu_{qi}],$$

$$1 \le q \le m, 1 \le i \le n; 1 \le t \le p \tag{3.5}$$

TABLE 3.1

Notations

Notation	Meaning
x_t	tth attribute
x_t^i	ith pattern of the tth attribute
v_{tq}	qth cluster of the tth attribute
μ_{Fiq}	membership of the tth attribute in qth cluster
$\overline{v_t}$	mass mean of the centers of the tth attribute
m	number of clusters
m_o	Optimal cluster number
m_t	Optimal cluster number for attribute t

where c denotes the number of clusters determined using cluster validity indices given in Section 4.2, n represents the number of attribute values and m represents the fuzziness coefficient. Each attribute x_t has a $m \times n$ fuzzy partition matrix $U = [\mu_{qi}]$, and V denotes the cluster centers for all m clusters of p attributes. Fuzzy partition is defined by the pairs (U, V). $\left\| x_t^i - v_{tq} \right\|$ is the Euclidean distance of attribute x_t to the cluster center v_q. The FCM method optimizes partitioning in iterations by improving U and V in each iteration, and it terminates when stable conditions are reached.

The fuzzy clustering of the continuous attribute in the input space X is described in the following pseudo-code.

Prerequisites: ε
Input: *attributes* x_t; $t = 1, \dots, p$
Output: Partition Matrix $U = \left[\mu_{F_{tq}}(x_t^i) \right]_{m \times n}$ for each attribute x_t,
Algorithm:
For each attribute x_t in the input space
　　If x_t is a discrete attribute then
　　　　Generate fuzzy partitions as fuzzy singletons
　　else
　　　for $m = 2:9$
　　　　Step1: iteration $= 0$.
　　　　Initialize $U^{(\text{iteration})} = \mu_{F_{tq}}(x_t^i)$; such that, $\sum_{q=1}^{m} \mu_{F_{tq}}(x_t^i) = 1$
　　　　Step2: iteration $=$ itearation $+ 1$;
　　　　Compute the center vectors $V^{(\text{iteration})} = \left[v_{tq} \right]$

$$v_{tq} = \frac{\sum_{i=1}^{n} \left(\mu_{F_{tq}}(x_t^i) \right)^r x_t^i}{\sum_{i=1}^{n} \left(\mu_{F_{tq}}(x_t^i) \right)^r}, 1 \le q \le m$$

Step 3: for each attribute value, update $U^{(\text{iteration})}$

$$\left(\mu_{F_{tq}}\left(x_t^i\right)\right) = \frac{1}{\sum\limits_{p=1}^{m}\left(\frac{\left|x_t^i - v_q\right|}{\left|x_t^i - v_p\right|}\right)^{2/(r-1)}}, 1 \le q \le m, 1 \le i \le n;$$

    end

Step 4: if $\left\|\left(U^{(\text{iteration})} - U^{(\text{iteration}-1)}\right)\right\| > \varepsilon$ then

        Go to step2

      else

      end

Step 5: Determine the cluster validity indices //**Refer to Section 3.4.2**

end

Step 6: Calculate the optimal number of clusters m_t // **Refer to Section 3.4.2**

Step 7: To compute the best partition matrix, repeat steps 1–4.

$$U = \left[\mu_{F_{tq}}\left(x_t^i\right)\right]_{m \times n}$$

    end

end

$\mu_{F_{tq}}(x_t^i)$ is the degree of membership of the ith value of an attribute x_t in the fuzzy set F_{tq}. n is the number of patterns, and m is the number of clusters. The weighting exponent r is given with the formal value of 2 (Bezdek, 1976). Step 6 computes the optimal cluster number m_t based on the cluster validity indices chosen in Step 5.

3.4.2 CLUSTER VALIDITY INDICES AND OPTIMALITY CONDITION (NARAYANAN ET AL., 2017)

In general, determining the number of clusters is a crucial step. There are different ways to approach this problem. As a part of explainable FDT where each continuous attribute is partitioned into several fuzzy sets, determining the optimal cluster number using cluster validity indices explains why a particular cluster number is used during FDT generation. Different cluster validity indices used are Separation and Compactness, compact overlap (Fukuyama, 1989, Xie and Beni, 1991) Partition Entropy, Fuzzy Hyper Volume, PBMF, and Partition Coefficient. The equation of indices and the process of obtaining optimal cluster numbers is as follows.

3.4.2.1 Separation and Compactness (SC) (Zahid et al., 1999)

$$V_{SC}(U,V;x_t,m) = SC_1(U,V;x_t,m) - SC_2(U,V;x_t,m)$$

$$SC_1(U,V;x_t,m) = \frac{\sum_{q=1}^{m} \left\| v_{tq} - \overline{v_t} \right\|^2 / m}{\sum_{q=1}^{m} \left(\sum_{i=1}^{n} (\mu_{F_{iq}}(x_t^i))^r) \left\| (x_t^i) - v_{tq} \right\|^2 / \sum_{t=1}^{n} (\mu_{F_{iq}}(x_t^i)) \right)}; t = 1,...p$$

$$SC_2(U,V;x_t,m) = \frac{\sum_{q=1}^{m-1} \sum_{l=i+1}^{m} \left(\sum_{i=1}^{n} \left(\min\left(\mu_{F_{iq}}(x_t^i), \mu_{F_{il}}(x_t^i)\right)\right)^2 \right) / \sum_{i=1}^{n} \left(\min\left(\mu_{F_{iq}}(x_t^i), \mu_{F_{il}}(x_t^i)\right)\right)}{\sum_{i=1}^{n} \left(\max_{1 \leq q \leq m} \mu_{F_{iq}}(x_t^i)\right)^2 / \sum_{i=1}^{n} \max_{1 \leq q \leq m} \mu_{F_{iq}}(x_t^i))}$$

Optimal Cluster Number: $m_t = \left\{ m_o : \ V_{SC}(U,V;x_t,m_o) = \min_{2 \leq m \leq 9} \left\{ V_{SC}(U,V;x_t,m\right\}\right\}$

3.4.2.2   Compact Overlap (CO) (Zalik, 2010)

$$V_{CO}(U;x_t,m) = C(U;x_t,m) - O(U;x_t,m)$$

$$C(U;x_t,m) - O(U;x_t,m) = \frac{1}{n} \sum_{i=1}^{n} \left(\sum_{q=1}^{m} C_{qi}(U;x_t,m) - \sum_{a=1}^{m-1} \sum_{b=a+1}^{m} O_{abi}(U;x_t,m)) \right)$$

$$C_{ki}(U;x_t,m) = \begin{cases} \mu_{F_{iq}}(x_t^i) & if\left(\mu_{F_{iq}}(x_t^i) - \mu_{F_{il}}(x_t^i)\right) \geq T_m, q \neq l, l = 1,..m, t = 1,...,p \\ 0 & \text{otherwise} \end{cases}$$

$$O_{abi}(U;x_t,m) = \begin{cases} 1 - (\mu_{F_{ia}}(x_t^i) - \mu_{F_{ib}}(x_t^i)) & if\left(\mu_{F_{ia}}(x_t^i) - \mu_{F_{ib}}(x_t^i)\right) \geq T_o \text{ and } a \neq b \\ 0 & \text{otherwise} \end{cases}$$

Optimal Cluster Number:

$$m_t = \left\{ m_o : \ V_{CO}(U;x_t,m_o) = \max_{2 \leq m \leq 9} \left\{ V_{CO}(U;x_t,m\right\}\right\}$$

3.4.2.3   Fukuyama and Sugeno (FS) (Fukuyama, 1989)

$$V_{FS}(U,V;x_t,m) = \sum_{q=1}^{m} \sum_{i=1}^{n} (\mu_{F_{iq}}(x_t^i))^m \left(\left\| (x_t^i) - v_{tq} \right\|^2 - \left\| v_{tq} - \overline{v_t} \right\|_A^2 \right); t = 1,...,p$$

Optimal Cluster Number:

$$m_t = \left\{ m_o : \quad V_{FS}(U,V;x_t,m_o) = \min_{2 \le m \le 9} \{ V_{FS}(U,V;x_t,m) \} \right\}$$

3.4.2.4 Xie and Beni (XB) (Xie and Beni, 1991)

$$V_{XB}(U,V;x_t,m) = \frac{\sum_{q=1}^{m} \sum_{i=1}^{n} (\mu_{F_{tq}}(x_t^i))^m \left\| (x_t^i) - v_{tq} \right\|^2}{n \left(\min_{\{q,p=1,......,m\},q \ne p} \left\| v_{tq} - v_{tp} \right\|^2 \right)} ; \quad t = 1,..,p$$

Optimal Cluster Number:

$$m_t = \left\{ m_o : \quad V_{XB}(U,V;x_t,m_o) = \min_{2 \le m \le 9} \{ V_{XB}(U,V;x_t,m) \} \right\}$$

3.4.2.5 Partition Entropy (Bezdek, 1974, 1981, Gath and Geva, 1989)

$$V_{PE}(U;x_t,m) = \frac{1}{n} \sum_{q=1}^{m} \sum_{i=1}^{n} \mu_{F_{tq}}(x_t^i) \log_a \mu_{F_{tq}}(x_t^i) \quad ; t = 1,..,p$$

Optimal Cluster Number:

$$m_t = \left\{ m_o : \quad V_{PE}(U;x_t,m_o) = \min_{2 \le m \le 9} \{ V_{PE}(U;x_t,m) \} \right\}$$

3.4.2.6 Fuzzy Hyper Volume (FHV) (Halkidi et al., 2001, Pakhira et al., 2004)

$$V_{FHV}(U,V;x_t,m) = \sum_{q=1}^{m} \left\| F_q \right\|^{1/2}$$

$$F_q(U,V;x_t,m) = \frac{\sum_{i=1}^{n} \left(\mu_{F_{tq}}(x_t^i) \right)^r \left(x_t^i - v_{tq} \right) \left(x_t^i - v_{tq} \right)^T}{\sum_{i=1}^{n} \left(\mu_{F_{tq}}(x_t^i) \right)^r} ; q = 1,..,m; t = 1,..,p$$

Optimal cluster number:

$$m_t = \left\{ m_o : \quad V_{PBMF}(U,V;x_t,m_o) = \min_{2 \le m \le 9} \{ V_{PBMF}(U,V;x_t,m) \} \right\}$$

3.4.2.7   PBMF (Trauwaert, 1988)

$$V_{PBMF}(U,V;x_t,m) = \frac{1}{m} \times \frac{E1 \times \max_{\{q,p=1,\dots,m\},q \neq p} \left\| v_{tq} - v_{pq} \right\|}{\sum_{q=1}^{m} \sum_{i=1}^{n} \mu_{F_{tq}}(x_t^i))^r \left\| (x_t^i) - v_{tq} \right\|}; \quad t=1,\dots,p$$

$$E_1 = \sum_{i=1}^{n} \mu_{F_{tq}}(x_t^i))^r \left\| x_t^i - v_t \right\|$$

Optimal cluster number:

$$m_t = \left\{ m_o : \quad V_{PBMF}(U,V;x_t,m_o) = \min_{2 \leq m \leq 9} \left\{ V_{PBMF}(U,V;x_t,m) \right\} \right\}$$

3.4.2.8   Partition Coefficient (Gath and Geva, 1989, Weber, 1992)

$$V_{PC}(U;x_t,m) = \frac{1}{n} \sum_{q=1}^{m} \sum_{i=1}^{n} (\mu_{F_{tq}}(x_t^i))^2$$

Optimal cluster number:

$$m_t = \left\{ m_o : \quad V_{PC}(U;x_t,m_o) = \min_{2 \leq m \leq 9} \left\{ V_{PC}(U;x_t,m) \right\} \right\}$$

3.4.3   Basics of Developing Fuzzy ID3

The Fuzzy ID (Quinlan, 1986) is a fuzzy variation of the ID3 originally established by Quinlan [30] for crisp partitions. ID3 is a prominent strategy for the induction of FDT. The root node selection during the generation of FDT is using the fuzzy classification entropy measure. It follows a probabilistic distribution approach to choose the optimal node which is further partitioned into several fuzzy sets (paths). For each optimal fuzzy set F_{tq} of the attribute x_t, the certainty factor concerning the lth class is defined as

$$\beta_{tq}^l = \frac{\sum_{i=1}^{n} \min\{\mu_{F_{tq}}(x_t^i), \mu_l(y^i)\}}{\sum_{i=1}^{n} \mu_{F_{tq}}(x_t^i)}; 0 \leq \beta_{tq}^l \leq 1 \tag{3.6}$$

The fuzzy classification entropy of F_{tq} is defined as

$$Entr_{tq} = -\sum_{l=1}^{s} \beta_{tq}^l \times \log_2(\beta_{tq}^l) \tag{3.7}$$

The averaged fuzzy classification entropy of x_t is defined as

$$E_t = \sum_{q=1}^{c_t} w_{tq} \times Entr_{tq} \tag{3.8}$$

where w_{tq} denotes the weight of the qth fuzzy set of the tth attribute and is defined as

$$w_{tq} = \frac{\sum_{i=1}^{n} \mu_{F_{tq}}(x_t^i)}{\sum_{q=1}^{m_t}\left(\sum_{i=1}^{n} \mu_{F_{tq}}(x_t^i)\right)} \tag{3.9}$$

The following is a general approach for creating FDT with Fuzzy ID3:

Requirements: A fuzzy partition space with the optimum number of clusters, leaf selection threshold β_{th}, and best node selection criterion.

Procedure:
WHILE candidate nodes exist *DO*

    Using a search method, choose one of the attributes as the root node,
    Create its child nodes,
    The leftover child nodes form new candidate nodes, while the child nodes that
        reach the leaf threshold become leaf nodes. This process continues till the
        stopping condition is met.

End

3.5   CASE STUDY: EXPLAINABLE FDT FOR HCV MEDICAL DATA

HCV data (https://archive.ics.uci.edu/ml/datasets/HCV+data.) from the UCI reposi-tory (Blake, 1998) is a multivariate dataset including blood donor and Hepatitis C patient laboratory values. The collection has 615 instances and 14 integer and real attributes. The dataset is suitable for classification tasks. Among the 14 attributes ALB, ALP, ALT, AST, BIL, CHE, CHOL, CREA, GGT, and PROT are labora-tory values, patient id, age and sex, and demographic attributes. The classification target attribute is a category (1- Suspect blood donor, 2- Hepatitis C, 3- Fibrosis, 4- Cirrhosis, an 5- Blood donor)

    To explain the process of explainable FDT, in this chapter, eight FDTs are con-structed with optimal fuzzy partitions for each node. The optimal clusters are obtained using FCM clustering and cluster validity measures are utilized to determine the best cluster number. For this process, clusters of 2–9 are chosen and validity measures are applied to these clusters to know the optimal cluster number. This helps in avoiding the trial-and-error approach or choosing the cluster number randomly. Based on the data available, the cluster validity measure helps in determining the optimal cluster number, and also FCM supports obtaining quality clusters. The process is explained

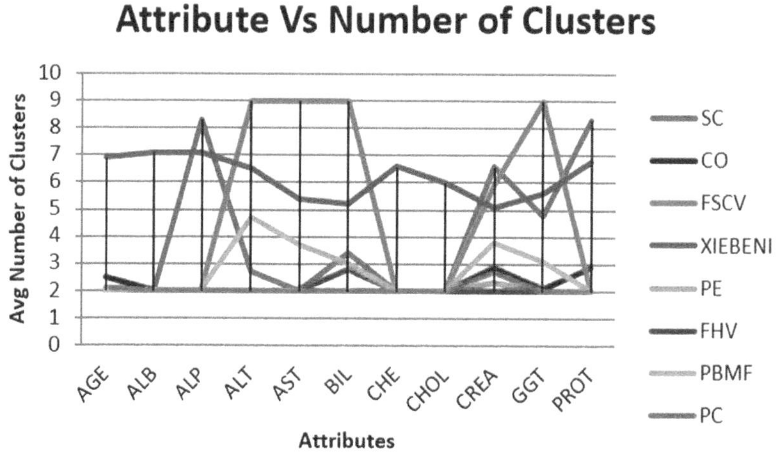

Attribute Vs Number of Clusters

FIGURE 3.2 Cluster validity measures and optimal cluster numbers.

in detail in Section 3.4. The best number of clusters determined by each of the cluster validity measures is shown in Figure 3.2.

The FDT induction process using FHV cluster validity indices as presented in Sections 3.4.2 and 3.4.3 is applied to generate FDT as shown in Figure 3.3.

The fuzzy rules extracted from the above FDT are:

IF **AST** is LOW and **ALB** is LOW and **CHE** is LOW and **BIL** is High THEN Suspect blood donor = 0, Hepatitis C = 0, Fibrosis = 0, Cirrhosis = 1, Blood donor = 0.

IF **AST** is LOW and **ALB** is LOW and **CHE** is HIGH THEN Suspect blood donor = 0, Hepatitis C = 0.0523, Fibrosis = 0.0701, Cirrhosis = 0.8682, Blood donor = 0.0093.

IF **AST** is LOW and **ALB** is HIGH and **BIL** is HIGH THEN Suspect blood donor = 0, Hepatitis C = 0, Fibrosis = 0, Cirrhosis = 1, 5- Blood donor = 0.

IF **AST** is HIGH THEN Suspect blood donor = 0, 2- Hepatitis C = 0.0269, Fibrosis = 0.0227, Cirrhosis = 0.0275, Blood donor = 0.9229.

These rules play a major role in explainable FDT which tells the experts how a decision is made and which rules are considered for inference using the product sum reasoning mechanism. In this experiment, a total of 8 FDTs are generated utilizing the optimal cluster numbers proposed by each of the cluster validity measures. Table 3.2 displays the classification accuracy and total number of fuzzy rules.

The results from each fold are shown in Tables 3.3 and 3.4. The results presented are an average of ten-fold cross-validation performed over the dataset. Following a uniform class distribution, the given dataset is divided into ten equal proportions to perform the 10-fold method. Nine of these ten parts are employed in training, while one is used in testing. The test data is interchanged with one part of training data for every fold. This ensures that each portion is tested at least once and trained nine times.

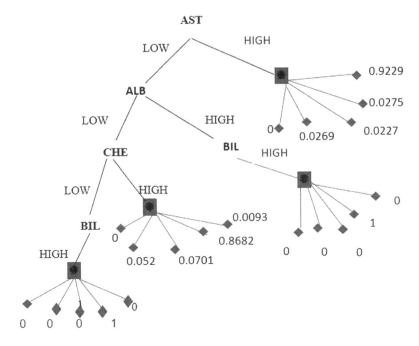

FIGURE 3.3 Fuzzy ID3 for HCV dataset.

TABLE 3.2
Average Classification Accuracy and Average Number of Rules with Different Cluster Validity Measures for FDT Induction

Dataset	SC	CO	FSCV	Xiebeni	PE	FHV	PBMF	PC
Accuracy	90.00	90.00	92.00	91.00	90.00	90.00	91.00	90.00
Number of Rules	66	8	90	102	5	4	34	6

TABLE 3.3
Ten-fold Classification Accuracy

Dataset	Fold 1	Fold 2	Fold 3	Fold 4	Fold 5	Fold 6	Fold 7	Fold 8	Fold 9	Fold 10
SC	90.00	91.67	88.33	91.67	90.00	91.67	90.00	86.67	91.67	88.33
CO	90.00	91.67	90.00	88.33	90.00	91.67	91.67	86.67	91.67	88.33
FSCV	95.00	90.00	88.33	95.00	91.67	96.67	93.33	86.67	95.00	90.00
Xiebeni	88.33	90.00	88.33	90.00	91.67	93.33	93.33	91.67	95.00	91.67
PE	88.33	91.67	90.00	88.33	90.00	91.67	91.67	88.33	91.67	88.33
FHV	90.00	91.67	88.33	88.33	90.00	91.67	91.67	88.33	91.67	88.33
PBMF	90.00	91.67	90.00	93.33	91.67	93.33	93.33	90.00	93.33	88.33
PC	88.33	91.67	90.00	88.33	90.00	91.67	91.67	88.33	91.67	88.33

TABLE 3.4
Ten-fold Number of Rules

Dataset	Fold 1	Fold 2	Fold 3	Fold 4	Fold 5	Fold 6	Fold 7	Fold 8	Fold 9	Fold 10
SC	68	30	97	52	69	47	78	83	75	65
CO	7	6	9	11	6	9	8	11	7	7
FSCV	67	83	105	80	78	112	72	99	103	106
Xiebeni	74	110	105	67	102	95	76	123	104	168
PE	4	5	8	7	6	5	4	5	4	6
FHV	4	5	4	4	6	5	4	3	10	4
PBMF	37	32	30	72	36	9	33	30	35	35
PC	4	5	8	7	6	10	4	5	4	6

From the results obtained, it is evident that the FDT are providing good accuracy and at the same time, the process involved in decision-making is transparent and easily the experts can conclude why a decision is made and confirm using their expertise about the decision made is correct or not. This helps domain experts as well as model developers in many ways to understand how a model works.

3.6 CONCLUSION AND FUTURE WORK

FDT are used to generate fuzzy rules and to infer classification label for the given test data. The explainable nature of rules is well accepted by health care physicians as it helps them to understand the model's predictions making it explainable. In this proposed work, the use of eight FDTs with optimal fuzzy partitions to offer fuzzy labels and the development of FDT to provide fuzzy rule bases considerably improves understandability and allows medical professionals to have a better knowledge of the relationships between patient descriptions and medical class derived from fuzzy rules. In the process of FDT generation, the optimal cluster number is used for partitioning of the attributes using FCM clustering. In this method, clusters ranging from 2 to 9 are selected for each selected attribute, and validity metrics are used for these clusters to determine the optimal cluster number. This helps to alleviate the trial-and-error approach of selecting the cluster number randomly. Based on the data supplied, the cluster validity measure assists in identifying the appropriate cluster number, and FCM assists in obtaining optimal clusters. This proposed system's effectiveness is thoroughly validated on the HCV medical datasets from the UCI repository. The contribution of this chapter lies in proposing FDT as explainable ML model where the generation of FDT is focused with explainable AI procedures in every step of FDT modeling. Using advanced knowledge interpolation techniques to deal with missing variables that typically occur in clinical contexts and explainable deep learning to handle diverse difficulties with health care data is also an interesting future work.

REFERENCES

Alonso, Jose M., Javier Toja-Alamancos, and Alberto Bugarín. "Experimental study on generating multi-modal explanations of black-box classifiers in terms of gray-box classifiers." 2020 *IEEE International Conference on Fuzzy Systems* (FUZZ-IEEE). IEEE, Glasgow, 2020.

Bezdek, James C. "Cluster validity with fuzzy sets." *Journal of Cybernet* 3, (1973): 58–73.

Bezdek, James C. "Numerical taxonomy with fuzzy sets." *Journal of Mathematical Bbiology* 1, no. 1 (1974): 57–71.

Bezdek, James C. "A physical interpretation of fuzzy ISODATA." *IEEE Transactions on Systems, Man, and Cybernetics* 5, (1976): 387–389.

Bezdek, James C. *Pattern Recognition with Fuzzy Objective Function Algorithms.* Plenum Press Publishers, New York, 1981.

Blake, Catherine. "UCI repository of machine learning databases." https://www.ics. uci. edu/~mlearn/MLRepository. html (1998).

Bloch, Louise, and Christoph M. Friedrich. "Data analysis with Shapley values for automatic subject selection in Alzheimer's disease data sets using interpretable machine learning." *Alzheimer's Research & Therapy* 13, no. 1 (2021): 1–30.

Chatterjee, Riddhi, Ratula Ray, Satya Ranjan Dash, and Om Prakash Jena. "Conceptualizing Tomorrow" healthcare through digitization." *Computational Intelligence and Healthcare Informatics* 2021 (2021): 359–376.

Chen, Tianhua, Changjing Shang, Pan Su, Elpida Keravnou-Papailiou, Yitian Zhao, Grigoris Antoniou, and Qiang Shen. "A decision tree-initialised neuro-fuzzy approach for clinical decision support." *Artificial Intelligence in Medicine* 111, (2021): 101986.

Chen, Tianhua, Pan Su, Yinghua Shen, Lu Chen, Mufti Mahmud, Yitian Zhao, and Grigoris Antoniou. "A dominant set-informed interpretable fuzzy system for automated diagnosis of dementia." *Frontiers in Neuroscience* 16, (2022): 1–18.

El-Sappagh, Shaker, Jose M. Alonso, S. M. Islam, Ahmad M. Sultan, and Kyung Sup Kwak. "A multilayer multimodal detection and prediction model based on explainable artificial intelligence for Alzheimer's disease." *Scientific Reports* 11, no. 1 (2021): 1–26.

Fernandez, Guillermo, Juan A. Aledo, Jose A. Gamez, and Jose M. Puerta. "Factual and counterfactual explanations in fuzzy classification trees." *IEEE Transactions on Fuzzy Systems* 30, no.12 (2022): 5484–5495.

Frank, Andrew, and Arthur Asuncion. "HCV dataset from UCI machine learning repository." https://archive.ics.uci.edu/ml/datasets/HCV+data.

Fukuyama, Yoshiki. "A new method of choosing the number of clusters for the fuzzy c-mean method." In *Proceedings of the Fifth Fuzzy System Symposium*, 247–250, 1989.

Gath, Isak, and Amir B. Geva. "Unsupervised optimal fuzzy clustering." *IEEE Transactions on Pattern Analysis and Machine Intelligence* 11, no. 7 (1989): 773–780.

Halkidi, Maria, Yannis Batistakis, and Michalis Vazirgiannis. "Clustering algorithms and validity measures." In *Proceedings Thirteenth International Conference on Scientific and Statistical Database Management*, SSDBM, 3–22. IEEE, Fairfax, VA, 2001.

Hu, Chang, Lu Li, Weipeng Huang, Tong Wu, Qiancheng Xu, Juan Liu, and Bo Hu. "Interpretable machine learning for early prediction of prognosis in sepsis: A discovery and validation study." *Infectious Diseases and Therapy*, 2022 (2022): 1–16.

Ibrahim, Lujain, Munib Mesinovic, Kai-Wen Yang, and Mohamad A. Eid. "Explainable prediction of acute myocardial infarction using machine learning and shapley values." IEEE *Access* 8, (2020): 210410–210417.

Ieracitano, Cosimo, Nadia Mammone, Amir Hussain, and Francesco Carlo Morabito. "A novel explainable machine learning approach for EEG-based brain-computer interface systems." *Neural Computing and Applications*, 2021 (2021): 1–14.

Islam, Mir Riyanul, Mobyen Uddin Ahmed, Shaibal Barua, and Shahina Begum. "A systematic review of explainable artificial intelligence in terms of different application domains and tasks." *Applied Sciences* 12, no. 3 (2022): 1353.

Jain, Anil K., and Richard C. Dubes. *Algorithms for Clustering Data.* Prentice-Hall, Inc., Upper Saddle River, NJ, 1988.

Kim, Kwang Hyeon, Hae-Won Koo, Byung-Jou Lee, Sang-Won Yoon, and Moon-Jun Sohn. "Cerebral hemorrhage detection and localization with medical imaging for cerebrovascular disease diagnosis and treatment using explainable deep learning." *Journal of the Korean Physical Society* 79, no. 3 (2021): 321–327.

Kokkotis, Christos, Charis Ntakolia, Serafeim Moustakidis, Giannis Giakas, and Dimitrios Tsaopoulos. "Explainable machine learning for knee osteoarthritis diagnosis based on a novel fuzzy feature selection methodology." *Physical and Engineering Sciences in Medicine* 45, no. 1 (2022): 219–229.

Li, Jianqiang, Cheng Wang, Jie Chen, Heng Zhang, Yuyan Dai, Lingwei Wang, Li Wang, and Asoke K. Nandi. "Explainable cnn with fuzzy tree regularization for respiratory sound analysis." *IEEE Transactions on Fuzzy Systems* 30, no. 6 (2022): 1516–1528.

Narayanan, Swathi Jamjala, Cyril Joe Baby, Boominathan Perumal, Rajen B. Bhatt, Xiaochun Cheng, Muhammad Rukunuddin Ghalib, and Achyut Shankar. "Fuzzy decision trees embedded with evolutionary fuzzy clustering for locating users using wireless signal strength in an indoor environment." *International Journal of Intelligent Systems* 36, no. 8 (2021): 4280–4297.

Narayanan, Swathi Jamjala, Rajen B. Bhatt, and Ilango Paramasivam. "An improved second order training algorithm for improving the accuracy of fuzzy decision trees." *International Journal of Fuzzy System Applications (IJFSA)* 5, no. 4 (2016a): 96–120.

Narayanan, Swathi Jamjala, Rajen B. Bhatt, and Ilango Paramasivam. "User localisation using wireless signal strength-an application for pattern classification using fuzzy decision tree." *International Journal of Internet Protocol Technology* 9, no. 2–3 (2016b): 138–150.

Narayanan, Swathi Jamjala, Rajen B. Bhatt, Ilango Paramasivam, M. Khalid, and B. K. Tripathy. "Induction of fuzzy decision trees and its refinement using gradient projected-neuro-fuzzy decision tree." *International Journal of Advanced Intelligence Paradigms* 6, no. 4 (2014): 346–369.

Narayanan, Swathi J., Ilango Paramasivam, Rajen B. Bhatt, and M. Khalid. "A study on the approximation of clustered data to parameterized family of fuzzy membership functions for the induction of fuzzy decision trees." *Cybernetics and Information Technologies* 15, no. 2 (2015): 75–96.

Narayanan, Swathi Jamjala, Ilango Paramasivam, and Rajen B. Bhatt. "On the estimation of optimal number of clusters for the induction of fuzzy decision trees." *International Journal of Data Science* 2, no. 3 (2017): 221–245.

Pakhira, Malay K., Sanghamitra Bandyopadhyay, and Ujjwal Maulik. "Validity index for crisp and fuzzy clusters." *Pattern Recognition* 37, no. 3 (2004): 487–501.

Panigrahi, Niranjan, Ishan Ayus, and Om Prakash Jena. "An expert system-based clinical decision support system for Hepatitis-B prediction & diagnosis." *Machine Learning for Healthcare Applications* 2021 (2021): 57–75.

Paramesha, K., H. L. Gururaj, and Om Prakash Jena. "Applications of machine learning in biomedical text processing and food industry." *Machine Learning for Healthcare Applications* 2021 (2021): 151–167.

Pattnayak, Parthasarathi, and Amiya Ranjan Panda. "Innovation on machine learning in healthcare services-An introduction." In *Technical Advancements of Machine Learning in Healthcare*, 1–30. Springer, Singapore, 2021.

Patra, Sudhansu Shekhar, Om Praksah Jena, Gaurav Kumar, Sreyashi Pramanik, Chinmaya Misra, and Kamakhya Narain Singh. "Random forest algorithm in imbalance genomics classification." *Data Analytics in Bioinformatics: A Machine Learning Perspective* 2021 (2021): 173–190.

Peng, Junfeng, Kaiqiang Zou, Mi Zhou, Yi Teng, Xiongyong Zhu, Feifei Zhang, and Jun Xu. "An explainable artificial intelligence framework for the deterioration risk prediction of hepatitis patients." *Journal of Medical Systems* 45, no. 5 (2021): 1–9.

Quinlan, J. Ross. "Induction of decision trees." *Machine Learning* 1, no. 1 (1986): 81–106.

Rabcan, Jan, Elena Zaitseva, Vitaly Levashenko, Miroslav Kvassay, Pavol Surda, and Denisa Macekova. "Fuzzy decision tree based method in decision-making of COVID-19 patients' treatment." *Mathematics* 9, no. 24 (2021): 3282.

Sahu, Barnali, Sitarashmi Sahu, and Om Prakash Jena. "Impact of ensemble-based models on cancer classification, its development, and challenges." In *Machine Learning and Deep Learning in Efficacy Improvement of Healthcare Systems*, 155–172. United Kingdom: CRC Press, 2022.

Stenwig, Eline, Giampiero Salvi, Pierluigi Salvo Rossi, and Nils Kristian Skjærvold. "Comparative analysis of explainable machine learning prediction models for hospital mortality." *BMC Medical Research Methodology* 22, no. 1 (2022): 1–14.

Suzuki, Hirofumi, Hiroaki Iwashita, Takuya Takagi, Keisuke Goto, Yuta Fujishige, and Satoshi Hara. "Explainable and local correction of classification models using decision trees." *Association for the Advancement of Artificial Intelligence*, Virtual Conference, 2022.

Trauwaert, Etienne. "On the meaning of Dunn's partition coefficient for fuzzy clusters." *Fuzzy Sets and Systems* 25, no. 2 (1988): 217–242.

Ultsch, Alfred, Jörg Hoffmann, Maximilian Röhnert, Malte Von Bonin, Uta Oelschlägel, Cornelia Brendel, and Michael C. Thrun. "An explainable AI system for the diagnosis of high dimensional biomedical data." *arXiv e-prints*, (2021): arXiv-2107.

Weber, Rosina. "A class of methods for automatic knowledge acquisition." In *Proceedings of the Second International Conference on Fuzzy Logic and Neural Networks*, Iizuka, 1992.

Xie, Xuanli Lisa, and Gerardo Beni. "A validity measure for fuzzy clustering." *IEEE Transactions on Pattern Analysis & Machine Intelligence* 13, no. 08 (1991): 841–847.

Zahid, Noureddine, Mohamed Limouri, and Abderrahmane Essaid. "A new cluster-validity for fuzzy clustering." *Pattern Recognition* 32, no. 7 (1999): 1089–1097.

Žalik, Krista Rizman. "Cluster validity index for estimation of fuzzy clusters of different sizes and densities." *Pattern Recognition* 43, no. 10 (2010): 3374–3390.

Zhang, Yiming, Ying Weng, and Jonathan Lund. "Applications of explainable artificial intelligence in diagnosis and surgery." *Diagnostics* 12, no. 2 (2022): 237.

4 Statistical Algorithm for Change Point Detection in Multivariate Time Series of Medicine Data Based on Principles of Explainable Artificial Intelligence

D. Klyushin and A. Urazovskyi
Taras Shevchenko National University of Kyiv

4.1 INTRODUCTION

In the opinion of the World Health Organization (WHO 2021), an artificial intellect offers great opportunities to improve health care worldwide, but only if ethics and human rights are at the center of its development and use. The advantages of using artificial intelligence can easily include the use of advanced medical experience where there are not enough specialists, optimization of resources in the healthcare system, and much more. But its shortcomings are not so obvious.

For artificial intelligence to be useful, WHO proposes to observe a number of principles in the development, implementation and use of advanced systems in healthcare, in particular, to keep the control of healthcare systems in the hands of a human; give the right to make decisions regarding health, only to the human; it is necessary to ensure the privacy and confidentiality of data as well as strict compliance with the requirements for the safety, accuracy and efficiency of the use of artificial in health care, etc. Among the many principles listed by the WHO, there is a principle that directly relates to the concept of explainable artificial intelligence (XAI): "The principles for implementing artificial intelligence in healthcare should be made as clear as possible to users." Compliance with these conditions, according to WHO, will ensure the usefulness of artificial intelligence in achieving the main goal of providing comprehensive and high-quality health services.

Now, the explainability of modern AI techniques becomes a problem (Pattnayak and Jena 2021, Patra et al. 2021, Chatterjee et al. 2021, Sahu et al. 2022, Panigrahi

DOI: 10.1201/9781003257721-4

et al. 2021, Paramesha et al. 2021). Complex neural networks provide high accuracy of diagnostics and prognostics, but to understand how they made this decision is usually impossible. On the opposite, old-school pattern recognition techniques often guarantee not only high accuracy but also the explainability of decisions and algorithms. Namely, methods, based on the concept of statistical depth of data allow ranking multivariate data, detect the most probable data and detect the least probable data (outliers and anomalies). Due to this concept, we may say about the individual risk of a patient (from almost certain diagnosis to doubt decision depending on the probability or rank of data) and classify the data in multidimensional space.

The purpose of the chapter is to present a novel nonparametric algorithm of change point detection in multivariate time series based on the concept of statistical depth and confidence ellipsoids, proposed in Petunin and Rublev (1999) and developed in Lyashko et al. (2013), and to demonstrate its prevalence and application in medicine.

In Section 4.2 we describe the state of the art in the domain of detection of change points in multivariate time series. In Section 4.3 we consider the algorithm of construction of Petunin's ellipsoids and analyze its properties. In Section 4.4 we provide the results of numerical experiments with wide spectrum of distributions. In Section 4.5 possible applications of the proposed algorithm are considered. As an example, we use a case of a hypothetical coronavirus patient that can be in different states (tachycardia, physical activity, panic attack, etc.) and measures (heart rate, oxygen saturation in blood and body temperature) that must be monitored. In all the cases we estimate the accuracy of change point detection.

4.2 DETECTION OF CHANGE POINTS IN MULTIVARIATE TIME SERIES

The problems of detection and localization of change points in random multivariate time series arise in a variety of problem domains. A change point is a point of a time series such that before this point the time series obey one probability distribution, but after this point, it has another probability distribution. Close, but different, the concept is anomaly. It is a point that differs in some sense from other points. As a rule, a point is considered an anomaly if it lies out of some confidence region.

The existing approaches to the problems of determining the change point in multivariate time series are divided into algorithms for online and offline data. Online data comes one after the other, and offline data is given as a whole. A great selective survey of method of change point detection in offline multivariate time series was made in Truong et al. (2020). Since we propose a nonparametric online method, we restrict ourselves to online algorithms described in the modern publications.

One of the most difficult features of such problems is the so-called "curse of dimensionality." In Alippi et al. (2016), the problem of identifying the change point in time series was solved using the log-likelihood function and the Kullback–Leibler divergence over distributions in different time windows. The authors have shown that the visibility of a change in a given value deteriorates as the dimension of the data increases.

In the paper by Wang et al. (2019), the authors present a method that works for online data flow using a large matrix, depending on the dimension of the source data space. The analogous methods are considered in Romano et al. (2021) where the authors have proposed an algorithm named Functional Online CuSUM (FOCuS). It is based on the concept of a moving window and simultaneously running early developed methods for all sizes of a window. The practical utility of the method was demonstrated by detecting anomalies in computer server data.

Paper Wang and Zwetsloot (2021) are devoted to the problem of the curse of dimensionality. The authors proposed an algorithm for change point detection based on a control chart. Their algorithm allows the detecting sparse shifts in the mean vector of high-dimensional heteroscedastic processes. It is robust to deviation from the preposition on normality, but it is not sensitive enough.

The task of detection the change point can be divided into two subtasks: determining the very fact of a change in the distribution and determining the coordinates of the change point. In Shin et al. (2022), a framework was developed that determines the fact of a change of distribution, but the coordinates of the change point are determined with unsatisfactory accuracy. The Bayesian method described in Sorba and Geissler (2021) works in a linear time from the number of points, but it forces you to choose between the calculation speed and accuracy.

The method we propose is designed to process an online stream, recognizes outliers well and does not use assumptions about the type of data distribution. Consider papers where authors tried to do the same. In Wendelberger et al. (2021), the authors extended Bayesian Online Changepoint Detection (BOCPD), a method proposed in Adams and MacKay (2007) devoted to the analysis of geographic information, outliers were studied that corrupted the data and led to false positive conclusions about the area under study. The same applies to (Cooney and White 2021), where the proposed method was oriented exclusively to exponential models. In (Castillo-Matteo 2021), to determine the greater accuracy of functioning, assumptions were made about the type of data distribution. In Hallgren et al. (2021), information about the distribution class made it possible to optimize the algorithm from a computational point of view. The paper (Fotoohinasab et al. 2021) also has a similar drawback, in which, in order to search for change point points in the model, it is required to know preliminary biological information about the data. To more accurately determine the change points of a multivariate time series, pre-processing of data is often necessary (Fearnhead and Rigaill 2018). In Harle et al. (2014), the authors proposed a Bayesian approach for multivariate time series segmentation using the MCMC method and the Gibbs sampling. It was shown that the transition points are reliably detected and localized with the help of an implicit study of the dependency structure or a preliminary explicit assumption about the structure. Similar ideas were presented in paper (Renz et al. 2021) devoted to gesture recognition using Changepoint-Modulated Pseudo-Labelling (CMPL). In Gallagher et al. (2021), the estimation of change points using a Yule-Walker moment estimator is affected by large shifts in the mean values, making the algorithm unstable.

The algorithm published in Navarro et al. (2021) showed a very efficient performance of an efficient algorithm for convex network clustering, but it requires high computational costs. One of the main methods for recognizing change points, described in Tickle et al. (2021), like most modern methods for detecting change points (in this case with application to global terrorism incidence), assumes that the data flow is independent of time. This criterion is resistant to the violation of this condition, but at the same time, it becomes possible to reduce its power.

The analysis of the literature shows that the most desirable properties of algorithms for change point detection in multivariate time series are (1) high accuracy, (2) stability, (3) independency from underlying distributions, and (4) low computational cost. Below, we describe such an algorithm base on so-called Petunin's ellipsoids. The algorithm of construction of Petunin's ellipsoids is investigated in Lyashko et al. (2013). The authors proved that (1) Petunin's ellipsoids provides uniqueness of random points ranking in multidimensional spaces, (2) the probability that a point is covered by a Petunin's ellipsoid as exact and is equal to $n-1/n+1$, where n is the number of random points, (3) using Petunin's ellipsoids we may find the deepest point and outlier (anomaly), since the Petunin's ellipsoids covering a set of random points are concentric and uniquely rank them according to their statistical depth, 4) the ranking of random points using Petunin's ellipsoids is independent on underlying distributions This amazing properties of Petunin's ellipsoids make it a wonderful tool for change point detection in multivariate time series.

4.3 PETUNIN'S ELLIPSES AND ELLIPSOIDS

Let us divide the algorithm into two versions depending on the dimension d of initial space.

Case $d = 2$. Let us consider the algorithm of construction of concentric Petunin's ellipses covering a set of random points $(x_1, y_1), ..., (x_n, y_n)$

> *Step 1.* Construct the convex hull of points $(x_1, y_1), ..., (x_n, y_n)$. Determine the diameter of the convex hull and find its ends (x_k, y_k) and (x_l, y_l). Draw the line L passing through them (Figure 4.1).

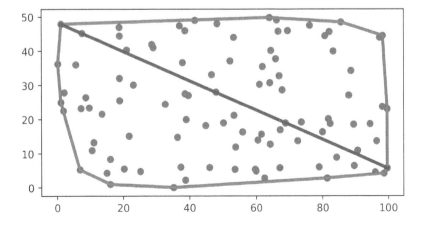

FIGURE 4.1 Two most distant points.

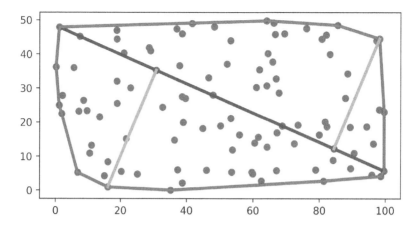

FIGURE 4.2 Two most distant points from L.

Step 2. Determine the most distant points from $L : (x_r, y_r)$ and (x_q, y_q). Draw the lines L_1 and L_2 in parallel to L through the points (x_r, y_r) and (x_q, y_q) (Figure 4.2).

Step 3. Draw the lines L_3 and L_4 orthogonally to L through (x_k, y_k) and (x_l, y_l). Lines L_1, L_2, L_3 and L_4 form a rectangle with sides a and b (let $a \leq b$) (Figure 4.3).

Step 4. Transform the rectangle into a square using translation, rotation and normalizing with shrinking coefficient $\alpha = \dfrac{a}{b}$. Denote the center of the square as (x'_0, y'_0). Compute distances $r_1, r_2, ..., r_n$ from the center (x'_0, y'_0) to the mappings of the origin points (x'_1, y'_1), (x'_2, y'_2), ..., (x'_n, y'_n). Find $R = \max(r_1, r_2, ..., r_n)$. Construct a circle with the center (x'_0, y'_0) and the radius R. Thus, the points (x'_1, y'_1), $(x'_2, y'_2), ..., (x'_n, y'_n)$ are covered by this circle and determine the concentric circles (Figure 4.4).

Step 5. Making the inverse transformations of the concentric circles, we obtain the concentric ellipses (Figure 4.5). The computational complexity of the algorithm is equal to the computational complexity of the convex hull construction, i.e. $O(n \lg n)$.

Case $d > 2$. Construct the convex hull of points $\vec{x}_1, \vec{x}_2, ..., \vec{x}_n$. Determine a diameter of the convex hull connecting point $\vec{x}_k$ and $\vec{x}_l$. Rotating and translating the axes align the diameter along to $O\vec{x}_1$. Projecting the points $\vec{x}_1, \vec{x}_2, ..., \vec{x}_n$ to the orthogonal complement to $O\vec{x}_1$. Repeat this procedure until the orthogonal complement becomes a 2D plane. Apply two-dimensional Petunin's algorithm and construct Petunin's rectangular Π. Reversing all the operations, construct a parallelogram P in d-dimensional space containing the mappings $\vec{x}_1', \vec{x}_2', ..., \vec{x}_n'$ of initial points. Shrink P to hypercube C. Find the center x_0 of C and distances $r_1, r_2, ..., r_n$ from x_0 to $\vec{x}_1', \vec{x}_2', ..., \vec{x}_n'$. Find $R = \max(r_1, r_2, ..., r_n)$. Construct a hypersphere with the center x_0 and radius R. Performing inverse transformations, construct Petunin's ellipsoid in the input space.

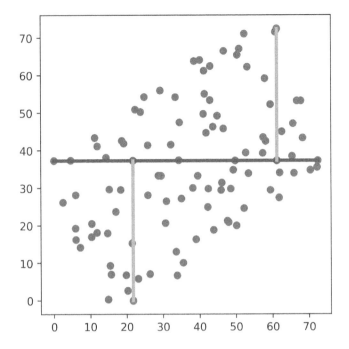

FIGURE 4.3 Translation, rotation, and scaling.

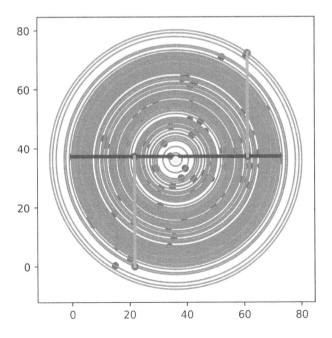

FIGURE 4.4 Construction of concentric circles.

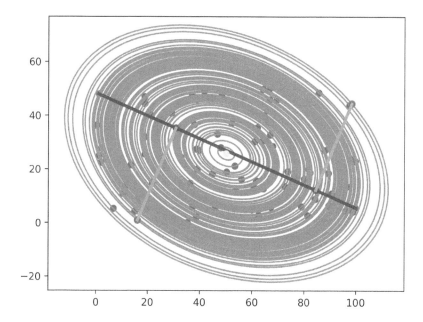

FIGURE 4.5 Construction of concentric ellipses.

Note 4.1. At Petunin's ellipses and ellipsoids only one initial point lay. Thus, using concentric Petunin's ellipses and ellipsoids, we uniquely arrange random points according to their statistical depth (rank of an ellipse or ellipsoid).

Note 4.2. The probability that random points from the same distribution lays within Petunin ellipse or ellipsoid is equal to $\frac{n-1}{n+1}$.

Thus, we have the *exact* probability and may find both the deepest point and outliers. Interpreting values of time series components as random points in a multidimensional space, we can find change points as outliers from Petinin's and ellipsoids. If a point falls out of a Petunin's ellipsoid, it is considered as outlier or anomaly. Moving a time window and constructing Petunin's ellipsoids further, we may detect that distribution of random points is changed and the overlapping of Petunin's ellipsoids is decreasing. In such a case, we detect a change point. If further point falls into the previous Petunin's ellipsoid, we consider the outlier as an anomaly.

4.4 NUMERICAL EXPERIMENTS

The purpose of our quasi-real experiments is to determine the accuracy of the proposed algorithm using the 3D version of Petunin's algorithm. To do this, we used three time series T_1, T_2, and T_3 consisting of different combinations of samples obeying different distributions. Every experiment was repeated 1000 times and error measures were averaged. We computed five error measures: mean absolute error (MAE), mean squared error (MSE), mean squared deviation (MSD), root mean squared error (RMSE), and normalized root mean squared error (NRMSE). To classify experiments on accuracy, we used the last measure. As well-known, if NRSMR > 0.5, the results are considered random. If NRMSE is close to 0, then results are considered good.

4.4.1 Almost Non-overlapped Uniform Distributions with Different Locations

Time series in Figure 4.6 has a clear stepwise form. This is typical for sharply changed states (Table 4.1). The NMRSE is 0.12 (see Table 4.2). This is a satisfactory error measure.

4.4.2 Uniform Distributions with Different Locations that Initially Are Strongly Overlapped, then Slightly Overlapped, and Finally Are Not Overlapped

Time series in Figure 4.7 has a more complex form. Here, we see the combination of overlapped and non-overlapped segments (Table 4.3). This is typical for intersected samples at different time intervals. The NRMSE is 0.32 (see Table 4.4). This is a quite satisfactory error measure.

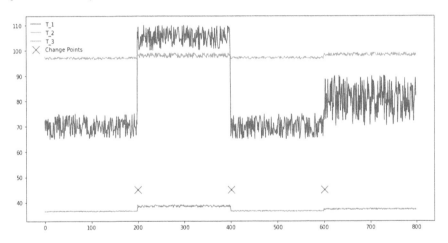

FIGURE 4.6   An example of time series consisting of samples from almost non-overlapped uniform distributions with different means and their change points.

TABLE 4.1
Time Intervals and Uniform Distributions with Different Means

Time Interval	Distribution T_1	Distribution T_2	Distribution T_3	Discovered Change Points
0–199	U(65;75)	U(96.5;97.5)	U(36.4;36.7)	[201, 401, 601]
200–399	U(100;110)	U(97.0;99.0)	U(38.0;39.0)	
400–599	U(65;75)	U(96.5, 97.5)	U(36.4;36.7)	
600–799	U(70;90)	U(97.5;99.0)	U(37.0;37.5)	

TABLE 4.2
Error Measures for Uniform
Distributions with Different Means

Error Measure	Value
MAE	33.48
MSE	7339.60
MSD	19.49
RMSE	46.35
NRMSE	0.12

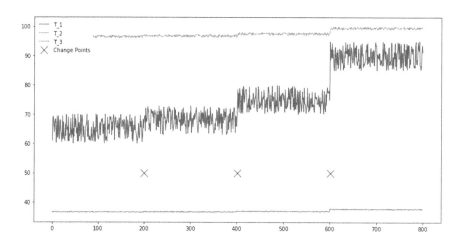

FIGURE 4.7 Time series consisting of samples from uniform distributions with different locations that initially are strongly intersected, then slightly intersected, and finally are not intersected, and their change points.

TABLE 4.3
Time Intervals and Uniform Distributions with Different Locations that Initially Are Strongly Intersected, then Slightly Intersected, and Finally Are Not Intersected

Time Interval	Distribution T_1	Distribution T_2	Distribution T_3	Discovered Change Points
0–199	U(60;70)	U(96.0;97.0)	U(36.4;36.7)	[201, 401, 601]
200–399	U(63;73)	U(96.3;97.3)	U(36.5;36.8)	
400–599	U(70;80)	U(97.0, 98.0)	U(36.7;37.0)	
600–799	U(85,95)	U(99.0;99.9)	U(37.5;37.8)	

TABLE 4.4

Error Measures for Uniform Distributions with Different Locations that Initially Are Strongly Intersected, then Slightly Intersected, and Finally Are Not Intersected

Error Measure	Value
MAE	86.19
MSE	34,898.77
MSD	63.61
RMSE	126.65
NRMSE	0.32

4.4.3 ALMOST NON-OVERLAPPED NORMAL DISTRIBUTIONS WITH DIFFERENT LOCATIONS

Time series in Figure 4.8 consists of non-intersecting and slightly overlapped samples. Here, we see both sharp changes and overlapped fragments in time series (Table 4.5). This is typical for combined samples with almost non-overlapped distributions with different locations. The NRMSE is 0.09 (see Table 4.6). This is a very satisfactory error measure.

4.4.4 NORMAL DISTRIBUTIONS WITH THE SAME LOCATION AND SCALES THAT ARE GRADUALLY BEGIN TO DIFFER

Time series in Figure 4.9 consists of strongly and slightly overlapped samples. This is typical for samples from distributions with the same location and gradually increasing

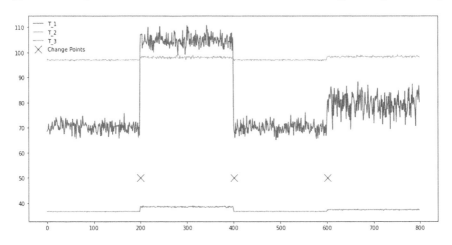

FIGURE 4.8 Time series consisting of samples from almost non-overlapped normal distributions with different locations.

TABLE 4.5

Time Intervals and Almost Non-Overlapped Normal Distributions with Different Locations

Time Interval	Distribution T_1	Distribution T_2	Distribution T_3	Discovered Change Points
0–199	N(70;2)	N(96.0;0.15)	N(36.5;0.05)	[201, 401, 601]
200–399	N(105;2)	N(96.3;0.33)	N(38.5;0.15)	
400–599	N(70;2)	N(97.0, 0.15)	N(36.5;0.05)	
600–799	N(80,4)	N(99.0;0.25)	N(37.3;0.98)	

TABLE 4.6

Error Measures for Almost Non-Overlapped Normal Distributions with Different Locations

Error Measure	Value
MAE	25.81
MSE	4560.03
MSD	11.45
RMSE	37.31
NRMSE	0.09

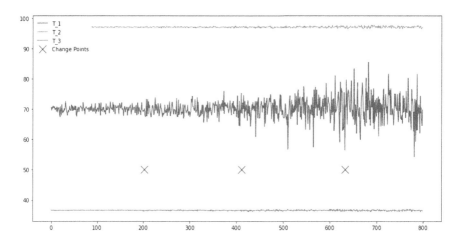

FIGURE 4.9 Time series consisting of samples from normal distributions with the same locations and scales that gradually begin to differ, and their change points.

TABLE 4.7

Time Intervals and Normal Distributions with the Same Locations and Scales that Are Gradually Begin to Differ

Time Interval	Distribution T_1	Distribution T_2	Distribution T_3	Discovered Change Points
0–199	N(70;1)	N(97.0;0.10)	N(36.55;0.05)	[203, 411, 632]
200–399	N(70;2)	N(96.3;0.15)	N(38.55;0.10)	
400–599	N(70;3)	N(97.0;0.20)	N(36.55;0.15)	
600–799	N(70,5)	N(97.0;0.30)	N(37.25;0.20)	

TABLE 4.8

Error Measures for Normal Distributions with the Same Locations and Scales that Are Gradually Begin to Differ

Error Measure	Value
MAE	128.14
MSE	40,361.07
MSD	111.47
RMSE	173.39
NRMSE	0.43

scales (Table 4.7). This case is more complex than previous ones for change point detection. The NRMSE is 0.43 (see Table 4.8). This is rather unsatisfactory error measure, since it is close to 0.5 (random case).

4.4.5 Normal Distributions with the Same Locations and Strongly Different Scales

Time series in Figure 4.10 consists of strongly overlapped samples. This is typical for samples from distributions with the same location and strongly and gradually increasing scales (Table 4.9). This case is much more complex than the previous case for change point detection. The NRMSE is 0.19 (Table 4.10). This is quite satisfactory error measure.

4.4.6 Exponential Distributions with Different Parameters

Time series in Figure 4.11 consists of strongly overlapped samples from the same distribution. This is typical for samples from exponential distributions with different parameters (Tables 4.11–4.13). This case is one of the most complex cases for change point detection. The NRMSE is 0.50 (Table 4.12). This is an unsatisfactory error measure because the prediction is random.

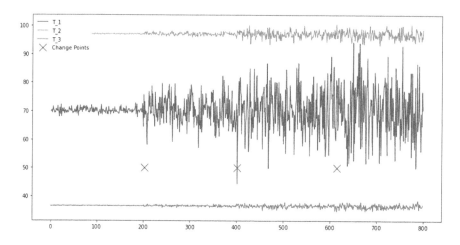

FIGURE 4.10   Time series consisting of samples from normal distributions with the same locations and strongly different scales, and their change points.

TABLE 4.9

Time Intervals and Normal Distributions with the Same Location and Strongly Different Scales

Time Interval	Distribution T_1	Distribution T_2	Distribution T_3	Discovered Change Points
0–199	N(70;1)	N(97.0;0.10)	N(36.55;0.05)	[203, 401, 615]
200–399	N(70;5)	N(96.3;0.15)	N(38.55;0.25)	
400–599	N(70;7)	N(97.0,1.00)	N(36.55;0.5)	
600–799	N(70,10)	N(97.0;1.50)	N(37.25;0.75)	

TABLE 4.10

Error Measures for Normal Distributions with the Same Location and Strongly Different Scales

Error Measure	Value
MAE	57.02
MSE	9099.77
MSD	39.66
RMSE	76.49
NRMSE	0.19

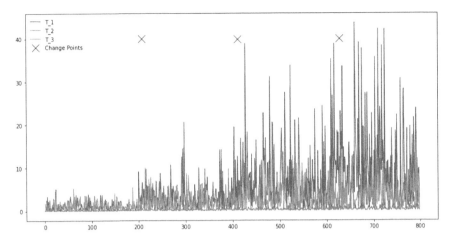

FIGURE 4.11 Time series consisting of samples from exponential distributions with different parameters, and their change points.

TABLE 4.11

Time Intervals and Exponential Distributions with Different Parameters

Time Interval	Distribution T_1	Distribution T_2	Distribution T_3	Discovered Change Points
0–199	Exp(1)	Exp(1)	Exp(0.1)	[208, 417, 628]
200–399	Exp(3)	Exp(2)	Exp(0.3)	
400–599	Exp(7)	Exp(3)	Exp(0.7)	
600–799	Exp(10)	Exp(4)	Exp(0.4)	

TABLE 4.12

Error Measures for Exponential Distributions with Different Parameters

Error Measure	Value
MAE	150.87
MSE	50,728.06
MSD	130.44
RMSE	199.42
NRMSE	0.50

TABLE 4.13

Time Intervals and Gamma-Distributions with the Same Location and Different Scales

Time Interval	Distribution T_1	Distribution T_2	Distribution T_3	Discovered Change Points
0–199	$\Gamma(12,1)$	$\Gamma(6,0.5)$	$\Gamma(10.0.1)$	[232, 430, 603]
200–399	$\Gamma(6,2)$	$\Gamma(3,1)$	$\Gamma(5.0.2)$	
400–599	$\Gamma(4,3)$	$\Gamma(1,3)$	$\Gamma(2,0.5)$	
600–799	$\Gamma(3,4)$	$\Gamma(0.5,6)$	$\Gamma(1.1)$	

4.4.7 GAMMA-DISTRIBUTIONS WITH THE SAME LOCATION AND DIFFERENT SCALES

Time series in Figure 4.12 consists of strongly overlapped samples from the same distribution. This is typical for samples from gamma distributions with the same location and different scales (Table 4.13). This case is the most complex for change point detection. The NRMSE is 0.67 (Table 4.14). This is an unsatisfactory error measure because the prediction is random.

4.4.8 GAMMA-DISTRIBUTIONS WITH DIFFERENT LOCATIONS AND THE SAME SCALE

Time series in Figure 4.13 consists of strongly overlapped samples. This is typical for samples from gamma distributions with different locations and the same scale. (Table 4.15). This case is the most complex case for change point detection. The NRMSE is 0.80 (Table 4.16). This is an unsatisfactory error measure because the prediction is random.

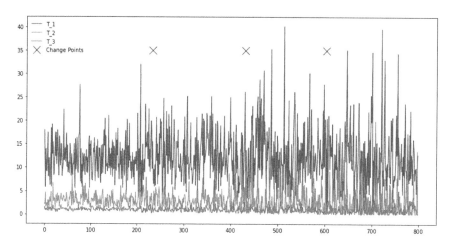

FIGURE 4.12 Time series consisting of samples from gamma-distributions with the same locations and different scales, and their change points.

TABLE 4.14

Error Measures for Gamma-Distributions with the Same Location and Different Scales

Error Measure	Value
MAE	209.18
MSE	84,773.08
MSD	181.34
RMSE	269.36909572994523
NRMSE	0.67

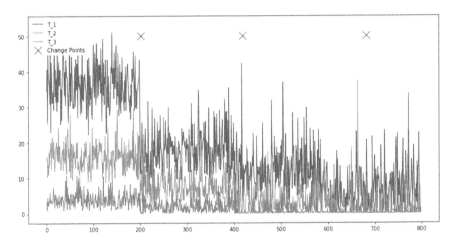

FIGURE 4.13 Time series consisting of samples from gamma-distributions with different locations and the same scale, and their change points.

TABLE 4.15

Time Intervals and Gamma-Distributions with Different Locations and the Same Scale

Time Interval	Distribution T_1	Distribution T_2	Distribution T_3	Discovered Change Points
0–199	$\Gamma(36,1)$	$\Gamma(16,1)$	$\Gamma(4, 1)$	[202, 419, 682]
200–399	$\Gamma(9,2)$	$\Gamma(4,2)$	$\Gamma(1,2)$	
400–599	$\Gamma(4,3)$	$\Gamma(1,4)$	$\Gamma(0.25,4)$	
600–799	$\Gamma(1,6)$	$\Gamma(0.25,8)$	$\Gamma(0.0625,8)$	

TABLE 4.16

Error Measures for Gamma-Distributions with Different Locations and the Same Scale

Error Measure	Value
MAE	274.49
MSE	112,349.50
MSD	259.84
RMSE	318.70
NRMSE	0.80

4.4.9 Gumbel Distributions with Different Locations and the Same Scale

Time series in Figure 4.14 consists of strongly overlapped samples with the exception of the first component. This is typical for samples from Gumbel distributions with different locations and the same scale (Table 4.17). Due to the stepwise form of the first component we have obtained quite high accuracy of change point detection. The NRMSE is 0.14 (Table 4.18). This is quite satisfactory error measure.

4.4.10 Gumbel Distributions with the Same Location and Different Scales

Time series in Figure 4.15 consists of strongly overlapped samples with a gradually increasing range. This is typical for samples from Gumbel distributions with the same location and different scales (Tables 4.19 and 4.20). The NRMSE is 0.30 (Table 4.18). This is quite satisfactory error measure.

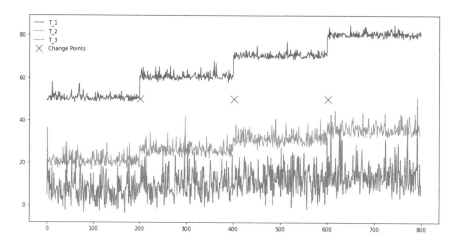

FIGURE 4.14 Time series consisting of samples from Gumbel distributions with different locations and the same scale, and their change points.

TABLE 4.17

Time Intervals and Gumbel Distributions with Different Locations and the Same Scale

Time Interval	Distribution T_1	Distribution T_2	Distribution T_3	Discovered Change Points
0–199	G(50,1)	G(20,2)	G(5,5)	[201, 401, 601]
200–399	G(60,1)	G(25,2)	G(7,5)	
400–599	G(70,1)	G(30,2)	G(9,5)	
600–799	G(80,1)	G(35,2)	G(11.5)	

TABLE 4.18

Error Measures for Gumbel Distributions with Different Locations and the Same Scale

Error Measure	Value
MAE	39.94
MSE	10,154.08
MSD	27.39
RMSE	56.02
NRMSE	0.14

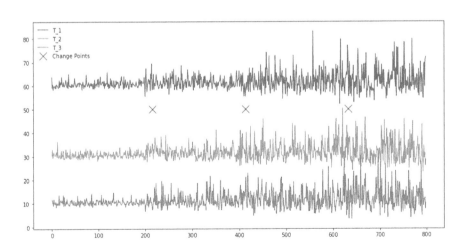

FIGURE 4.15 Time series consisting of samples from Gumbel distributions with the same location and different scales, and their change points.

TABLE 4.19
Time Intervals and Gumbel Distributions with the Same Location and Different Scales

Time Interval	Distribution T_1	Distribution T_2	Distribution T_3	Discovered Change Points
0–199	G(60,1)	G(30,2)	G(10,1)	[216, 414, 633]
200–399	G(60,2)	G(30,2)	G(10,2)	
400–599	G(60,3)	G(30,3)	G(10,3)	
600–799	G(60,4)	G(30,4)	G(10.4)	

TABLE 4.20
Error Measures for Gumbel Distributions with the Same Location and Different Scales

Error Measure	Value
MAE	99.13
MSE	23,019.27
MSD	72.66
RMSE	121.84
NRMSE	0.30

4.4.11 RAYLEIGH DISTRIBUTIONS WITH DIFFERENT SCALES

Time series in Figure 4.16 is similar to previous ones. This is typical for samples from distributions with different scales (Tables 4.21 and 4.22). This case also is one of the most complex cases for change point detection, due to the similarity of time

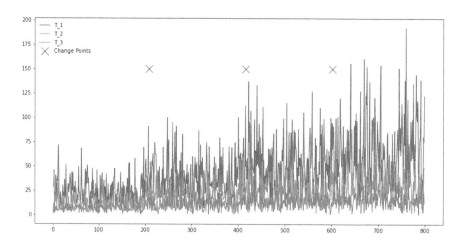

FIGURE 4.16 Time series consisting of samples from Rayleigh distributions with different scales.

TABLE 4.21

Time Intervals and Rayleigh Distributions with Different Scales

Time Interval	Distribution T_1	Distribution T_2	Distribution T_3	Discovered Change Points
0–199	R(20)	R(10)	R(6)	[208, 415, 603]
200–399	R(30)	R(15)	R(8)	
400–599	R(40)	R(20)	R(10)	
600–799	R(50)	R(25)	R(12)	

TABLE 4.22

Error Measures for Rayleigh Distributions with Different Scales

Error Measure	Value
MAE	188.07
MSE	69,601.50
MSD	158.77
RMSE	239.69
NRMSE	0.60

series segments. The NRMSE is 0.60 (Table 4.18). This is unsatisfactory error measure because the prediction is random.

4.4.12 LAPLACE DISTRIBUTIONS WITH DIFFERENT MEANS AND THE SAME VARIANCE

Time series in Figure 4.17 has a stepwise form with slightly and strongly overlapped segments. This is typical for samples from Laplace distributions with different locations and the same scale (Table 4.23). The NRMSE is 0.24 (Table 4.24). This is quite satisfactory error measure.

4.4.13 LAPLACE DISTRIBUTIONS WITH THE SAME LOCATION AND DIFFERENT SCALES

Time series in Figure 4.18 consists of overlapped samples from Laplace distributions with the same location and different scales. This case belongs to the group most complex time series for change point detection due to the similarity of its segments (Table 4.25). The NRMSE is 0.50 (Table 4.26). This is unsatisfactory error measure because the prediction is random.

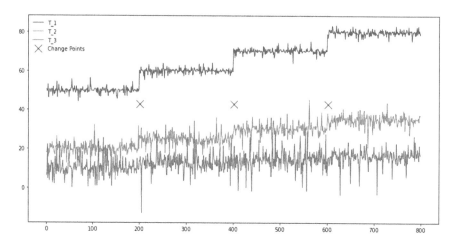

FIGURE 4.17   Time series consisting of samples from Laplace distributions with different locations and the same scale.

TABLE 4.23

Time Intervals and Laplace Distributions with Different Means and the Same Scale

Time Interval	Distribution T_1	Distribution T_2	Distribution T_3	Discovered Change Points
0–199	L(50,1)	L(20,2)	L(10,3)	[205, 401, 645]
200–399	L(60,1)	L(25,2)	L(12,3)	
400–599	L(70,1)	L(30,2)	L(14,3)	
600–799	L(80,1)	L(35,2)	L(16,3)	

TABLE 4.24

Error Measures for Laplace Distributions with Different Means and the Same Scale

Error Measure	Value
MAE	68.51
MSE	21,592.69
MSD	47.85
RMSE	96.90
NRMSE	0.24

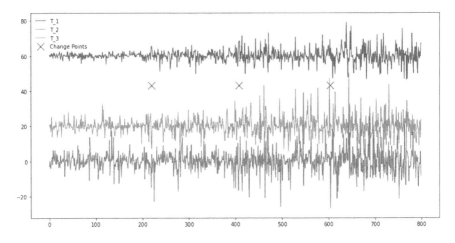

FIGURE 4.18 Time series consisting of samples from Laplace distributions with the same locations and different scales.

TABLE 4.25

Time Intervals and Laplace Distributions with Same Locations and Different Scales

Time Interval	Distribution T_1	Distribution T_2	Distribution T_3	Discovered Change Points
0–199	L(60,1)	L(20,2)	L(0,3)	[220, 408, 603]
200–399	L(60,2)	L(20,3)	L(0,4)	
400–599	L(60,3)	L(20,4)	L(0,5)	
600–799	L(60,4)	L(20,5)	L(0,6)	

TABLE 4.26

Error Measures for Laplace Distributions with Same Locations and Different Scales

Error Measure	Value
MAE	156.16
MSE	52,935.07
MSD	129.13
RMSE	201.09
NRMSE	0.50

4.4.14   LOGISTIC DISTRIBUTIONS WITH DIFFERENT LOCATIONS AND THE SAME SCALE

Time series in Figure 4.18 has a stepwise form where one component has a strong stepwise form with non-overlapped segments and other components are mixed ones (Table 4.27). This case belongs to the group most simple time series for change point detection due to the non-overlapped segments of the first component. The NRMSE is 0.50 (Table 4.28). This is unsatisfactory error measure because the prediction is random (see Figure 4.19).

4.4.15   LOGISTIC DISTRIBUTIONS WITH THE SAME LOCATION AND DIFFERENT SCALES

All the components of time series in Figure 4.20 consist of overlapped segments (Table 4.29). Therefore, this case is complex for change point detection. The NRMSE is 0.49 (Table 4.30). This is unsatisfactory error measure because the prediction is random.

4.4.16   CONCLUSION ON NUMERICAL EXPERIMENTS

The massive experiment with numerous and various distributions described above demonstrates high average accuracy of the proposed algorithm based on Petunin's

---

TABLE 4.27

Time Intervals and Logistic Distributions with Different Locations and the Same Scale

Time Interval	Distribution T_1	Distribution T_2	Distribution T_3	Discovered Change Points
0–199	Logis(50,1)	Logis(20,2)	Logis(0,4)	[201, 401, 601]
200–399	Logis(60,1)	Logis(25,2)	Logis(2,4)	
400–599	Logis(70,1)	Logis(30,2)	Logis(4,4)	
600–799	Logis(80,1)	Logis(35,2)	Logis(6,4)	

TABLE 4.28

Error Measures for Logistic Distributions with Different Locations and the Same Scales

Error Measure	Value
MAE	89.69
MSE	32,563.88
MSD	73.50
RMSE	125.86
NRMSE	0.31

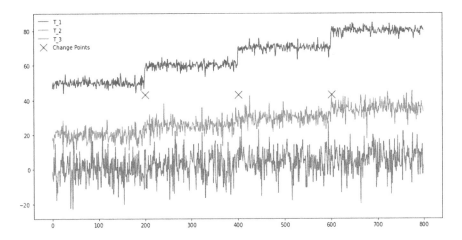

FIGURE 4.19 Time series consisting of samples from logistic distributions with different locations and the same scale.

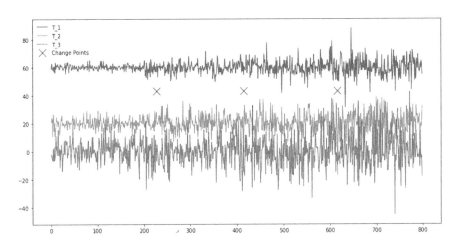

FIGURE 4.20 Time series consisting of samples from logistic distributions with the same location and different scales.

TABLE 4.29
Time Intervals and Logistic Distributions with the Same Location and Different Scales

Time Interval	Distribution T_1	Distribution T_2	Distribution T_3	Discovered Change Points
0–199	Logis(60,1)	Logis(20,2)	Logis(0,4)	[209, 402, 617]
200–399	Logis(60,2)	Logis(20,3)	Logis(0,5)	
400–599	Logis(60,3)	Logis(20,4)	Logis(0,6)	
600–799	Logis(60,4)	Logis(20,5)	Logis(0,6)	

TABLE 4.30

Error Measures for Logistic Distributions
with the Same Location and Different Scales

Error Measure	Value
MAE	152.34
MSE	49,238.10
MSD	128.96
RMSE	194.41
NRMSE	0.49

ellipsoids. As we see, this algorithm has extremely high average accuracy when at least one of its components has a stepwise form. In addition, in other cases, this algorithm is stable and has satisfactory average accuracy compared with the widely accepted significance level of 5%.

For uniform and normal distributions (Tables 4.1–4.10) with different locations and the same scales NRMSE is 0.12 and 0.09. If the location is the same and scales are different MRMSE varies from 0.19 to 0.43. Therefore, the results vary from quite satisfactory to rather unsatisfactory, but they are not random.

For exponential and gamma-distribution (Tables 4.1–4.16) with different location and scale parameters the algorithm has NRMSE varying from 0.5 to 0.8. Thus, the results are random. This is explained by the fact, that time series in these experiments were very similar.

For Gumbel, Rayleigh, and Laplace distributions (Tables 4.17–4.26) we achieved NRMSE in the range from 0.14 (Gumbel distributions) to 60% (Rayleigh distributions). The results of experiments with samples from Gumbel distribution were quite satisfactory (NRMSE is 0.14 and 0.30). The results of experiments with samples from Rayleigh distributions and Laplace distributions with the same location and different scales were random (NRMSE is 0.60 and 0.50). However, in the experiment with Laplace distributions with different means and the same scale, the results were satisfactory (NRMSE = 0.24).

When at least one of the components of a multivariate time series obeying a logistic distribution had a stepwise form, we obtained quite satisfactory result (NRMSE = 0.31). Otherwise, the results were rather random (NRMSE = 0.49).

Thus, we may state that the proposed algorithm of change point detection in random time series is accurate and stable in a wide spectrum of distributions with different locations and the same scale. Otherwise, the accuracy of the algorithm is low.

4.5 QUASI-REAL EXPERIMENTS

For realistic conditions, demonstrating the practical value of the algorithm, let us imagine that we are monitoring a patient using three measures: heart rate (HR), oxygen saturation in blood (SPO_2), and body temperature (T). For this purpose, we generated time series that are close to real time series observed in clinics.

4.5.1 SIMULATION OF TACHYCARDIA

Time series in Figure 4.21 is similar to Figure 4.6. This is typical for sharply changed states as in an attack of tachycardia (Table 4.31). The NRMSE is 0.07 (Table 4.32). The high accuracy of the change point detection algorithm is explained by the sharp jumps of HR.

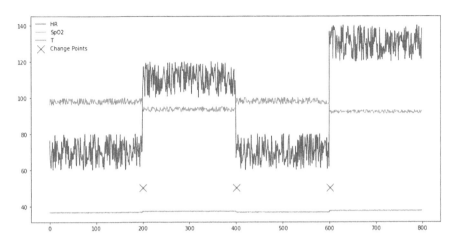

FIGURE 4.21 Time series of heart rate, oxygen saturation in blood and body temperature in patient with tachycardia.

TABLE 4.31
Time Intervals and Distributions, Imitating Tachycardia

Time Interval	Heart Rate	SpO$_2$	Temperature	Discovered Change Points
0–199 (normal)	U(60,80)	U(96,100)	U(35.5,37.2)	[201, 401, 601]
200–399 (tachycardia)	U(100,120)	U(92,95)	U(37,37.2)	
400–599 (normal)	U(60,80)	U(96,100)	U(35.5,37.2)	
600–799 (strong tachycardia)	U(120,140)	U(91,93)	U(37.2,37.5)	

TABLE 4.32
Error Measures for Distributions, Imitating Tachycardia

Error Measure	Value
MAE	17.3
MSE	1946.79
MSD	3.56
RMSE	26.40
NRMSE	0.07

4.5.2 SIMULATION OF CORONAVIRUS PNEUMONIA

Time series in Figure 4.21 is similar to Figure 4.6 but here we see jumps of SpO_2. This is typical in this case it is coronavirus patient (Table 4.33). The NRMSE is 0.06 (Table 4.34). The high accuracy of the change point detection algorithm is explained by the sharp jumps of HR. The high accuracy of the change point detection algorithm is explained by the sharp changing of SpO_2 (see Figure 4.22).

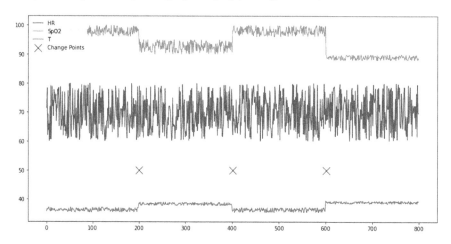

FIGURE 4.22 Time series of heart rate, oxygen saturation in blood and body temperature in patient with coronavirus pneumonia.

TABLE 4.33
Time Intervals and Distributions, Imitating Coronavirus Pneumonia

Time Interval	Heart Rate	SpO$_2$	Temperature	Discovered Change Points
0–199 (normal)	U(60,80)	U(96,100)	U(35.5,37.2)	[201, 401, 601]
200–399 (fever and hypoxia)	U(60,80)	U(92,95)	U(37.8,37.2)	
400–599 (normal)	U(60,80)	U(96,100)	U(35.5,37.2)	
600–799 (strong fever and hypoxia)	U(60,80)	U(88,90)	U(38.5,39.5)	

TABLE 4.34
Error Measures for Distributions, Imitating Coronavirus Pneumonia

Error Measure	Value
MAE	16.76
MSE	1898.63
MSD	4.41
RMSE	24.10
NRMSE	0.06

4.5.3 SIMULATION OF CANCER LUNG

The state of a hypothetical patient with cancer lung (Figure 4.23) is similar to the state of a hypothetical coronavirus patient but here, in addition to jumps of SpO_2, we see jumps in HR (Table 4.35). The NRMSE is 0.11 (Table 4.36). The high accuracy of the change point detection algorithm is explained by the sharp jumps of HR. The high accuracy of the change point detection algorithm is explained by the sharp changing of SpO_2.

4.5.4 SIMULATION OF PHYSICAL ACTIVITY

Here, we are monitoring the physical activity of a hypothetical coronavirus patient (Figure 4.24). The state of such a patient is similar to the state of a hypothetical patient with lung cancer. We see both jumps of SpO_2 and HR (Table 4.37). The NRMSE is 0.10 (Table 4.38). The high accuracy of the change point detection algorithm is explained by the sharp jumps of HR and SpO_2.

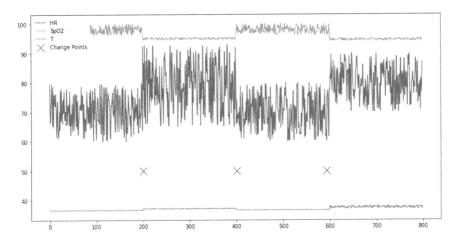

FIGURE 4.23 Time series of heart rate, oxygen saturation in blood and body temperature in patient with cancer lung, and their change points.

TABLE 4.35
Time Intervals and Distributions, Imitating Cancer Lung

Time Interval	Heart Rate	SpO_2	Temperature	Discovered Change Points
0–199 (normal)	U(60,80)	U(96,100)	U(35.5,37.2)	[201, 401, 601]
200–399 (fever and hypoxia)	U(65,93)	U(92,95)	U(37.8,37.2)	
400–599 (normal)	U(60,80)	U(96,100)	U(35.5,37.2)	
600–799 (strong fever and hypoxia)	U(60,80)	U(88,90)	U(38.5,39.5)	

TABLE 4.36
Error Measures for Distributions, Imitating Cancer Lung

Error Measure	Value
MAE	31.24
MSE	4112.34
MSD	17.21
RMSE	45.28
NRMSE	0.11

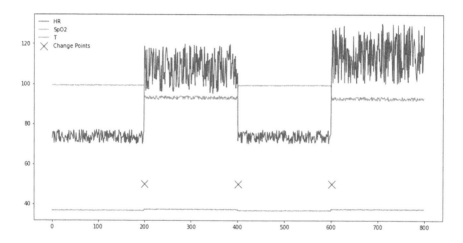

FIGURE 4.24 Time series of heart rate, oxygen saturation in blood and body temperature in patient with physical activity, and their change points.

TABLE 4.37
Time Intervals and Distributions, Imitating Physical Activity

Time Interval	Heart Rate	SpO$_2$	Temperature	Discovered Change Points
0–199 (quiescence)	U(70,77)	U(99,99.4)	U(36.5,36.7)	[203, 401, 601]
200–399 (physical activity)	U(95,120)	U(92,94)	U(37,37.3)	
400–599 (quiescence)	U(70,77)	U(99,99.4)	U(36.5,36.7)	
600–799 (strong physical activity)	U(100,130)	U(91.5, 93.5)	U(37.1,37.4)	

TABLE 4.38

Error Measures for Distributions, Imitating Physical Activity

Error Measure	Value
MAE	27.40
MSE	5108.74
MSD	13.02
RMSE	38.79
NRMSE	0.10

4.5.5 SIMULATION OF STRESS/PANIC ATTACK

Here, we are monitoring the state of a hypothetical coronavirus patient suffering from a panic attack (Figure 4.25). The state of such a patient is similar to the state of a hypothetical patient with tachycardia (Tables 4.39 and 4.40). We see slight jumps of

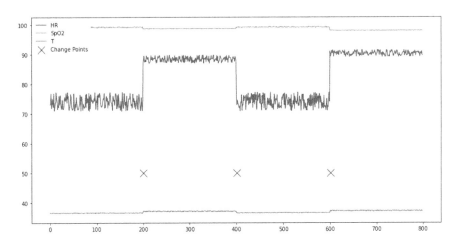

FIGURE 4.25 Time series of heart rate, oxygen saturation in blood and body temperature in patient with stress, and their change points.

TABLE 4.39

Time Intervals and Distributions, Imitating Stress/Panic Attack

Time Interval	Heart Rate	SpO$_2$	Temperature	Discovered Change Points
0–199 (quiescence)	U(70.9,77.3)	U(99,99.4)	U(36.5,36.7)	[203, 401, 601]
200–399 (stress)	U(87,89.8)	U(98.6,98.8)	U(37,37.3)	
400–599 (quiescence)	U(70.9,77.3)	U(99,99.4)	U(36.5,36.7)	
600–799 (strong stress)	U(89.1,91.5)	U(97.9, 98.1)	U(37.1,37.4)	

TABLE 4.40
Error Measures for Distributions,
Imitating Stress/Panic Attack

Error Measure	Value
MAE	39.78
MSE	8677.40
MSD	23.18
RMSE	54.66
NRMSE	0.14

SpO_2 and sharp jumps of HR. The NRMSE is 0.14 (Table 4.38). The high accuracy of the change point detection algorithm is explained by the sharp jumps of HR.

4.5.6 CONCLUSION ON QUASI-REAL EXPERIMENTS

The high accuracy and stability of the proposed algorithm in the case of monitoring hypothetical patients with tachycardia, coronavirus pneumonia, cancer lung, physical activity, and stress/panic attack are explained by the stepwise form of one of the components of a multivariate time series. In every hypothetical situation, we see jumps of HR, SpO_2, or both. Thus, the proposed algorithm has practical value for application in clinics.

4.6 CONCLUSION

The chapter outlines a nonparametric method for detecting a transition point in multivariate time series using tolerant ellipsoids. Both numerical and quasi-real experiments demonstrate the high accuracy and stability of the proposed algorithm in a wide range of distributions and hypothetical clinical cases. This method provides a clear and understandable human interpretation of both the results and the process of obtaining them. This means that this algorithm has a high theoretical and practical value for modern XAI systems developed in clinics, in particular, for monitoring the condition of patients with coronavirus using pulse oximeters. In the future, it would be useful to develop fast algorithms for constructing multidimensional tolerant ellipsoids using the achievements of modern computational geometry and compare their accuracy with alternative methods.

REFERENCES

Adams, P. and D. Mackay. 2007. Bayesian Online Changepoint Detection. arXiv preprint arXiv:0710.3742v1, 2007. https://arxiv.org/pdf/0710.3742.pdf. doi: 10.48550/arXiv.0710.3742.
Alippi, C., Boracchi, G., Carrera, D. and M. Roveri. 2016. Change Detection in Multivariate Datastreams: Likelihood and Detectability Loss. *Twenty-Fifth International Joint Conference on Artificial Intelligence (IJCAI-16)*, 2016, pp. 1368–1374. https://arxiv.org/pdf/1510.04850.pdf. doi: 10.48550/arXiv.1510.04850.

Castillo-Mateo, J. 2021 Distribution-Free Changepoint Detection Tests Based on the Breaking of Records. https://arxiv.org/abs/2105.08186. 2021. doi: 10.48550/arXiv.2105.08186.

Chatterjee, R., Ray, R., Dash, S. R., and O. M. Jena. 2021. Conceptualizing Tomorrow Healthcare Through Digitization. In: *Computational Intelligence and Healthcare Informatics*, ed. O. P. Jena, A. R. Tripathy, A. A. Elngar, and Z. Polkowski, 359–376. Beverly, MA: Scrivener Publishing LLC. doi: 10.1002/9781119818717.ch19

Cooney, P. and A. White. 2021 Change-point Detection for Piecewise Exponential Models. https://arxiv.org/pdf/2112.03962.pdf. doi: 10.48550/arXiv.2112.03962.

Fearnhead, P. and G. Rigaill. 2018. Changepoint Detection in the Presence of Outliers. *Journal of the American Statistical Association* 114, pp. 169–183. doi: 10.1080/01621459.2017.1385466.

Fotoohinasab, A., Hocking, T. and F. Afghah. 2021. A Greedy Graph Search Algorithm Based on Changepoint Analysis for Automatic QRS Complex Detection. *Computers in Biology and Medicine* 130, 104208. https://www.ncbi.nlm.nih.gov/pmc/articles/PMC8026760/pdf/nihms-1664921.pdf. doi:10.1016/j.compbiomed.2021.104208.

Gallagher, C., Killick, R., Lund, R. and X. Shi. 2021. Autocovariance Estimation in the Presence of Changepoints. https://arxiv.org/pdf/2102.10669.pdf. doi: 10.48550/arXiv.2102.10669.

Hallgren, K. L., Heard, N. A. and M. J. M. Turcotte. 2021. Changepoint Detection on a Graph of Time Series. https://arxiv.org/pdf/2102.04112.pdf doi: 10.48550/arXiv.2102.04112.

Harlé, F., Chatelain, F., Gouy-Pailler, C. and S. Achard. 2014. Rank-based Multiple Change-point Detection in Multivariate Time Series. *22nd European Signal Processing Conference (EUSIPCO)*, 2014, pp. 1337–1341. doi: 10.5281/zenodo.43927.

Lyashko, S. I., Klyushin, D. A., and V. V. Alexeyenko. 2013. Mulrivariate Ranking Using Elliptical Peeling. *Cybernetics and Systems Analysis* 4, pp. 29–36. doi: 10.1007/s10559-013-9536-x.

Navarro, M., Allen, G. I. and M. Weylandt. 2021. Network Clustering for Latent State and Changepoint Detection. https://arxiv.org/pdf/2111.01273.pdf. doi: 10.48550/arXiv.2111.01273.

Panigrahi, N., Ayus, I., and O. Jena. 2021. An Expert System-Based Clinical Decision Support System for Hepatitis-B Prediction & Diagnosis. In: *Machine learning in Healthycare Applications*, ed. S. N. Mohanty, G. Nalinipriya, O. P. Jena, A. Sarkar, 57–75. Beverly, MA: Scrivener Publishing LLC. doi: 10.1002/9781119792611.ch4.

Paramesha, K., Gururaj, H. L. and O. Jena. 2021. Applications of Machine Learning in Biomedical Text Processing and Food Industry. In: *Machine Learning in Healthycare Applications*, ed. S. N. Mohanty, G. Nalinipriya, O. P. Jena, A. Sarkar, 151–167. Beverly, MA: Scrivener Publishing LLC. 10.1002/9781119792611.ch10.

Patra, S., Jena, O. P., Kumar, G., Pramanik, S, Misra, C, and K. Singh. 2021. Random Forest Algorithm in Imbalance Genomics Classification. In: *Data Analytics in Bioinformatics: A Machine Learning Perspective*, ed. Hoboken, NJ: Wiley. R. Satpathy, T. Choudhury, S. Satpathy, S. N. Mohanty, and Xiaobo Zhang, 173–190. doi: 10.1002/9781119785620.ch7.

Pattnayak, P. and O. Jena. 2021. Innovation on Machine Learning in Healthcare Services-An Introduction. In: *Machine Learning in Healthycare Applications*, ed. S. N. Mohanty, G. Nalinipriya, O. P. Jena, A. Sarkar, 151–167. Beverly, MA: Scrivener Publishing LLC. 10.1002/9781119792611.ch1.

Petunin, Y. I. and B. V. Rublev. 1999. Pattern Recognition with the Help of Quadratic Discriminant Functions. *Journal of Mathematical Sciences* 97, pp. 3959–3967. doi:10.1007/BF02366387.

Renz, K., Stache, N. C., Fox, N., Varol, G. and S. Albanie. 2021. Sign Segmentation with Changepoint-Modulated Pseudo-Labelling. https://arxiv.org/pdf/2104.13817.pdf. doi: 10.48550/arXiv.2104.13817.

Romano, G., Eckley, I., Fearnhead, P. and G. Rigaill. Fast Online Changepoint Detection via Functional Pruning CUSUM statistics. https://arxiv.org/pdf/2110.08205.pdf. doi: 10.48550/arXiv.2110.08205.

Sahu, B., Sahu, S. and O. Jena. 2022. Impact of Ensemble-Based Models on Cancer Classification, Its Development, and Challenges. In: *Machine Learning and Deep Learning in Efficacy Improvement of Healthcare Systems*, ed. Jena, O. M., Bhishan, B., Rakesh, N., Astya, P., and Y. Farhaoui,155-172. Boca Raton, FL: CRC-Press Taylor & Fransics Group. doi: 10.1201/9781003189053-8.

Shin, J., Ramdas, A. and A. Rinaldo. 2022. E-detectors: A Nonparametric Framework for Online Changepoint Detection. https://arxiv.org/pdf/2203.03532.pdf. doi: 10.48550/arXiv.2203.03532.

Sorba, O. and C. Geissler, 2021. Online Bayesian Inference for Multiple Changepoints and Risk Assessment. https://arxiv.org/pdf/2106.05834.pdf. doi: 10.48550/arXiv.2106.05834.

Tickle, S. O., Eckley, I. A. and P. Fearnhead. 2020. A Computationally Efficient, High-dimensional Multiple Changepoint Procedure with Application to Global Terrorism Incidence. https://arxiv.org/pdf/2011.03599.pdf. doi: 10.1111/rssa.12695.

Truong, C., Oudre, L. and N. Vayatis. 2020. Selective Review of Offline Change Point Detection Methods. *Signal Processing*, 167, 107299. https://arxiv.org/pdf/1801.00718.pdf. doi: 10.1016/j.sigpro.2019.107299.

Wang, Z. and I. M. Zwetsloot. 2021. A Change-Point Based Control Chart for Detecting Sparse Changes in High-Dimensional Heteroscedastic Data. https://arxiv.org/pdf/2101.09424.pdf. Data. doi: 10.48550/arXiv.2101.09424.

Wang, Z., Lin, X., Mishra, A. and R. Sriharsha. 2021. Online Changepoint Detection on a Budget. *2021 International Conference on Data Mining Workshops (ICDMW)*, 414–420. https://arxiv.org/pdf/2201.03710.pdf. doi:10.1109/ICDMW53433.2021.00057.

Wendelberger, L., Gray, J., Reich, B. and A. Wilson. 2021. Monitoring Deforestation Using Multivariate Bayesian Online Changepoint Detection with Outliers. https://arxiv.org/pdf/2112.12899.pdf. doi: 10.48550/arXiv.2112.12899.

WHO. 2021. Ethics and Governance of Artificial Intelligence for Health. https://www.who.int/publications/i/item/9789240029200.

Wu, H. and D. S. Matteson. 2020. Adaptive Bayesian Changepoint Analysis and Local Outlier Scoring. https://arxiv.org/pdf/2011.09437.pdf. doi:10.48550/arXiv.2011.09437. https://arxiv.org/pdf/2011.09437.pdf.

5 XAI and Machine Learning for Cyber Security
A Systematic Review

Gousia Habib and Shaima Qureshi
National Institute of Technology Srinagar

5.1 INTRODUCTION TO EXPLAINABLE AI

Artificial intelligence (AI) refers to a set of methods and models for extracting knowledge from enormous volumes of data. The quality of data, the methods, the responsibilities, and the experience of the AI engineer used by AI systems make humans unable to trust them. Other software development approaches might be regarded as peers to AI-based solutions in cyber security and cannot be trusted.

Whether there can be faith in AI-based cyber security solutions or not? It is not easy to answer a question that encompasses data, methodology, and expert accountability. However, researchers have been working on comprehensible AI to defend the AI-based solutions' reliability, capacity, and trustworthiness in imitation of answering that query (XAI).

A number of distinct explanations for learned decisions have been presented. Some people try to explain the concept in its entirety, while others strive to fully replace it with a model that is intrinsically understandable, such as a decision tree. Other approaches try to guide the model through the learning process to a more explainable state, or focus on just explaining single predictions, such as by highlighting important features or contrasting it to another decision.

John McCarthy first coined the term AI in 1956 when he invited a group of researchers from a variety of disciplines including language simulation, neuron nets, complexity theory, and more to a summer workshop called the Dartmouth Summer Research Project on Artificial Intelligence to discuss what would ultimately become the field of AI (Andresen, 2002). Explainable artificial intelligence (XAI) that focuses on improving model transparency is known as XAI. As the name suggests, XAI provides humans with an insight into why a machine made a specific decision. When humans act on judgments produced by a computer system, the results must be understandable. With the boundaries of XAI, there is a difference between global interpretability, which allows understanding how the model performs in any situation, and local explanations, which explain why a choice was reached in a given case.

DOI: 10.1201/9781003257721-5

Using interpretability methodologies in conjunction with a person keeping a decision-maker in the loop improves trustworthiness and security processes associated with machine learning systems (Andresen, 2002). However, recent investigations in the image recognition sector have revealed that explainable approaches are weak and potentially vulnerable to malevolent manipulations. Post-hoc approaches are fragile, as evidenced by recent research; considering safety and security, a slight change in the input can dramatically affect the interpretations, this vulnerability is unwelcome. Part of the reason for this brittleness (2) is the black-box nature of the underlying models that post-hoc approaches seek to explain, and the explanations themselves are fragile (Rudin, 2019). The achievement of systems based on machine learning (ML), specifically deep learning (DL), in a range of domains, as well as the complexity of these complicated models has sparked much interest in XAI methods. Over the past decade, there has been a dramatic increase in clinical publications, meetings, and symposia about XAI (Pattnayak 2001). As a result, some domain-unique and context-unique methodologies for coping with ML version interpretation and human rationalization system had been created. Over the previous decade, the phenomenal rise in the quality of ML algorithms and DL has contributed considerably to the rise in XAI analysis outputs. DL has a wide range of applications, from e-commerce to gaming (Lapuschkin et al., 2019), as well as applications in criminal justice (Rudin, 2019), healthcare (Fellous et al., 2019), computer vision (Barredo Arrieta et al., 2020), and military simulations (Fellous et al., 2019). Figures 5.1 and 5.2 are the most acceptable representations of the many reasons for Explainability in ML models.

These additions to Figure 5.1 are intended to broaden the range of goals that XAI approaches to pursue. Model explainability, trustworthiness, and privacy awareness are added to complement the claimed relevance of purposes and targeted audiences.

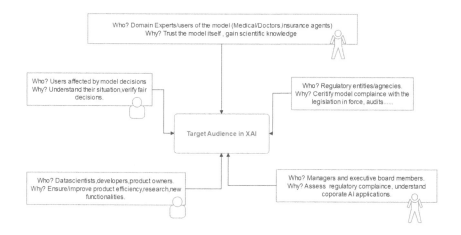

FIGURE 5.1   Diverse uses of XAI in Deep Learning models sorted by audience profiles (Montavon et al., 2017).

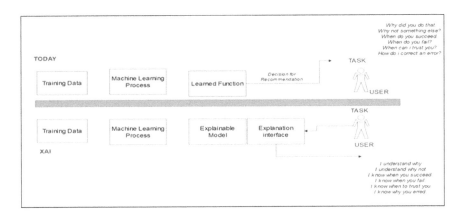

FIGURE 5.2 XAI visualization (Montavon et al., 2017).

5.2 PRINCIPLES FOLLOWED BY XAI ALGORITHM

Comprehensibility: Comprehension is defined as the capability of an algorithm to correspond to learned information in a human-readable approach (Craven, 1996).

Interpretability involves explaining or offering meaning in terms that are understandable to a human being.

Explainability is linked to the notion of explainability of a decision-maker interface that allows for both accurate and understandable communication between humans and machines.

Transparency: If a model is understandable, it is transparent. Transparent models are split into three groups based on their degree of understandability. Models that are decomposable, simulation-based, and algorithmically transparent (Lötsch et al., 2021).

Understandability appears as the essential notion in XAI in all preceding classifications. Transparency and interpretability go hand in hand with this term: A model's transparency refers to how easily a human can understand it on its own. Understandability is how well a human can understand its decisions. Understandability is linked to comprehension in that understanding the information contained in a model is dependent on the audience's ability to comprehend it. Model understandability and human understandability are the two categories of understandability. The various goals of XAI trustworthiness AI are given in Figure 5.3 and summarized in Table 5.1.

- Explainability attributes Scholars use the concepts of "explainability" and its characteristics to define the concept. Some specific clusters have been identified.

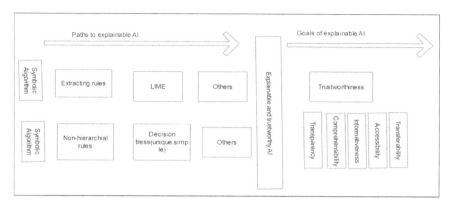

FIGURE 5.3   Goals and paths to XAI.

TABLE 5.1
Summarized Notions Associated with the Idea of Comprehensibility

A Concept	Summary
Transparency in algorithmic design	It is the degree of trust in a learning algorithm's ability to behave ethically in general.
Ability to act	Learning systems must be able to provide new information to users.
Causality	The capacity of a method to explain the link between inputs and outputs is referred to as explainability.
Completeness	The amount to which explanations may describe an underlying inferential system.
Comprehensibility	The quality of a method's language in terms of explainability.
Cognitive relief	The "surprise value" is a metric that determines how much cognitive dissonance exists between the explanandum and the user's point of view. This causes the user to question their viewpoints after reading the explanandum.
Correct ability	An explainability approach allows end users to make technical modifications to an underlying model.
Effectiveness	The ability of an explainability strategy to help users make better decisions.
Efficiency	How an explainability method can assist users in making faster decisions.
Explicability	The degree of correlation between a robot's expected behavior and its actual observed behaviors to complete assigned tasks or goals.
Explicitness	The ability of the strategy to deliver clear and concise explanations promptly.
Faithfulness	The ability of an explainability technique to choose relevant features.
Intelligibility	The ability to understand something solely by the use of one's intellect.
Interpretability	The ability to describe or explain an abstract concept.
Transparency	A method's ability to describe how a system works, even when it performs unexpectedly.
Transferability	The ability of an explainability approach to transfer existing knowledge to new contexts.
Understandability	The ability of an explainability method to make a model intelligible.

5.3 TYPES OF EXPLAINABILITY

The following forms of post-hoc explanations may be considered for opaque models (SVM, GAN'S, Bayesian Networks, GAM's, KNN, and linear regression) in particular.

Text explanations use symbols to create understandable representations, such as natural language text. Propositional symbols, for example, are used to explain the model's behavior by defining abstract ideas that represent high-level processes.

The goal of **visual explanation** is to provide visualizations that aid in the comprehension of a model. Despite certain inherent problems (such as our incapacity to perceive more than three dimensions), the established methodologies can aid in understanding the decision boundary or how features interact with one another.

Local explanations try to explain how a model works in a specific situation. As a result, the explanations that follow do not always extend to a global scale, indicating the model's overall behavior.

To demonstrate how the model works, **explanations by example** pull typical cases from the training dataset. In many circumstances, this is comparable to how humans approach explanations, where they use unique examples to convey a more general process.

Explanations via simplification are approaches for approximating an opaque model with a simpler, easier-to-understand one. The fundamental difficulty arises from the fact that the basic model must be adaptable enough to accurately represent the complicated model.

Feature relevance explanations aim to quantify the importance of each input variable on a model's decision. As a result, a ranking of importance scores is produced, with higher scores indicating that the related variable was more significant to the model.

5.4 SOME CRITICAL APPLICATIONS OF EXPLAINABILITY

Explainability is crucial in a variety of fields, but not all of them, such as health care. For years, algorithms in other sectors, such as aeroplane collision avoidance, have operated without human contact and without providing explanations. When there is some degree of incompleteness, explainability is required. To be clear, incompleteness is not the same as uncertainty. Uncertainty is a concept that may be codified and dealt with using mathematical models. Incompleteness, on the other hand, refers to a feature of the problem that cannot be well represented in the model. Explainability is required, according to Lipton, anytime, and the aim for which the prediction model was built differs from the actual usage of the model after it is deployed. In other words, explainability is required because there is a mismatch between what a model can explain and what a decision-maker wants to know. Explainability and interpretability are also crucial features of DL models, which rely on a large number of weights and parameters to reach a determination. The parameters are frequently abstract and distant from the real world, making the results of deep model hard to comprehend and explain.

There is an increased interest in techniques in the medical field, especially during the COVID-19 epidemic. However, AI applications must be trustworthy, transparent, interpretable, and explainable, especially for clinical decision-making (Holzinger et al., 2017). For example, Soares, Angelov, Biaso, et al. proposed a DL technique for the detection of COVID-19 using computed tomography (CT) scans. In terms of accuracy, F1 score, and other statistical metrics of performance, the proposed approach was reported to outperform mainstream DL approaches such as ResNet, GoogleNet, and VGG-16, but more importantly, this approach is based on prototypes, which, in this case, represent a CT scan that a radiologist can clearly understand. CT scans of patients with and without COVID are used to create the prototypes.

The criminal justice system is another example of XAI in action. Automated algorithms are being utilized in some nations, such as the United States, to predict where crimes will most likely occur, who will most likely conduct a violent crime, who will most likely fail to appear at their court hearing, and who will most likely re-offend at some point in the future. Correctional Offender Management Profiling for Alternative Sanctions (COMPAS) is one such commonly utilized criminal risk assessment tool. XAI is also useful for NLP-based applications. Based on LIME, Mathews presented an explainable strategy for Twitter data classification. Different writers look into XAI algorithms for anomaly and fraud detection as a way to improve consumer confidence.

Autonomous systems (which can be aerial, marine, or land-based individual vehicles with a control system or swarms) are another application sector in which there is a rising number of applications and interest in XAI. Self-driving automobiles, for example, are automated systems that will be employed in a potentially unknown environment.

Military expert systems: Expert systems can be used by the military, for example, in the training of soldiers. A user in a military simulation environment must achieve a specific aim. The user receives useful information on how to achieve the goal more efficiently – thanks to explainable ML (van Lent et al., 2004).

Explainable recommendations assist system designers in understanding why a recommender system suggests a specific product to a specific user group. It aids in the improvement of a recommender system's performance as well as the clarity of a conclusion.

5.5   RELATED WORK

Since its inception in the mid-twentieth century, AI has been strongly tied to both ML and logic and symbolic forms of reasoning. Due to an extraordinary rise in the volume and complexity of data available (today the bulk of data is unstructured, with much more images/videos as well as text/speech than in the previous century), ML and data-driven statistical techniques have gained traction in recent years. Decision trees, symbolic AI, expert systems, fuzzy logic, and automated reasoning, as well as some forms of artificial neural networks were among the first AI methodologies (ANNs).

Explainability has become a hot topic in recent years, not only among scientists but also among the general public, regulators, and politicians. As AI and ML (and, in particular, DL) become more widely used and interwoven with human-centric applications, and algorithmic judgments become more important to individuals and society, the focus has turned back to explainability.

Users can be easily fooled by complex and "black box" (Rudin, 2019) models, which can lead to severe or even catastrophic results. Not just for societal acceptance but also for regulatory purposes, it is vital to open the "black box." (The Algorithmic Accountability Act was enacted by the US Congress in 2019, and the EU enshrined the consumer's entitlement to an explanation.

For some of the most successful (in terms of accuracy) variants of ML, such as SVMs, DLs, and many of the ANNs, the topic of explainability is an open research question (Abed et al., 2022).

5.6 HISTORICAL ORIGINS OF THE NEED FOR EXPLAINABLE AI

System expertise in terms of knowledge representation

There is nothing new about explainable AI. In the 1980s and 1990s, AI systems were extensively studied. Predicate logic and graphs, which include directed acyclic graphs (DAG), fuzzy reasoning, and Dempster-Shafer theory, as well as some sorts of approximation reasoning, were used to describe human knowledge in a precise and formal manner. The Gene Ontology knowledge base, for example, is one of the world's most effective knowledge-based systems. However, one of these systems' major bottlenecks is that it is necessary for ML to have manually created knowledge representation before it can begin working. This problem appears to be best solved by algorithms that act intelligently (Preece, 2018).

Knowledge-based systems

The underlying ML system can be adequately explained using a sound scientific theory. A transparent choice based on AI can be made. The reliable system can make logical deductions from this theory to arrive at its findings, similar to Kepler's astronomy rules for predicting planet locations. A forecast's scope and accuracy can be estimated using sound scientific theory systems.

Skill-based systems

It is common for ML systems to be used for tasks in which a scientific theory is not yet presented or understood. It is now possible to diagnose patients using ML methods based on gene expression data, even when the molecular mechanisms involved in the disease are only partly understood. Typically, ML literature only measures the "quality" of diagnostic systems by assessing their accuracy on small data sets that did not form the basis of the system's development (training, learning, adaptation, and tuning), i.e., "test data" (Preece, 2018).

The constraints of skill-based ML systems will perform well for a very compact data structure to the training data. The skill-based ML algorithm will fail if the data has a different structure. It may not even notice that the data has a different structure than its skill domain, similar to the epicycle model of planetary motion in astronomy.

Using a specific learning technique to create a model from data is challenging. There has been a vast quantity of work devoted to exploring and defining the concept of explainability, resulting in a wide range of explanations and the construction of numerous qualities and structures. After performing a comprehensive literature

TABLE 5.2

XAI Models and Their Degree of Explainability

Model	Simulatability	Decomposability	Algorithmic Transparency
Linear/Logistic Regression	Predictors are human-readable and interactions among them are kept to a minimum	Too many interactions and predictors	Variables and interactions are too complex to be analyzed without mathematical tools
Decision Trees	Haman call understand without mathematical background	Rules do not modify data and are understandable	Humans can understand the prediction model by traversing tree
K-Nearest Neighbors	The complexity of the mode] matches human naive capabilities for simulation	Too many variables, but the similarity measure and the set of variables can be. Analyzed	Complex similarity measuie. too many variables to be analyzed without mathematical tools
Rule Based Learners	Readable variables, size of rules is manageable by a human	Size of rules is too large to be analyzed	Rules so complicated that mathematical tools are needed
General Additive Models	Variables, interactions and functions must be understandable	Interactions too complex to be simulated	Due to their complexity, variables and interactions cannot be analyzed without mathematical tools
Bayesian Models	Statistical relationships and variables should be understandable by the target audience	Relationships involve too many variable s	Relationships and predictors are so complex that mathematical tools are needed
Tree Ensembles	Not applicable	Not applicable	Not applicable
Support Vector	Not applicable	Not applicable	Not applicable

review, the notions related to the concept of XAI are summarized in Table 5.2, given on the proceeding page.

Several theories about how scholars report their explanations for ad-hoc applications; a model's prediction, its causes, context, and consequences, as well as their ordering may be explained using the model's various components, including or excluding. Summarized notions associated with the idea of comprehensibility are given in Table 5.1.

5.7   TAXONOMY OF MAP OF EXPLAINABILITY APPROACHES

The taxonomy of XAI approaches can be best visualized by figure 5.4 as (Barredo Arrieta et al., 2020).

The overall picture of DL model classification and their level of explainability can be best illustrated in a tabular form, as given in Table 5.2:

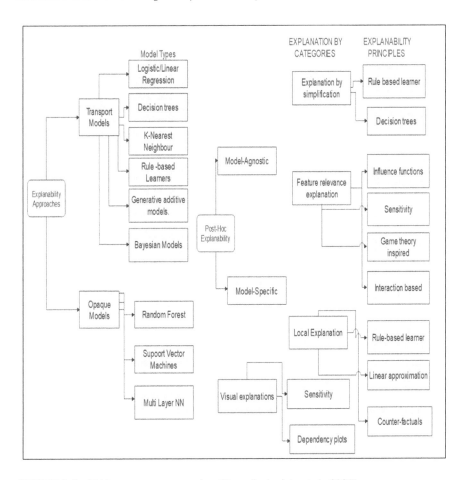

FIGURE 5.4   XAI taxonomy approaches (Barredo Arrieta et al., 2020).

5.8   CHALLENGES POSED BY XAI

Explainability: It is both a theoretically and socially fascinating topic. XAI is a tremendously powerful descriptive tool that can deliver information well beyond what standard linear models could. Various challenges posed by XAI are given as:

   Confidentiality: Some algorithms are confidential, trade secrets, or may compromise security if disclosed.

   Complexity: Algorithms are sometimes simple to understand but quite difficult to implement. As a result, a layperson's comprehension is ludicrous, and this is an area where XAI techniques may be effective.

   Unreasonableness: Algorithms that produce not reasonable, prejudiced, or out of line.

   Injustice: We may grasp how an algorithm works, but we need further information on how it complies with a legal or moral code. The summary of XAI challenges posed can be best visualized in Figure 5.5.

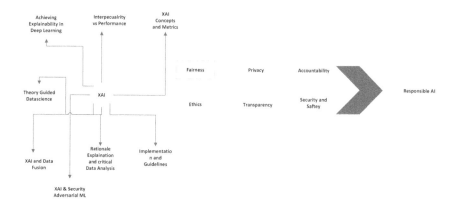

FIGURE 5.5 Summarized XAI challenges.

5.8.1 A BLACK-BOX ATTACK ON XAI IN CYBERSECURITY

Attacks targeting consistency, correctness, and confidence

Depending on which part of the system is targeted, attacks on the underlying system's confidence can be divided into two categories: (1) CI attacks, which target both the classifier and its coupled interpreter, and (2) I Attacks, which target only the interpreter while leaving the classifier alone. According to the threat, the attacker is subject to additional restrictions: The exploit is carried out in a black-box environment, meaning the intended attacker has no information on the model's fundamental design, hyperparameters, or training data distributions. Changing the initial instance x into xadv = x + δ should be a sparse perturbation, and xadv must be understandable. The attack can be performed, keeping these constraints into consideration. The attack is performed using the black-box attack, the invader gathers a small collection of n-test data and begins querying each pattern's prediction and rationalization report. Although test sample outputs can be used to build a surrogate classifier, data n may be restricted. The invader is devoid of information on the distributions of the actual learning data on which the model was trained.

5.8.2 MANIPULATION OF ADVERSARIAL MODELS TO DECEIVE NEURAL NETWORK INTERPRETATIONS

Two essential methods are used to perform adversarial attacks on NN as passive and active fooling. Active fooling is described as causing the interpretation procedures to produce erroneous explanations on purpose. An adversarial model can be fine-tuned with an objective function that combines the standard classification loss with an interpretation penalty term to achieve adversarial model manipulation.

Passive fooling is defined as causing interpretation methods to produce uninformative explanations. Fooling one interpretation technique can also fool other interpretation methods, with various success rates depending on the fooling kind, model architecture, and other factors.

5.8.3 Geometry is Responsible for the Manipulation of Explanations

Explanation techniques have recently gained popularity among practitioners. Among the main reasons for this unforeseen vulnerability is the vast curvature of the decision function of the network. Models themselves remain unchanged as only the explanation process has been smoothed. By increasing the model's robustness to manipulations, its performance can be significantly improved. Explanation approaches aim to make neural networks more reliable and understandable. Explanations can be modified randomly by adding barely detectable perturbations to the input that keep the network's output close to constant.

5.8.4 Saliency Method's Unreliability

The goal of saliency approaches is to explain how deep neural networks make predictions. These strategies are unreliable when explanations contain elements that do not contribute to the model prediction. The condition that a saliency approach mirrors the model's sensitivity concerning input transformations is known as input invariance. In this chapter, using various examples, the saliency approaches that do not satisfy input invariance and can lead to erroneous attribution will be presented.

5.8.5 Misleading Black-Box Explanations are
Used to Manipulate User Trust

Existing black-box explanation tactics are primarily concerned with fidelity or ensuring that the explanations appropriately match the black-box model's predictions. These approaches that are based on the notion model's biases will be reproduced in the explanation unless the black-box model has high fidelity. However, whether this holds in practice is debatable. High fidelity assures that the explanation's predictions and the black box's predictions are highly correlated.

There are also further problems with post-hoc explanations that the fidelity measure does not address: They likely missed causal connections between input features and black-box predictions. (1) Many high-fidelity explanations may appear qualitatively different for the same black box. (2) They may not be resilient, varying dramatically even when input data is perturbed.

Due to these difficulties, it is more likely that explanations provided using present methodologies will encourage the decision-maker to trust a problematic black box.

5.9 VARIOUS SUGGESTED SOLUTIONS FOR
XAI SECURITY CHALLENGES

5.9.1 Addressing Manipulation of User Trust Through
Misleading Black Box Explanations

Two approaches were discussed to address the problem mentioned in Section 5.5. First, recent research has recommended viewing explanations as an interactive conversation in which end users can inquire or explore several black-box explanations (referred to as viewpoints). MUSE is built to support interaction. For example, how will the black box generate predictions for defendants of different races and genders? A judge could ask MUSE this question. MUSE would specifically address race and gender in the if-then clauses on the outside edges. In the if-then clauses on the out-side edges, MUSE would only respond to race and/or gender questions. Recently, researchers have attempted to elucidate causal relationships between input features and black-box predictions.

Besides being inaccurate, correlation-based explanations lack robustness and causal explanations to address these concerns.

5.9.2 Improved Interpretability of DL

It is critical to explain deep neural network (DNN) models when used in security-sensitive domains.

Assisting users in comprehending the inner workings of DNNs, a variety of inter-pretation models have been proposed. What factors does a DNN consider while deciding on a given input? By integrating humans into the decision-making process, better interpretability provides a sense of security. Interpretability, however, is sus-ceptible to malicious manipulations due to its data-driven nature.

5.9.3 Heat-Map Explanations Defense Against Adversarial Cyber Attacks

When ML models are deployed for more sensitive applications, interpretability methods are applied to verify that no distinguishing features were employed. Fair-washing, or modifying a model such that more benign attributes are shown to be necessary instead of the traits used in reality, could be a source of concern. A simple combination of multiple explanation approaches can make the network resistant to manipulation, even if the attacker knows the model weights and explanation proce-dures. Other methods for enhancing the robustness of explanations are given below:

5.9.4 Curvature Minimization

To achieve curvature minimization, the training technique is altered so that a small value of the Hessian Frobenius norm is part of the goal. The loss function is modified to penalize the Frobenius norm for this to work.

5.9.5 Weight Decay

Second, the neural network's weights affect the Hessian Frobenius norm.

5.9.6 Smoothing Activation Functions

Third, the network's Hessian is determined by the maximum values of the first and second derivatives of the activation function. Therefore, the explanations will be more precise if activations with lower values are selected for these maximal values (Abed, Amira Hassan et al., 2021; Chatterjee, Riddhi et al., 2021; Patra, Sudhansu et al., 2021).

5.10   CONCLUSION

Despite the increasing ubiquity of AI models in cyber security applications (e.g., interruption identification frameworks (IDS)), XAI has retained its relevance, progressively vital to deciphering the AI model. To improve executives' trust by permitting human specialists to comprehend the hidden information proof and causal thinking. The critical job of trusting the executives, as indicated by IDS, is to understand the effect of awful information to identify any interruption.

XAI, which has recently been developed as a fundamental criterion for adopting ML methodologies in real-world applications, has been the focus of this overview. The authors of this study expanded research on XAI in two steps. First, by explaining the various principles that underpin model explainability. Second, by demonstrating various motivations for the hunt for better interpretable ML algorithms.

Data availability and material

The necessary data and material used for critical analysis are cited in the paper.

ACKNOWLEDGMENT

We would like to thank the anonymous reviewers for their future constructive comments. We would also like to ask the Cybersecurity journal editor-in-chief for considering this paper for the review process.

Funding: No funding is available.

REFERENCES

Abed, Amira Hassan, Essam M. Shaaban, Om Prakash Jena, and Ahmed A. Elngar. "A Comprehensive survey on breast cancer thermography classification using deep neural network." In *Machine Learning and Deep Learning in Medical Data Analytics and Healthcare Applications*, pp. 169–182. CRC Press, 2022. https://doi.org/10.1201/9781003226147

Andresen, Scott L. "John McCarthy: Father of AI." *IEEE Intelligent Systems* 17, no. 5 (2002): 84–85.

Arrieta, Alejandro Barredo, Natalia Díaz-Rodríguez, Javier Del Ser, Adrien Bennetot, Siham Tabik, Alberto Barbado, Salvador García et al. "Explainable Artificial Intelligence (XAI): Concepts, taxonomies, opportunities and challenges toward responsible AI." *Information Fusion* 58 (2020): 82–115.

Chatterjee, Riddhi, Ratula Ray, Satya Ranjan Dash, and Om Prakash Jena. "Conceptualizing tomorrow's healthcare through digitization." *Computational Intelligence and Healthcare Informatics* 2020 (2021): 359–376.

Concept.https://livingconceptmap.blogspot.com/2021/05/machine-learning-conceptmap.html.

Craven, Mark William. *Extracting Comprehensible Models from Trained Neural Networks.* The University of Wisconsin-Madison, Madison, 1996.

Fellous, Jean-Marc, Guillermo Sapiro, Andrew Rossi, Helen Mayberg, and Michele Ferrante. "Explainable artificial intelligence for neuroscience: Behavioral neurostimulation." *Frontiers in Neuroscience* 13 (2019): 1346.

Holzinger, Andreas, Georg Langs, Helmut Denk, Kurt Zatloukal, and Heimo Müller. "Causability and explainability of artificial intelligence in medicine." *Wiley Interdisciplinary Reviews: Data Mining and Knowledge Discovery* 9, no. 4 (2019): e1312.

Lapuschkin, Sebastian, Stephan Wäldchen, Alexander Binder, Grégoire Montavon, Wojciech Samek, and Klaus-Robert Müller. "Unmasking Clever Hans predictors and assessing what machines really learn." *Nature Communications* 10, no. 1 (2019): 1–8.

Lötsch, Jörn, Dario Kringel, and Alfred Ultsch. "Explainable artificial intelligence (XAI) in biomedicine: Making AI decisions trustworthy for physicians and patients." *BioMed Informatics* 2, no. 1 (2021): 1–17.

Multaheb, Samim, Fabian Bauer, Peter Bretschneider, and Oliver Niggemann. "Learning Physically Meaningful Representations of Energy Systems with Variational Autoencoders." Stuttgart, 2022.

Pattnayak, Parthasarathy and Amiya Ranjan Panda. "Innovation on machine learning in healthcare services-An introduction." In *Technical Advancements of Machine Learning in Healthcare*, pp. 1–30. Springer, Singapore, 2021.

Patra, Sudhansu Shekhar, Om Praksah Jena, Gaurav Kumar, Sreyashi Pramanik, Chinmaya Misra, and Kamakhya Narain Singh. "Random forest algorithm in imbalance genomics classification." *Data Analytics in Bioinformatics: A Machine Learning Perspective* 2021 (2021): 173–190.

Preece, Alun. "Asking 'Why' in AI: Explainability of intelligent systems-perspectives and challenges." *Intelligent Systems in Accounting, Finance and Management* 25, no. 2 (2018): 63–72.

Rudin, Cynthia. "Stop explaining black box machine learning models for high stakes decisions and use interpretable models instead." *Nature Machine Intelligence* 1, no. 5 (2019): 206–215.

Van Lent, Michael, William Fisher, and Michael Mancuso. "An explainable artificial intelligence system for small-unit tactical behavior." In *Proceedings of the National Conference on Artificial Intelligence*, pp. 900–907. AAAI Press; MIT Press, Menlo Park, CA; Cambridge, MA; London, 1999, 2004.

WSKM, G. Montavon. "Methods for interpreting and understanding deep neural networks." *Digital Signal Processing* (2018).

6 Classification and Regression Tree Modelling Approach to Predict the Number of Lymph Node Dissection among Endometrial Cancer Patients

Prafulla Kumar Swain, Manas Ranjan Tripathy,
Pravat Kumar Sarangi, and Smruti Sudha Pattnaik

6.1 INTRODUCTION

Classification and regression tree (CART) is a non-parametric statistical modelling technique (Zhang and Singer, 1999). For simplicity in modelling and interpretation, it has been widely used as a knowledge discovery tool in the field of Statistics, Health Science, Computer Science, Metrological Science, etc. (Faraway, 2016). This technique was first pioneered by Morgan and Sonquist (1963) and later developed by Breiman et al. (1984). CART analysis is an innovative and powerful data analytics technique with significant clinical utility. It has been used in the field of disease dynamics (Aguiar et al., 2012; Kareem et al., 2010) including breast cancer survival prediction by Ganggayah et al. (2019) and weight loss prediction among head and neck cancer patients by Cheng et al. (2018). The complex modelling of cancer treatment for outcome prediction and advising can be automated using CART models to aid physicians to make informative decisions. Barlin et al. (2013) implemented a CART analysis to evaluate how the clinicopathologic factors influenced the overall survival of endometrial carcinoma.

Particularly, endometrial cancer (EC) arises from uterine adenomyosis, and its diagnosis may be challenging as the patients usually refuse to report themselves or report at an advance stage. It has become a major issue in public health. Rathod et al. (2014), in their study, revealed that the high-grade tumour (Grade 3) is one of the significant predictors in higher nodal lymph node dissection with increasing depth of myometrial invasion. Biswas et al. (2013) suggested that histology, disease stage, and tumour size were significant predictors for overall survival of EC patients.

The identification of the number of positive lymph node in an early stage may prevent the progress of advance stage cancer among the patients. The effective number of lymph node dissection may vary and is based on the characteristics of different cancers (Yang et al., 2010, Giuliani et al., 2004). Detection and dissection of affected lymph node significantly improves the survival of the advanced cancer patients (Woo et al., 2017). Among EC patients with pelvic nodal status, the median number of lymph nodes dissection was observed as 30 (Panici et al., 2008).

It is worth to mention here that unnecessary lymph nodes dissection may cause vaginal bleeding, nerve or vessel damage, wound infection, blood clots and damage to nearby tissues. It was also found that EC patients whose lymph node dissection was performed at an early stage, i.e., Stage-1 is more likely to experience surgery-related morbidity compared to patients without any lymph node dissection (May et al., 2010). Therefore, it has been suggested to identify the patients at higher risk and prevent their critical condition by dissecting the required number of lymph nodes at the right time. Positive pelvic lymph nodes and lymph vascular invasion may help to identify a subgroup of high-risk patients (Mariani et al., 2004). The knowledge on tumour size at surgery or preoperatively by hysteroscopy will help to identify the patients, who are at a high risk for lymph node metastasis (Schink et al., 1987). The combined pelvic and paraaortic lymph node dissection is recommended in the intermediate and high-risk EC patients for their longer survival (Todo et al., 2010).

Literature suggests that the EC patients whose lymph node dissection was delayed are likely to have a greater number of positive nodes and longer hospitalization (Faries et al., 2010). Therefore, it is very important to detect the patients at higher risk and extract the required number of lymph nodes as soon as possible. Researchers are looking for ways to estimate the number of lymph nodes that needs to be dissected from the patients using information on different covariates such as age, sex, stage, grade, co-morbidities, etc. But, the limitation of this method is that it only considers the covariates and ignores their levels. To overcome these limitations and to identify and prevent the critical conditions of the patients, here we have proposed a CART model to predict the required number of lymph node dissection using the information on selected covariates and their levels.

The increasing demand of machine learning (ML) technique can be experienced in various healthcare sectors (Chatterjee et al., 2021; Sahu et al., 2022). This technique also helps in mapping and treating different diseases (Pattnayak and Jena, 2021), which can be regarded as an important achievement in medical treatment sector. Explainable artificial intelligence (XAI) has gained popularity in recent years across various research fields (Gunning et al., 2019). The ML technique is a part of XAI (Letzgus et al., 2021) and CART is one technique among several ML techniques. Recently, several CART models have also been developed using the XAI technique (Vieira et al., 2020; Mahbooba et al., 2021; Gong et al., 2022). Further, random forest (RF) technique also been used to improve the accuracy of CART models (Patra et al., 2021).

This chapter has six sections. After a brief introduction, Section 6.2 explains the data source. In Section 6.3, the materials and methods have been discussed. In Section 6.4, the applications to EC data have been demonstrated. Finally, Sections 6.5 and 6.6 includes discussion and conclusion of the study, respectively.

6.2 DATA SOURCE

The data for this chapter was collected on total number of lymph node dissection and covariates, namely age, postmenopausal bleeding, obstetrics history, status, tumour size, histology, grade, myometrial invasion, lymph vascular space invasion, and cervical extension from 170 patients with EC who underwent a scientific and routine pelvic, combined pelvic and paraaortic lymph node dissection during the period of 2011–2017 at Acharya Harihar Post Graduate Institute of Cancer (AHPGIC), Cuttack, Odisha.

6.3 METHODS USED

The CART model can be applied on both quantitative and qualitative data. In particular, regression tree operates when the response variable is quantitative (interval or continuous) in nature. On the other hand, classification tree can be used when the response variable is qualitative (nominal or categorical) (Ma et al., 2018). The regression tree is not burdened by variation in the data and p-values as the conventional regression models. Its main thrust is finding the patterns in the data and doing prediction. Statistically, it is an exploratory procedure associated with inductive or data driven process.

Let us consider a regression problem with a continuous response variable Y_i ($i = 1$, $2, ..., n$) as the number of lymph nodes dissected from ith endometrial cancer (EC) patient and let there be p predictors $x_1, x_2, ..., x_p$. Some of them are continuous, and some are discrete variables, namely, age, postmenopausal bleeding, obstetrics history, status, tumour size, histology, grade, myometrial invasion, lymph vascular space invasion, and cervical extension.

The underlying data structure can be described by Zhang and Singer (1999);

$$Y = f(x_1, x_2, ..., x_p) + \varepsilon \tag{6.1}$$

where f is an unknown smooth function and ε is the measurement error with unknown distribution with mean zero.

In an ordinary regression model $f(x) = \sum_{i=1}^{n} x_i \beta_i$ and the parameter $\beta_i's$ can be easily estimated. However, if the underlaying data structure suffers from restrictive assumptions, then the results we get are a poor fit. This limitation can be overcome by the non-parametric approaches based on recursive partitioning technique such as regression trees and multivariate adaptive regression splines (Friedman, 1991). Regression tree fits a constant to its response variable within each terminal node, and it is well known as the step function model. The CART model provides important predictor(s) which can effectively predict the response variable. An important advantage CART modelling technique is simplicity, and it is very easy to interpret its result.

6.3.1 REGRESSION TREE

6.3.1.1 Model Description

In order to construct a regression tree model, two criteria are adopted. Node splitting criterion and cost complexity criterion can be applied to develop a tree-based model. The node splitting criterion is used to grow a large tree, and then a cost complexity criterion is used to prune the large tree (Gail et al., 2009).

To make a regression tree, we have the data that consists of a response variable Y_i and p predictors x_{ij}, each having n observations. In ordered pair, we can define the data set (y_i, x_i) with $x_i = (x_{i1}, x_{i2, ...}, x_{ip})$ for $= 1, 2, ..., n$. Let us consider that the data space is divided into M regions, i.e., $R_1, R_2, ..., R_M$. Then, we can model the response as c_m $(constant)$ in each region where $f(x)$ becomes:

$$f(x) = \sum_{m=1}^{M} c_m \ I(x \in R_m) \tag{6.2}$$

where c_m is the output value that lies in the region R_m and $I(.)$ is an indicator function which will decide that the value will lies in the region R_m or not.

Now, our objective is to minimize the error sum of square and is given by;

$$ESS = \sum_{c \in \ leaves(t_i)} \sum_{i \epsilon c} (y_i - f(x_i))^2 \tag{6.3}$$

Then, the best value of $\hat{c}_m$ can be achieved by taking the average value of y_i in the region R_m:

$$\hat{c}_m = average(y_i \mid x_i \epsilon R_m) \tag{6.4}$$

6.3.1.2 Splitting Rule

Then, branch and bound algorithm can be performed by splitting the variable (preferably a binary split). Starting with all the available data, consider a splitting variable j and a split point s. Then, divide the data space into two half planes R_1 and R_2 such that;

$$R_1(j, s) = \{x \mid x_j \le s\} \quad and \quad R_2(j, s) = \{x \mid x_j \rangle s\} \tag{6.5}$$

Now, the value of j and s can be obtained by solving the following expression;

$$\min_{j,\,s} \left[\min_{c_1} \sum_{x_i \in R_1(j,\,s)} (y_i - c_1)^2 + \min_{c_2} \sum_{x_i \in R_2(j,\,s)} (y_i - c_2)^2 \right] \quad (6.6)$$

And, the inner minimization can be achieved for best possible value of (j, s) as follows;

$$\hat{c}_1 = \text{average}\left(y_i \big| x_i \epsilon R_1(j, s)\right) \quad \text{and} \quad \hat{c}_2 = \text{average}\left(y_i \big| x_i \epsilon R_2(j, s)\right) \quad (6.7)$$

Since the number of data points is less and finite, we can estimate the best possible value of (j, s). After getting the best split point, we can partition the data space into two regions and repeat this splitting process on each of the two resultant regions. This process can be repeated on all the resulting subregions.

6.3.1.3 Stopping Rule

It is clear that if we continue growing, then we reach at a large tree and make a lot of decisions which essentially end up the tree to individual data point. So, it is a way of overfitting and not considered as a good way to fit the data. On the other hand, if we stop growing the tree very early, we may miss out on finding the interesting pattern in the data.

Splitting of the tree nodes is undertaken only if the decrease in sum of squares achieved due to the split. This strategy is a time-taking process and involves a lot of complex calculations. Therefore, an alternative strategy is adopted to grow a large tree and stop the splitting process only when the minimum node size (say 5) is reached (Hastie et al., 2009). Then the large tree is pruned (collapse the internal nodes of the tree) to get the optimal tree size. There are several methods of pruning regression tree like, reduced error pruning, cost complexity pruning, etc. A detailed description is given in Hastie et al. (2009).

6.3.2 Optimal Threshold Value (Cut Off Point)

Consider we have two sets of information: one on a test variable and another on a state variable as $x_1, x_2,...., x_n$ and $y_1, y_2,...., y_{n^-}$, respectively. Their cumulative distribution functions are $f(x)$ and $g(y)$, respectively. For a given threshold value t (say) we have, Sensitivity $(t) = 1 - f(t)$ and Specificity $(t) = g(t)$ (Faraggi and Reiser, 2005). Hence, the Youden index for the optimal threshold value is defined as;

$$J = Max_t \{g(t) - f(t)\} = Max_t \{\text{Sensitivity}(t) + \text{Specificity}(t) - 1\} \quad (6.8)$$

The value of t, which achieves the maximum value of Youden index, can be considered as optimal threshold value or cut off point (Youden, 1950).

6.3.3 Regression Tree Algorithm

The growing algorithm of a basic regression tree is discussed below;

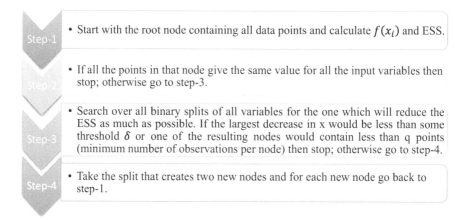

Step-1 • Start with the root node containing all data points and calculate $f(x_i)$ and ESS.

Step-2 • If all the points in that node give the same value for all the input variables then stop; otherwise go to step-3.

Step-3 • Search over all binary splits of all variables for the one which will reduce the ESS as much as possible. If the largest decrease in x would be less than some threshold δ or one of the resulting nodes would contain less than q points (minimum number of observations per node) then stop; otherwise go to step-4.

Step-4 • Take the split that creates two new nodes and for each new node go back to step-1.

6.3.4 VALIDATION OF MODELS

The validation of a predictive model can be performed using different measures such as sensitivity, specificity, positive predictive value, negative predictive value and area under ROC curve (Kareem et al., 2010). These measures can be calculated by using various values given in the following table and described as follows.

		Predicted value	
		Category-1	**Category-2**
Actual value	Category-1	a (True positive)	b (False positive)
	Category-2	c (False negative)	d (True negative)

Sensitivity is the true positive value divided by all the predicted value(s) in category-1 and is defined as;

$$Sensitivity = \frac{a}{(a+c)} \qquad (6.9)$$

Specificity is the true negative value divided by all the predicted value(s) in category-2 and is defined as;

$$Specificity = \frac{d}{(b+d)} \qquad (6.10)$$

Positive predictive value (PPV) is the true positive value divided by all the actual value(s) in category-1 and is defined as

$$PPV = \frac{a}{(a+b)} \qquad (6.11)$$

Negative predictive value (NPV) is the true negative value divided by all the actual value(s) in category-2 and is defined as:

$$NPV = \frac{d}{(c+d)} \tag{6.12}$$

The ROC curve is plotted between sensitivity vs. 1-specificity for different predicted values. This curve shows the predictive performance of the prediction model and the measured value in terms of the area under the curve. The larger the area under the curve, the better is the prediction. The prediction accuracy can be measured by the number of correctly predicted cases divided by all the cases in that study and can be defined as:

$$Accuracy = \frac{(a+d)}{(a+b+c+d)} \tag{6.13}$$

All the statistical analysis and plotting were done by using R (version 3.6.2) and SPSS (version 20). All the predictors are considered as significant at p<0.05.

6.4 APPLICATIONS TO EC DATA

The detailed descriptive statistics of the patients under study is shown in Table 6.1. A total of 170 EC patients are considered for this analysis. The mean age of the patients was 56.86 ± 9.01 years with the range 55 (25, 80) years. Majority patients are from the age group ≥ 57 years (54.7%). About 53% of the patients have tumour size ≥3 cm with the range 7.9 (0.5, 8.4) cm. The mean tumour size was observed to be 02.87 ± 1.49 cm with the range 7.9 (0.5, 8.4). Most of the patients (68.2%) suffered with postmenopausal bleeding in less than 1-year (approx.) with average 381.34 ± 622.18 days and range 2920 (0, 2920) days. The nodal dissection of the patients ranged between (0, 20) with mean number of nodes 09.56 ± 5. 68. Less than 13 lymph node dissections were done among most of the patients (i.e., 85.9%). Considering obstetrics status, almost 70% of the patients had one or more children (multipara) and remaining did not have even a single child (nullipara). Most of the patients are with grade-2 (62.4%), and there are 15.3% and 22.3% patients with grade-1 and grade-3, respectively. The histology status shows that the endometrial glands are present in nearly 85%. More than 80% of the patients have less than 50% myometrial invasion. Only 13.5% and 10.6% of the patients have cervical extension and lymph vascular space invasion positive status, respectively. Majority of the patients (i.e., 57.1%.) are with pelvic nodal status.

Here, Table 6.2 shows the results of multiple regression modelling on EC patient data to determine significant covariates affecting the number of lymph nodes. Two covariates namely nodal status and tumour size are found to be significant (P-value < 0.05) to predict the number of lymph nodes. Other variables are not found to be significant in our multiple regression analysis. Now in an effort to see the big picture and determine what truly matters in the evaluation of lymph node dissection in the EC patients, CART analysis was performed.

TABLE 6.1
Descriptive Statistics of Endometrial Cancer Patients

Patient's Characteristics		Mean ± SD	Range (min, max)
Age (in years)		56.86 ± 9.01	55 (25, 80)
Tumour size (in cm)		02.87 ± 1.49	7.9 (0.5, 8.4)
Postmenopausal bleeding (in days)		381.34 ± 622.18	2920 (0, 2920)
Node dissection (in numbers)		09.56 ± 5.68	20 (0, 20)
Covariate (code)	n_i (%)	Covariate (code)	n_i (%)
Age		Grade	
<57 years (0)	77 (45.3%)	Grade-1 (0)	26 (15.3%)
≥57 years (1)	93 (54.7%)	Grade-2 (1)	106 (62.4%)
Tumour size		Grade-3 (2)	38 (22.3%)
<3 cm (0)	90 (52.9%)	Lymph vascular Space invasion	
≥3 cm (1)	80 (47.1%)	Negative (0)	152 (89.4%)
Postmenopausal bleeding		Positive (1)	18 (10.6%)
<381 days (0)	116 (68.2%)	Cervical extension	
≥381 days (1)	54 (31.8%)	Negative (0)	147 (86.5%)
Obstetrics history		Positive (1)	23 (13.5%)
Nullipara (0)	52 (30.6%)	Nodal Status	
Multipara (1)	118 (69.4%)	pelvic (0)	97 (57.1%)
Histology		paraaortic (1)	73 (42.9%)
Nonendometrioid (0)	26 (15.3%)	Number of nodes dissect	
Endometrioid (1)	144 (84.7%)	<13 (0)	146 (85.9%)
Myometrial invasion		≥13 (1)	24 (14.1%)
<50% (0)	138 (81.2%)		
≥50% (1)	32 (18.8%)		

TABLE 6.2
Results of Multiple Regression Modelling

Co-factor	Category (Code)	Estimate	Std. Error	t-value	Pr(>|t|)
(Intercept)		2.794	2.864	0.975	0.331
Age	<57 years (0)	Ref.			
	≥57 years (1)	0.035	0.043	0.818	0.415
Postmenopausal bleeding	<381 days (0)	Ref.			
	≥381 days (1)	0.000	0.001	−0.04	0.968
Obstetric history	Nullipara (0)	Ref.			
	Multipara (1)	−0.385	0.862	−0.446	0.656
Nodal status	pelvic (0)	Ref.			
	paraaortic (1)	2.245	0.754	2.979	**0.003**
Tumour size	–	1.509	0.263	5.734	**0.001**
Histology	Nonendometrioid (0)	Ref.			
	Endometrioid (1)	−0.851	1.260	−0.676	0.500

(Continued)

TABLE 6.2 (*Continued*)
Results of Multiple Regression Modelling

Co-factor	Category (Code)	Estimate	Std. Error	*t*-value	Pr(> | *t* |)
Grade	Grade-1(0)	Ref.			
	Grade-2(1)	−0.179	1.060	−0.169	0.866
	Grade-3(2)	1.402	1.353	1.036	0.302
Myometrial invasion	<50% (0)	Ref.			
	≥50% (1)	1.167	1.009	1.157	0.249
Lymphovascular space invasion	Negative (0)	Ref.			
	Positive (1)	−0.508	1.408	−0.361	0.719
Cervical extension	Negative (0)	Ref.			
	Positive (1)	0.880	1.192	0.739	0.461

All the covariates with pr(>|t|) < 0.05 are said to be significant at 5% level of sifnificance and highlited as bold text.

At the beginning, a regression tree holds all the data points in its root node. Further, we need a splitting criterion to split the root node. Starting with covariate tumour size and the cut-point 1.9 cm, all the women with tumour size < 1.9 cm are splitted into the left daughter node and the rest into the right daughter node. A total of 56 women went to the left node and 114 women to the right node (Figure 6.1). The choices, tumour size and 1.9 cm are the best cut-point to split the root node.

```
node), spliting variable(xᵢ), number of data points (n), deviance value, response value(y)

1) Root 170 5357.912 9.558
    2) Tumor Size< 1.9 56 1650.982 3.732
        4) Grade=1,2 50 1226.580 2.780
            8) Tumor Size>=1.45 29 366.758 1.206 *
            9) Tumor Size< 1.45 21 688.952 4.952
                18) Grade=2 16 447.937 3.562
                    36) Obstetric History=1 11 216.909 2.090
                        72) Age< 64 6  0.000 0.000 *
                        73) Age>=64 5 159.200 4.600 *
                    37) Obstetric History=0 5 154.800 6.800 *
                19) Grade=1 5 111.200 9.400 *
        5) Grade=3 6  1.333 11.666 *
    3) Tumor Size>=1.9 114 871.789 12.421
        6) Nodal Status=0 59 310.169 10.881 *
        7) Nodal Status=1 55 271.709 14.072 *
```

FIGURE 6.1   Splitting strategy in CART modelling (*for terminal node & --for parallel nodes).

To verify how good the given split is, here we use variance criterion. The variance of the number of lymph nodes of all women in the root node is 32.26. Now, the variance of number of lymph nodes of all women in the left node (tumour size < 1.9 cm) is 30.02 and in the right node is 7.71. So, by splitting the root node, the variances of the subsets of the data went down. We can measure overall reduction in variance by using a weighted sum of the variances of the data in daughter nodes known as goodness of split. So, here in this split, the goodness of the split $= (56/170) \times 30.02 + (114/170) \times 7.71 = 15.05$. A low variance means less variation and the data hovers around the mean (9.56) of the data. The goal is to find the cut-point for which the goodness of the split is minimum. Equivalently, we can also find the cut-point for which the weighted average of daughters' variances is minimum. Thus, rationally, we need to find a cut-point so that the data in each daughter node is less variable as much as possible. Similarly, for each covariate, we can find out the best cut-point. There are also several other ways to achieve less variability such as two-sample permutation test. If the size of a node is 5 or less, it will not split the node. The splitting strategy is shown step by step in Figure 6.1.

Figure 6.2 shows splitting performance of CART model and their determinants. The root or the principal discriminating predictor for predicting lymph node dissection is found as tumour size. The data space splits into two daughter branches; one

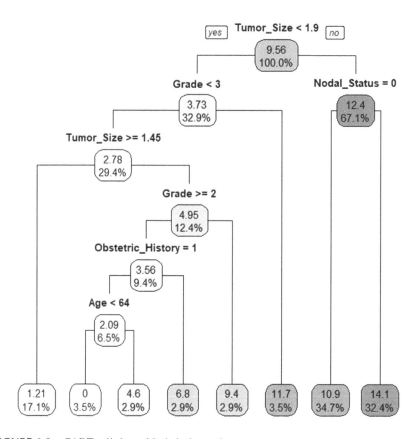

FIGURE 6.2 CART splitting with their determinants.

in left and one in right for tumour size <1.9 cm and ≥1.9 cm, respectively. Then the two daughter nodes are divided into two parts separately, each after going through a binary condition. The second split is done on the daughter node grade as <3 and ≥3 (terminal node). Next split is done at the tumour size ≥1.9 cm, which divides the information on nodal status as pelvic (terminal node) and paraaortic (terminal node). Further, patients with grade <3 (i.e., 1 and 2) are divided into two parts as tumour size ≥1.45 cm (terminal node) cm and <1.45 cm. Patients having tumour size <1.45 cm are partitioned again by grade ≥2 and <2 (terminal node). Subsequently, the patients with grade ≥2 are further split by obstetric status as: nullipara (0: terminal node) and multipara (1). Finally, multipara patients are divided by the last determinant age as <64 (terminal node) and ≥64 years (terminal node).

Finally, the splitting of nodes stops after seventh split. At each node the mean number of lymph node dissection and size (%) of the root or leaf node are reported. This tree has eight terminal nodes. The covariates tumour size, nodal status, grade, obstetric history and age play an important role to construct the regression tree. However, the variables such as postmenopausal bleeding, obstetrics history, histology, myometrial invasion, lymph vascular space invasion, cervical extension have no role in the regression tree. Figure 6.3 shows modified splitting in the CART model by ignoring the insignificant predictors. The model outcomes with their significant predictors are consistent with the multiple regression analysis (see Table 6.2).

The output of CART model demonstrates that there are two significant predictors for predicting lymph node dissection and they are tumour size and nodal status.

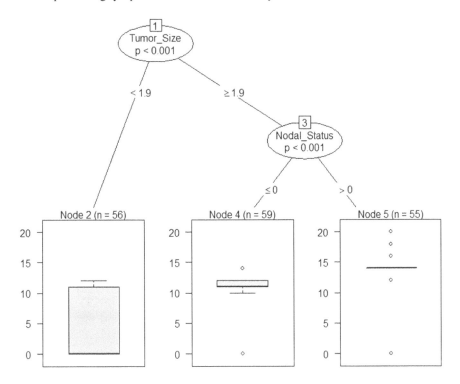

FIGURE 6.3 Modified CART splitting with their determinants.

The outcomes of the model states that the patients with tumour size ≥1.9 cm are at higher risk of extracting additional lymph node compared to the patients having tumour size <1.9 cm. Similarly, the patients with nodal status as paraaortic are at high risk of extracting additional lymph node compared with the patients having pelvic nodal status. Thus, it is more important to dissect an additional lymph node of the patients having tumour size ≥1.9 cm and paraaortic nodal status.

We have checked the model adequacy by plotting the residuals of both multiple and CART model (not shown here). It was also verified that the observed data coincide with reference line passing through origin, hence validating the assumption of normality of the error term in the model.

From Figure 6.4, it can be clearly observed that the number of lymph nodes is mostly scattered in the upper part of the blue horizontal line, indicating that the majority of patients have ≥10 nodes. Further, the upper data is more scattered towards the right-hand side of the blue vertical line, indicating the major patients those ≥10 lymph nodes dissected are belongs to age ≥50. It is clear that, the age predictor of the patients is explaining the high and low risk of extraction of lymph node. Hence, the patients under study can be classified into two major groups based on their ages i.e., <50 and ≥50 (Cheng, 2018).

The information gained from the above stratification can be used to stratify the continuous response variable with a binary threshold. Hence, we can take age as state variable and number of nodes dissected as test variable. Then, we have obtained the measures of Youden index as shown in Table 6.3. From Table 6.3, the maximum value of Youden index is 0.082, which is associated with the value of the test variable

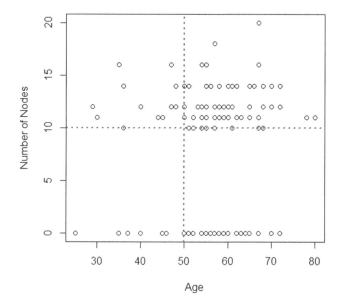

FIGURE 6.4   Scatter plot between age and number of node-dissect of the patients.

TABLE 6.3

Measurement of Youden Index

Test Variable: Number of Nodes Dissect
State Variable: Age and Value of State Variable: 50

Positive if Greater Than or Equal To	Sensitivity	1- Specificity	Youden Index (Sensitivity+Specificity-1)
−1.00	1.000	1.000	0
5.00	.750	.759	−0.009
10.50	.750	.684	0.066
11.50	.500	.481	0.019
13.00	.417	.335	**0.082**
15.00	.000	.044	−0.044
17.00	.000	.013	−0.013
19.00	.000	.006	−0.006
21.00	.000	.000	0

(i.e., number of nodes dissected) that is 13. Therefore, we can take 13 as an optimal threshold value for the dependent variable, and it can be stratified as <13 and ≥13 groups, which can be used further for validating and comparing the predictive models. Table 6.4 shows cross tabulation of predicted vs actual value for both multiple regression & CART model. CART model gives less misclassification error as compared to multiple regression model.

In order to compare the predictive power of the CART model with the multiple regression model, we draw two ROC curves as shown in Figure 6.5. The area under the ROC curve (AUC) is 0.965 in the CART model and 0.883 in the multiple regression model. This shows the predictive power is expected to be more in the CART model than in the multiple regression model. We can also compare the performance of two predictive models by comparing their R-squared value. The R-squared value of multiple regression and CART model are 0.334 and 0.754, respectively (Table 6.5). Hence, the CART model gives better performance than the multiple regression model by explaining the variations in the number of lymph nodes with the existing information on independent covariates. Other comparison characteristics are given in the Table 6.5.

TABLE 6.4

Cross Tabulation of Predicted vs Actual Value for Multiple Regression

Multiple Regression				CART			
		Predictions				Predictions	
		<13	≥13			<13	≥13
Actual	<13	106	6	Actual	<13	110	2
	≥13	40	18		≥13	5	53

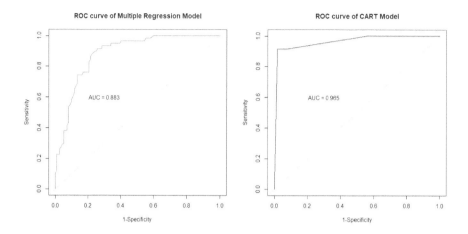

FIGURE 6.5   Comparison of ROC curves obtained by multiple regression & CART model.

TABLE 6.5
Comparison of Prediction Models for <13 vs ≥13 Lymph Node Dissection

Parameters	Multiple Regression Model	CART Model
Area under the curve (AUC)	0.883	0.965
Sensitivity	0.726	0.956
Specificity	0.750	0.963
Positive predictive value	0.946	0.982
Negative predictive value	0.310	0.913
Accuracy	0.729	0.959
R^2	0.334	0.754

In more detail, Table 6.5 shows the value of different parameters for comparing multiple regression model and CART model. Sensitivity, specificity, PPV, NPV and accuracy are 0.726, 0.750, 0.946, 0.310 and 0.729, respectively for multiple regression model and 0.956, 0.963, 0.982, 0.913 and 0.959, respectively for the CART model. The accuracy of CART model over multiple regression model shows that CART can be considered as a better alternative to multiple regression model particularly for analysing EC data.

6.5   DISCUSSION

We have considered the CART model to derive a diagnostic classification scheme for appropriate lymph node dissection among EC patients. CART analysis is a robust, analytical technique of ML. In our analysis, we have used the number of involved lymph nodes as our outcome variable as it is a clinically important marker for EC patients.

The importance of prediction of lymph node dissection can be experienced by the patient under treatment as well as the physicians. While delay in lymph node dissection may causes serious illness for the patients, unnecessary lymph node dissection makes the patient morally and physically weak. It has also been found that EC patients with low risk of lymph node metastasis do not get any benefit from lymph node dissection (Todo et al., 2014).

Systematic pelvic and paraaortic lymph node dissection did not improve the survival of patients with early stage I and II endometrioid EC at intermediate and high risk of recurrence (Ignatov et al., 2020). However, the improvement of survival can be achieved at an advance stage cancer if combined pelvic and paraaortic lymph node dissection has been performed (Todo et al., 2010).

Therefore, it is very important for the EC patients to develop a model which can be used to predict the number of lymph node dissection based on selected covariates. Based on our CART analysis, the most important variables for prediction of lymph node dissection are tumour size and nodal status (pelvic and paraaortic). These results could be useful for clinicians in making a decision regarding lymph node dissection.

We have compared the predictive capability and accuracy of two predictive models and observed that the CART model has more predictive capability and accuracy in comparison to multiple regression model. In a previous study, it was also found that the CART model has more accurate predictive power for explaining the factors responsible among the cancer patients compared to other ML techniques (Park and Lee, 2021). Hence, it is recommended to use the CART model to deal with EC data. The CART model reveals tumour size as the principal discriminating predictor, which is congruous with the previous studies where tumour size was the significant risk factor for predicting lymph node and survival status (Schink et al., 1987; Shah et al., 2005; Mahdi et al., 2015). In addition to this, it was also found that the nodal status has a significant role in predicting the number on lymph node dissection among EC patients.

Our model provides critical variables threshold (lymph node dissection) and their directional influence on the outcomes. The high accuracy of our CART model allows prompt use in a population of EC patients. Further, the advantages of CART are that it is simple, interactions between the variables can be identified directly from the model and probability can be displayed in the tree. Its simple structure makes it easy for the clinician to understand the data displayed, unlike some other statistical methods.

It is worth here to note the limitations of our study; the sample is small and taken from a single centre only. The result may be interpreted with caution. Thus, further confirmative of the result needs to verify with a larger data set.

6.6   CONCLUSION

CART analysis is a robust analytical technique, which can produce meaningful results using only a few important covariates. The proposed CART model is able to predict the number of lymph node dissection of EC patients with an accuracy of 95.9% based on the selected risk factors and validated using ROC curve. It is also found that the CART model has potential advancement over multiple regression model and can be used as an alternative method for predicting lymph node dissection among EC patients. Further, we have also found that the information on tumour size and nodal status helps us to predict the required number of lymph node dissection(s) with a greater accuracy. It is also suggested that the regression tree approach increases the prediction accuracy by means of discovering hidden information.

REFERENCES

Aguiar, Fabio S., Luciana L. Almeida, Antonio Ruffino-Netto, Afranio Lineu Kritski, Fernanda CQ Mello, and Guilherme L. Werneck. "Classification and regression tree (CART) model to predict pulmonary tuberculosis in hospitalized patients." *BMC Pulmonary Medicine* 12, no. 1 (2012): 1–8.

Barlin, Joyce N., Qin Zhou, Caryn M. St Clair, Alexia Iasonos, Robert A. Soslow, Kaled M. Alektiar, Martee L. Hensley, Mario M. Leitao Jr, Richard R. Barakat, and Nadeem R. Abu-Rustum. "Classification and regression tree (CART) analysis of endometrial carcinoma: Seeing the forest for the trees." *Gynecologic Oncology* 130, no. 3 (2013): 452–456.

Biswas, Ahitagni, Firuza Patel, Pankaj Kumar, Radhika Srinivasan, Anjan Bera, Suresh C. Sharma, and Arvind Rajwanshi. "Uterine sarcoma-current management and experience from a regional cancer centre in North India." *Archives of Gynecology and Obstetrics* 288, no. 4 (2013): 873–882.

Breiman, Leo, Jerome Friedman, Richard Olshen, and Charles Stone. "Classification and regression trees. *Wadsworth International Group* 37, no. 15 (1984): 237–251.

Chatterjee, Riddhi, Ratula Ray, Satya Ranjan Dash, and Om Prakash Jena. "Conceptualizing tomorrow's healthcare through digitization." *Computational Intelligence and Healthcare Informatics* 2021 (2021): 359–376.

Cheng, Zhi, Minoru Nakatsugawa, Chen Hu, Scott P. Robertson, Xuan Hui, Joseph A. Moore, Michael R. Bowers et al. "Evaluation of classification and regression tree (CART) model in weight loss prediction following head and neck cancer radiation therapy." *Advances in Radiation Oncology* 3, no. 3 (2018): 346–355.

Faraway, Julian J. *Extending the Linear Model with R: Generalized Linear, Mixed Effects and Nonparametric Regression Models*. New York: Chapman and Hall/CRC, 2016.

Faries, Mark B., John F. Thompson, Alistair Cochran, Robert Elashoff, Edwin C. Glass, Nicola Mozzillo, Omgo E. Nieweg et al. "The impact on morbidity and length of stay of early versus delayed complete lymphadenectomy in melanoma: Results of the Multicenter Selective Lymphadenectomy Trial (I)." *Annals of Surgical Oncology* 17, no. 12 (2010): 3324–3329.

Fluss, Ronen, David Faraggi, and Benjamin Reiser. "Estimation of the Youden Index and its associated cutoff point." *Biometrical Journal: Journal of Mathematical Methods in Biosciences* 47, no. 4 (2005): 458–472.

Friedman, Jerome H. "Multivariate adaptive regression splines." *The Annals of Statistics* 19, no. 1 (1991): 1–67.

Gail, Mitchell, Klaus Krickeberg, J. Samet, Anastasios Tsiatis, and Wing Wong. "Statistics for biology and health." (2007).

Ganggayah, Mogana Darshini, Nur Aishah Taib, Yip Cheng Har, Pietro Lio, and Sarinder Kaur Dhillon. "Predicting factors for survival of breast cancer patients using machine learning techniques." *BMC Medical Informatics and Decision Making* 19, no. 1 (2019): 1–17.

Giuliani, Andrea, A. Caporale, M. Corona, M. Di Bari, M. Demoro, T. Ricciardulli, P. Gozzo, G. Galati, and A. Tocchi. "Lymphadenectomy in gastric cancer: influence on prognosis of lymph node count." *Journal of Experimental and Clinical Cancer Research* 23 (2004): 215–224.

Gong, Houwu, Miye Wang, Hanxue Zhang, Md Fazla Elahe, and Min Jin. "An explainable AI approach for the rapid diagnosis of COVID-19 using ensemble learning algorithms." *Frontiers in Public Health* 10 (2022): 874455.

Gunning, David, Mark Stefik, Jaesik Choi, Timothy Miller, Simone Stumpf, and Guang-Zhong Yang. "XAI-Explainable artificial intelligence." *Science Robotics* 4, no. 37 (2019): eaay7120.

Hastie, Trevor, Robert Tibshirani, Jerome H. Friedman, and Jerome H. Friedman. *The Elements of Statistical Learning: Data Mining, Inference, and Prediction*. Vol. 2. New York: Springer, 2009.

Ignatov, Atanas, Stylianos Ivros, Mihaela Bozukova, Thomas Papathemelis, Olaf Ortmann, and Holm Eggemann. "Systematic lymphadenectomy in early stage endometrial cancer." *Archives of Gynecology and Obstetrics* 302, no. 1 (2020): 231–239.

Kareem, Sameem Abdul, S. Raviraja, Namir A. Awadh, Adeeba Kamaruzaman, and Annapurni Kajindran. "Classification and regression tree in prediction of survival of aids patients." *Malaysian Journal of Computer Science* 23, no. 3 (2010): 153–165.

Letzgus, Simon, Patrick Wagner, Jonas Lederer, Wojciech Samek, Klaus-Robert Müller, and Grégoire Montavon. "Toward explainable AI for regression models." arXiv preprint arXiv:2112.11407 (2021).

Ma, Xin. *Using Classification and Regression Trees: A Practical Primer*. IAP, 2018.

Mahbooba, Basim, Mohan Timilsina, Radhya Sahal, and Martin Serrano. "Explainable artificial intelligence (XAI) to enhance trust management in intrusion detection systems using decision tree model." *Complexity* 2021 (2021): 1–11.

Mahdi, Haider, Adnan R. Munkarah, Rouba Ali-Fehmi, Jessica Woessner, Shetal N. Shah, and Mehdi Moslemi-Kebria. "Tumor size is an independent predictor of lymph node metastasis and survival in early stage endometrioid endometrial cancer." *Archives of Gynecology and Obstetrics* 292, no. 1 (2015): 183–190.

Mariani, Andrea, Gary L. Keeney, Giacomo Aletti, Maurice J. Webb, Michael G. Haddock, and Karl C. Podratz. "Endometrial carcinoma: Paraaortic dissemination." *Gynecologic Oncology* 92, no. 3 (2004): 833–838.

May, Katie, Andrew Bryant, Heather O. Dickinson, Sean Kehoe, and Jo Morrison. "Lymphadenectomy for the management of endometrial cancer." *Cochrane Database of Systematic Reviews* 1 (2010): 1–43.

Morgan, James N., and John A. Sonquist. "Problems in the analysis of survey data, and a proposal." *Journal of the American Statistical Association* 58, no. 302 (1963): 415–434.

Panici, Pierluigi Benedetti, Stefano Basile, Francesco Maneschi, Andrea Alberto Lissoni, Mauro Signorelli, Giovanni Scambia, Roberto Angioli et al. "Systematic pelvic lymphadenectomy vs no lymphadenectomy in early-stage endometrial carcinoma: Randomized clinical trial." *JNCI: Journal of the National Cancer Institute* 100, no. 23 (2008): 1707–1716.

Park, Young Min, and Byung-Joo Lee. "Machine learning-based prediction model using clinico-pathologic factors for papillary thyroid carcinoma recurrence." *Scientific Reports* 11, no. 1 (2021): 1–7.

Patra, Sudhansu Shekhar, Om Praksah Jena, Gaurav Kumar, Sreyashi Pramanik, Chinmaya Misra, and Kamakhya Narain Singh. "Random forest algorithm in imbalance genomics classification." In *Data Analytics in Bioinformatics: A Machine Learning Perspective* (2021): 173–190. United States: CRC Press, Scrivener Publishing LLC.

Pattnayak, Parthasarathi, and Om Prakash Jena. "Innovation on machine learning in healthcare services-An introduction." *Machine Learning for Healthcare Applications*, 2021 (2021): pp. 3–15.

Rathod, Praveen S., P. N. Shakuntala, V. R. Pallavi, Rajashekar Kundaragi, B. Shankaranand, C. R. Vijay, K. Uma Devi, and Uttam D. Bafna. "The risk and pattern of pelvic and para aortic lymph nodal metastasis in patients with intermediate and high risk endometrial cancer." *Indian Journal of Surgical Oncology* 5, no. 2 (2014): 109–114.

Sahu, Barnali, Sitarashmi Sahu, and Om Prakash Jena. "Impact of ensemble-based models on cancer classification, its development, and challenges." In *Machine Learning and Deep Learning in Efficacy Improvement of Healthcare Systems* (2022), pp. 155–172. New York: CRC Press.

Schink, Julian C., John R. Lurain, C. B. Wallemark, and Joan S. Chmiel. "Tumor size in endometrial cancer: A prognostic factor for lymph node metastasis." *Obstetrics and Gynecology* 70, no. 2 (1987): 216–219.

Shah, Chirag, E. Blair Johnson, Elise Everett, Hisham Tamimi, Benjamin Greer, Elizabeth Swisher, and Barbara Goff. "Does size matter? Tumor size and morphology as predictors of nodal status and recurrence in endometrial cancer." *Gynecologic Oncology* 99, no. 3 (2005): 564–570.

Todo, Yukiharu, Hidemichi Watari, Sokbom Kang, and Noriaki Sakuragi. "Tailoring lymphadenectomy according to the risk of lymph node metastasis in endometrial cancer." *Journal of Obstetrics and Gynaecology Research* 40, no. 2 (2014): 317–321.

Todo, Yukiharu, Hidenori Kato, Masanori Kaneuchi, Hidemichi Watari, Mahito Takeda, and Noriaki Sakuragi. "Survival effect of para-aortic lymphadenectomy in endometrial cancer (SEPAL study): A retrospective cohort analysis." *The Lancet* 375, no. 9721 (2010): 1165–1172.

Vieira, Carla Piazzon Ramos, and Luciano Antonio Digiampietri. "A study about explainable articial intelligence: Using decision tree to explain SVM." *Revista Brasileira de Computação Aplicada* 12, no. 1 (2020): 113–121.

Woo, Yanghee, Bryan Goldner, Philip Ituarte, Byrne Lee, Laleh Melstrom, Taeil Son, Sung Hoon Noh, Yuman Fong, and Woo Jin Hyung. "Lymphadenectomy with optimum of 29 lymph nodes retrieved associated with improved survival in advanced gastric cancer: A 25,000-patient international database study." *Journal of the American College of Surgeons* 224, no. 4 (2017): 546–555.

Yang, Hao-Xian, Ying Xu, Jian-Hua Fu, Jun-Ye Wang, Peng Lin, and Tie-Hua Rong. "An evaluation of the number of lymph nodes examined and survival for node-negative esophageal carcinoma: Data from China." *Annals of Surgical Oncology* 17, no. 7 (2010): 1901–1911.

Youden, William J. "Index for rating diagnostic tests." *Cancer* 3, no. 1 (1950): 32–35.

Zhang, Heping, and Burton Singer. *Recursive Partitioning in the Health Sciences*. New York: Springer Science & Business Media, 1999.

7 Automated Brain Tumor Analysis Using Deep Learning-Based Framework

Amiya Halder and Rudrajit Choudhuri
St. Thomas College of Engineering and Technology

Apurba Sarkar
Indian Institute of Engineering Science
and Technology, Howrah

7.1 INTRODUCTION

Advancements in artificial intelligence and image processing have revolutionized various domains in recent times and have had a huge impact on the healthcare and biomedical industries [1–3]. The era of automated analysis for computer-aided diagnosis has impacted the clinical domain in profound ways. Medical image processing is now relevant [4–6] in the early detection of various diseases and has been able to analyze different organs of the human body, including the brain, heart, lungs, liver, and spleen, among many others.

Brain image analysis for automated diagnosis, including tissue segmentation [7], injury detection [8], tumor detection [9], and classification [10] has greatly helped in early-stage treatment and surgery planning. A brain tumor is an anomaly in the human brain that arises due to a collection of abnormal cells and has the capability of causing severe damage to the human nervous system. Brain magnetic resonance imaging (MRI) [11] is an imaging technique that provides a significant advantage over other imaging methods when it comes to multimodal image acquisition for the immaculate study of the human brain. Accurate detection and classification of tumors from MRI images potentially increases the chances of survival and can tremendously help in treatment. The manual process of tumor detection and identification requires an in-depth study of images and domain expertise. The process lacks reproducibility, is rigorous, and is time-consuming. Automated tumor detection and tumor-type identification are extensive research domains lying at the core of medical image analysis. Over the years, the foundations have been laid across areas related to enhancement, noise reduction, feature extraction, and segregation for accurate classification.

DOI: 10.1201/9781003257721-7

Brain tumors [12] can be majorly subdivided into two categories: the benign and the malignant tumor grades. Benign types generally develop outside brain tissues but inside the human skull and can cause a critical life condition. Meningioma and pituitary tumors are the most common participants in the benign tumor group. Meningioma tumors generally do not spread across the brain and can be extracted through surgery. Pituitary tumors originate in the pituitary gland and malfunction the hormonal controls and regulatory functions of the brain, leading to hormonal deficiency and loss of vision, among other symptoms. The malignant category of tumor is capable of reproducing and spreading across the brain in a disorganized and uncontrolled fashion. They can cause structural changes in normal tissues and can even destroy them. Glioma is the most common malignant tumor type. It is often the cause of brain cancer, and it rapidly escalates across the human body.

Over the years, statistical machine learning and deep learning techniques [13] have proved to be strong paragons for brain image classification. However, the problem with such detailed classifications is manifold. First, brain images have overlapping regions and highly correlated features. Second, the acquisition techniques often inject inhomogeneities and other artifacts, which makes classification more difficult. Finally, the most challenging problem is the lack of sufficiently large datasets with detailed annotations. Medical images are hard to annotate as they have to be done manually by radiologists. These problems have imposed a bottleneck in image segmentation and classification, and it is very difficult to achieve high accuracy given these situations. At the same time, without high accuracy, the automated tools cannot be incorporated into real-time systems as they would endanger human life arising due to inaccurate analysis.

Transfer learning [14] has gained popularity due to its ability to develop robust prediction models with limited data. To simply state, transfer learning is reusing a pre-trained prediction model for a new class classification. With prior knowledge from past learning experiences, these models can achieve high prediction accuracy with fine-tuning for a particular use case. Training a neural network from scratch is computationally expensive, as the network should be familiar with latent feature extraction along with case-specific feature extraction. Transfer learning comes in handy during these times, as the pre-trained networks are so chosen that they are already resilient in latent space feature extraction (they are trained to classify between a significantly large set of classes). With a reduced need for feature-based prediction training, the need for large datasets and computation expenses is also reduced. Modifying final layers can effectively make the network reliable in case-specific feature extraction, thus developing a robust prediction model.

In this chapter, we leverage the use of deep learning and transfer learning for the development of a robust brain MR image analysis pipeline targeted at automated brain tumor diagnosis. First, a deep convolutional denoising autoencoder architecture is reported targeted at Gaussian noise removal from brain MR images. In digital image acquisition, Gaussian noise is a common problem that arises due to sensor limitations. This may occur due to low lighting conditions or other faults that hinder the sensors from efficiently capturing scene details. Gaussian noise is common in medical images due to faults in acquisition sensors and/or the acquisition environment (magnetic field, radio coils, etc.). After the denoising step is complete, the images are passed on to the tumor detection and tumor grade identification stages. We use a transfer learning paradigm for the development of tumor detection and grade prediction models. For this purpose, five pre-trained deep convolutional neural networks, namely ResNet50 [15], Xception [16], MobileNet [17], EfficientNetB2, and EfficientNetB3 [18] architectures, are fine-tuned for catering to the required problem. The detection networks are trained to classify between normal and tumor samples, while the grade identification networks are trained to classify four classes of brain MRI images (normal, glioma, meningioma, and pituitary). If no tumor is detected in a sample, it is labeled as normal. The normal class of brain images is also included in the grade identification models for handling outliers of detection models (if any). After rigorous experimentation and evaluation, it is noticed that the architectures attain stable and remarkable performances and establish themselves as a new standard for brain tumor detection and tumor type classification.

The main contributions of this chapter are:

1. A denoising convolutional autoencoder architecture is reported in this chapter targeted at Gaussian noise removal from brain MR image samples. The model is generalizable across different medical image analysis tasks. It accentuates image feature extraction and specifically aids in segmentation and classification.
2. Five fine-tuned deep convolutional neural networks are presented for brain tumor detection and type identification. The architectural settings and the training procedure are detailed in this chapter.
3. A new standard in automated brain tumor analysis is established after extensive experimentation and performance analysis on the most cutting-edge methods currently available.

The rest of this chapter is structured as follows: The related works in literature are discussed in Section 7.2. Background about the use of deep convolutional networks is summarized in Section 7.3. Section 7.4 presents the data acquisition, preprocessing, model architectural design, and training phase summarization. Experimental results are analyzed, and inferences are presented in Section 7.5. Finally, the conclusion is derived in Section 7.6.

7.2   RELATED WORKS

Automated tumor detection [19,20] is an active research area in the biomedical domain. Over a long period, several techniques based on the intersections of feature engineering, machine learning, deep learning, computer vision, and image processing have come into existence. Machine learning-based techniques assimilated with statistical feature extraction laid the foundation stones for tackling the problem. In the last few years, different algorithmic techniques have tried to tackle the problem of tumor detection. Feature extraction using Gray Level Co-occurrence Matrix (GLCM) followed by classification using Kernel SVM [21], brain tumor detection using Naïve Bayes classification [22], probabilistic neural network based classification [23], convolutional neural net (CNN)-based classification [24], and a hybrid CNN – GLCM tumor detection [25] are some of the robust techniques in the domain. A multistage framework with statistical classifiers targeted at tumor grade classification [26] was proposed back in 2009. The framework can predict glioma tumor grades with a peak accuracy of 85%. In 2018, a possibilistic neural net for GLCM feature-based brain tumor classification came into existence. The technique achieves accuracies in the range of 83–84%. In the same year, a statistical-based MRI feature extraction with the help of the Gabor filter and discrete wave transformation was proposed. The technique uses multilayer perceptron to achieve an accuracy of 91.9% [27].

The statistical feature extraction-based classification techniques require human understanding for the selection of prospective features needed for prediction model training. This manual process is heavily dependent on specific domain experience. Also, the selected features might not always be exhaustive enough, which can hamper the accuracy and reliability of the classification models.

For this reason, deep learning-based feature extraction and classification have gained prominence and popularity in the research community. A standard Conv Net-based multi-class MRI classification [28] can predict tumor classes with the highest overall performance accuracy of 96.7%. Another approach combining standard Convolutional Neural Nets with Genetic Algorithm-based optimization [29] for classifying tumor types from brain MRIs became a part of the literature, obtaining a rough 94% accuracy. Ghosal et.al. proposed a tumor classification model in 2019, based on ResNet architecture Squeeze and Excitation Deep Neural Network [30]. This technique achieves an accuracy of 93.8% on the brain tumor identification task. Some of the other recently proposed techniques [31] have further set high benchmarks in brain tumor detection and grade identification. In 2022, Rizwan et al. proposed a Gaussian CNN [32] which achieves an average accuracy of 98.4% in the context of brain tumor grade identification. Furthermore, a technique merging a CNN architecture with GLCM feature extraction [33] targeted at brain tumor classification claims a classification rate of 99%.

Incorporating transfer learning into the use of pre-trained models has boosted the performance of tumor classification. The use of AlexNet, VGGNet, and GoogleNet for tumor detection and grade classification is presented in [34]. The architectures have shown promising results, with accuracy as high as 98.69% in the detection and classification domains.

7.3 BACKGROUND

This section briefly discusses the preliminary background necessary for the comprehension of the different phases of the presented diagnosis tool. First, an overview of autoencoders and convolutional autoencoders is described. Following that, a concise description of the various pre-trained classification architectures employed in the methodology pipeline is covered.

7.3.1 AUTOENCODERS

Autoencoders are based on unsupervised learning paradigms that use artificial neural networks for the task of representation learning. An autoencoder tries to learn an approximation for function identification using a backpropagation technique. Given a set of unlabeled training inputs ($I \in [0, 1]^d$), the model first encodes it to a hidden representation space ($y \in [0, 1]^d$) using a deterministic mapping. The latent space representation (y) is then decoded to obtain the reconstructed data point (J) using a similar mapping. The model parameters are optimized to minimize reconstruction errors (which can be quantified by monitoring mean squared loss or cross entropy loss).

An autoencoder consists of:

1. **Encoder**: The encoder accepts input and performs deterministic latent space mapping.
2. **Decoder**: The decoder accepts the latent space mapping and reconstructs it to get data having a similar shape as the input.

Overall, first, the network accepts data (corrupted medical image in this context). Next, it compresses the data into a latent space representation and finally reconstructs it to get the output data.

7.3.2 Convolutional Autoencoders

Convolutional autoencoders are substructured on standard autoencoder architectures. The model uses convolutional encoding and decoding layers. These types of autoencoders are better suited for image processing as they utilize convolutional neural nets in full capacity for feature extraction and understanding of image structure. Here, the weights are shared among all input locations, which helps in preserving the local spatial information in images. A feature map is represented as follows:

$$l^i = s\left(x * W^i + b^i\right) \tag{7.1}$$

where bias is broadcast to the entire map, * denotes a 2D convolution operation, W represents a model parameter, b represents bias, and s represents an activation. A single bias is used per latent map and the reconstructed data point is obtained as

$$y = s\left(\sum_{i \in Z} l^i * F^i + c\right) \tag{7.2}$$

where c is bias per input channel, Z is a group of latent feature maps, and F is a flip operation over both weight dimensions. Backpropagation is used for parameter-based gradient computation of the error function.

7.3.3 Pre-trained Deep Classification Architectures

ResNet50 architecture: In 2016, Microsoft Research came up with Residual Networks (ResNets) [15] based on a residual learning paradigm for ease in training deep networks. Instead of unreferenced learning from layer inputs, the architecture formulates each layer as a residual learning function. It is proved that this modification helps in the easier optimization of deeper networks along with increased accuracy for deep architectures. ResNet-50 is one such architecture in the ResNet category. The network consists of 48 convolutional layers structured into four residual modules.

Xception architecture: Xception [16] was developed by Google back in 2017, with an idea based on depth-wise separable convolutional layers (DSC). DSC is designed by performing channel-based convolution followed by linear integration of the outputs amalgamated with spatial point-wise convolutions. The architecture is substructured upon the Inception architecture family with the mentioned extrapolations, and thus it was coined "Extreme Inception". The idea was to decouple spatial and cross-channel correlations in feature maps of CNNs. For feature extraction, the architecture consists of 36 convolution layers (3 × 3) structured into 14 modules.

Around each of the modules (except for the first and last ones) there exist residual connections. The architecture can be summed up to be a linear pile of depth separable 2D Conv layers coupled with linear residual connections.

MobileNet architecture: The MobileNet architecture [17] was also proposed by Google and succeeds the Xception model. It also implements DSC and applies single filters to each of the image channels. There are layers for filtering and combining outputs. The architecture consists of 28 feature extraction layers (standard Conv Layers and DSC layers) each incorporated with batch normalization [35] and Rectified Linear Unit (ReLU) activation layers (a simple activation function that directly outputs the maximum of the input value and zero). MobileNet also provides width and resolution multipliers for improving upon computational requirements and making the model faster when necessary.

EfficientNet architecture: EfficientNets B0-B7 [18] is a class of convolutional neural network family developed by Google AI in 2019. The large convolutional models that are too deep often quickly saturate, thus not being very efficient in use cases. The EfficientNets have been developed keeping this in mind, and thus are scaled in a disciplined approach. The basic substructure or the backbone is the same for all the networks in the family: the stem in each network contains rescaling, normalization, padding, convolution, batch normalization, and activation layers. These layers have varying numbers of sub-blocks which are gradually increased as we move from EfficientNet B0 – B7. For this paper, we limit ourselves to using only the B2 and B3 architectures as they suit best to our use case.

Xception, MobileNet, ResNet, and EfficientNet architectures are available in the TensorFlow and PyTorch libraries. All the networks are trained on the ImageNet [36] dataset. It comprises a large collection of high-resolution images with a wide gamut of classes. The networks are tested on various object detection and classification datasets. For this chapter, we use the TensorFlow libraries for designing and fine-tuning the networks. A detailed view of the architecture (tabularized and pictorial views), including each layer along with its attributes, is available in [15–18].

7.4 PROPOSED METHODOLOGY

The section details the proposed methodology incorporated for automated brain tumor analysis from MR images. The image preprocessing phase focused on

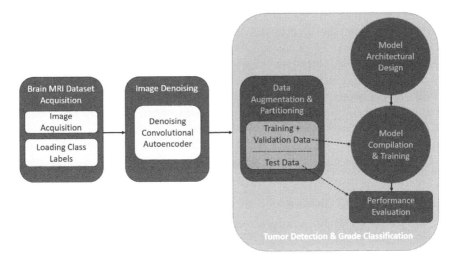

FIGURE 7.1 Stages of the proposed automated brain tumor diagnosis pipeline.

Gaussian noise removal, followed by the image classification phase for tumor detection and tumor type identification, is discussed at length in the subsequent subsections. Figure 7.1 presents a block diagram representing the different stages in the analysis pipeline.

7.4.1 IMAGE DENOISING

In this section, a denoising convolutional autoencoder is constructed using convolutional layers that is then used for efficient denoising of brain MR images. The model restores corrupted images by removing noise and thereby enhances the performance of further processing tasks. The presented architecture has minimalistic training requirements and computational costs. Using limited samples, the presented method manages to have a decent performance in noise reduction from images. The underlying idea incorporates converting images into latent space where noise is removed, following which the image is reconstructed in order to get rid of any corruption present in the image. The technique is based on convolution, which allows the approach to pick out useful features from the images while denoising them. These features can be important in classification and segmentation tasks. Upon rigorous experimentation, the presented approach achieves significant performance both qualitatively and quantitatively and proves to be a reliable approach when it comes to brain medical image denoising. This section details the different phases incorporated in the construction of the denoising convolutional autoencoder in chronological order. First, we discuss the data acquisition and noisy data generation, followed by the model architectural setting. Finally, we summarize the model compilation and training phase. Model performance evaluation and comparison with existing methods are detailed in the result section.

Data acquisition: Two datasets, namely, BR35H: Brain Tumor Dataset 2020 [37] and Brats-2015 [38] are used in this project for model training and performance evaluation. The low-resolution images are removed and all the images are resized to 224 × 224 prior to model training. A total of 3000 images (split in a 60:20:20 ratio) are used for training and evaluation.

Adding Gaussian Noise to images: For training the model first, the images are corrupted by stochastically adding Gaussian noise to them. The added noise follows a random normal distribution (factor = 0.08, mean = 0, variance = 1). This operation is performed to simulate the noisy image acquisition scenario that commonly occurs during medical image acquisition. Figure 7.2 shows a collection of original and noisy image samples from the dataset.

7.4.1.1 Model Architecture

We use a convolutional denoising autoencoder targeted at Gaussian noise removal from brain MR images. This is a stochastic extension to the classic denoising autoencoders [39], i.e., the model is forced to learn input reconstruction given its noisy version. As the data is already stochastically corrupted, it is passed on to the presented autoencoder network, where the noisy pixels are reconstructed using image features and local spatial information. A block diagram for the denoising autoencoder pipeline is shown in Figure 7.3.

Encoder network: The first layer for the encoder network is a 2D convolution layer with 64 kernels (kernel size 3 x 3). A ReLU [40] activation is attached to the layer. The next layer in the pipeline is a 2D Max Pooling layer used for data subsampling (pooling size = (2, 2)). After subsampling, another 2D convolution layer with 64 kernels (kernel size 3 x 3) and a ReLU activation function are used, followed by a final Max Pooling layer with a pool size of (2, 2). Figure 7.4 presents a block representation of the encoder architecture.

Note: The same padding is used in all the layers. ReLU is a piecewise linear activation function that clips any negative input value to 0. It is the most commonly used

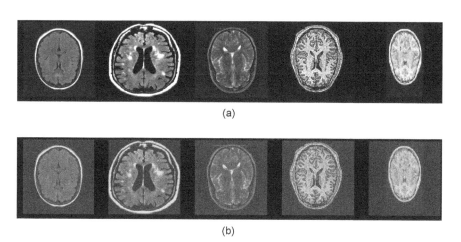

(a)

(b)

FIGURE 7.2   (a) Original and (b) Gaussian Noise corrupted brain MR image samples.

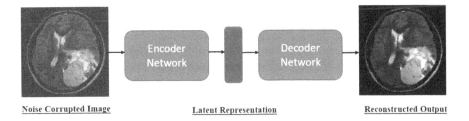

Noise Corrupted Image   Latent Representation   Reconstructed Output

FIGURE 7.3 Denoising convolutional autoencoder pipeline.

FIGURE 7.4 Block representation of the encoder network architecture.

activation function as it is simple and aids in the prevention of exponential growth in the computation required to operate the network.

Decoder network: A 2D convolution layer consisting of 64 kernels (kernel size 3 x 3) is the first layer in the decoder network. ReLU activation is associated with the convolution layer. Next, a 2D upsampling layer (size = (2, 2)) is used for data upsampling. These two layers are again repeated in the pipeline. The final layer in the network is a 2D convolution layer with 1 kernel (size = 3 x 3) assimilated with the sigmoid activation function [41]. Figure 7.5 presents a compact block view of the decoder network architecture.

Note: The same padding is used in each layer. Sigmoid activation is a probabilistic activation function commonly used in output layers to bring in non-linearity, i.e. allow networks to find non-linear relationships between data features.

Model compilation and training: The model is compiled using the Adaptive Moment Estimation (ADAM) [42] optimization algorithm in order to update the weights of the network iteratively based on the input data. It is a straightforward stochastic optimization technique that is computationally effective. Without an optimization algorithm, immense computational power and time would be required, even for a small network. Binary cross entropy serves as the loss function, and the model robustness is monitored using the validation set loss. The model is trained for 100 epochs with a batch size of 32. The best model obtained has a validation loss of 0.37.

FIGURE 7.5 Block representation of the decoder network architecture.

7.4.2 TUMOR DETECTION AND TUMOR GRADE CLASSIFICATION

After the noise reduction phase, we pass the images through two classification pipe-lines. The first pipeline detects the presence of a tumor in an image sample. If a tumor is detected in a brain MR image sample, it is passed through the second classification pipeline where the type of the tumor is identified. We leverage the use of transfer learning for detecting tumors and determining the tumor type. For these purposes, five pre-trained deep convolutional neural networks, namely ResNet50, Xception, MobileNet, and EfficientNet B2, B3 architectures are fine-tuned. The detection networks are trained to classify two classes of brain MRI images (normal & tumor samples). On the other hand, the type identification networks are trained to classify four classes of brain MRI images (normal, glioma, meningioma, and pituitary). The normal sample class in the tumor type prediction pipeline tackles any outliers that were not captured in the detection pipeline. In this section, we first discuss MR image data acquisition. Next, the experimental setup is detailed. Finally, the model training procedure is discussed.

7.4.2.1 Data Acquisition

For model training and performance evaluation, it is important to have a standard-ized dataset. For tumor detection classifier training, the BR35H: Brain Tumor Dataset 2020 [37] is used. The dataset comprises 3000 brain MRI images (1500 samples per class) collected from over 280 patients. The low-resolution images are preprocessed before the classification models are trained. Figure 7.6 presents data samples cor-responding to each image class. Data augmentation by varying the brightness and contrast of the original images, horizontal and vertical flipping, and rotation opera-tions (up to 7%) were also performed.

For training tumor-grade classification models, the Figshare [43] dataset is used for all experiments in this project. It encompasses a wide range of brain MRI data col-lected over five years from hospitals and medical universities in China. The dataset

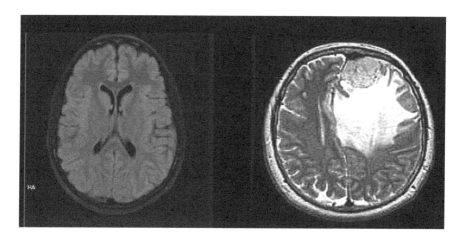

FIGURE 7.6 Data samples corresponding to each image class (tumor detection dataset).

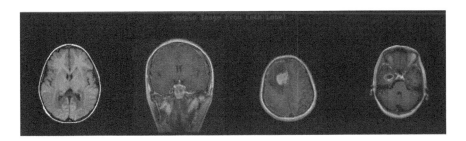

FIGURE 7.7 Data samples corresponding to each image class (grade classification dataset).

comprises 3064 MR image data samples collected from 200+ patients. Figure 7.7 shows MRI data samples corresponding to each image class. The low-resolution images in the dataset are preprocessed before model training is performed.

7.4.2.2 Experimental Setup: Fine-Tuning the Architectures

The first step in the classification pipeline is designing the model architectures. The architectures (ResNet-50, Xception, MobileNet, and EfficientNet B2, B3) are imported with ImageNet weights. The top layers (layers responsible for class prediction) are removed from the architecture. After this, a 2D global average pool layer is attached for data subsampling. This allows faster computations with fewer features (abstracted data) without hampering accuracy. Next, a 0.5 dropout layer is attached to prevent data overfitting. As these models are already trained on a huge data sample, the architectures should be designed such that the crucial features from image samples are the determining factors without a clutter of data coming into the decision-making picture.

Next, a dense fully connected neural net layer (the number of neurons is based on the number of classes) is attached with softmax activation. The function is applied to the neural net output to represent image classes using probabilities. The function uses a probability distribution over all the classes to normalize the final layer output. The model is compiled using cross entropy as the loss function (binary cross entropy for detection models and categorical cross entropy for grade identification models), prediction accuracy as the evaluation metric, and Adaptive Moment Estimation (ADAM) as the stochastic optimization algorithm for weight upgradation. Figure 7.8 summarizes the architectural design and presents a compact view of the experimental setup.

7.4.3 Model Training

Tumor detection: The models are trained for 6 epochs with a batch size of 32 and a validation set size of 10%. ResNet-50 model achieves 98.22% training accuracy with 98.16% validation set accuracy. The Xception model attains 98.61% training accuracy with 98.33% validation set accuracy. Fine-tuned MobileNet model achieves 99.83% training accuracy with 98.83% validation set accuracy. Finally, EfficientNet B2 and B3 models have the best performance among the lot, and they attain a training accuracy of 99.78% and 99.94% with a validation set accuracy of 99.33% and

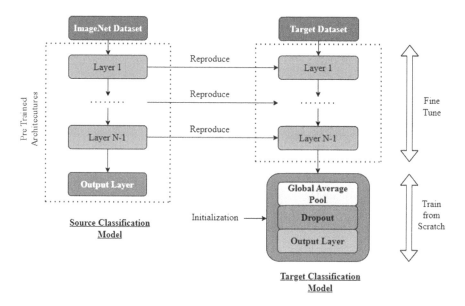

FIGURE 7.8 Architectural design for fine-tuning the pre-trained models for brain tumor detection and tumor type identification.

99.88% respectively. The accuracy and loss curves corresponding to each of these models are presented in Figures 7.9–7.13. The robustness of the models in tumor detection can be overtly noticed and is further clarified in the result section.

Grade classification: The fine-tuned models are trained for 12 epochs with a batch size of 32 and a validation set size of 10%. The ResNet-50 model attains 99.81% training accuracy (t-AUC) and 96.6% validation set accuracy (v-AUC).

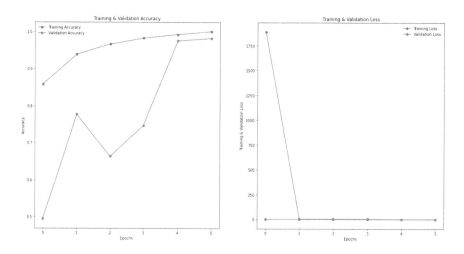

FIGURE 7.9 Accuracy and loss curve for ResNet50 model training.

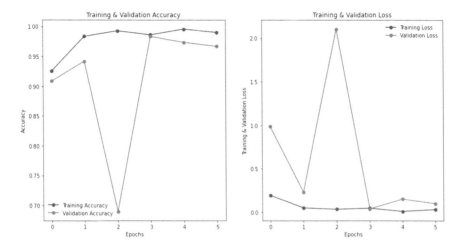

FIGURE 7.10   Accuracy and loss curve for Xception model training.

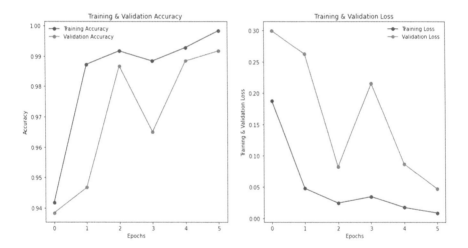

FIGURE 7.11   Accuracy and loss curve for MobileNet model training.

Xception architecture attains a training accuracy of 99.85% with a 97.27% v-AUC. EfficientNet B2 is able to achieve 99.7% training accuracy while having 97.9% validation accuracy. EfficientNet B3 performs similarly (99.67% t-AUC and 98.29% v-AUC). The MobileNet architecture tops all the performances and attains 99.9% training accuracy with 98.5% validation accuracy. It is to be noted that transfer learning leverages and drastically makes the prediction performance robust with just 12 epochs of training. Thus, it saves a lot of computation requirements that would have been needed in training a network from scratch. The accuracy and loss curves for the models during training are presented in Figures 7.14–7.18.

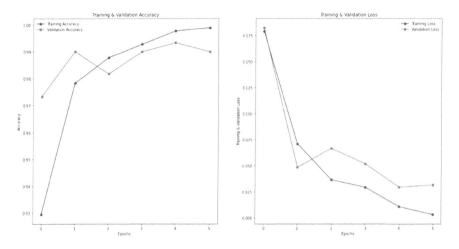

FIGURE 7.12   Accuracy and loss curve for EfficientNet B2 model training.

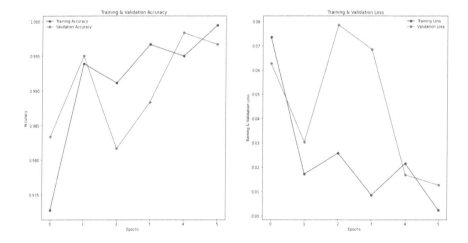

FIGURE 7.13   Accuracy and loss curve for EfficientNet B3 model training.

7.5   RESULT ANALYSIS

Quantitative evaluation metrics are crucial for judging the robustness of a processing or analysis technique. A brief description of the evaluation metrics used across different experiments in the context of the scope of this chapter is summarized in the following subsection.

7.5.1   EVALUATION METRICS

Evaluation of the denoising techniques is performed using image quality metrics including Root Mean Squared Error (RMSE), Peak Signal-to-Noise Ratio (PSNR), and Structural Similarity Measure (SSIM). RMSE measures the deviation between

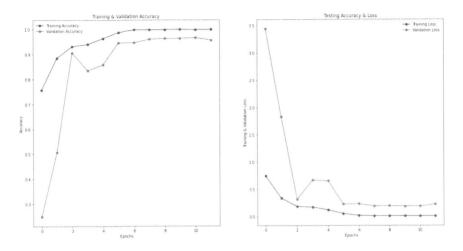

FIGURE 7.14 Accuracy and loss curve for ResNet50 model training.

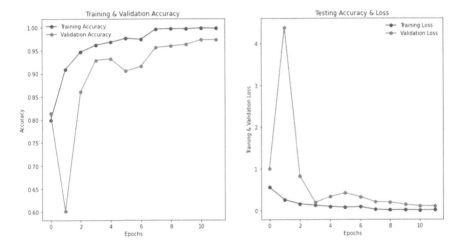

FIGURE 7.15 Accuracy and loss curve for Xception model training.

the original and the regenerated image, thus highlighting the resiliency flaw in enhancement techniques. PSNR and SSIM quantify the quality of regeneration, thereby defending algorithmic robustness. A low RMSE value along with high PSNR and SSIM values quantitatively highlights the reliability of a processing technique. The metrics are defined as follows:

$$\text{RSME} = \frac{1}{M \times N} \sqrt{\sum_{i=1}^{M} \sum_{j=1}^{N} \left(x_{i,j} - y_{i,j} \right)^2} \tag{7.3}$$

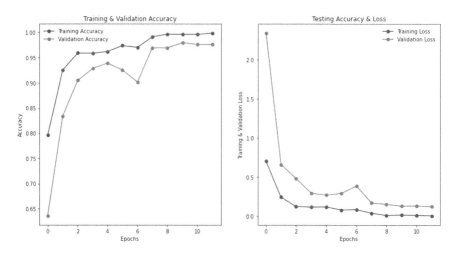

FIGURE 7.16   Accuracy and loss curve for MobileNet model training.

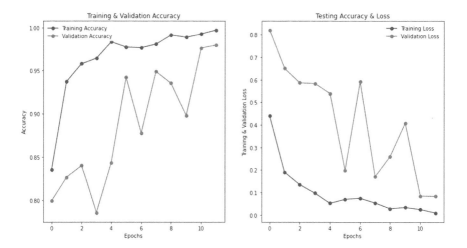

FIGURE 7.17   Accuracy and loss curve for EfficientNet B2 model training.

$$PSNR = 20log_{10}\left(\frac{255^2}{RMSE}\right) \tag{7.4}$$

$$SSIM = \frac{\left(2\mu_x\mu_y + c_1\right)\left(2\sigma_{xy} + c_2\right)}{\left(\mu_x^2 + \mu_y^2 + c_1\right)\left(\sigma_x^2 + \sigma_y^2 + c_2\right)} \tag{7.5}$$

where $x_{i,j}$ and $y_{i,j}$ are pixels of image x and y of size M×N respectively. μ_x and μ_y are the average intensities of the images x and y. σ_x, σ_y represent the standard deviations,

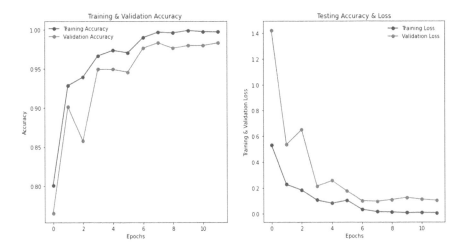

FIGURE 7.18   Accuracy and loss curve for EfficientNet B3 model training.

and σ_{xy} denotes the covariance measure. Finally, c_1 and c_2 are constants and are set to be $(0.01 \times 255)^2$ and $(0.03 \times 255)^2$ respectively.

For judging the resiliency of the classifiers (tumor detection and type identification models), different quantitative metrics are used which include:

Prediction accuracy: Prediction Accuracy is a strong quantitative evaluation metric for classification models. The accuracy metric demonstrates model resiliency across output class predictions and upholds the reliability of the model. Prediction Accuracy is calculated as follows:

$$\text{Prediction Accuracy} = \frac{\text{Total Correct Predictions}}{\text{Total Predictions}}$$

The total predictions encompass the true predictions (true positives and negatives) along with the false predictions ((false positives and negatives (type- I and II error))). The correct predictions correspond to the true predictions only.

Specificity: The specificity of a classifier measures its true negative rate. This simply boils down to the proportion between correctly identified negatives and the actual negatives. It is described as follows:

$$\text{Specificity} = \frac{\text{Total True Negatives}}{\text{Total True Negatives} + \text{Total False Positives}}$$

For a multi-class classification, it presents an average true negative rate across classes which denotes reliability against class misclassification.

Recall: The metric denotes model sensitivity, a.k.a. the true positive rate. To put it in simple words, it is a measure of a classifier's ability to accurately classify a sample corresponding to its original class. It is defined as the proportion of correctly identified positives to actual positives. Recall metric computation is defined as follows:

$$\text{Recall} = \frac{\text{Total True Positives}}{\text{Total True Positives} + \text{Total False Negatives}}$$

Precision: The precision metric is crucial in understanding the model's ability to predict positives (correct true class predictions) that are relevant. It denotes the quality of a positive prediction made by the classifier. The Precision metric is described as:

$$\text{Precision} = \frac{\text{Total True Positives}}{\text{Total True Positives} + \text{Total False Positives}}$$

It is to be noted that the specificity, recall, and precision metrics are averaged across all classes to evaluate model performance in multi-class classification.

7.5.2 PERFORMANCE EVALUATION

In this subsection, we first report the performance of the presented denoising convolutional autoencoder model. Subsequently, the performance of the classifiers in the context of tumor detection and tumor grade classification is analyzed, and the results and observations are reported.

Figure 7.19 qualitatively analyzes the performance of the presented autoencoder. It shows the original image, a Gaussian noise corrupted image, and finally an image denoised using the presented autoencoder network. The visual results are indicative of the better performance of the proposed architecture. The average quantitative results obtained over twenty brain MR images are reported in Table 7.1. The autoencoder architecture obtains high PSNR and SSIM values, thus defending the robustness of the approach. The technique also achieves a low RMSE value, thus signifying minimal deviation from the original uncorrupted image samples.

Next, the performance of the tumor detection models is evaluated. We compare the performance of the models with the existing state-of-the-art algorithms. CNN, GLCM-KSVM, Naïve Bayes, CNN-GLCM, AlexNet, GoogleNet, and VGG16

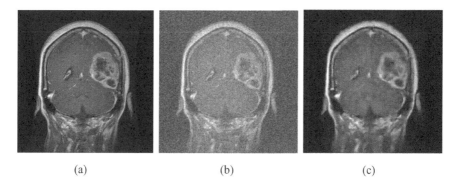

(a)   (b)   (c)

FIGURE 7.19 (a) Original (b) 8% Gaussian noise corrupted, and (c) Denoising convolutional autoencoder filtered brain MR image sample.

TABLE 7.1

Average Evaluation Metrics Corresponding to Convolutional Autoencoder Based Denoising Algorithm (up to 8% Gaussian Noise) Using Obtained Over Twenty Brain MR Images

ALGORITHM	RMSE	PSNR	SSIM
Convolutional Denoising Autoencoder	10.53	27.68	0.99

architectures. The test dataset consists of 600 image samples (300 per class). The confusion matrix related to the presented architectures is shown in Figure 7.20 and the quantitative performance results are reported in Table 7.2.

We see that the Xception, ResNet50, MobileNet, EfficientNet B2, and EfficientNet B3 models attain 98.16%, 98.66%, 98.83%, 99.50%, and 99.66% test set accuracies, respectively. The MobileNet and EfficientNet models have the best performance results, which are significantly better than their peers. The acquired precision and recall highlight the resiliency of the deep learning-based classifiers and set a standard in tumor detection based on the classification paradigm. In addition to this, the obtained specificity defends the reliability of the models against misclassification.

For the performance evaluation of the tumor type identification pipeline, we compare the presented architectures with other benchmark algorithms mentioned in the literature. For comparison with other statistical feature extraction methods, we evaluate GLCM-MLP [27]. Deep learning-based architectures, including standard ConvNet [28], SE-ResNet101 [30], fine-tuned AlexNet, GoogleNet, and VGG16 architectures [34] are also evaluated. The test dataset consists of 327 image samples (54 normal samples, 104 pituitary samples, 78 meningioma samples, and 90 glioma samples).

The confusion matrix related to the presented architectures is shown in Figure 7.21, and the quantitative performance results are tabularized in Table 7.3. The ResNet50, EfficientNet B2 and B3 models attain 98.16%, 98.47%, and 98.77% test set accuracy, respectively. We observe that the EfficientNet B3 and MobileNet architectures achieve the best performance results with test set accuracies as high as 98.8% and 99.08%, which is better than all of their peers. The acquired precision and recall are high, signifying the model's accurate class prediction ability. Also, the observed specificity highlights the reliability of the models against misclassification.

Why should the presented AI systems be trusted? – Using visual analytics for XAI In the domain of biomedical analysis, transparency in AI systems are in demand as a lack of trust in the black box functioning may often lead to unwanted issues. Explainable AI (XAI) is an evolving research domain that answers why a model performs the way it does and explains its predictions [A]. The XAI pipeline is crucial when it comes to deploying responsible and reliable AI systems for real-life scenarios. The field of visual analytics leverages the domain of XAI as it assists in easy comprehension of AI systems by providing visualizations that make exploration and explanation intuitive and simple.

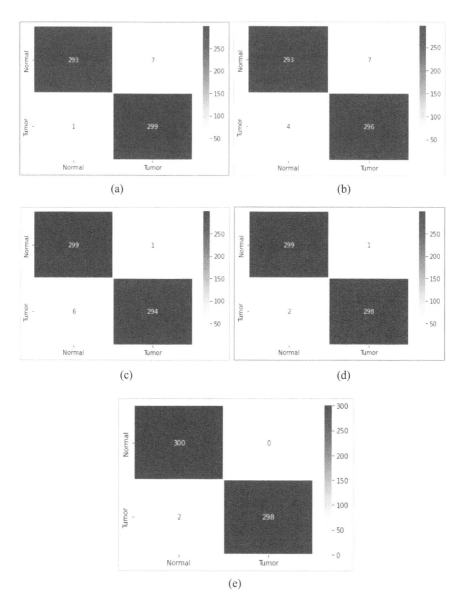

FIGURE 7.20 Confusion matrix corresponding to test data predictions using (a) ResNet50, (b) Xception, (c) MobileNet, (d) EfficientNet B2, and (e) EfficientNet B3 models.

In this chapter, we use class activation maps (CAM) [44] to visually demonstrate the reliability of the presented deep neural network models. To do so, we present a case study where random brain MR image samples are passed through three of the presented networks (ResNet, MobileNet, and Xception) and the corresponding visualizations and inferences are reported. Before jumping into the analysis, it is important to understand why CAM is a good measure for explaining the model predictions.

TABLE 7.2

Average Tumor Detection Model Performance Metric Values Over All Image Classes

Classifier	Specificity	Recall	Precision	Accuracy (%)
GLCM-KSVM	0.92	0.89	0.90	91.16
Naïve Bayes	0.94	0.90	0.91	92.50
CNN	0.95	0.93	0.95	94.16
CNN-GLCM	0.95	0.94	0.96	96.00
AlexNet	0.96	0.95	0.97	97.4
GoogleNet	0.97	0.96	0.98	98.07
VGG16	0.98	0.98	0.98	98.18
ResNet50	0.98	0.98	0.98	98.66
Xception	0.98	0.98	0.97	98.16
MobileNet	0.99	0.98	0.99	98.83
EfficientNet B2	0.99	0.99	0.99	99.50
EfficientNet B3	1.00	0.99	1.00	99.66

A CAM simply is a weighted activation map that is generated for an image. It helps in region quantification (the region the classifier focuses on during prediction) in a weakly supervised fashion. Initially, after an image is passed, the class prediction of the network is obtained and the weights corresponding to the output neurons are stored in addition to the output of the final convolutional layer. Next, CAM is computed by a dot product of the activation layers and their corresponding weights. Lastly, a bilinear upsampling is performed for the size extension of the map to fit the size of the input sample. An in-depth explanation is provided in [45].

Coming to the case study, we pick a tumor sample for analyzing the CAM for the tumor detection predictor models. Figure 7.22 shows an original tumor sample and the activation maps corresponding to the ResNet 50 and MobileNet models. As it can be clearly noticed, the tumor region is most activated (yellow region) among the network feature maps and is thus most responsible for the prediction. The detected CAM regions successfully highlight the reliability of the detector models.

Next, a glioma tumor sample is picked for analyzing the CAMs for the grade classification models (presented in Figure 7.23). We present the CAMs corresponding to the ResNet50 and Xception architectures. Here, as noticed again, the tumor region is most activated – signifying the contribution of the highlighted region in class prediction.

Overall, along with performance evaluation, the robustness and reliability of the systems are also visually analyzed and the rationale behind the predictions is clearly demonstrated. The AI systems stand out and can be efficiently incorporated into real-life medical scenarios to aid doctors and domain experts in brain tumor diagnosis.

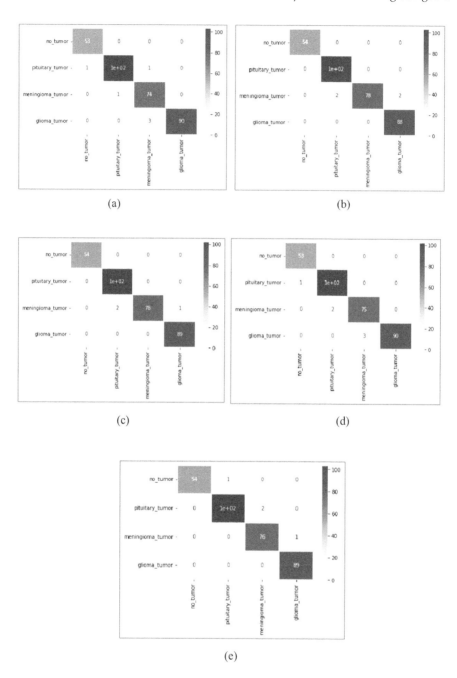

FIGURE 7.21 Confusion matrix corresponding to test data predictions using (a) ResNet50, (b) Xception, (c) MobileNet, (d) EfficientNet B2, and (e) EfficientNet B3 models.

TABLE 7.3

Average Grade Classification Model Performance Metric Values Over All Image Classes

Classifier	Specificity	Recall	Precision	Accuracy (%)
GLCM-MLP	0.94	0.92	0.92	91.9
SE-ResNet101	0.96	0.92	0.95	93.83
ConvNet	0.97	0.94	0.96	96.74
AlexNet	0.96	0.95	0.97	97.4
GoogleNet	0.97	0.96	0.98	98.07
VGG16	0.98	0.98	0.98	98.18
ResNet50	0.98	0.98	0.98	98.16
Xception	0.99	0.99	0.99	98.77
MobileNet	0.99	0.99	0.99	99.08
EfficientNet B2	0.98	0.98	0.98	98.47
EfficientNet B3	0.99	0.99	0.99	98.8

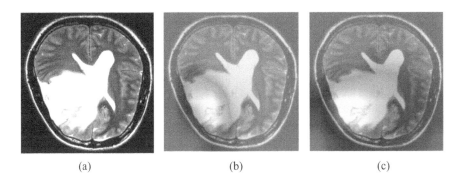

(a)   (b)   (c)

FIGURE 7.22 Visualizing the CAMs for tumor detection models: (a) Original tumor sample (b) CAM corresponding to ResNet 50 and (c) CAM corresponding to MobileNet models.

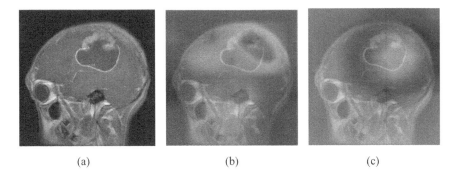

(a)   (b)   (c)

FIGURE 7.23 Visualizing the CAMs for tumor grade identification models: (a) Original glioma tumor sample (b) CAM corresponding to ResNet 50 and (c) CAM corresponding to Xception models.

7.6 CONCLUSION

This chapter tackles the challenge of brain MR image classification targeted at tumor detection and tumor-grade identification. The network architectures used in the work establish a new benchmark performance in the domain. The peak accuracies achieved by the classifier networks corresponding to tumor detection as well as type identification suggest the resiliency of these architectures. Additionally, a robust denoising autoencoder architecture is presented targeted at Gaussian noise removal from MR images. Experiments suggest the reliability and the standard performance of the denoiser across image samples. Overall, the deep neural network architectures incorporated for the presented use case stand out to be fault tolerant and efficient across varied image types and can be incorporated into medical systems for real-time applications. In the future, the next big step will be exploring other learning paradigms with even reduced computational requirements while still maintaining the reliability benchmark.

REFERENCES

1. Oguz, Mustafa and Andrew P. Cox. "Machine learning biopharma applications and overview of key steps for successful implementation."
2. Sahu, Barnali, Sitarashmi Sahu, and Om Jena. Impact of ensemble-based models on cancer classification, its development, and challenges, 2022. 10.1201/9781003189053-8.
3. Om Jena, K. Paramesha, and H. L. Gururaj. (2021). Applications of machine learning in biomedical text processing and food industry. 10.1002/9781119792611.ch10.
4. Patra, Sudhansu, M. Mittal, and Om Jena. Multiobjective evolutionary algorithm based on decomposition for feature selection in medical diagnosis, 2022. 10.1016/B978-0-323-99864-2.00005-6.
5. Abed, Amira, E. Shaaban, Om Jena, and A. Elngar. A comprehensive survey on breast cancer thermography classification using deep neural network, 2022. 10.1201/9781003226147-9.
6. Jena, Om, N. Panigrahi, and Ishan Ayus. An expert system-based clinical decision support system for Hepatitis-B prediction & diagnosis, 2021. 10.1002/9781119792611.ch4.
7. Dora, Lingraj, et al. "State-of-the-art methods for brain tissue segmentation: A review." *IEEE Reviews in Biomedical Engineering* 10 (2017): 235–249.
8. Sun, Yu, Bir Bhanu, and Shiv Bhanu. "Automatic symmetry-integrated brain injury detection in MRI sequences." *2009 IEEE Computer Society Conference on Computer Vision and Pattern Recognition Workshops*. IEEE, Miami, FL, 2009.
9. Kapoor, Luxit, and Sanjeev Thakur. "A survey on brain tumor detection using image processing techniques." *2017 7th International Conference on Cloud Computing, Data Science & Engineering-Confluence*. IEEE, Noida, 2017.
10. Abiwinanda, Nyoman, et al. "Brain tumor classification using convolutional neural network." *World Congress on Medical Physics and Biomedical Engineering 2018*. Springer, Singapore, 2019.
11. Vlaardingerbroek, Marinus T., and Jacques A. Boer. *Magnetic Resonance Imaging: Theory and Practice*. Springer Science & Business Media, Springer-Verlag Berlin Heidelberg New York, 2013.
12. Herholz, K., K. J. Langen, C. Schiepers, and J. M. Mountz. (2012, November). Brain tumors. In *Seminars in Nuclear Medicine* (Vol. 42, No. 6, pp. 356–370). Elsevier, WB Saunders, United Kingdom.

13. Cai, Lei, Jingyang Gao, and Di Zhao. "A review of the application of deep learning in medical image classification and segmentation." *Annals of Translational Medicine* 8.11 (2020): 1–15.

14. Zhuang, Fuzhen, et al. "A comprehensive survey on transfer learning." *Proceedings of the IEEE* 109.1 (2020): 43–76.

15. He, Kaiming, et al. "Deep residual learning for image recognition." *Proceedings of the IEEE Conference on Computer Vision and Pattern Recognition*, Las Vegas, NV, 2016.

16. Chollet, François. "Xception: Deep learning with depthwise separable convolutions." *Proceedings of the IEEE Conference on Computer Vision and Pattern Recognition*, Honolulu, HI, 2017.

17. Howard, A. G., M. Zhu, B. Chen, D. Kalenichenko, W. Wang, T. Weyand ... and H. Adam. Mobilenets: Efficient convolutional neural networks for mobile vision applications, 2017. *arXiv preprint arXiv:1704.04861.*

18. Tan, Mingxing, and Quoc Le. "Efficientnet: Rethinking model scaling for convolutional neural networks." *International Conference on Machine Learning.* PMLR, Long Beach, CA, 2019.

19. Halder, A. and A. Sarkar. Automatic detection of tumor cell in brain MRI using rough-fuzzy feature selection with support vector machine and morphological operation. *Advanced Machine Learning Approaches in Cancer Prognosis Challenges and Applications* (pp. 221–246). Springer, 2021.

20. Arabahmadi, C., R. Farahbakhsh, and J. Rezazadeh. Deep learning for smart healthcare-a survey on brain tumor detection from medical imaging. *Sensors* 22.5 (2022 March): 1960.

21. Kadam, Megha, and Avinash Dhole. "Brain tumor detection using GLCM with the help of KSVM." *International Journal of Engineering and Technical Research* 7.2 (2017): 10–12.

22. Zaw, Hein Tun, Noppadol Maneerat, and Khin Yadanar Win. "Brain tumor detection based on Naïve Bayes Classification." *2019 5th International Conference on Engineering, Applied Sciences and Technology (ICEAST).* IEEE, 2019.

23. Abir, Tasnim Azad, et al. "Analysis of a novel MRI based brain tumour classification using probabilistic neural network (PNN)." *International Journal of Scientific Research in Science, Engineering Technology* 4.8 (2018): 65–79.

24. Hossain, Tonmoy, et al. "Brain tumor detection using convolutional neural network." *2019 1st International Conference on Advances in Science, Engineering and Robotics Technology (ICASERT).* IEEE, Dhaka, 2019.

25. Gurunathan, Akila, and Batri Krishnan. "A hybrid CNN-GLCM classifier for detection and grade classification of brain tumor." *Brain Imaging and Behavior* 16.3 (2022): 1410–1427.

26. Zacharaki, E. I., S. Wang, S. Chawla, D. Soo Yoo, R. Wolf, E. R. Melhem, and C. Davatzikos. Classification of brain tumor type and grade using MRI texture and shape in a machine learning scheme. *Magnetic Resonance in Medicine: An Official Journal of the International Society for Magnetic Resonance in Medicine* 62.6 (2009): 1609–1618.

27. Ismael, Mustafa R., and Ikhlas Abdel-Qader. "Brain tumor classification via statistical features and back-propagation neural network." *2018 IEEE International Conference on Electro/information Technology (EIT).* IEEE, Rochester, HI, 2018.

28. Sultan, Hossam H., Nancy M. Salem, and Walid Al-Atabany. "Multi-classification of brain tumor images using deep neural network." *IEEE Access* 7 (2019): 69215–69225.

29. Anaraki, Amin Kabir, Moosa Ayati, and Foad Kazemi. "Magnetic resonance imaging-based brain tumor grades classification and grading via convolutional neural networks and genetic algorithms." *Biocybernetics and Biomedical Engineering* 39.1 (2019): 63–74.

30. Ghosal, Palash, et al. "Brain tumor classification using ResNet-101 based squeeze and excitation deep neural network." *2019 Second International Conference on Advanced Computational and Communication Paradigms (ICACCP)*. IEEE, Gangtok, 2019.

31. Ali, S., J. Li, Y. Pei, R. Khurram, and T. Mahmood. A comprehensive survey on brain tumor diagnosis using deep learning and emerging hybrid techniques with multi-modal MR image. *Archives of Computational Methods in Engineering* 2022 (2022 May 9): 1–26.

32. Rizwan, M., A. Shabbir, A. R., Javed, M. Shabbir, T. Baker, and D. A. Obe. Brain tumor and glioma grade classification using gaussian convolutional neural network. *IEEE Access* 10 (2022 February 21): 29731–29740.

33. Gurunathan, A. and B. Krishnan. A hybrid CNN-GLCM classifier for detection and grade classification of brain tumor. *Brain Imaging and Behavior* 16.3 (2022 June): 1410–1427.

34. Rehman, Arshia, et al. "A deep learning-based framework for automatic brain tumors classification using transfer learning." *Circuits, Systems, and Signal Processing* 39.2 (2020): 757–775.

35. Bjorck, N., C. P. Gomes, B. Selman, and K. Q. Weinberger. Understanding batch normalization. *Advances in Neural Information Processing Systems* 2018(2018): 31.

36. Deng, J., W. Dong, R. Socher, L. J. Li, K. Li, and L. Fei-Fei. Imagenet: A large-scale hierarchical image database. *In 2009 IEEE Conference on Computer Vision and Pattern Recognition* (pp. 248–255), Miami, FL, 2009.

37. Hamada, A. Br35H: Brain tumor detection, 2020. https://www.kaggle.com/datasets/ahmedhamada0/brain-tumor-detection

38. Rao, Vinay, M. Shari Sarabi, and Ayush Jaiswal. "Brain tumor segmentation with deep learning." *MICCAI Multimodal Brain Tumor Segmentation Challenge* (BraTS) 59 (2015): 1–4.

39. Vincent, Pascal, Hugo Larochelle, Yoshua Bengio, and Pierre-Antoine Manzagol. "Extracting and composing robust features with denoising autoencoders." *In Proceedings of the 25th International Conference on Machine learning* (pp. 1096–1103), Helsinki, 2008.

40. Agarap, Abien Fred. "Deep learning using rectified linear units (relu)." arXiv preprint arXiv:1803.08375 (2018).

41. Narayan, Sridhar. "The generalized sigmoid activation function: Competitive supervised learning." *Information Sciences* 99.1–2 (1997): 69–82.

42. Kingma, D. P. and B. Jimmy. "Adam: A method for stochastic optimization." *arXiv preprint arXiv:1412.6980, 2014.*

43. Cheng, Jun. "Brain tumor dataset." figshare. *Dataset* 5 (2017): 1512427.

44. Doshi-Velez, F. and Kim, B. "Towards a rigorous science of interpretable machine learning," 2017, https://arxiv.org/abs/ 1702.08608.

45. Zhou, B., A. Khosla, A. Lapedriza, A. Oliva, and A. Torralba. Learning deep features for discriminative localization. *In Proceedings of the IEEE Conference on Computer Vision and Pattern Recognition* 2016 (pp. 2921–2929). Las Vegas, NV, 2016.

8 A Robust Framework for Prediction of Diabetes Mellitus Using Machine Learning

Sarthak Singh, Rohan Singh,
Arkaprovo Ghosal, and Tanmaya Mahapatra
Birla Institute of Technology & Science

8.1 INTRODUCTION

Diabetes has become a very common and widespread disease across the globe that it may be justifiable to be termed as a hidden pandemic. The disease itself is continually contributing to the ever rising burden of non-communicable diseases. This is promoted by declining exercise levels and the rise in obesity level [1,2]. According to the International Diabetes Federation (IDF): Diabetes Atlas [3], 527 million adults between 20 and 79 are living with diabetes. Also, one in ten people are unaware they have the disease. Diabetes is characterized by the body's inability to metabolize glucose and can lead to other severe and complex illnesses like kidney diseases and heart attacks. Diabetes mellitus is a disease which is characterized by too high sugar levels in the blood and urine. It is usually diagnosed by means of a glucose tolerance test (GTT). In the GTT, after an overnight fast, a patient is administered a substantial quantity of glucose upon arrival at the hospital (sugar in the form in which it usually appears in the bloodstream). Several measures of the patient's blood glucose concentration are taken throughout the next three to five hours, and these values are used to diagnose diabetes mellitus [4]. Diabetic patients require a supplement of insulin in the form of regular injections and tablets in addition to a modified diet to regulate glucose input. Glucose plays an important role in the food metabolism of any vertebrate tissue since it is a source of energy for all tissues and organs. Diabetes can be classified as Type 1 or Type 2. Type 1 diabetes is caused when the pancreas is unable to produce an adequate amount of insulin for the body, whereas, in Type 2 diabetes, the body is unable to use the produced insulin effectively because of which an inadequate amount of insulin is released into the bloodstream. A timely and accurate diagnosis of diabetes will help patients take precautions and appropriate medical care from an early stage. Diagnosing the disease at an early stage reduces the risk of complications and decreases medical costs by a large margin. However, the diagnosis and treatment are delayed in most cases because of limited healthcare facilities and

DOI: 10.1201/9781003257721-8

GTT being time-consuming and tedious. Diabetes has a relatively lengthy asymptomatic phase. The therapies that have a demonstrated positive influence on clinically significant outcomes are available, and screening technologies are safe, acceptable, and have acceptable sensitivity and accuracy. However, it remains uncertain due to the lack of clear evidence that detecting diabetes early in its natural course is genuinely advantageous for individuals. Testing blood sugar levels (GTT, as mentioned above) is the most common way to test diabetes in people, but we endeavor to predict diabetes using physical attributes and symptoms. Most people make assessments based on their symptoms but lack proper medical knowledge to make a sound decision. Using these common symptoms, building a prediction model bridges the lack of knowledge with a high accuracy model, which can be used as an early sign. Succinctly, this chapter contributes by (1) performing a narrative literature survey to distill the state-of-the-art ML methods used in predicting diabetes mellitus (Section 8.3), (2) conceptualizing a novel and robust ML method for easy prediction of diabetes mellitus (Section 8.4). In this regard, the goal is to build predictive models with high accuracy and lesser false negatives to detect diabetes at an early age. Multiple ML algorithms and their ensemble models are used and tested on our dataset. The models used in our conceptual approach include logistic regression, support vector machine (SVM), random forest (RF), XGBoost, and neural network. The many trainable parameters involved in the ML models help them classify the data points with very high accuracy and (3) provide a comparative discussion with all other existing works to demonstrate the efficiency of our approach over all others (Section 8.6). The best accuracy of 98.08%, achieved by using a neural network with two hidden layers, is highlighted in this context.

8.2 BACKGROUND

In this section, we briefly summarize the idea of machine learning (ML) and the working of various ML algorithms used in our approach for easy prediction of diabetes mellitus. ML is a subset of artificial intelligence (AI) that enables computers to learn from experience and improve without being explicitly programmed automatically. ML aims to develop computer models that can accept datasets and utilize them to train themselves. There are various types of ML, including supervised learning, unsupervised learning, and reinforcement ML, among others. Face recognition, audio recognition, object recognition, and translation are just some of the many tasks at which ML systems excel. Government, education, and healthcare are all sectors impacted by ML. It can be utilized by organizations specializing in marketing, social media, customer service, autonomous vehicles, and more. It is currently recognized as a fundamental instrument for decision-making. The ML procedure begins by introducing training data to the chosen algorithm. Training data consists of either known or unknown data for developing the final ML algorithm. The type of input training data affects the algorithm. New input data is given into the ML system to verify its functionality. The prediction and outcomes are subsequently compared. ML aims to replicate how humans (and other sentient organisms) acquire the ability to process sensory (input) data to achieve a goal. ML has two very advantageous features. First, it can replace tedious and repetitive human labor. Second, and more importantly, it has the capacity to discover more complex and subtle patterns in the input data than the average human observer. The training and testing procedure is the most crucial aspect impacting the success of ML. An effective training procedure enhances the quality of the created system. Researchers divide datasets into training and testing portions. The quantity of training and examinations has the most significant bearing on the success rate. If there is a strong association between the characteristics and the label, the training test set is split 50/50. This indicates that 50% of the data will be used for training and 50% for testing. However, if there is concern that success will decline, training can be accelerated. Less than 50% of the training data is undesirable because it will negatively impact the test outcomes. The researcher examines the test performance based on the criteria for performance evaluation. To prevent the scenario of unstable data, the research can be repeated by altering the training and test data during the training and testing procedure.

SVM [5] is one of the most common algorithms used, especially for classification problems. SVM works by creating a decision boundary in multidimensional space to classify the data points best lying on either side of the boundary. The dimension of the space depends on the number of features. It is supervised ML and when you give an SVM model sets of labeled training data for each category, it can put new content into those categories. They have two main advantages over newer algorithms like neural networks: they are faster and work better with a smaller number of samples (in the thousands). A simple example is the best way to understand what SVMs are and how they work. Let's say our data has two features, x and y, and our labels are red and blue. We want a classifier that, given a pair of coordinates (x,y), tells us whether the point is red or blue. A SVM takes these data points and outputs the hyperplane, which, in two dimensions, is just a line that best separates the tags. This line is the boundary for making a decision. Anything that falls on one side of it will be called blue, and anything that falls on the other side will be called red. We can sort vectors in a space with more than one dimension and work with data that is not linear.

Logistic regression [6,7] is used to determine the probability of an event based on the input variables. This is done by creating a linear combination of all the input variables and determining their optimal coefficients. The most common application of logistic regression in ML is a binary classification problem where the output can belong to only two distinct classes. It uses the logistic function, which restricts the range to 0–1. It is a predictive algorithm that uses independent variables to predict the dependent variable, just like linear regression, but the dependent variable should be a categorical variable. The independent variables can be either numeric or categorical, but the dependent variable will always be categorical. A categorical variable is one that can only take one of a small, usually fixed number of possible values. Logistic regression is a statistical model that models the conditional probability using the logistic function. Logistic functions model the exponential growth of a population, but they also take into account factors in the dataset that affect the growth. It's important to remember that the exponential function doesn't have an inflection point, but the logistic function does. An example of logistic regression is figuring out if someone will miss their credit card payment or not. A person's credit card balance, income, and other factors can all affect how likely it is that they won't make their credit card payment on time.

Decision trees [8] are based on sequential splitting of data based on conditions imposed on a feature. This splitting is done till either the node has the same value as the target or when splitting stops adding any value to the predictions. A decision tree is a way to show information that looks like an upside-down tree. It is similar to a flowchart. The goal of a decision tree is to break up a large dataset into smaller groups of cases with similar values so that you can see how likely different options are to turn out. Decision trees are used in supervised learning regression and classification algorithms to guess the class or value of target variables. Regression algorithms, which are also called continuous algorithms, use training data to predict all of a data instance's future values within a certain amount of time. Classification algorithms, on the other hand, use training data to predict the value of a single piece of data at a certain time. There are two kinds of decision trees: categorical and continuous/regressive. In a categorical decision tree, new data results are based on a single, discrete variable. On the other hand, the results of a continuous decision tree are based on the results of the previous decision nodes.

By putting together the results of several decision trees, you can make them more accurate. The RF is a classification algorithm consisting of many decision trees. Decision trees are made by looking at a set of labeled training examples and using that information to look at examples that have never been seen before. When good data is used to train a decision tree, it can make very accurate predictions. RF [9] is an ensemble technique based on decision trees, combining multiple decision trees to solve a classification or regression problem. These multiple decision trees work on different subsets of the training data and are combined in the end by a majority decision. This prevents overfitting and gives higher accuracy in general.

XGBoost [10], or extreme gradient boosting, is an ensemble technique based on decision trees that use gradient boosting to improve the performance of the base learners. It is a distributed gradient-boosted decision tree (GBDT) ML library that can be used on a large scale. It is the best ML library for regression, classification, and ranking problems, and it has parallel tree boosting. In ensemble learning, the gradient boosting algorithm is a common method. Ensemble learning is a type of ML in which multiple models work together to make predictions. Boosting algorithms are different from other ensemble learning methods because they build on a series of weak models to make stronger models. Gradient boosting algorithms use the gradient of a loss function that measures how well a model does to decide how to build a more powerful model. The XGBoost algorithm learns a model faster than many other ML models and works well with categorical data and small datasets.

Neural networks or artificial neural networks are the base of deep learning. These consist of nodes, an input layer, an output layer, and more hidden layers between them. Each node has a weight and threshold through which information passes in the feedforward network. Each value passing through a node is multiplied by its weight, and if it is more than the threshold value, information is passed through that node. In deep learning models, neurons are the nodes that data and computations flow through. They get one or more signals from the outside. These input signals can either come from the raw data set or come from neurons in a layer of the neural net that came before it. They do some math and then use a synapse to send signals to neurons further down in the neural network. In a deep learning model, the synapses between neurons can connect to more than one neuron in the layer below. Each synapse has a weight that affects how important the neuron before it is in the whole neural network. Weights are a very important part of deep learning because changing the weights of a model is the main way to train a deep learning model. Once a neuron gets its inputs from the neurons in the model's previous layer, it adds each signal's weight to it and sends the result to an activation function. The activation function works out what the neuron's output value will be. The next layer of the neural network then gets this output value through another synapse.

Optuna [11] is a framework for automatically finding the optimal hyperparameters using different samplers like grid search, Bayesian, random, and evolutionary algorithms. It efficiently searches large spaces and can easily parallelize over multiple threads. Stacking [12] is an ensemble technique that uses multiple models in parallel and combines them by using another model to train on these predictions. Unlike other ensemble techniques like bagging and boosting, which uses homogeneous models, stacking uses heterogeneous learners.

8.3 RELATED WORK

Researchers have studied RR-interval signals1, known as heart rate variability (HRV) signals and have put forth a methodology for classifying diabetic and normal HRV signals using deep learning architectures [13]. Using long short-term memory (LSTM), convolutional neural network (CNN), and its combinations, meaningful insights have been extracted from the input HRV data. These features are passed into SVM for classification. They obtained a performance improvement of 0.03% and 0.06% in CNN and CNN-LSTM architecture, respectively, compared to prior work done without using SVM. The accuracy of the above-proposed algorithm is around 95.7%. Another interesting comparative study has been done using the PIMA dataset ("PIMA Indians Diabetes Dataset" 2016) involving various ML algorithms [14]. Here, various classification models and ensemble techniques have been used to predict diabetes, including K-nearest neighbor (KNN), logistic regression (LR), decision tree (DT), SVM, gradient boosting (GB), and RF. The result shows that RF achieved higher accuracy compared to other ML techniques. Another interesting piece of work focused on detecting patterns with risk factors using R-Data manipulation tools [15]. The dataset used for analysis is the PIMA Indian dataset, and the ML algorithms were tested on the dataset such as linear kernel SVM (SVM), the radial basis function (RBF), KNN, artificial neural networks, and multi these dimensionality reduction (MDR). Boruta wrapper (feature selection tool related for dataset with all the attributes, and it yielded four attributes as in ns can be attributes, the accuracy, precision and recall, and other para were taken to each of the algorithms. Researchers have talked about fully with around embedded inside data mining pipelines to extract more ne of the features Here, the missing data were treated by means of in (HbA1c), hyper-care for class imbalance in the dataset, collected in accuracy of 83.8% 1000 data points. LR was used with stepwise included gender, age, body mass index (P tension, and smoking habit. After tail was achieved. Another work focused on using ML models to detect diabetes at an early stage by using features much more easily attainable than laboratory tests [20]. Attributes such as sudden weight loss and obesity are used for the prediction mode, which makes this model more understandable and applicable. They use six classical ML models to make a prediction model, including LR, SVM, RF, boosting, and artificial neural networks. Dataset used was from the UCI ML repository, collected from a hospital in Bangladesh. RF and ANN seem to perform better than LR, SVM, and decision trees. ANN achieved the highest accuracy of 96%

8.4　CONCEPTUAL APPROACH

In this section, we discuss the conceptual approach of our robust ML framework for diabetes prediction. We have used various models, optimized hyperparameters, and their combinations while stacking them together. Models include SVM, RF, XGBoost, and neural network. All the models have been trained at 70% of the data, which is cross-validated, by dividing it into five folds. In each iteration, it is trained on four folds and validated on one fold. Cross-validation is a technique for assessing the efficiency of a model by training it on a subset of input data and testing it on a subset of input data that it has never seen before. In the end, the results are concatenated from each iteration and averaged to make the final prediction. We have used LR as one of the baseline models for our study. LR works by representing the class as a linear combination of features by giving them optimal weights. We train our model over 500 iterations. One of the critical parameters is the inverse regularization strength (C) which by default is 1. We optimize it using optional, and the value comes out to be 257.92. The higher value for 'C' signifies the training data is close to real-world data and thus should be given more importance. Another model we have used as a baseline model is the SVM. SVM works by creating a hyperplane with the maximum margin between datapoint of distinct classes. We use the linear kernel, which creates a single line in a 2-D plane to classify the data points. We have optimized the regularization parameter 'C'. The model performs best for $C = 2.1$. The regularization parameter controls the penalty model suffers for misclassification. RF is an ensemble model using decision trees as a basic unit. The results from these uncorrelated trees are averaged to achieve the final output. We have fine tuned the depth ⌐ the estimators used in the model using Optuna. The n estimators represent the `er of trees used to build the RF. Max Depth is each tree's depth, representing `ber of splits a tree can have. The model performs best for estimators = 7 and `. = 13.74. XGBoost is a boosting technique where only one decision tree CA the real data, and all subsequent trees are trained on the previous tree's and r uses CART (Classification and Regression Trees) as their base unit. fine th rapidly show vital data links, automatically search for patterns, subsam structure in even the most intricate data. For this model, we have binary w of estimators, learning rate, L1 and L2 regularization terms, number of e maximum depth of the tree. L1 regularization produces error term m 0 to 1 for a model's features and is used to reduce the `imensional data collection. L2 regularization disperses `lting in more precise, custom-tailored final models.

Neural Networks are made up of nodes arranged in different layers, mainly the input layer, output layer, and hidden layers in between. Each node has an associated weight and threshold. Data only passes through the node if the incoming value, when multiplied by a weight, is more than the threshold value. Weights keep changing as the model is trained. This combination of weights and biases from nodes and layers helps in accurately predicting the final output accurately. We have stacked different models from the models mentioned above in different combinations. We have used these different models to generate predictions for the validation dataset and train a LR on these predictions from different models against the true class for that data point.

8.5 EVALUATION

In this section, we describe the results of the application of specific ML algorithms against our dataset. The source code of our implementation/experimentation can be found in a public GitLab repository.[1] Dataset One of the main limitations with building prediction models for medical use is the availability of public datasets. For the detection of diabetes, the two most used datasets available publicly are PIMA Indian Diabetes Dataset [21] and UCI Repository dataset [22]. PIMA Indian dataset uses attributes only attainable after going through medical tests. On the other hand, the dataset from the UCI repository contains physical attributes about the body, which are easy to collect and make predictions. Other datasets, such as the time series HRV dataset [19], are private and collected for specific studies. Also, another limitation is the size of datasets, the availability of new data points, and their credibility. The size of the PIMA dataset is 732 samples, and for the UCI dataset, it is 520 samples. This prevents us from having models trained over large amounts of data. This makes it challenging to make the ML models more robust. The dataset used in our approach is from the UCI ML repository, available publicly here.[2] This dataset was created using a survey conducted at Sylhet Diabetes Hospital, Bangladesh. One of the reasons to select this dataset is the similar geography and people relative to India. Also, the attributes in this dataset do not require any medical tests and can be collected quite easily. Therefore, the dataset is more understandable and accessible to people. There are in total 17 features, one of which is the class of patient, i.e., negative or positive to diabetes. This dataset includes data from 520 patients, of whom 320 are diabetes positive, and the rest are negative. Out of the 520 data points, we split them into 70% for the training dataset for various algorithms and the remaining 30% for the test dataset. Out of the 16 useful attributes, only age is a numerical feature. We use a min-max scalar to normalize the age while using an ordinal encoder [23] and one hot encoding [24] for categorical data. Our customized dataset can be found online with the following link.[3]

Logistic Regression Table 8.1 shows the coefficients for all the features obtained from the LR model. Gender, Polyuria, Polydipsia, Itching, and Irritability contribute the most to the model. Also, Polyuria, Polydipsia, sudden weight loss, Obesity,

---

[1] https://gitlab.com/mahapatra09/diabetes
[2] https://archive.ics.uci.edu/ml/datasets/Early+stage+diabetes+risk+prediction+dataset.#
[3] https://data.mendeley.com/datasets/vtv9fdctvv/1

TABLE 8.1

Coefficients for the Features Obtained from the Logistic Regression Model

Feature	Coefficient
Age	–0.04236754
Gender	–4.20007207
Polyuria	4.76788881
Polydipsia	4.92444541
Sudden Weight Loss	0.25806588
Obesity	0.64441296
Weakness	0.66976562
Polyphagia	1.12353558
Genital thrush	1.80860326
Visual blurring	1.85355942
Itiching	–3.16816322
Ittitability	2.78359415
Delayed healing	–0.77989157
Partial pareses	0.87967633
Muscle stiffness	–0.16638746
Alopecia	0.23253257

weakness, Polyphagia, Genital thrush, visual blurring, Irritability, partial pareses, and Alopecia have positive coefficients. Train and test scores have been compared against the size of the dataset in Figure 8.1. The accuracy achieved using this model is 92.94%. Table 8.2 shows the confusion matrix obtained for the same.

SVM: Figure 8.2 plots the test error for the SVM against folds. Running SVM for $C = 2.1$ gives us the best accuracy of 91.02%, which is lesser than the accuracy achieved by LR. Table 8.3 shows the confusion matrix obtained for the same. The decrease in the accuracy is at the cost of false negatives, which shows that SVM performs worse than LR, even though the accuracy between the two models is comparable.

Random forest: Figure 8.3 shows the training versus test scores for different data sizes. Since the scores for both converge as we cover the whole dataset, this tells us that the model is not underfitting or overfitting. For the optimized parameter obtained using Optuna, RF gives us an accuracy of 96.15%. This is a huge improvement from the previous models we considered. The confusion matrix for RF is summarized in Table 8.4. The false negatives are quite low, with a further improvement in the case of false positives.

XGBoost: Figure 8.4 shows the training versus test scores for the XGBoost model against different data sizes. Since the train and test scores are relatively high, this shows the model performs well for the dataset. For the optimized parameters, XGBoost gives us an accuracy of 96.15%, which is the same as the RF model. The confusion matrix for the same is given in Table 8.5. However, comparing the

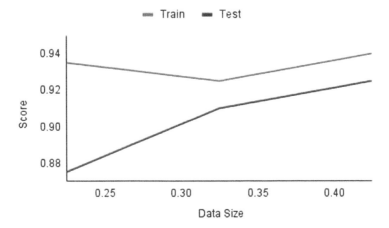

FIGURE 8.1   Logistic regression: Loss graph.

TABLE 8.2
Confusion Matrix for Logistic Regression Model

		Predicted	
		True	**False**
Actual	True	89	4
	False	7	56

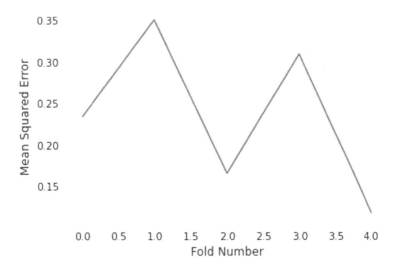

FIGURE 8.2   SVM: Loss graph.

TABLE 8.3

Confusion Matrix for SVM Model

		Predicted	
		True	**False**
Actual	True	86	7
	False	7	56

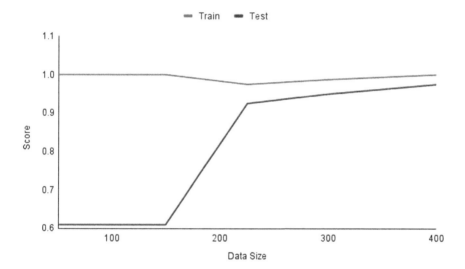

FIGURE 8.3   Random forest: Loss graph.

TABLE 8.4

Confusion Matrix for Random Forest Model

		Predicted	
		True	**False**
Actual	True	91	2
	False	4	59

confusion matrices for RF and XGBoost, we find that false negative for RF is lesser than that of XGBoost, making it a better model compared to RF.

Neural network: Neural network with two hidden layers performs the best with an accuracy of 98.08%. This is mainly because of the large number of trainable parameters that neural networks have, which help segregate the data points into

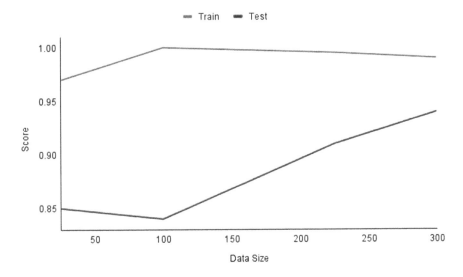

FIGURE 8.4   XGBoost: Loss graph.

TABLE 8.5
Confusion Matrix for XGBoost Model

		Predicted	
		True	**False**
Actual	True	90	3
	False	3	60

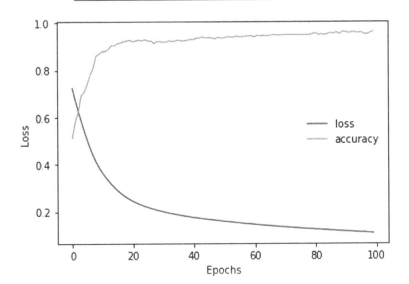

FIGURE 8.5   Neural network: Loss & accuracy graph.

TABLE 8.6

Confusion Matrix for Neural Network Model

		Predicted	
		True	**False**
Actual	True	100	2
	False	1	53

TABLE 8.7
Ensemble Models Metrics

Ensemble Models	Accuracy (%)	True Positives	False Negatives	False Negatives	False Negatives
LogReg + SVM	92.30	88	7	5	56
LogReg + Random Forest	93.58	90	7	3	56
LogReg + Random Forest + XGBoost	96.79	92	4	1	59
LogReg + Random Forest + Neural Network	95.51	90	4	3	59
LogReg + Random Forest + XGBoost + SVM	95.51	90	4	3	59

correct classes. Figure 8.5 shows the loss and accuracy of the model against the number of epochs. The false negatives in the case of ANN are only 1, which is exceptionally high. Compared to the previous models, the accuracy increases by almost 2%. The confusion matrix for the same is summarized in Table 8.6.

Ensemble methods: We run the individual models mentioned in the previous sections by stacking them in different combinations and using LR as a meta learner, which is trained on the predictions from the individual models. Table 8.7 mentions the confusion matrix's accuracy and metrics for all the five ensemble models used in this study. The ensemble model with LR, RF, and XGBoost performs the best with 96.79% accuracy. Also, the same model has the minimum number of false negatives across all the ensembles and the individual models considered.

8.6 DISCUSSION

An efficient prediction model to detect diabetes at an early stage will help patients get a timely and proper diagnosis. Early detection of diabetes dataset is used for our study as it is more easily accessible and understandable to common people. Further, we have pre-processed the numerical and categorical features separately to feed them to our ML algorithms. We have used Optuna open-source library for fine-tuning the hyper-parameters for all our models and analyzed their performance on the dataset using accuracy and false-negative rate as our metrics. We have built five prediction models, including LR, SVM, RF, XGBoost, and neural network, and five ensemble models by stacking these models. Table 8.8 shows the accuracy and false-negative rate for all the ten models we considered. The neural network gave the highest accuracy of 98.08%, while the ensemble model of RF, XGBoost, and LR had the lowest false negatives rate.

TABLE 8.8
ML Models: Accuracy and False-Negative Rates

Model	Accuracy (%)	False Negative Rate
Logistic Regression	92.94	4.30
SVM	91.02	7.52
Random Forest	96.15	2.15
XGBoost	96.15	3.22
Neural Network	98.08	1.96
LogReg + SVM	92.30	5.37
LogReg + Random Forest	93.58	3.22
LogReg + Random Forest + XGBoost	96.79	1.07
LogReg + Random Forest + Neural Network	95.51	3.22
LogReg + Random Forest + XGBoost + SVM	95.51	3.22

The more complex algorithms perform better as they have more trainable parameters. In the future, these models can be tested against new datasets with more data points. Also, we can use these models in the back end for a web-based application where people can enter their respective symptoms and have a resultant probability of having diabetes. This can act as a great early warning system for such cases.

8.7 CONCLUSION

Diabetes Mellitus is a chronic and widespread disease. Instant diagnosis of this disease is difficult as we have to rely on a GTT method for its detection. ML techniques can be leveraged in this area for better and more efficient prediction. Nevertheless, the state-of-the-art ML methods used by various researchers suffer from low prediction accuracy issues. In this chapter, we have discussed all the ML models used for diabetes prediction by researchers in the state-of-the-art and created a customized dataset for our approach. We have developed a robust framework for diabetes prediction using various ML algorithms, including their prediction accuracy. The best accuracy was 98.08%, achieved using a neural network with two hidden layers. The results demonstrated in our paper present a significant improvement in diabetes prediction using ML over the established state-of-the-art. As a future work, we intend to develop a web-based diabetes prediction system to be used by everyday users. We envision leveraging these models in the back end of a web-based application where people can enter their respective symptoms and have a resultant probability of having diabetes, which would potentially act as an early warning system for such cases.

REFERENCES

[1] Roglic, G., et al. (2016). WHO global report on diabetes: A summary. *International Journal of Noncommunicable Diseases*, 1 (1), 3.
[2] Aguiree, F., Brown, A., Cho, N. H., Dahlquist, G., Dodd, S., Dunning, T., ... others (2013). Idf diabetes atlas. Retrieved from https://dro.deakin.edu.au/view/ DU:30060687

[3] Sun, H., Saeedi, P., Karuranga, S., Pinkepank, M., Ogurtsova, K., Duncan, B. B., ... others (2022). Idf diabetes atlas: Global, regional and country-level diabetes prevalence estimates for 2021 and projections for 2045. *Diabetes Research and Clinical Practice*, 183, 109119.

[4] Eastham, R. D. (1983). *A Laboratory Guide to Clinical Diagnosis / r.d. eastham* (5th ed.). Bristol: J. Wright. (ISBN: 0723606536)

[5] Cristianini, N., and Ricci, E. (2008). Support vector machines. In M.- Y. Kao (Ed.), *Encyclopedia of Algorithms* (pp. 928–932). Boston, MA: Springer US.

[6] Morgan, S. P., & Teachman, J. D. (1988). Logistic regression: Description, examples, and comparisons. *Journal of Marriage and Family*, 50 (4), 929–936. Retrieved 2022-06-10, from https://www.jstor.org/stable/352104

[7] Cramer, J. (2002, December). The origins of logistic regression (<source>Tinbergen Institute Discussion Papers No. 02-119/4). Tinbergen Institute</source>. Retrieved from https:// ideas.repec.org/p/tin/wpaper/20020119.html

[8] Breiman, L. (2001, October 01). Random forests. *Machine Learning*, 45 (1), 5–32. Retrieved from https://doi.org/10.1023/A:1010933404324

[9] Quinlan, J. R. (1986, March 01). Induction of decision trees. *Machine Learning*, 1 (1), 81–106. Retrieved from https://doi.org/10.1007/BF00116251

[10] Chen, T., & Guestrin, C. (2016). Xgboost: A scalable tree boosting system. In *Proceedings of the 22nd ACM SIGKDD International Conference on Knowledge Discovery and Data Mining* (pp. 785–794). New York, NY, USA: Association for Computing Machinery. Retrieved from https://doi.org/10.1145/2939672.2939785

[11] Akiba, T., Sano, S., Yanase, T., Ohta, T., & Koyama, M. (2019). Optuna: A next-generation hyperparameter optimization framework. arXiv. Retrieved from https:// arxiv.org/abs/1907.10902

[12] Wolpert, D. (1992, 12). Stacked generalization. *Neural Networks*, 5, 241–259. 10.1016/ S0893-6080(05)80023-1

[13] Goutham, Swapna, Ravi, Vinayakumar, & K.P. Soman. (2018). Diabetes detection using deep learning algorithms. *ICT Express*, 4 (4), 243–246. Retrieved from https://www.sciencedirect.com/science/article/pii/S2405959518304624

[14] Soni, M., & Varma, S. (2020). Diabetes prediction using machine learning techniques. *International Journal of Engineering Research and Technology*, 9, 921–925.

[15] Kaur, H., & Kumari, V. (2022, Jan 01). Predictive modelling and analytics for diabetes using a machine learning approach. *Applied Computing and Informatics*, 18 (1/2), 90–100. Retrieved from https://doi.org/10.1016/j.aci.2018.12.004 doi:

[16] Patra, Sudhansu, Mittal, Mamta, & Jena, Om. (2022). Multiobjective evolutionary algorithm based on decomposition for feature selection in medical diagnosis. 10.1016/ B978-0-323-99864-2.00005-6.

[17] Abed, Amira, Shaaban, Essam, Jena, Om, & Elngar, Ahmed. (2022). A comprehensive survey on breast cancer thermography classification using deep neural network. 10.1201/9781003226147-9.

[18] Sahu, Barnali, Sahu, Sitarashmi & Jena, Om. (2022). Impact of ensemble-Based models on cancer classification, its development, and challenges. 10.1201/9781003189053-8.

[19] Dagliati, A., Marini, S., Sacchi, L., Cogni, G., Teliti, M., Tibollo, V., ... Bellazzi, R. (2017, May). Machine learning methods to predict diabetes complications. *Journal of Diabetes Science and Technology*, 12 (2), 295–302. Retrieved from https://doi.org/10.1177/1932296817706375 doi:

[20] Ma, J. (2020). Machine learning in predicting diabetes in the early stage. In *2020 2nd International Conference on Machine Learning, Big Data and Business Intelligence (MLBDBI)* (pp. 167–172), Chengdu, China.

[21] Smith, J. W., Everhart, J. E., Dickson, W., Knowler, W. C., & Johannes, R. S. (1988). Using the adap learning algorithm to forecast the onset of diabetes mellitus. In *Proceedings of the Annual Symposium on Computer Application in Medical Care* (p. 261), American Medical Informatics Association, United States.

[22] Islam, M. M. F., Ferdousi, R., Rahman, S., & Bushra, H. (2020, 01). Likelihood prediction of diabetes at early stage using data mining techniques. In (p. 113–125). doi: 10.1007/978-981-13-8798-2_12

[23] Potdar, K., Pardawala, T. S., & Pai, C. D. (2017). A comparative study of categorical variable encoding techniques for neural network classifiers. *International Journal of Computer Applications, 175* (4), 7–9.

[24] DelSole, M. (2018). What is one hot encoding and how to do it. Diambil kembali dari Medium: https://medium. com/@ michaeldelsole/whatis-one-hot-encoding-and-how-to-do-it-f0ae272f1179. Retrieved from https://medium.com/@michaeldelsole/what-is-one-hot-encoding-and -how-to-do-it-f0ae272f1179

9 Effective Feature Extraction for Early Recognition and Classification of Triple Modality Breast Cancer Images Using Logistic Regression Algorithm

Manjula Devarakonda Venkata
Pragati Engineering College

Sumalatha Lingamgunta
JNTUK

9.1 INTRODUCTION

Cells in the human body grow abnormally and affect other parts of the body as well, like the lung, skin, pancreas, and making the breast affected. The probability of the increase rate of breast cancer (BC) is higher than the other types of cancer. Many women in the age group of 30–65 are affected by BC. The most common malignancy among Indian women is BC, with a rate as high as 25.8 (per 100,000) women and a mortality rate of 12.7 per 100,000 women, according to the National Cancer Institute health ministry and estimates of at least 17,97,900 women in India might have this cancer by 2021. It has increased over the last few years, and the mortality rate has increased day by day due to its improper identification at an earlier stage. BC is a malignant tumor that enables the abnormal growth of cells that lie near the breast region [9]. BC treatment is complicated, and more research is desperately needed (Figure 9.1).

9.2 SYMPTOMS OF BREAST CANCER

BC is the growth of unhealthy cells abnormally. It forms as tumor in the very initial stage, which can be perceived as lumps in the image screening modalities. As per [6],

DOI: 10.1201/9781003257721-9

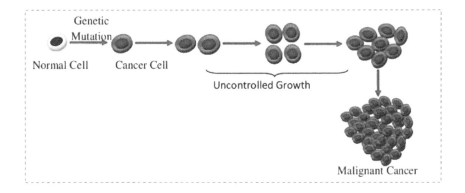

FIGURE 9.1 Growth of malignant cells.

a tumor is malignant if the cancerous cells spread toward the healthy tissue as well as other parts of the body. Irrespective of a woman's age, between 30 and 65, BC is curable when diagnosed at a very early stage. According to the research by NCI [7], the main symptoms of BC are listed as follows:

- A hard mass is found in the breasts (the formed mass varies in size, shape, and texture, mostly with non-smooth edges).
- Inflammation in some parts of the breast.
- Change in skin complexion in the breast.
- Pain observed for a prolonged time (in a few cases, pain may not be experienced).
- Redness (or) skin peeling is observed in the nipples.
- Discharge of transparent fluid from the nipples.

Lymph node swelling near the underarm that has lasted more than two weeks.

Stages of BC:

The cancer's stage, which impacts treatment choices and prognosis, is determined by the amount of the disease and its dissemination at the time of diagnosis. Depending upon the growth of the tumor, the stages of BC are determined and classified as follows:

Stage 0	It is a kind of BC that has an accumulation of cancerous cells but does not have the capacity to spread to other tissues. In particular, it does not spread to the lymph nodes near the affected region of the breast.
Stage 1	At this stage, tumors of less than 2 cm lie around the breast region and do not spread to other tissues as well as lymph nodes. Further, it is classified into 1A and 1B, in which 1A contains non-metastasized tissues and 1B contains micro metastases in 1–3 lymph nodes in the underarm area (National Cancer Institute (NCI), 2016). Stage 1A is curable, and some further examination is carried out in stage 1B.

(Continued)

Stage 2A	It has a tumor size of less than 2 cm, which gives a 100% survival rate. It has developed certain characteristics that are found in lymph nodes such as the arm, skin, and forms as metastases, and the small metastases are also found in the mammary glands.
Stage 2B	It has a tumor size of less than 2 and 5 cm in diameter. It is found in the internal organs. It does not have the potential to grow near the chest wall (or) skin. Its survival rate is about 93%.
Stage 3A	Here, the tumor size is not more than 5 cm and has spread slowly to the lymph nodes. In some cases, it spreads to the underarm of the lymph nodes in the mammary glands when the tumor size is increased to 9 cm.
Stage 3B	It has tumor cells, which spread faster to the chest, arm, and skin. It possesses some characteristics: i) Non-metastases in the lymph nodes ii) Have 1–3 micro meta states in mammary gland lymph nodes. It affects at least nine lymph nodes of mammary glands [11].
Stage 3C	This type will not depend on the size of the tumor. The survival rate is about 75%. It has characteristics such as: Under the arm area, 10 lymph nodes are affected by metastasis [10]. The areas under and above the collarbone are also affected.
Stage 4	Irrespective of the tumor size, in most cases, BC metastases are formed in the bones, liver, brain, or lungs. The survival rate is nearly 20%.

Lesions of BC

Irrespective of the tumor size, in most cases, BC metastases are formed in the bones, liver, brain, or lungs. The survival rate is nearly 20%.

a. **Calcifications:** Calcification is one of the important abnormalities observed on mammography images. The accumulation and the presence of calcium within the breast tissue are termed calcification. This is classified into two types: macro calcification and micro calcification. It is varied by the amount of calcium accumulation. On the other hand, macro calcification is the accumulation of a high amount of calcium, which comes under the class of benign, whereas micro calcification is the accumulation of a small amount of calcium, which is a sign of malignancy. Further, it is classified into different forms, viz., diffused, linear, scattered, and regional. Figure 9.2 illustrates different forms of calcification. Identification of these is based on clusters of calcification formation throughout the breast. The distribution of five or more calcifications is known as clustered calcification. Similar types of calcification present in the entire regions of the breast are diffuse and scattered; linear and regional calcification forms around the lines of ducts in mammary glands [12].

Based on the forms of calcification, the stage of the tumor is determined and classified into three sorts, namely, benign, intermediate, and malignant (Table 9.1).

b. **Mass:** A mass is defined as an estimated infected area of tissue in the breast region. Its shape, boundaries, and margins characterize it. In some cases, it

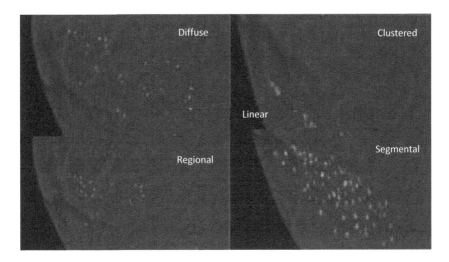

FIGURE 9.2   Different forms of calcification.

TABLE 9.1
Types of Calcification

Types of Calcification	Forms of Calcification
Benign	Diffuse or scattered, regional
Intermediate	Clustered
Malignant	Linear, Segmental

is determined manually without the existence of calcifications. The intensity level and morphology process between normal and abnormal breast tissue processes it. It is perceived that mass detection is a more complex process than the detection of calcification in the breast. Figure 9.3a and b represent the margin and shape descriptors of the breast mass.

Depending on the shapes of the breast mass [1–5], the shape descriptors and margin descriptors have been used to determine the severity type of BC, which is given in Table 9.2.

Along with clinical tests with respect to amount of calcification and mass analysis, Nipple Aspirate Fluid (NAF), breast biopsy and genetic tests, the screening methods [13] such as mammography, X-rays, MRI, CT, ultrasound, and self-examination are performed to derive "The goal of detecting and removing at an earlier stage in order to increase the survival rate" [6–8].

c. **Mammography: Screening process and its limitations**

Mammography is one of the oldest screening processes that examines the breast by producing low-dose amplitude X-rays. The calcium accumulation and the breast mass are evident on the mammogram images. Mammography's sensitivity in the general population is estimated to be between 75% and 90%, with a 25% positive predictive value.

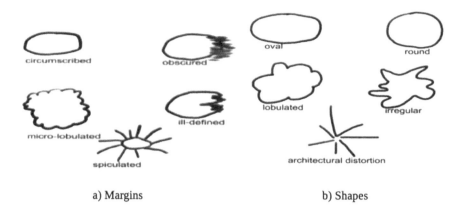

a) Margins   b) Shapes

FIGURE 9.3   Margins and shapes descriptors for breast mass estimation.

TABLE 9.2
Breast Mass Classifications Based on Shapes

Severity Types of Breast Cancer	Shape Descriptors	Margin Descriptors
Benign	Round, oval and lobular	Ill - defined,
Intermediate	Lobular	Obscured, ill - defined, microlobulated
Malignant	Irregular	Ill-defined and speculated

Limitations:
Studies have revealed that it is not well suited for women with high severity. It is not screening the breast for dense tissue, implants, hormone irregularities, fibrocystic breasts, and so on. When the density of the breast tissue increases, the ability of mammography to recognize the infected area becomes reduced. It works by compressing the breast tissue; in such a case, it slows down the recognition of encapsulated cancerous tumors. The encapsulated cancerous tumors are de-encapsulated by providing 22 pounds of pressure. In today's environment, at least 42 pounds of pressure is being applied to the equipment for mammograms. Depending on the locality of the tumor, this process releases the malignant cells into the bloodstream. Some risks are also perceived during the radiation treatment process. Compared to older women, young women are seriously affected by the effects of ionizing radiation. The detection of cancer at an earlier stage becomes a complex task using mammographic screening. Patients with carcinoma in situ are easily recognized by mammograms. On the other hand, women with dense breasts are also recognized by 68%. It is also suggested that some other techniques embedded with mammography have also helped to yield better results [10–15].

d. Ultrasound and its limitations:
Ultrasound is one of the latest tools that coordinates with mammography and the clinical examination process. It acts as an adjunctive tool, especially

in dense breast tissue cases. It makes the screening process easier for mammograms. It is observed that the functioning of mammography becomes sensitive when the tumor size increases (or) decreases. In this course of ascertaining facts, the ultrasound becomes insensitive toward the tumor size. It relied on three factors in order to assure their recognition accuracy, namely, the tool quality, the expert's knowledge toward image interpretation, and the deployment of a multidisciplinary approach. It has become a safe, portable, and inexpensive diagnostic modality for imaging anatomical structures, blood flow measurements, and tissue characterization.

Limitations:

The screening efficiency of the ultrasound process is determined by the efficiency of its signal processing. The received intensity level is transformed into the voltage signal. Then, the raw details of the images are captured. Since it operates on sectional images, an expert is needed to interpret the raw data obtained. Similar to that, the data acquisition process also demands an experienced consultant. Along with that, it is not an approachable one for screening multiple images in a single shot. Thus, it is a time-consuming process. In some cases, the intervention of noise is higher, which leads to an inaccurate structure of the objects. Compared to the other screening processes, the interpretation of an object becomes a more demanding task. The quality of the images is low. Thus, it poses noise-related issues for automatic detection and classification processes [10–15].

e. Magnetic Resonance Imaging and its limitations:

Magnetic resonance imaging (MRI) is one of the most efficient screening processes as it is a painless screening process. It is a kind of non-invasive process. It does not make use of ionizing radiation. Hence, it is known as non-ionizing radiation therapy. It is widely selected to deal with dense breasts. It can acquire the raw data from any orientation. Due to its capability of focusing on all parts and multi-focal properties, it recognizes the cancerous cells that lie near the chest walls effortlessly. It evaluates the recurrence of cancer in the case of lumpectomy.

Limitations:

Though it scans the entire body with high spatial resolution, even for hard and soft tissue, it consumes a lot of time for the data acquisition process. It penetrates deep into the dense breasts. It is very expensive [10–15].

Medical image-based diagnosis plays an active role in coordination with the traditional approaches, physical analysis, and the biopsy process. Because the processes involved in the biopsy cause pain in the breast, women are hesitant to undergo it. Therefore, the need for detection processes with non-invasive approaches is widely studied by researchers. The concept of medical imaging technology becomes an active part of the treatment and also reduces the fear of this deadly disease. In spite of the technological developments, the analysis and interpretation of images is still a cumbersome task. The acquisition of related information from the obtained images deals with implicit knowledge formation, data relationships, and other forms of data patterns. Further, the feature mining process is one of steps in data mining. It helps to design efficient classifiers. The preprocessed data is further analyzed by performing some segmentation techniques. In this step, it is combined with the segmentation techniques of the image processing system. The features are extracted on the basis of the shape, texture, and colors of an image. This further helps in constructing the training classifier.

Different screening modalities such as mammograms, MRI, ultrasound, PET, and so forth are available for examining the infected breast tissues. Despite the fact that each of the above screening modalities has provided numerous benefits, they do have some limitations. The main limitation resides in the image interpretability. Though the screening modalities have efficiently detected the lesions, the interpretability of the screening results has also played a vital role. While screening of breast tissue using three image screening modalities investigates performance issues [14–18], they have limitations such as:

a. **Mammography:** Sensitivity and specificity are limited.
b. **Ultrasound images:** Since it's an adjunctive tool of mammography, a higher accumulation of noise and time complexity are the main issues.

Magnetic resonance imaging: It is quite expensive. Even so, it is a widely adopted one. Only experts can advise on the diagnosis process, which brings challenges to non-experts. The inherent limitations of the above three screening methods individually have motivated us to study their common features, which will help in identifying the patterns and classifying the images [19–22].

9.3 NEED FOR EARLY DETECTION

- Increasing incidence of BC in younger age groups
- Rising numbers of cases of BC in India
- Late penetrations: This directly decreases long term survival of the patient
- Lack of awareness and Screening:
- Aggressive cancer in youngsters.

Figure 9.4 shows the review of BC and increasing incidence of BC in young women (20s–60s) -2019.

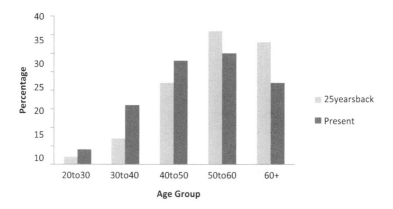

FIGURE 9.4   BC Statistics in India on Age Factor (www.breastcancerindia.net).

There is a need to develop a prominent feature extraction and classification system from BC imaging schemes, namely US, Mammo, and MRI, using ML tools for early diagnosis of BC and to analyze, evaluate, and compare the effectiveness of the three modalities

9.4   DATASETS USED

In recent years, ML and DL have made great strides. The success of AI in the medical industry has led to a large rise of medical AI applications. The purpose of AI research is to develop tools that employ AI to help physicians make choices about their patients. Surgery, illness diagnostics, and many other areas of medicine all make use of AI as shown in Figures 9.5 and 9.6 and the data is given in Table 9.3.

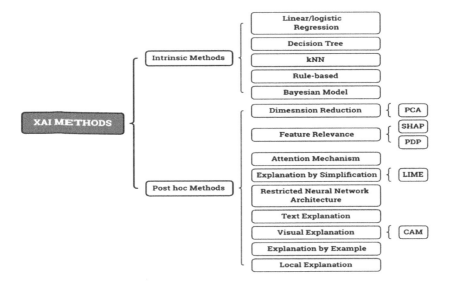

FIGURE 9.5   Taxonomy of XAI methods.

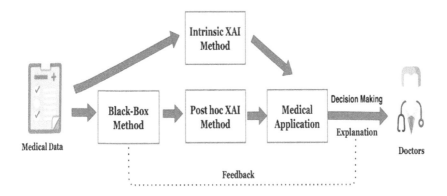

FIGURE 9.6   XAI methods: Intrinsic or post hoc decision-making, provides explanation to doctor.

anisotropic diffusion equation also called Perona-Malik filter is characterized by the following non- linear partial differential equation presented as Let $\Omega \subset R^2$ denote a subset of the plane and $I(.,t):\Omega \to R$ be a family of gray scale images. $I(., 0)$ is the input image Then anisotropic diffusion is defined as

$$\frac{\partial I}{\partial t} = \text{div}\big(c(x,y,t)\nabla I\big) = (\nabla c).\nabla I + c(x,y,t)I \tag{9.1}$$

where Δ denotes the Laplacian coefficient ∇ is gradient, div(...), & c(x, y, t) are divergence and diffusion operators. For t > 0, the output image is available as $I(.,t)$, with larger t producing blurrier images. $c(x,y,t)$ is often selected as a function of the picture gradient to regulate the pace of diffusion while maintaining the image's edges.

9.5.2 SEGMENTATION

Segmentation is a crucial step in the image recognition process that separates the targeted item from the image so that it may be examined. Cellular automata, mostly used medical image segmentation algorithm is used in this work, which consists of regular grid of cells in which each cell can have a finite number of possible states. The state of a cell at a given time step is updated in parallel and determined by the previous states of surrounding neighborhood of cells with the help of a specified transition rule. Thus, the rules of the CA are local and uniform. The transition function can be represented as

$$(t+1) = \delta\big(q(t), qi-1(t)1qi+1(t)\big) \tag{9.2}$$

where $qi(t + 1)$ $qi(t)$ denotes the state of the ith cell at time $t+1$ and t respectively, $qi-1(t)$ and $qi+1(t)$ represents the state of the left and right neighbor of the ith cell at time t, and δ is the next state function or the transition rule.

9.5.3 FEATURE EVALUATION AND SELECTING FEATURE VECTOR

Feature extraction is a vital step in carcinoma detection. because it helps distinguish between benign and malignant tumors.

9.5.4 CLASSIFICATION

For classification, logistic regression is often used successfully for predicting categorical outputs of biomedical data. The benefits of this algorithm are that it (1) requires fewer computation resources; (2) unrelated features to the output parameter are often eliminated; (3) is exclusively simple to implement and really efficient to coach. (4) Identify risk factors in a very patient's history and choose variables with a better probability of assessing the samples than choosing variables that reduce the sum of squared errors. The variable quantity and variable association are estimated using logistic regression. Finding independent variables by calculating probabilities employing a logistic or Sigmoid function. Then, these probabilities must be transformed into binary values to form predictions. This can be the Sigmoid function.

It's an S-shaped curve that takes any real-valued number and maps it into a value between the range of 0 and 1. Finally, these values between 0 and 1 are going to be transformed into either 0 or 1 employing a threshold classifier. Logistic regression analysis could acknowledge the anticipated results by doctors or radiologists, thereby aiding them in correcting the incorrect predictions. The output variable (y) must be binary or dichotomous (0 indicating no cancer, 1 indicating cancer). The procedure is

In Figure 9.8, Equation 9.3 associates each feature with a weight. This is the basis for the classification of logistic regression as a generalized linear model. The data given inside the range is then converted using the link function (0,1). Equation 9.4 demonstrates that the link function is a Sigmoid function and that the value of z is the probability that one of the events will occur.

Provided is a set of data (x, y), where x is a matrix of values with "m" samples and "n" characteristics, and y is a vector with "m" examples. The goal is to train the model to provide a classification prediction for the future value. A weight matrix with a random initialization is mostly created. Then multiply it by features.

$$\theta^T = w_0 + w_1 x_1 + w_2 x_2 + \dots\dots + w_n x_n \tag{9.3}$$

then pass the output obtained from Equation 9.4 to a link function.

$$g(z) = \frac{1}{1 + e^{-z}} \text{ where } z = \theta^T x_i \tag{9.4}$$

This is followed by calculating the cost for that iteration whose formula is

$$cost(w) = -\frac{1}{m} \sum_{i=1}^{m} y_i \log(\hat{y}_i) + (1 - y_i) \log(1 - \hat{y}_i) \tag{9.5}$$

The derivative of this cost function is calculated following which the weights are updated as in Equations 9.6 and 9.7 respectively.

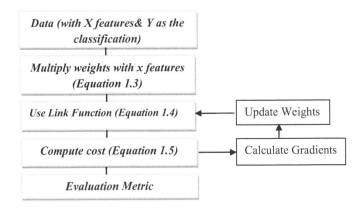

FIGURE 9.8 Steps of *LOGISTIC REGRESSION* algorithm.

$$\text{Gradient } dw_j = \sum_{i=1}^{n} \left(\widehat{y} - y \right) x_j^i \qquad (9.6)$$

$$\text{Update } w_i = w_j - \left(\alpha * dw_j \right) \qquad (9.7)$$

9.6 RESULTS

The features evaluated, observed and extracted are mentioned in comparison Table 9.4.

9.6.1 PREPROCESSED US IMAGES

Although ultrasound pictures offer a variety of advantages, such as being inexpensive, radiation-free, real-time, etc., they are distorted by many forms of noise that significantly impair the visual quality since they are low-resolution images produced by reflecting ultrasonic waves. In preprocessing, filtering and segmentation of a small area known as a region of interest (ROI) from the image contribute to the diagnosis. Color conversions and multidimensional filtering techniques are applied to remove noise, and segmentation is done to detect abnormal regions of the input images, as shown in Figure 9.9. All images are read, and 3D images are converted to single planes.

Features evaluated on segmented image

The features that are detected on ultrasound imaging are Shadowing, Spiculation, Tumor area, Mean Intensity, Minor -Axis Length, Major-Axis Length and Orientation.

Shadowing

After detecting abnormal region, first a posterior feature, shadowing of tumor region is detected. The segmented image and filtered image are multiplied to find the shadow of tumor region, and thereby the shadow feature of segmented image is obtained.

Spiculation

Although ultrasound scans offer a number of benefits, there is a type of marginal feature or edge detection to find the edge of the tumor. By measuring the angle of

---

TABLE 9.4
Medical Features Evaluation and Selection

Ultrasound	Mammography	MRI
• Shadowing	• Tumor size	• Spiculation
• Spiculation	• Shape of mass	• Area of segmented tumor
• Tumor area	• Area of tumor	• Tumor size
• Mean Intensity	• Mean Intensity	• Background Parenchyma Enhancement(BPE)
• Minor Axis Length	• Minor Axis Length	• Fibro glandular tissue
• Major Axis Length	• Major Axis Length	• Architectural distortion
• Orientation		

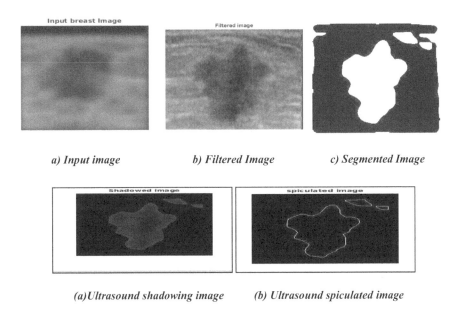

a) Input image   *b) Filtered Image*   *c) Segmented Image*

(a)Ultrasound shadowing image   *(b) Ultrasound spiculated image*

FIGURE 9.9   Stages of preprocessing of data set.

curvature at each contour pixel, spiculations of mass may be identified. The recorded angle of curvature at each pixel is compared with a range of angles to reveal the spiculated region, since the spiculated regions will have less angle of curvature. The spiculated angle range in this case is 45°–60°, and any pixels exhibiting this characteristic are flagged for examination. For example, ultrasonography is affordable, radiation-free, real-time, etc.

Area of mass

This is the function region property that is used to calculate a tumor's abnormal area. This function is used to find some other features like major axis and minor axis, centroid, orientation, etc. These kinds of features are extracted from segmented images and are shown in the command window. The result was a 1-by-Q vector containing the region's center of mass. The horizontal coordinate, or "x-coordinate," of the center of mass is the first component of a centroid. The vertical coordinate is the second component (or y-coordinate). All other elements of the centroid are in order of dimension. The bounding box represents the coordinates of the rectangular border that fully encloses the segmented image. The major axis length and minor axis length are the measures of the longest axis and smallest axis of the ROI. Orientation: parallel angle, given as a scalar, between the x-axis and the main axis of the ellipse that has the same second moments as the region. The range of the value, which is represented in degrees, is –90 to 90.

9.6.2 Preprocessed Mammogram Images

Features evaluated on segmented image

In segmentation, the white region shows fabil, the abnormal region and other techniques can be used to detect edges and curves. In this segmented image only, the following features are focused as given in Figures 9.10 and 9.11 and Table 9.5.

$$\text{Accuracy} = \frac{\text{True Negatives} + \text{True Positives}}{\text{True Positive} + \text{False Positive} + \text{True Negative} + \text{False Negative}}$$

$$\text{Sensitivity} = \frac{\text{Number of true positives}}{\text{Number of true postives} + \text{Number of false negatives}}$$

$$\text{Specificity} = \frac{\text{Number of true negatives}}{\text{Number of true negatives} + \text{Number of false positives}}$$

A logistic regression analysis tool is used to validate the results of three modalities. The above features are extracted and evaluated in every imaging technique and estimate its performance using accuracy, sensitivity, and specificity parameters, displaying the corresponding values. It is revealed that MRI modality gives good accuracy in identifying malignant tumors.

AI has started to be profoundly integrated with mammography, MRI, ultrasound and other diagnostic techniques in recent years as a result of the advancement of AI and the amassing of medical data. This will help doctors diagnose diseases. Logistic regression algorithm is XAI intrinsic method used to assess our model using an actual mammography reports and contrast it with US and MRI widely used interpretable approaches. The experimental findings demonstrate that our interpretable findings are more in line with clinical diagnostic standards.

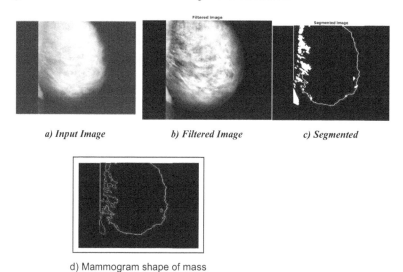

a) Input Image   b) Filtered Image   c) Segmented

d) Mammogram shape of mass

FIGURE 9.10   Preprocessed MRI images.

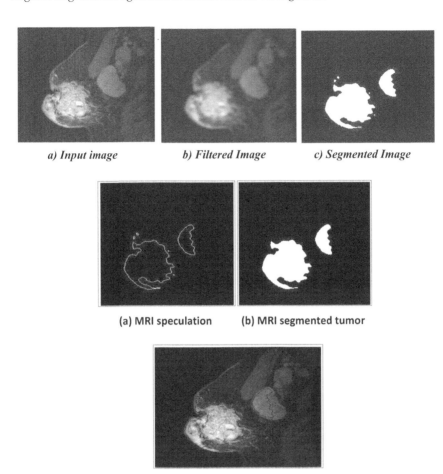

a) Input image   b) Filtered Image   c) Segmented Image

(a) MRI speculation   (b) MRI segmented tumor

c) MRI Architectural distortion

FIGURE 9.11   MRI speculation, segmented and distortion images.

TABLE 9.5
Comparison of Three Imaging Techniques

Data Sets	Accuracy (%)	Sensitivity (%)	Specificity (%)
MRI	95.00	95.00	95.00
Mammogram	93.33	93.33	93.33
Ultrasound	90.00	100.00	80.00

9.7   CONCLUSION

The goal of this effort is to detect the suspicious and tiny malignant masses in BC images. It compares the three widely used BC imaging techniques, such as mammography, MRI, and ultrasound. Prominent features, such as medical features, are extracted and evaluated against each modality to classify the benign and malignant breast masses using classifier metrics MRI proved to be effective in identifying suspicious malignant masses. Patients with architectural distortion/skin thickening have a higher probability of being diagnosed with BC, which is 18 times higher than patients with normal classification. These advancements in imaging techniques aid in detecting BC patients and can help the doctors and radiologists treat the patients. The system gave a better accuracy of 95%, sensitivity of 95%, and specificity of 95% for MRI images when compared with two other modalities. Our findings suggest that the performance of classifiers for MRI images may be superior to mammograms and US for the early detection of malignant tumors.

REFERENCES

[1] Singh, Deepika, and Ashutosh Kumar Singh. 2020. "Role of image thermography in early breast cancer detection-past, present and future." *Computer Methods & Programs in Biomedicine* 183: p. 105074. doi: 10.1016/j.cmpb.2019.105074

[2] Badwaik, Rahul. 2019. "Precision medicine: Emerging trends in cancer therapy." *Journal of Clinical & Diagnostic Research.*

[3] PDQ Adult Treatment Editorial Board. 2016. "Mycosis Fungoides and the Sézary Syndrome Treatment." (PDQ®) Patient Version, Bethesda. https://www.ncbi.nlm.nih.gov/books/NBK65878.2/?report=reader

[4] McGale. 2014. "Effect of radiotherapy after mastectomy and axillary surgery on 10-year recurrence and 20-year Breast cancer mortality": Meta-analysis of individual patient data for 8135 women in 22 randomized trials. *Lancet* 383, no. 9935: pp. 2127–2135. doi: 10.1016/S0140-6736(14)60488-8

[5] Mitsuk, Anzhelika. 2016. "Breast cancer information for young women": A project for Terveysnetti. Thesis book. https://www.theseus.fi/bitstream/handle/10024/123683/thesis%2020.12%20new.pdf?sequence=1

[6] Nitsche et al. 2015."Cardiac toxicity after radiotherapy for breast cancer- myths and facts." *Breast Care Journal* 10, no. 2: pp. 131–135. doi: 10.1159/000376560

[7] Munagala, Radha. 2011. "Promising molecular targeted therapies in breast cancer." *Indian Journal of Pharmacology* 43, no. 3: pp. 236–245. doi: 10.4103/0253-7613.81497.

[8] Smith, Robert A., et al. 2016. "Cancer screening in the United States: A review of current American Cancer Society guidelines and current issues in cancer screening." *CA: A Cancer Journal for Clinicians* 66, no. 3: pp. 184–210. doi: 10.3322/caac.21557

[9] Silva, Orlando E., Stefano Zurrida, et al. 2005. *Breast Cancer: A Practical Guide.* Elsevier Health Sciences.

[10] Runowicz, Carolyn D., et al. 2016. "American cancer society/American society of clinical oncology breast cancer survivorshipcare guidelines." *CA: A Cancer Journal for Clinicians* 66, no. 1: pp. 43–73. doi: 10.3322/caac.21319

[11] Gaikwad, Varsha J. 2015. "Detection of breast cancer in mammogram using support vector machine." *International Journal of Scientific Engineering and Research* 2015: pp. 19–21.

[12] Kourou, Konstantina, et al. 2015. "Machine learning applications in cancer prognosis and prediction." *Computational and Structural Biotechnology Journal* 13: pp. 8–17. doi: 10.1016/j.csbj.2014.11.005

[13] Chaurasia, Vikas, & Saurabh Pal. 2014. "Data mining techniques: To predict and resolve breast cancer survivability." *International Journal of Computer Science and Mobile Computing* 2014, pp. 10–22.

[14] Goyal, Kashish, et al. 2019. "Comparative analysis of machine learning algorithms for breast cancer prognosis." In *Proceedings of 2nd International Conference on Communication, Computing and Networking*, pp. 727–734. Springer, Singapore.

[15] Gan, Wensheng, et al. 2021. "Beyond frequency: Utility mining with varied item-specific minimum utility." *ACM Transactions on Internet Technology (TOIT)* 21, pp. 1–32.

[16] Yasmin, Mussarat, et al. 2013. "Survey paper on diagnosis of breast cancer using image processing techniques." *Research Journal Recent Sciences* 2, no. 10: pp. 88–98. ISSN 2277-2502.

[17] Constantine, Rostom Mennour, and Mohamed Batouche. 2015. "Drug discovery for breast cancer based on big data analytics techniques." In *2015 5th International Conference on Information & Communication Technology and Accessibility (ICTA)*, pp. 1–6. IEEE.

[18] Jena, Om, & Parthasarathi Pattnayak. 2021. "Innovation on machine learning in healthcare services: An introduction. 10.1002/9781119792611.ch1.

[19] Patra, Sudhansu Shekhar, Om Jena, Gaurav Kumar, Sreyashi Pramanik, Chinmaya Misra, & Kamakhya Singh. 2021. "Random forest algorithm in imbalance genomics classification." 10.1002/9781119785620.ch7.

[20] Chatterjee, Riddhi, Ratula Ray, Satya Ranjan Dash, & Om Prakash Jena. 2021. "Conceptualizing tomorrow healthcare through digitization," Chapter 19. 10.1002/9781119818717.ch19.

[21] Patra, Sudhansu Shekhar, Mittal Mamta, & Om Jena. 2022. "Multi objective evolutionary algorithm based on decomposition for feature selection in medical diagnosis." In *Predictive Modeling in Biomedical Data Mining and Analysis*. doi: 10.1016/B978-0-323-99864-2.00005-6.

[22] Abed, Amira Hassan, Essam M. Shaaban, Om Jena, & Ahmed Elngar. 2022. "A comprehensive survey on breast cancer thermography classification using deep neural network." In *Machine Learning and Deep Learning in Medical Data Analytics and Healthcare Applications*. doi: 10.1201/9781003226147-9.

10 Machine Learning and Deep Learning Models Used to Detect Diabetic Retinopathy and Its Stages

S. Karthika and M. Durgadevi
SRM Institute of Science and Technology

10.1 INTRODUCTION

In recent years, DR is the major cause of blindness and a disease that affects people all over the world. It is a prevalent condition that affects people between the ages of 20 and 50. As a result, early diagnosis of DR is critical in therapy. Diabetes affects 80%–90% of adults. It does not cause any symptoms in the early stage. According to the WHO, more than 30–31 million people in India get affected by diabetics, and this is anticipated to climb to 79.4 million by 2030. ML and DL algorithms are used to predict diseases using advanced techniques in healthcare services (Chatterjee et al. 2021; Pattnayak et al. 2021). Diabetics are more likely to develop DR (Kayal et al. 2014). Blood flows to the retina through blood capillaries cause high blood sugar levels. If significant levels of glucose accumulate in the blood circulation, as a result of insufficient oxygen transport to the cells, the blood vessels begin to collapse (Agurto et al. 2010). A blockage in these arteries results in serious eye disorder. Therefore, aberrant blood vessels and slow metabolic rate resulting in DR. DR symptoms include microaneurysms (MA), hemorrhage (HEM), exudates (EX), and aberrant blood vessel growth (Krause et al. 2018). MA is the initial stage of DR. This condition causes changes in blood vessel size. Non-Proliferative_DR (NPDR) and Proliferative_DR (PDR) are two types of DR, with five DR stages: normal, mild, moderate, severe, and proliferative. Figure 10.1 depicts various levels of DR ranging from normal, moderate, mild, severe, and proliferate as shown below.

- In the normal stage, a person with no DR symptoms is observed, and the class is referred to as normal.
- Mild (NPDR) is defined as a microaneurysm in the retina blood vessels with a tiny balloon-like swelling.

DOI: 10.1201/9781003257721-10

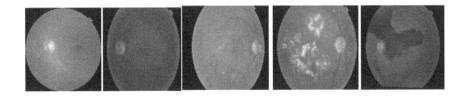

FIGURE 10.1   Levels of DR images (normal, moderate, mild, severe, and proliferate).

- If swelling and the number of MA increase leads to a block in blood flow to the retina. If MA is less than 15 or if HEM is less than 5, it leads to a moderate stage.
- The severe stage includes several vessels blocking and blocking off blood flow to some areas of the retina. This signal results in the expansion of new vessels. MA greater than or equal to 15 or HEM greater than or equal to 5 is considered as exudates.
- Proliferative_DR is the serious stage, which causes neovascularization (NV) which refers to new growth of blood vessels (Mahendran et al. 2014). These newly grown blood vessels are very dangerous, causing damage to blood fluids. This leakage of fluids causes severe eye disease and even blindness. This includes many signs including EXs, HEM, and MA, Internal Microvascular Abnormalities (IRMA). Table 10.1 explains different DR grades and their features.

Computer-aided diagnosis (CAD) is gaining importance in ophthalmologist in terms of time, costs, and personnel for DR screening and some diagnosis factors. CAD can efficiently diagnose the early stage of DR and manage DR patients with fewer issues in the eye. Commonly used imaging techniques for investigating the DR include Optical Coherence Tomography Angiography (OCTA).

TABLE 10.1
DR Levels and Features

Levels	Observations	Features
Normal_DR	MA is equal to 0 and HEM is equal to 0	No DR
Mild_NPDR	MA ranges from 0 to less than or equal to 5 & HEM is equal to 0	Signs of Microaneurysm
Moderate_ NPDR	MA ranges from 5 to less than 15 or (HEM ranges from 0 to less than 5) and (NV is equal to 0))	Presents of Exudates, Hemorrhage, and Microaneurysms
Severe_NPDR	(MA ranges from 15 or more) or (HEM is higher than or equal to 5) or (NV is equal to one))	The unusual features are shown in each quadrant of the retina
PDR	NV is equal to one	Aberrant blood vessels growth

This chapter suggests using XAI techniques (Pawar et al. 2020) to explain to healthcare holders the reason behind predictions of diseases provided by AI-based systems in order to reap the following benefits:

- XAI approaches to increase the transparency of how AI systems work and can increase levels of trust since they explain why an AI system made a particular decision.
- Using the explanations produced by XAI methods, it is possible to identify the variables that the AI system took into account when making a prediction.
- When making a forecast, AI systems learn from the data. Sometimes incorrect learning rules can result in incorrect predictions (Khedkar et al. 2019).

This chapter reviews the overview of DR with different machine and deep learning (DL) methodologies for DR disease prediction. In addition, a detailed comparison of segmentation methods used in DR is also discussed for existing models. The performance measures used in the medical sector are also reviewed. Chapter 11 is arranged below as Section 10.2 reviews the existing ML and DL methods in a detailed way. Section 10.3 explains the existing datasets used in the medical field. Section 10.4 explains the DR detection process used in general. Section 10.5 reviews the evaluation metrics of commonly used existing methods and Section 10.6 explains the conclusion of the DR survey.

10.2 CONVENTIONAL ML & DL ALGORITHMS

10.2.1 ML – SUPPORT VECTOR MACHINE (ML – SVM)

Cortes et al. (1995) proposed a well-known supervised learning algorithm called SVM. The goal is to create a decision boundary or line for separating the classes based on n-dimensional space. SVM uses a hyperplane for separating the best decision boundary. Consider an example, a decision boundary or line can separate DR stages such as S1, S2, S3, S4, and S5 into classes according to the presence of retinopathy in patients. If the properties are satisfied, the classes are separated based on the severity levels of patients using the algorithm. The training and testing data requires user-defined parameters and might be over-fitted with an excessive amount of input data.

10.2.2 ML – K_NEAREST NEIGHBORS (ML – KNN)

Cover et al. (1967) designed a most basic machine learning algorithm called as KNN, a type of supervised learning technique for solving classification & regression problems. It is also known as "lazy learning" and is predominantly used as a classifier. It assumes the similarity between new data points and classifies based on the nearest data points. Due to equal weighting, the standard ANN classifiers suffer from an imbalance between the data samples. During the bindings between classes, the classification remains uncertain and can be resolved traditionally using ANN, thereby reducing the K value (constant) or by minimizing the distances to every nearest associated class.

10.2.3 ML – RANDOM FOREST (ML – RF)

Breiman (2001) created a random forest method that uses ensemble learning to solve classification and regression issues. To solve a difficult problem, RF creates a decision tree based on various facts or information for classification, it uses just the highest votes, and for regression, it uses the average. Classification and Regression Trees (CART) are trained on similar-sized data known as "bootstraps," which are created based on a randomly sampled training set. The test set is taken from the original set based on the record in datasets once the tree is constructed. The error rate is estimated based on the out-of-bag test sets (Patra et al. 2021).

10.2.4 ML – NEURAL NETWORKS (ML – NN)

McCulloch et al. (1943) created NN which is basically a traditional learning system that makes use of networks to understand and translate the input into an adorable output. Neural networks learn by themselves based on some weights which specify the output classes normally belonging to the probability of input. In order to achieve this, NN recognizes some features while obtaining the results (severity DR) based on the known input data. To set the parameters some manual works need to be done regularly. Alternatively, neural networks are used to extract features and send them to the classifiers.

10.2.5 DEEP LEARNING

One of the most widely used types is deep learning (DL) was introduced by Dechter (1986) with high features and training data used to weigh the exact features and to map input to output data labels. The core of DL methods is deep convolutional neural networks (CNN), one of the most successful techniques in picture classification and prediction. The CNN uses 15 convolutional filters to transform the inputs and enable the spatial distribution of the weights. The DL algorithm requires fewer user specifications than traditional ML systems, but it may not be clear what properties affect its classifications.

10.2.6 DL – CLASSIC NEURAL NETWORKS

The structure and functions of neural cells with multi-layered perceptron properties are described by Fully Connected Neural Networks (FCNN), also known as Classic Neural Networks. Basheer et al. (2000) a psychologist, devised a continuous layer in 1958 that shows how to adapt the FCNN model to binary input. This includes three functionalities in the mode

- Linear
- Nonlinear
- Rectified Linear Unit

10.2.7 DL – Convolutional Neural Networks (DL – CNN)

LeCun et al. (1989) were the first to enhance DL – CNN. LeNet-5 is a hierarchical artificial neural network that may be used to distinguish handwriting digits. Because it has several layers, LeNet-5, like other networks, can be utilized with a backpropagation method. These are more sophisticated challenges, such as large-scale picture and video classification. With Alexnet's success, many works have been proposed to increase performance. Nowadays, CNN is quite successful in terms of picture categorization performance. It employs the latest deep CNN and discussed the quality of these models using the DR image datasets, in addition to learning how to transmit and fine-tune hyperparameters. A retinopathy comparative review includes studies on model performance. The transfer learning approach is used to remove the final completely connected layer of the previously trained CNN and presents a feature extractor. It extracts all functions from medical pictures and trains the classifier using a new dataset. If these parameters aren't set by the network, they'll have to be tweaked and improved depending on the DR imaging results to increase performance.

10.2.8 DL – LSTMNs (Long Short-Term Memory Networks)

Long short-term memory networks (LSTMN) is a sort of recurrent neural network (RNN) that can learn and strike a book's lengthy dependencies. The default behavior is to recall past information over long periods of time and retains information based on time (Hochreiter et al. 1997). They're helpful in time-series prediction as a result of previous inputs. The LSTMN is a four-layer, interconnected chain-like structure that has a special manner of communicating. Along with time-series forecasts, LSTMN is commonly utilized in other applications such as voice recognition, music production, and pharmaceutical research.

10.2.9 DL – Recurrent Neural Networks (DL – RNN)

RNNs are a powerful and long-lasting sort of neural network, and because they have internal storage, they're one of the most promising algorithms now in use, proposed by McClelland et al. (1986). Many DL approaches, like RNNs, are quite old. They were built in 1980, but it has only been in the last few years that their actual ability has been realized. RNNs have gained popularity as a result of increased computer power, vast volumes of data that need to work with, as well as the discovery of LSTM to boost performance through imaging. RNNs can be quite accurate in forecasting what will happen next since they can remember significant information about the input they received in their internal memory. This is why they are the preferred set of rules for sequential facts such as time collecting, voice, text, monetary data, audio, video, weather, and many more. RNNs can shape a lot more information about a series and its surroundings in comparison to other algorithms.

10.2.10 DL – GENERATIVE ADVERSARIAL NETWORKS (DL – GAN)

Goodfellow et al. (2014) creared Generative Adversarial Networks (GAN) a neural network technique that combines two DL neural networks known as generator and discriminator. The Generator (G) continues to create new data that is similar to the original data, and the Discriminator (D) distinguishes between real and fake data. If a library of photographs is needed, for example, the network generator will generate data that looks like the real thing. It would next build the deconvolution neural network to distinguish between the images, which is followed by a network of image detectors. Below equation explains that Pda(x1) = distribution_real data, P(k) = distribution_generator, q = sample from Pda(x1), z = sample from P(k), D(b) = Discriminator_network, G(a) = Generator_network.

$$min\ max\ V\ D,\ G = E_{q\text{-}(xl)} \log D\ b + E_{z\text{-}pz}(k) \log (1 - D(G(a))) \qquad (10.1)$$

10.2.11 DL – REINFORCEMENT LEARNING

Sutton et al. (1998) proposed a reinforcement learning method, the process through which an agent interacts with its environment to modify its state. The agent may look about and react to what it sees. By engaging with the scenario, the agent helps a network achieve its goal. The state of the environment serves as the input layer, and there is input, output, and several hidden multiple levels in this design. The model operates by attempting to forecast the future payoff for each action made under the given conditions on a continuous basis.

10.3 RETINAL IMAGE DATASETS USED IN DR DETECTION

Datasets are generally a collection of information or records about various sectors. There are lots of private and public datasets available across the world for medical sectors that are discussed in this review. DR datasets contain image datasets as well as CSV files. Researchers mainly use publicly available datasets, which are also named as a benchmark or common datasets for experiments such as DRIVE, Kaggle, STARE, and so on, that can be accessed through some specific kind of links.

Public datasets
- Hamilton Eye Institute Macular Edema Dataset (HEI-MED) images are used for the detection of exudates which includes 115 unusual and 45 wholesome data. All those images are taken 45-fold view using PRO fundus-digital digicam (Bilal et al. 2021). The pixel of all images is 2196×1958.
- MESSIDOR Digital Retinal Images (Messidor) generally make use of DR for HEM, exudates, and MA detection with 1200 images. Messidor2 includes 1784 retinal fundus images for the automated identification of DR in Abràmoff et al. (2016).
- Kaggle contains 88,702 photos of the retinal fundus. The dataset was created with the aid of EyePACS, which gives the researcher access to 53,576 efforts at fundus images and 35,126 attempts at education in order to identify DR (Gulshan et al. 2016).

- DRIVE (Niemeijer et al. 2004) dataset that comprises 20 fundus images for experimentation as well as 20 fundus images for education. The images are captured by the 3CCD camera, and the image decision is 786×584 for normal blood vessels, HEMs, exudates, and MA detection.
- CHASE (Child Health and Study England) consists of 28 retinal images collected from 14 children. The researchers (Mo et al. 2017) utilize it to segment retinal blood vessels.
- A TOP-CON-TRV 50 fundus camera with 35-folds is used to capture images for the Structured Analysis of the Retina (STARE) database. There are 400 photos to choose from, with a total of 605×700 options. To detect normal blood vessels, HEM, EX, and MA (Hoover et al. 2000).
- e-ophtha_EX contains 40+ exudate images with 30–35 no lesion images, whereas e-ophtha_MA contains 200+ no lesion images and 140+ images with mild HEM and MA. These datasets are used for exudates and MA (Decenciere et al. 2013).
- Retinopathy online challenge (ROC) features 1100+ images with three different pixel sizes 768, 1058 and 1389. These photographs, which were taken with a Canon camera, are used to spot MA (Niemeijer et al. 2009).
- The datasets DR1 and DR2 are open-source. Digital retinal fundus images for DR1 and DR2 will each contain 234 and 520 images, respectively. The DR was discovered through switch research, and DR1 and DR2 were utilized to identify difficult exudates (Naqvi et al. 2015).
- DIARETB0 and DIARETB1 images have a 50-fold view with a resolution of 1500×1152. DIARETB0 contains 110 photos of diabetic retinopathy (DR) and 20 images of common retinopathy. For identifying abnormal blood vessels, HEM, EX, and MA. DIARETB1 consists of 84 images of DR and 5 images of common retinopathy (Kalviainen et al. 2007).

10.4   DR PROCESS DETECTION

DR should be detected and treated as soon as possible because the disease's progression can be slowed. The vast majority of the strategies rely exclusively on laser technology. To avoid leaks, laser coagulation effectively burns blood vessels in the attention. Laser therapy has the disadvantage of reducing retinal thickness. Preventing retinal edema with this method is a viable alternative. This medication reduces the likelihood of creative and precognitive decline by 40%–50%. It will worsen in some cases due to a lack of imagination and foresight. That is the primary motivation for researchers, to invest in specific technologies and methods for detecting DR in the early stage. Figure 10.2 depicts the flow of DR detection that is entirely dependent on retinal image features.

10.4.1   Non-Proliferative_DR

Non-Proliferative_DR (NPDR) is a kind of DR that has little or no signs and symptoms. With NPDR, the blood vessels get damaged. MA or minute bulges in blood

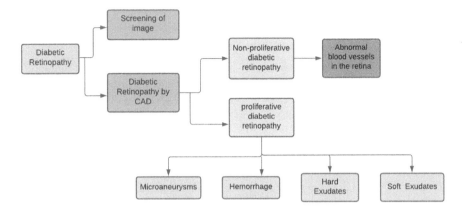

FIGURE 10.2 DR process detection.

vessels can potentially cause fluid to flow into the retina. This leaking could cause the macula to expand.

10.4.2 Proliferative_DR

Proliferative_DR (PDR) is a severe form of the condition where the retina suffers from poor blood circulation causing a gel-like fluid that fills in the retina with the growth of new vessels. Blood from the new blood vessels could flow into the vitreous, causing vision to be obstructed. PDR can also result in retinal detachment as a result of scar tissue proliferation, as well as the development of glaucoma. Glaucoma is an eye disease in which the optic nerve is injured in an unusual way. PDR can cause significant creative and precognitive loss, as well as blindness if left untreated.

10.4.2.1 Techniques for Detecting Microaneurysms

MA are DR's first symptom. MA must be diagnosed (Patra et al. 2022) in order to detect DR early. MA, which is produced by substantial dilatation of tiny blood arteries, is the most common symptom of NPDR. Microaneurysm detection is critical since these formations are the most easily identifiable function of DR. The earliest studies that linked these structures to DR recovery were published in the 1980s. This section discusses the different techniques created to recognize such as MA. MA are the earliest sign of DR. MA must be identified in order to diagnose DR early. PNR causes AM, which is produced by a massive dilatation of tiny blood vessels. Microaneurysm detection is critical since these structures are the most recognizable function closer to DR. This section discusses numerous applications for detecting red lesions, such as MA, that have been developed. Table 10.2 explains the methods used to detect MA.

In Pan et al. (2020), the author proposes a deep learning-based classification system using FFA images for DR detection. Dense Net was the most consistent and

TABLE 10.2

Detection of Microaneurysms Using Different Variants of Methods

Authors	Database	DL/ML Technique	Performance
Pan et al.	Zhejiang University School of Medicine	CNNs	Sensitivity-98.00%
		DenseNet	Specificity-77.30%
		VGG16	Sensitivity-99.80%
			Specificity-14.60%
		ResNet50	Sensitivity-97.60%
			Specificity-22.70%
Manasi et al.	COKMCM	Hybrid detection	Accuracy-91.55%
			Sensitivity-96.1%
			Specificity-78.2%
Carson et al.	e-Ophtha	CNN	Accuracy-95%
Krishna et al.	MESSIDOR	Contrast limited adaptive histogram equalization	Accuracy-92%
Roy et al.	DIARETDB1	Morphological operation & Canny edge detection	Sensitivity-89.50% Specificity-82.10%
Waleed et al. (2017)	DIARETDB1	CNNs	Accuracy-95.40%
Shan et al. (2016)	DIARETDB1	Stacked Sparse Autoencoder	Accuracy-97.54% F- Score-91.30%
Deepthi et al. (2015)	DIARETDB1	Segmentation & Morphological operation	Accuracy-98.75% Sensitivity-97.80% Specificity-97.50%

reliable using CNN architectures for detecting MA, leaks, and laser scars. The multi-label classification algorithm reduces ophthalmologist workload and repetitive tasks in clinical practice, resulting in better DR diagnosis and treatment. To detect lesions using picture patches, DL algorithms have been constructed (Purandare et al. 2016). 243 retinal pictures were used as a dataset in this procedure, which was verified by two ophthalmologists. The image patches in the Kaggle input dataset include HEM, MA, EX. CNN were used by the authors to detect and classify them into five groups. MA have been discovered using a collection-based architecture (Lam et al. 2018). There are two steps to the recommended procedure. Preprocessing and network vascular structure analysis are the two key procedures. Preprocessing is done in the initial stage using structure analysis of retinal vascular. The ability to detect aberrant from normal images in a fractal scan improves the effectiveness of computer scanning program. Next stage is to use morphological operations and Canny edge detection to identify MA as aberrant image. The calculations for 89 fundus images were done using a database that was easily available. Following that, the approach attained the greatest sensitivity and specificity of 82.1% and 89.5% (Krishna et al. 2013). Researchers published a method for categorizing blood vessel, microaneurysm, and exudate lesions (Roy et al. 2013).

10.4.2.2 Techniques for Detecting Hemorrhage

HEM is usually found in the shallow and deep retina causing blood flows in blood vessels. In this scenario, accurate and rapid bleeding detection is crucial, as it can aid in the timely treatment of diabetics. The shallow retina has linear bright red HEM, whereas the deep retina has surrounding formed and brilliant red HEM.

10.4.2.3 Techniques for Detecting Exudate

The buildup of proteins and lipids in the retina is known as exudate. The retina is frequently affected by glossy, shiny, white, or milky lesions. It suggests a higher risk of retinal edema due to greater vascular permeability. This is a symptom of retinal fluid retention, not a visual hazard; nonetheless, they appear around the macula's center and are thought to cause serious harm. In the majority of cases, it was discovered that they had a hidden ailment. EX is a crucial indicator of DR that can be avoided during the initial inspection (Kayal et al. 2014).

10.4.2.4 Techniques for Detecting Macular Edema

Wherever light is directed, the macula serves as the focal point. The macula is the center of the tissue layer in the bodily structure image, which is dark in color due to excessive melanin synthesis. The image is interpreted and sent to the brain. The macula is three millimeters in size. A dark lesion forms when lipoid protein begins to gather around or on the macula. A common term for this condition is called as Macular edema. Macular edema is divided into two types. non-clinically significant macular edema (NCSME). At this time, the patient has no visible symptoms and is unaware that they are diagnosed with macular edema. The body waste begins to leak, soaking the tissue layer like a sponge. Exudate away from the fovea has no effect on the patient's vision. Most of the blood arteries inside the retina are compromised by clinically significant macular edema (CSME), and there are numerous ways to escape it. The liquid settled in fovea central after the exudate leaked. The detected images don't appear to be appropriately focused on the target, which has a major impact on eyesight.

10.5 DR LESION SEGMENTATION

The retinal blood vessels can be seen clearly using digital fundus imaging. For DR sufferers, this method provides the optimal fitness window. Certain image processing algorithms can be used to extract the vasculature from an RGB image's inexperienced component (Acharya et al. 2009). The segmentation and detection of retinal vessels is critical because it gives information about various retinal disorders such as hypertension, age-related macular degeneration, DR, and glaucoma. Detecting blood vessels within the retina and its divisions may also aid in the detection of aberrant coronary heart and brain abnormalities within the retinal vasculature. Studies on retinal vascular segmentation are more useful and important for non-surgical fundus pictures.The input images are converted to RGB images using the following equations, where ri, gi, and bi from equations known as mean standards with illuminations:R_q, G_q, B_q. R1, G2, B3 represent individual pixels in each channel (Karthika and Durgadevi 2022).

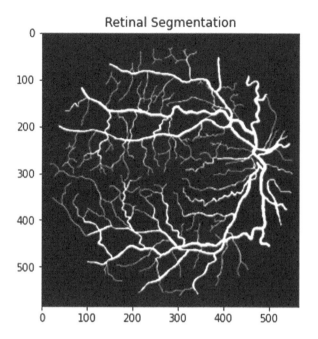

FIGURE 10.3 Segmented image.

Figure 10.3 shows the retinal segmentation and identification from DR images. In Table 10.3, the implementation details for each article are shown.

$$R1 = \text{minimum } \{R1 \text{ /mean } (R_q) \cdot ri, 255\} \tag{10.2}$$

$$G2 = \text{minimum } \{G2 \text{ /mean } (G_q) \cdot gi, 255\} \tag{10.3}$$

$$B3 = \text{minimum } \{B3 \text{ / mean } (B_q) \cdot bi, 255\} \tag{10.4}$$

The blood vessels are discovered using morphological characteristics. Anomalies can be more precisely recognized after discovering anomalous spots within the retinal fundus image. The effects of the experiments are assessed using 30+ retinal images from hospital (Shami et al. 2014). The Sensitivity (Sens) is 85%, while the common specificity is 99%. Researchers invented a system for detecting blood vessel, MA, and EX lesions (Fraz et al. 2013). The suggested method employs images to categorize retinal stages and is fully based on artificial neural networks. A neural network (NN) method is used to classify pixels (Abed et al. 2022). The linear discriminant analysis (May et al. 2016) is a technique for segmenting retinal arteries that is entirely dependent on pixel classification. The Gabor filter's reaction is used to determine pixel-based vessel measurements, and the characteristic vector includes a modified multiscale line operator. In Raja et al. (2014), it describes a method for categorizing blood arteries that uses DL and retinal imaging. The approach outlined above is based on ordinary unsupervised learning. Ensemble members are subjected

TABLE 10.3
Segmentation Based Studies in DR Detection

Authors Info	Methods Used	Datasets Used	Performance Measures
Shami et al.	Image processing using morph operation	Eye Hospital-Nikookari	Sens-85.82% Spec-99.98%
Fraz et al.	Multiscale line detection and Gabor filtering method	STARE DRIVE MESSIDOR	Accuracy (Acc)-95% Sens-73% Spec-97% Acc-94% Sens-73% Spec-97% Acc-96% Sens-73% Spec-98%
May et al.	ANN	DIARECTDB1	Acc-96%
Raja et al.	Markov Operation	DRIVE	Sens-78.63% Spec-97%
Lahiri et al.	Ensemble-based Deep Neural Method	DRIVE	Accs-95%
Wang et al.	Classification framework using cascade method	DB1 STARE	Acc-96.03% Sens-95.41% Spec-96.40% Acc-96.03% Sens-95.41% Spec-96.40%

to a variety of noise discounting techniques and automated coding stacks. In Lahiri et al. (2016), the SoftMax classifier is used to classify blood arteries from the DRIVE and Kappa datasets. MA, retinal blood vessels, and exudates were identified using morphological procedures in segmentation techniques. Using BPNN and one rule classifiers, they used PCA to identify the fundus images as DR or NO_DR, and they used Haar wavelet modification for characteristic extraction and selection (Wang et al. 2019).

10.6 PERFORMANCE METRICS

The use of the fundus camera was documented in retinal fundus images for an early analysis of DR. After capturing photographs, the images will be subjected to a number of preprocessing procedures before being subjected to image processing algorithms. Common filtering, scaling, adaptive histogram equalization, and holomorphic are some of the preprocessing procedures. In clinical treatment, medical facts are usually separated into two categories: the present ailment's location and facts, and the location of the available statistics where the ailment has no longer been recognized. For confidentiality and self-evaluation, the severity of the sickness is determined. To test the Specificity (Spec) and Sensitivity (Sen) of each image, fundus images are extensively employed in clinical technologies in DR. The clinical treatment will be better if the specificity and sensitivity levels are high. True −ve (T−) is used to represent no lesion pixels, while True +ve (T+) is used to denote the entire combination of lesion pixels. The False −ve (F−) and False +ve (F+) values represent the number of lesion pixels and non-lesion pixels that aren't recognized. Furthermore, the total performance of a set of rules can be represented as a table, which is referred to as a confusion matrix (CM) for supervised learning and a matching matrix for unsupervised learning. The matrix is represented in two dimensions as an actual condition and test result. For example, if someone wants to check whether or not he/she is having has a selected disease or not, this matrix table is used based on the subsequent overall performance measures. For example, if someone wants to check whether or not he/she is having has a selected disease or not, this matrix table is used based on the subsequent overall performance measures.

$$Sen = (T+)/(T+ + F-) \tag{10.5}$$

$$Spec = (T-)/(T- + F+) \tag{10.6}$$

10.6.1 TRUE POSITIVE

Postive values are identified as positive. That is, the test is positive and the patient is suffering from the disease.

10.6.2 TRUE NEGATIVE

Postitve values are identified as negative. That is, the test is negative and the patient is not suffering from the disease.

10.6.3 FALSE POSITIVE

Positive values are identified as negative. That is, the test is positive but the patient is not suffering from the disease.

10.6.4 FALSE NEGATIVE

Negative values are identified as positive. That is, the test is negative but the patient is suffering from the disease.

From the above four instances, the fourth case i.e., False −ve (Type 2 error) is risky as it may cause the life of the patient due to an error in the test.

So, generally, false negative instances are taken into consideration to be extra risky than false positive; however, in a few applications like software program testing, false positive instances (Type 2 error) are attempted to be minimized. Table 10.4 shows the confusion matrices with its measurements.

TABLE 10.4
Confusion Matrix

		Actual Condition		
		Positive [have DR]	Negative [No DR]	
Test Outcome	**Test outcome Positive [have DR]**	True +ve (TP)	False +ve (FP) **Type 1 Error**	PPV (Precision)
	Test outcome Negative [No DR]	False –ve (FN) **Type 2 Error**	True –ve (TN)	NPV
		TPR (Sensitivity)	TNR (Specificity)	ACC F-Measurement

NPV = –ve Predictive value; PPV = +ve Predictive value

10.7 CONCLUSION

Recent DR detection research has focused on automatic approaches referred to as CAD structures. The CAD system has two essential processes for DR: the first is the type and severity of DR, and the second is the segmentation of lesions, as well as MA, HEM, and EX. The majority of research in the literature has used various standard approaches for diagnosing and segmenting DR. This chapter has examined the current review of research conducted in the DR utilizing various DL and ML approaches for illness detection. A thorough examination of the techniques under consideration also aids the region in gaining a better knowledge of the existing models to investigate the overall performance evaluation of ML and DL algorithms. Research is still needed to address issues with model-agnostic XAI approaches' rising computational costs and assumption-based operation. For improved advancements in its adoption and use, the XAI domain needs to be continuously researched and utilized in AI-based healthcare systems.

REFERENCES

Abed, Amira Hassan, Essam M. Shaaban, Om Prakash Jena, and Ahmed A. Elngar. "A comprehensive survey on breast cancer thermography classification using deep neural network." *Machine Learning and Deep Learning in Medical Data Analytics and Healthcare Applications* (2022): 169–182.

Abràmoff, Michael David, Yiyue Lou, Ali Erginay, Warren Clarida, Ryan Amelon, James C. Folk, and Meindert Niemeijer. "Improved automated detection of diabetic retinopathy on a publicly available dataset through integration of deep learning." *Investigative Ophthalmology & Visual Science* 57, no. 13 (2016): 5200–5206.

Acharya, Udyavara R., Choo M. Lim, E. Yin Kwee Ng, Caroline Chee, and Toshiyo Tamura. "Computer-based detection of diabetes retinopathy stages using digital fundus images." *Proceedings of the Institution of Mechanical Engineers, Part H: Journal of Engineering in Medicine* 223, no. 5 (2009): 545–553.

Agurto, Carla, Victor Murray, Eduardo Barriga, Sergio Murillo, Marios Pattichis, Herbert Davis, Stephen Russell, Michael Abràmoff, and Peter Soliz. "Multiscale AM-FM methods for diabetic retinopathy lesion detection." *IEEE Transactions on Medical Imaging* 29, no. 2 (2010): 502–512.

Basheer, Imad A., and Maha Hajmeer. "Artificial neural networks: Fundamentals, computing, design, and application." *Journal of Microbiological Methods* 43, no. 1 (2000): 3–31.

Bilal, A., G. Sun, and S. Mazhar. "Survey on recent developments in automatic detection of diabetic retinopathy." *Journal Français d'Ophtalmologie* 44, no. 3 (2021): 420–440.

Breiman, Leo. "Random forests." *Machine Learning* 45, no. 1 (2001): 5–32.

Chatterjee, Riddhi, Ratula Ray, Satya Ranjan Dash, and Om Prakash Jena. "Conceptualizing tomorrow's healthcare through digitization." *Computational Intelligence and Healthcare Informatics* (2021): 359–376.

Cortes, Corinna, and Vladimir Vapnik. "Support-vector networks." *Machine Learning* 20, no. 3 (1995): 273–297.

Cover, Thomas, and Peter Hart. "Nearest neighbor pattern classification." *IEEE Transactions on Information Theory* 13, no. 1 (1967): 21–27.

Decenciere, Etienne, Guy Cazuguel, Xiwei Zhang, Guillaume Thibault, J-C. Klein, Fernand Meyer, Beatriz Marcotegui et al. "TeleOphta: Machine learning and image processing methods for teleophthalmology." *IRBM* 34, no. 2 (2013): 196–203.

Dechter, Rina. "Learning while searching in constraint-satisfaction problems." In *Proceedings of the 5th National Conference on Artificial Intelligence*, vol. 1, pp. 178–185. Philadelphia, PA, 1986.

Fraz, M. M., P. Remagnino, A. Hoppe, and S. A. Barman. "Retinal image analysis aimed at extraction of vascular structure using linear discriminant classifier." In *2013 International Conference on Computer Medical Applications (ICCMA)*, pp. 1–6. IEEE, Sousse, 2013. doi: 10.1109/ICCMA.2013.6506180

Gondal, Waleed M., Jan M. Köhler, René Grzeszick, Gernot A. Fink, and Michael Hirsch. "Weakly-supervised localization of diabetic retinopathy lesions in retinal fundus images." In *2017 IEEE International Conference on Image Processing (ICIP)*, pp. 2069–2073. IEEE, Beijing, 2017.

Goodfellow, Ian, Jean Pouget-Abadie, Mehdi Mirza, Bing Xu, David Warde-Farley, Sherjil Ozair, Aaron Courville, and Yoshua Bengio. "Generative adversarial networks." *Communications of the ACM* 63, no. 11 (2020): 139–144.

Gulshan, Varun, Lily Peng, Marc Coram, Martin C. Stumpe, Derek Wu, Arunachalam Narayanaswamy, Subhashini Venugopalan et al. "Development and validation of a deep learning algorithm for detection of diabetic retinopathy in retinal fundus photographs." *JAMA* 316, no. 22 (2016): 2402–2410.

Hochreiter, Sepp, and Jürgen Schmidhuber. "Long short-term memory." *Neural Computation* 9, no. 8 (1997): 1735–1780.

Hoover, A. D., Valentina Kouznetsova, and Michael Goldbaum. "Locating blood vessels in retinal images by piecewise threshold probing of a matched filter response." *IEEE Transactions on Medical Imaging* 19, no. 3 (2000): 203–210.

Kalviainen, R. V. J. P. H., and H. Uusitalo. "DIARETDB1 diabetic retinopathy database and evaluation protocol." In *Medical Image Understanding and Analysis*, vol. 2007, p. 61. Citeseer, 2007.

Karthika, S., and M. Durgadevi. "Detection of MA based on iris blood vessel segmentation and classification using convolutional neural networks (ConvNets)." In *Communication and Intelligent Systems*, pp. 393–410. Springer, Singapore, 2022.

Kayal, Diptoneel, and Sreeparna Banerjee. "A new dynamic thresholding based technique for detection of hard exudates in digital retinal fundus image." In *2014 International Conference on Signal Processing and Integrated Networks (SPIN)*, pp. 141–144. IEEE, Noida, 2014.

Khedkar, Sujata, Vignesh Subramanian, Gayatri Shinde, and Priyanka Gandhi. "Explainable AI in healthcare." In *Healthcare (April 8, 2019). 2nd International Conference on Advances in Science & Technology (ICAST)*. K J Somaiya Institute of Engineering & Information Technology, Mumbai, 2019.

Krause, Jonathan, Varun Gulshan, Ehsan Rahimy, Peter Karth, Kasumi Widner, Greg S. Corrado, Lily Peng, and Dale R. Webster. "Grader variability and the importance of reference standards for evaluating machine learning models for diabetic retinopathy." *Ophthalmology* 125, no. 8 (2018): 1264–1272.

Krishna, N. Venkata, N. Reddy, M. Venkata Ramana, and E. Prasanna Kumar. "The communal system for early detection microaneurysm and diabetic retinopathy grading through color fundus images." *International Journal of Scientific Engineering and Technology* 2, no. 4 (2013): 228–232.

Lahiri, Avisek, Abhijit Guha Roy, Debdoot Sheet, and Prabir Kumar Biswas. "Deep neural ensemble for retinal vessel segmentation in fundus images towards achieving label-free angiography." In *2016 38th Annual International Conference of the IEEE Engineering in Medicine and Biology Society (EMBC)*, pp. 1340–1343. IEEE, Orlando, FL, 2016.

Lam, Carson, Caroline Yu, Laura Huang, and Daniel Rubin. "Retinal lesion detection with deep learning using image patches." *Investigative Ophthalmology & Visual Science* 59, no. 1 (2018): 590–596.

LeCun, Yann, Bernhard Boser, John S. Denker, Donnie Henderson, Richard E. Howard, Wayne Hubbard, and Lawrence D. Jackel. "Backpropagation applied to handwritten zip code recognition." *Neural Computation* 1, no. 4 (1989): 541–551.

Mahendran, G., R. Dhanasekaran, and K. N. Narmadha Devi. "Identification of exudates for Diabetic Retinopathy based on morphological process and PNN classifier." In *2014 International Conference on Communication and Signal Processing*, pp. 1117–1121. IEEE, Melmaruvathur, 2014.

McClelland, James L., David E. Rumelhart, and Geoffrey E. Hinton. *The Appeal of Parallel Distributed Processing*. MIT Press, Cambridge MA 3 (1986): 44.

McCulloch, Warren S., and Walter Pitts. "A logical calculus of the ideas immanent in nervous activity." *The Bulletin of Mathematical Biophysics* 5, no. 4 (1943): 115–133.

Mo, Juan, and Lei Zhang. "Multi-level deep supervised networks for retinal vessel segmentation." *International Journal of Computer Assisted Radiology and Surgery* 12, no. 12 (2017): 2181–2193.

Naqvi, Syed Ali Gohar, Muhammad Faisal Zafar, and Ihsan ul Haq. "Referral system for hard exudates in eye fundus." *Computers in Biology and Medicine* 64 (2015): 217–235.

Niemeijer, M., Staal, J. J., Ginneken, B., Loog, M., and Abramoff, M. D. (2004). DRIVE: digital retinal images for vessel extraction. Methods for evaluating segmentation and indexing techniques dedicated to retinal ophthalmology. *IEEE Transactions on Medical Imaging* 23 (2004): 501–509.

Niemeijer, Meindert, Bram Van Ginneken, Michael J. Cree, Atsushi Mizutani, Gwénolé Quellec, Clara I. Sánchez, Bob Zhang et al. "Retinopathy online challenge: automatic detection of microaneurysms in digital color fundus photographs." *IEEE Transactions on Medical Imaging* 29, no. 1 (2009): 185–195.

Paing, May Phu, Somsak Choomchuay, and M. D. Rapeeporn Yodprom. "Detection of lesions and classification of diabetic retinopathy using fundus images." In *2016 9th Biomedical Engineering International Conference (BMEiCON)*, pp. 1–5. IEEE, Laung Prabang, 2016.

Pan, Xiangji, Kai Jin, Jing Cao, Zhifang Liu, Jian Wu, Kun You, Yifei Lu et al. "Multi-label classification of retinal lesions in diabetic retinopathy for automatic analysis of fundus fluorescein angiography based on deep learning." *Graefe's Archive for Clinical and Experimental Ophthalmology* 258, no. 4 (2020): 779–785.

Patra, Sudhansu Shekhar, Mamta Mittal, and Om Prakash Jena. "Multiobjective evolutionary algorithm based on decomposition for feature selection in medical diagnosis." In *Predictive Modeling in Biomedical Data Mining and Analysis*, pp. 253–293. Academic Press, 2022.

Patra, Sudhansu Shekhar, Om Praksah Jena, Gaurav Kumar, Sreyashi Pramanik, Chinmaya Misra, and Kamakhya Narain Singh. "Random forest algorithm in imbalance genomics classification." *Data Analytics in Bioinformatics: A Machine Learning Perspective*, pp. 173–190, 2021.

Pattnayak, Parthasarathi, and Amiya Ranjan Panda. "Innovation on machine learning in healthcare services-An introduction." In *Technical Advancements of Machine Learning in Healthcare*, pp. 1–30. Springer, Singapore, 2021.

Pawar, Urja, Donna O'Shea, Susan Rea, and Ruairi O'Reilly. "Explainable ai in healthcare." In *2020 International Conference on Cyber Situational Awareness, Data Analytics and Assessment (CyberSA)*, pp. 1–2. IEEE, Dublin, 2020.

Prasad, Deepthi K., L. Vibha, and K. R. Venugopal. "Early detection of diabetic retinopathy from digital retinal fundus images." In *2015 IEEE Recent Advances in Intelligent Computational Systems (RAICS)*, pp. 240–245. IEEE, Trivandrum, 2015.

Purandare, Manasi, and Kevin Noronha. "Hybrid system for automatic classification of Diabetic Retinopathy using fundus images." In *2016 online International Conference on Green Engineering and Technologies (IC-GET)*, pp. 1–5. IEEE, Coimbatore, 2016.

Raja, J. Benadict, and C. G. Ravichandran. "Automatic localization of fovea in retinal images based on mathematical morphology and anatomic structures." *International Journal of Engineering and Technology* 6, no. 5 (2014): 2171–2183.

Roy, Rukhmini, Srinivasan Aruchamy, and Partha Bhattacharjee. "Detection of retinal microaneurysms using fractal analysis and feature extraction technique." In *2013 International Conference on Communication and Signal Processing*, pp. 469–474. IEEE, Melmaruvathur, 2013.

Shami, Foroogh, Hadi Seyedarabi, and Ali Aghagolzadeh. "Better detection of retinal abnormalities by accurate detection of blood vessels in retina." In *2014 22nd Iranian Conference on Electrical Engineering (ICEE)*, pp. 1493–1496. IEEE, Tehran, 2014.

Shan, Juan, and Lin Li. "A deep learning method for microaneurysm detection in fundus images." In *2016 IEEE First International Conference on Connected Health: Applications, Systems and Engineering Technologies (CHASE)*, pp. 357–358. IEEE, Washington, DC, 2016.

Sutton, Richard S., and Andrew G. Barto. "Introduction to reinforcement learning." (1998): 551283.

Wang, Xiaohong, Xudong Jiang, and Jianfeng Ren. "Blood vessel segmentation from fundus image by a cascade classification framework." *Pattern Recognition* 88 (2019): 331–341.

11 Clinical Natural Language Processing Systems for Information Retrieval from Unstructured Medical Narratives

S. Lourdumarie Sophie and S. Siva Sathya
Pondicherry University

11.1 INTRODUCTION

Natural language processing (NLP) is a branch of artificial intelligence (AI) that assists machines in reading, analyzing, and deriving meaning from human language. It is applied across various areas of study such as agriculture (Prasad and Prasad 2008), education (Devi and Ponnusamy 2018; Khaled 2014), health care (Basyal, Rimal, and Zeng 2020; Devi and Ponnusamy 2018; Iroju and Olaleke 2015), urban governance, management (M. Cai 2021), etc. The main objective of these NLP systems is to interpret the text or speech to evaluate its significance, thereby allowing the computer applications to interact with humans efficiently. Traditional NLP engines utilize enormous corpora of text, usually books or other composed records, to decide how the language is organized and how the sentence structure is framed.

Figure 11.1 represents the input and output of an NLP system; the input is usually unstructured data (written text or voice record). In the case of written text, the NLP system uses the lexical, syntactic, and semantic understanding of the language, whereas, in the case of a spoken language, it is done by using all information required to analyze a written text and the organization of speech sounds. The output is generally a targeted representation in a language that is recognized by the application program.

Electronic health record (EHR) is a repository for longitudinal health-related information on patients. It is an electronic representation of a patients' medical

FIGURE 11.1 Input and output for an NLP system.

DOI: 10.1201/9781003257721-11

record, including demographic profile, illnesses, prescription medications, treatment plans, clinical examination, vaccinations, previous medical history, laboratory findings, and radiological results. The medical text data are generally unstructured, and there is no proper standard technique to ensure consistency in their format, quality, or contents. As a result, converting these unstructured clinical texts into meaningful, quantifiable information is a daunting task. NLP provides a computerized method for analyzing these types of clinical texts. Applying NLP techniques to EHR data makes it more convenient for clinicians to discover meaningful patterns from patient information. Evaluating a patient's health state from the EHR data requires a two-phase analysis,

    i. **Information etraction phase**: In this, the NLP system extracts clinical terms (diagnosis, symptoms, drugs, etc.) from the unstructured EHR data using medical knowledge resources like Unified Medical Language System (UMLS);

    ii. **Classification phase**: It uses machine learning or deep learning models to derive specific outcomes/analyses from the retrieved terms.

Though EHRs provide several advantages over conventional paper records, like effective data storage and retrieval, the present EHR system struggles with usability issues, resulting in inefficient workflows and dissatisfied users. These usability issues necessitate a critical demand for the EHR to assist users in readily locating information essential to give treatment.

Healthcare system is a complex sector with a lot of room for development. Due to the use of newer technology in the field of health care, there have been significant breakthroughs. One such technological advancement is Clinical Natural Language Processing (CNLP). Clinical NLP is a subset of NLP specializing in health care that helps computers decipher the complex context contained in a doctor's prescription, discharge summary, radiology reports, etc. Applying NLP in the health care industry significantly improves patient care delivery, aids in disease diagnosis, brings down health care expenses, and enhances the process. Since NLP is used in several aspects of the health care domain and very few literature reviews have been done, this chapter throws light on various facets of NLP and their usage in healthcare, covering several topics as detailed below.

The remaining part of this chapter is organized as follows: Section 2 gives the components of NLP and Section 3 presents the various stages/ phases of NLP, followed by the applications of the NLP system in section 4. Section 5 gives an elaborated analysis of various NLP systems employed in the clinical sector for retrieving vital information from medical reports. Finally, Section 6 concludes the paper.

The NLP system has two major components, as depicted in Figure 11.2.

11.1.1 Natural Language Understanding

Natural Language Understanding (NLU) converts the given data into a meaningful format that the machine can recognize. NLU aims to infer the user's intention by analyzing the text. Business applications frequently depend on NLU to interpret what

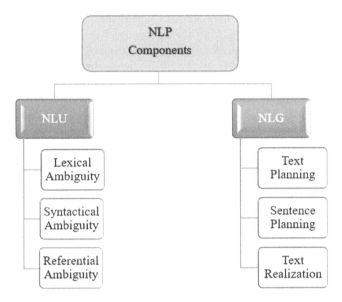

FIGURE 11.2   Components of NLP.

an individual says both in written and spoken language. This information enables virtual assistants to identify the user's objective and direct them to the appropriate task. NLU also aids in the analysis of linguistic ambiguities such as,

- **Lexical ambiguity***:* This ambiguity highlights words with multiple claims. That is, it refers to two or more possible meanings for a single word. For instance, the term "cold" can be referred to as a freezing environment or the common cold.
- **Syntactical ambiguity***:* This kind of ambiguity occurs when a statement's form or syntax produces uncertainty. It denotes two or more possible meanings within a sentence. For instance, the term "bank" in the phrase " I'll see you at the bank" has two possible meanings. This can also happen when a statement lacks punctuation marks, thereby obscuring its meaning.
- **Referential ambiguity***:* This kind of ambiguity occurs whenever a word or phrase in a statement's context relates to two or more characteristics or objects. That is, it refers to a word in a sentence relating to two or more entities. It is sometimes apparent from the context which interpretation is meant, although that may not be the case always. For instance, in the phrase "Jordan is a big celebrity icon," it is unclear whether the term "big" implies fat or famous without the context.

11.1.2   NATURAL LANGUAGE GENERATION

Natural Language Generation (NLG) generates meaningful output in the form of natural language (human language) using some internal representation. It involves,

- **Text planning**: It identifies the information that has to be delivered by retrieving specific terms from the knowledge base and organizing them based on the aims and preferences of the reader and the writer. In general, the key contents of the text are chosen for the specific readership and structured effectively, and the text organization concepts/theories are utilized to select appropriate information ordering.
- **Sentence planning**: It divides the information content into sentences and paragraphs with proper usage of pronouns, adjectives, etc. The approaches employed here include grammaticalization, lexicalization, referring expressions, and aggregation. Sentence planning aims to select suitable words, generate meaningful sentences, and set the correction tone.
- **Text realization**: It is responsible for generating grammatically acceptable sentences by mapping sentence plan to sentence structure. The mapping process uses grammatical knowledge of the specified language. Text realization also performs syntax selection and inflection for the given text.

11.2   STAGES OF NLP

NLP is generally practiced at the stages shown below, as seen in Figure 11.3. Regardless of granularity, the stages could be distributed in varied orders based on the application.

11.2.1   Phonological Analysis

Phonology is the study of a language's acoustic patterns. The phonological analysis phase is considered only if the input is a speech. The sound of speech will reveal a lot about the context of a word or a phrase. This analysis relates to how speech sounds are interpreted within and through words. Homophones are terms that refer to words that share the same pronunciation but have distinct meanings; differentiating these

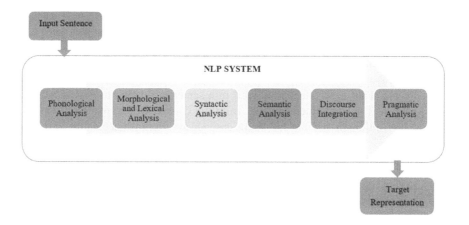

FIGURE 11.3   Stages involved in an NLP system.

words is a more significant challenge. Hanumanthappa, Rashmi, and Jyothi (2014) suggested that creating a homophone dictionary is an efficient and effective approach for resolving phonological ambiguity, and it also discusses various concepts for creating a consistent and well-ordered phonetic dictionary that focuses on homophones.

11.2.2 MORPHOLOGICAL AND LEXICAL ANALYSIS

Morphology is the study of the formation of words and their relationship with other words in the same language. It deals with recognizing distinct words based on morphemes (the smallest significant part of a word). Biomedical data used in the health care domain requires high morphological information because of the complex procedure terms and chemical names (e.g., di-hydro-thym-ine) (Friedman and Johnson 2006). Morphological analysis enhances the NLP system to handle new terms efficiently.

Lexical analysis is typically the first phase of the compilation process when the given input is text. This phase scans the given text character by character and produces a sequence of tokens. A token is a set of characters with common sense, such as names, keywords, punctuation marks, white space, and comments (Iroju and Olaleke 2015). A specific instance of a token is termed a Lexeme that includes nouns, adjectives, and verbs (Friedman and Johnson 2006). According to Farhanaaz and Sanju (2016), a Lexeme is an abstract unit of morphological analysis in linguistics. These tokens are then stored in the symbol table and sent as input for the next phase. The lexical analysis phase is responsible for keeping track of errors irrespective of the stage (Farhanaaz and Sanju 2016). An elaborated review of recent approaches and challenges in the lexical analysis phase is presented in Pai T and Aithal (2020).

11.2.3 SYNTACTIC ANALYSIS

Syntactic analysis/Parsing refers to the arrangement of words to form a well-defined sentence in a language (Trivedi 2018). The main objective is to check grammar and word arrangements in the sentence, which affects their context. A hierarchical rewriting of the parsing phase is presented in Massa Cereda, Miura, and Neto (2018) to address the context-sensitivity issue in NLP systems. Also, this phase reduces the number of interpretations of the sentence (Bessmertny et al. 2017) as it is dictionary-dependent. Syntactic analysis is associated with the correct arrangement of terms and their effect on semantics.

11.2.4 SEMANTIC ANALYSIS

This analysis is associated with the word or phrase meaning in a language. Semantics is required to analyze any natural language. Reference (Rajani S and Computer 2016) presents various techniques to perform semantic analysis for NLP systems, of which Latent Semantic Analysis (LSA) is proved to be more effective. Most of the terms used in biomedical data are polysemous; there may be two or more possible meanings for a particular word. For example, the word "discharge" has two separate meanings in the subsequent sentences; "*The patient was prescribed with clindamycin upon discharge*" and "*The patient suffered from vaginal discharge*," this led to the ambiguation problem. Word Sense Disambiguation (WSD) is a technique that instantly addresses these ambiguities and is an essential step in text understanding (Stevenson and Guo 2010). According to Vij and Pruthi (2018), Both medical and English dictionaries are utilized as a knowledge base in WSD to eliminate uncertainty in terms of both domain and non-domain aspects. WSD takes only one meaning for the word depending on the usage of the word in a sentence.

11.2.5 Discourse Integration

This analysis deals with the sense of context. In the discourse integration stage, a sentence's meaning depends upon the preceding and succeeding sentence; that is, the sense of a single sentence is determined by the meaning of the preceding sentences and may affect the meaning of the subsequent sentences. For example, the word "it" in the sentence "Joe wanted it" is dependent on the previous discourse context. Once the exact reference for "it" is known, it becomes easy to figure out to which it is being referred.

11.2.6 Pragmatic Analysis

The pragmatic analysis is the last phase of the NLP system; it applies a set of rules to identify how a particular sentence is interpreted in the way in which it has been used. This stage requires some real-world knowledge. For example, a mass in a brain CT report implies a brain tumor, whereas a mass in a religious journal implies a ceremony (Friedman and Johnson 2006). The goal is to determine the underlying meaning of a particular text and derive conclusions. In short, this stage concentrates on revealing a user's views, perceptions, emotions, desires, and the message they wish to convey by analyzing the text, thereby discovering the intended effect depending on the context.

11.3 APPLICATIONS AND TECHNIQUES

This section covers the predominant applications and techniques used in a clinical NLP system.

11.3.1 Optical Character Recognition

Optical character recognition (OCR) is a technique employed to convert handwritten documents (scanned images) or printed text into a machine-readable format, that is, digitizing a document image into its constituent character (Vasudeven and James 2015). It scans the unstructured data, extracts the text and tables, and displays the information in an editable format. OCR is utilized in a variety of research projects by employing machine learning algorithms (Decision Tree, Support Vector Machine, k-Nearest Neighbor (Lorigo and Govindaraju 2006; Trenkle et al. 2001)), and deep learning approaches (Lecun, Bengio, and Hinton 2015). Studies suggest that OCR using deep learning techniques has better performance and accuracy (Breuel et al.

2013). OCR is widely used in the healthcare industry to digitize case reports, patient health records, admission forms, and other documents. Other application areas of OCR include an automatic number plate recognition system (Qadri and Asif 2009), a signature verification system (Chakravarthi and Chandra 2017; Sangwan and Sihag 2015; Shahane, Choukade, and Diyewar 2015) that helps visually impaired people to read the text (H. Shen and Coughlan 2012), and so on.

11.3.2 Named Entity Recognition

Named entity recognition (NER) is the process of extracting specific elements from documents; this process of extraction aids in finding the key information from unstructured data. NER is a two-stage process; the first stage focuses on detecting and determining entities from the textual data, whereas the second stage focuses on selecting and extracting those entities. Generic named entity focuses on extracting general terms from the text, such as the person's name, location, and so on. Domain-specific named entity extracts terms related to a specific domain such as medicine, manufacturing, and so on.

In the healthcare domain, extraction of clinical entities (such as drug, symptom, diagnosis, procedures, etc.) from clinical narratives (electronic medical reports, lab reports, discharge summaries, etc.) is one of the fundamental tasks. Most clinical NLP systems, such as MedLEE (Friedman et al. 2004; Friedman 1997), MetaMap (Aronson 2001; Aronson and Lang 2010; Denecke, n.d.), cTAKES (Denecke, n.d.; Névéol et al. 2018; Savova et al. 2010), and KnowledgeMap (Denny, Irani, et al. 2003; Denny, Smithers, et al. 2003), extract clinical entities using rule-based approaches that depend on traditional biomedical vocabularies (Tang et al. 2013). Recent technological advancements in machine learning and deep learning have cleared the path for clinical NLP systems to incorporate these approaches for clinical NER applications (Abed et al. 2022; Behera and Jena 2021; Pattnayak and Jena 2021). Among different machine learning algorithms, conditional random fields (CRFs) and support vector machines (SVM) are the most frequently used approaches for NER tasks (Patra et al. 2021; Tang et al. 2013; Z. Liu et al. 2017). Recurrent neural network (RNN) is a widely used deep learning model for entity recognition in clinical texts (Y. Wu et al. 2017; Z. Liu et al. 2017). Figure 11.4 gives a classic example of NER in medical documents.

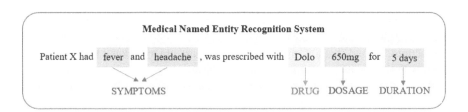

FIGURE 11.4   Example of medical domain-specific NER system.

11.3.3 QUESTION ANSWERING

Question Answering (QA) models are built to retrieve precise answers to questions posed in natural human language. Users can utilize Question-Answering techniques to acquire specific responses to requests given in natural language. Although several QA systems have been developed for clinical/ diagnosis purposes for the past few years, most medical QA systems use the UMLS, a comprehensive database of medical terminology and semantics.

A clinical question answering (CliniQA) system specifically for pancreatic cancer using MetaMap to extract the clinical terms from the medical phrase and a MetaMap Transfer (MMTx) program to classify the question and extract precise answers using a simple heuristic approach is developed in (Zahid et al. 2018). Andrenucci (2008) compares three medical QA (Template-based, Deep NLP, Information Retrieval enhanced by Shallow NLP) techniques. A template-based approach is best suited for web-based medical applications aiming for multilingual retrieval. The deep NLP approach is ideal for situations where the precision of the recovered data is critical, such as decision-making or evidence-based treatment. IR improved by shallow NLP is more suited as a search engine can only return factual replies. The authors in Cairns et al. (2011) developed a rule-based Multi-source Integrated Platform for Answering Clinical Questions (MiPACQ) that combines many information retrievals and NLP tools into a flexible QA system; it has proven to outperform Medpedia, a wiki-style medical article database. A semantic approach for QA is proposed by Ben Abacha and Zweigenbaum (2015), which suggests that along with the NLP technique and semantic web technologies for extracting answers, a query relaxation method has opted that addresses the weaknesses or faults in the NLP approaches. Manually acquiring QA annotations is time-consuming and impossible, especially when it comes to the medical domain; a system to create an electronic medical record question-answering corpus termed emrQA is proposed in Pampari et al. (2018) so that it can be used for corpus generation and model analysis. The resultant corpus of the emrQA is proven to include nearly 1 million medical queries and approximately 400,000 QA evidence pairings for the same. Developing a credible medical QA system necessitates massive QA labels that adequately reflect the complex nature of medical narratives. Also, privacy violations about disclosing individuals' health records and the tedious process of integrating response annotations across all longitudinal patient records should be considered while building the system.

11.3.4 CHATBOTS

The chatbot is one of the significant applications of the QA system. It utilizes NLP to comprehend language, which is commonly done through text or voice recognition interactions. AI and chatbots are the two game-changing techniques that have altered the way how patients and clinicians view healthcare.

AI interactive diet planner bot that gives suggestions and plans to the user to stay fit is developed in Bennet Praba et al. (2019); the authors focus on overcoming the morphological ambiguity in comprehending medical terms and providing an appropriate response to the user by breaking it down into smaller subdivisions.

Diagnostic chatbots have been a popular study subject in NLP to make the health-care system more participatory. A Fuzzy Support Vector Machine (Omoregbe et al. 2020), Decision tree-based (Kidwai and Rk 2020) diagnostic chatbots communicate with patients or physicians to assist them in predicting a diagnosis for their disease based on their symptoms. These virtual assistant bots/chatbots benefit from serving as medical reference books, educating patients about their illnesses, and enhancing their quality of life (Mahajan et al. 2020). These healthcare chatbots can potentially reshape the healthcare sector by delivering predictive diagnosis or other services such as appointment scheduling (Kandpal et al. 2020).

11.3.5 MACHINE TRANSLATION

Machine translation is the automated process of converting written or spoken words between two natural languages while preserving the meaning and generating natu-ral-sounding material in the target language. A physician faced with communica-tion barriers and no qualified interpreter could utilize a machine translation to help communicate with a patient during a clinical visit (Randhawa et al. 2013). Recent research proves that neural machine translation techniques maximize the translation performance of the healthcare domain compared to traditional statistical ones (Wołk and Marasek 2015). Physicians might use machine translation to understand patient histories, review a clinical diagnosis, or reiterate the recommended treatment plan and follow-up to aid comprehension. They may also advise patients to enter text into the translator to encourage them to ask questions regarding the treatment plan or any other concerns.

11.3.6 SENTIMENT ANALYSIS

Sentiment Analysis or Opinion Mining analyzes and extracts hidden emotion from spoken or written data. It does by giving the text a polarity (positive, negative, or neu-tral) to identify the underlying mood inside a sentence or phrase by utilizing a combi-nation of NLP and Machine Learning (ML) approaches. Naïve Bayes (Chintalapudi et al. 2021; Vij and Pruthi 2018), Logistic Regression (Vij and Pruthi 2018), and Support Vector Machine (Garcia and Berton 2021) are widely used ML methods for performing opinion mining.

Sentiment analysis plays a significant role in the medical sector as it evaluates clinical records and makes decision-making easier for doctors. For instance, when a patient is ill, the physician utilizes symptomatic data to diagnose the patient's condi-tion, and these diagnostic reports are kept in the EHR system. Researchers can use these data to determine whether or not a diagnosis exists in an individual; if pres-ent, the certainty of the diagnosis and the severity of the disease can be anticipated (Denecke and Deng 2015). Furthermore, in the EHR, the physician can express their thoughts or observations to comprehend patient feedback better. Thus, opinion min-ing helps grasp the patient's opinion about the healthcare sector's significant aspects. Online platforms, including social media, blogs, and websites, have become the pri-mary means through which doctors and patients discuss healthcare services and the difficulties they've encountered (Yadav et al. 2019).

11.3.7 Topic Modeling

Topic modeling is an unsupervised method that automatically groups together words and phrases most closely associated with a topic based on their frequency and similarity across several sources. Applying topic modeling to EHR data gives a better understanding of the patients and reveals unexpected patterns between patients' clinical notes and biological variables like genetics (Chan et al. 2013). Therefore, the clinical information in the topic model output of patient reports might be highly beneficial (Sarioglu, Yadav, and Choi 2013).

The topic model generally groups similar words or documents based on their semantic relations (J. K. Lee 2019) and automatically identifies the "topic" the document deals with. For this purpose, several approaches such as LSA, Probabilistic Latent Semantic Analysis (pLSA), Latent Dirichlet Allocation (LDA), and deep learning-based lda2vec are employed. Among these techniques, LDA (Chan et al. 2013; Chiudinelli et al. 2020; Geletta, Follett, and Laugerman 2019; Sarioglu, Yadav, and Choi 2013) is the most prevalent type of topic modeling; it uses algorithms to find semantic links between different words and phrases and classify them accordingly. Figure 11.5 gives the abstract view of topic models that aid in identifying the hidden topical patterns that appear across the collection.

11.3.8 Automatic Text Summarization

A summary is a simplified version of the original document's narrative. Text summarization reduces the source document into a summary document by specifying the most significant points with the least duplication. Thus, it consolidates data to make it easier for users to find and process critical information more efficiently and precisely, also aids in reducing the size of the document. Text summarization falls into two categories: abstractive and extractive summarization (M. Afzal et al. 2020). The former method looks at the text and constructs a new summarized text close to the original. On the other hand, the latter approach identifies the most significant element of the text, extracts it, and produces it exactly.

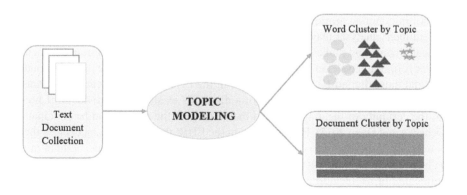

FIGURE 11.5 Overview of topic modeling.

The vast amount of textual data in the biomedical area is constantly a barrier, prompting researchers to create new domain-specific text processing methods. In addition, clinical documents (medical records, trail reports) are getting extremely massive daily, making it more difficult to extract and manage the information contained inside them (Moradi and Ghadiri 2019). Automatic text summarization (ATS) is a potential way to quickly assist doctors and researchers in obtaining the basic idea of a clinical document by creating a textual or graphical summary (Mishra et al. 2014). As a result, automatic text summarizing might become a powerful tool to help physicians and researchers organize their information and expertise.

11.3.9 Co-reference Resolution

The co-reference resolution technique discovers linguistic phrases in natural language that relate to the same real-world entity. The objective of the co-reference resolution is to locate all text expressions that represent the same thing. For example, "Have reviewed the MRI report. It shows that the extra-axial fluid collections around the cerebral hemispheres remain unchanged but no evidence of recurrence or leptomeningeal metastasis." The phrases "the MRI" and "It" refer to the same concept, that is, the magnetic resonance imaging (MRI).

This technique plays a significant role in many NLP applications such as text/ document summarizing, question answering, and information extraction that need natural language comprehension. Unfortunately, research on co-reference resolution in clinical narratives has not progressed significantly. The differences across summary forms; the examination of contextual information, such as dose, amounts, and section titles; and clinical domain expertise are the key hurdles in resolving co-reference linkages within patient discharge summaries (Dai et al. 2012). Most works on applying co-reference resolution to clinical texts make use of the Ontology Development and Information Extraction (ODIE) corpus (J. Zheng et al. 2011; 2012) to lay the groundwork for methodologies in the clinical domain. With the help of this technique, Sentences become self-contained, and the machine can grasp their meaning without any further context.

11.3.10 Disease Prediction

Environment and modern lifestyles contribute to a wide range of illnesses plaguing today's population. On the whole, predicting disease in the initial stage is essential. Disease prediction recognizes a patient's health by applying specific ML and data mining techniques (Dahiwade, Patle, and Meshram 2019; Dinesh et al. 2018; Pasha and Mohamed 2020) on patient medical history to forecast case severity. Most models built on disease prediction use the risk assessment score module (Coquet et al. 2019; D. Van Le et al. 2018; Moon et al. 2019) to categorize patients as low, moderate, or high-risk signs of a medical condition depending on the symptoms extracted.

The disease prediction models aid in anticipating medical issues and help physicians get a second opinion, thereby decreasing the incidences of misdiagnosis (Chatterjee et al. 2021; Patra, Mittal, and Jena 2022). Applying prediction techniques to EHR data to estimate patient health status has proven beneficial (Aswathy, Rathi, and P 2019; Zhang et al. 2017). Early detection of a diagnosis in a patient may minimize unfavorable outcomes. Hence, predictive models have the potential to assist physicians in quick clinical decision-making (Sheikhalishahi et al. 2019), thereby preventing or delaying the onset of disease and enhancing patient care.

11.3.11 TEXT CLASSIFICATION

Text classification categorizes texts based on their content; it automatically analyzes text and assigns specified tags or categories depending on its context. Clinical or medical text classification is complicated because medical text usually contains standardized medical terms referring to certain concepts or abbreviations used in the clinical field.

Medical text classification relieves physicians of the burden of dealing with unstructured clinical narratives (Venkataraman et al. 2020). A healthcare professional, for example, may utilize text classification to identify at-risk patients based on key terms or phrases in their medical records. ML techniques are beneficial for clinical text classification applications (Ikonomakis, Kotsiantis, and Tampakas 2005). However, an efficient ML model demands significant human labor to collect labeled training data and execute feature engineering (Y. Wang, Sohn, et al. 2019). Therefore, most research works create clinical text classification paradigms depending on deep convolutional neural networks (Hughes et al. 2017; Yao, Mao, and Luo 2019) to minimize human efforts and eliminate feature engineering requirements.

11.3.12 COGNITIVE ASSISTANT

Using AI machines to aid humans in their daily lives laid the path for cognitive assistant (CA) development. CAs are self-learning, multi-modal human–computer interfaces, and customized conversation systems that consider voice, gestures, and facial emotions (N. T. Le and Wartschinski 2018). It aims to assist humans in solving a wide range of complex tasks in various fields, from well-defined to ill-defined problems (N. T. Le, Loll, and Pinkwart 2013). Well-defined problems are the ones that have concrete objectives, optimum solution paths, or anticipated solutions and ill-defined problems are entirely contradictory to them; they lack realistic targets and defined solutions. Chatbots and CAs are two different applications except that they are both designed to aid in human–computer interaction. Chatbots are structured dialogue-based systems configured to respond to a limited number of queries and fail to respond to complex questions that are not coded into them (Kidwai and Rk 2020). On the other hand, CA analyzes emotions in natural language, allowing them to improve their communication abilities even more. In addition, some systems adopt artificial neural network models to learn from circumstances, recognize, categorize, and make predictions based on analysis.

Healthcare CA systems utilize ML, pattern recognition, and NLP programs that let clinicians connect with patients more proactively (Preum et al. 2021). The technology provides patients with automated and relevant recommendations about doctors, treatment plans, consultation decisions, and mental health support. Figure 11.6 depicts the abstract picture of user interaction with the CA system.

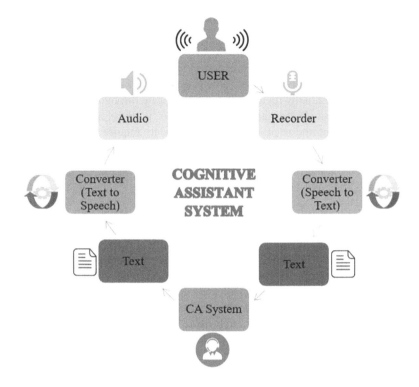

FIGURE 11.6 An overview of cognitive assistant application.

11.3.13 Automatic Speech Recognition

Automatic speech recognition (ASR) application converts human speech into a written representation. Acoustic and linguistic modeling techniques accomplish speech recognition. The former defines the relation between the audio signal and other linguistic speech sounds, and the latter links sound with a sequence of words (Chiu et al. 2018; Pakhomov, Schonwetter, and Bachenko 2001). Hidden Markov models (HMM), Gaussian mixture models (GMM), N-grams, Neural networks, and Speaker Diarization (SD) are the predominantly employed speech recognition algorithms to detect potential next words by analyzing the given input speech sounds (K. Lee and Park 2014; Kumah-Crystal et al. 2018).

The healthcare sector claims that most physicians spend a lot of time manually documenting patients' medical notes, reports, and other documents, which affects their productivity. Employing an ASR system in healthcare automates the data entry process by retrieving vital information at the time of service rather than a manual transcription of medical documents (Vogel et al. 2015). This technology frees clinicians from their time-consuming chore of documenting summary reports and helps them concentrate on diagnosing and treating patients. Apart from enhancing the clinical documentation process, ASR detects stress and anxiety in patients with psychological disorders using speech signals (Latif et al. 2021). Regardless of the benefits, speech recognition technology poses a few challenges, such as the inability to detect the exact words due to user accent, eliminating background noise during voice capture, etc. Several research works are carried out in medical ASR systems concentrating on the aforementioned factors (Mani, Palaskar, and Konam 2020).

ASR generates a digitalized record based on a patient's past medical history that the clinician may eventually review rather than navigate through several paper documents during the visit (Dodiya and Jain 2016). Thus, it allows medical practitioners to focus on providing the necessary care that patients require and guarantees that clinical documentation is precise and comprehensive.

11.4   NLP SYSTEMS IN HEALTH CARE

This section presents a list of predominantly used NLP systems in the healthcare domain to extract clinical terms from patients' EHR data (Kreimeyer et al. 2017). Table 11.2 shows the predominantly used NLP systems along with their references in the healthcare sector. Our review approach was designed to adhere to the PRISMA criteria for comprehensive literature reporting (Moher et al. 2009). The references include only the articles that have employed/compared the respective NLP system. After reviewing PRISMA recommendations, the reference papers were extracted by performing a literature query search using unique keywords and availing the advanced database search options from BioKDE (Biomedical Knowledge Discovery Engine), PubMed, Science Direct, and Google Scholar. These databases can access authentic and trustworthy resources such as Elsevier, Springer, Research Gate, etc. The popular NLP systems in the healthcare sector are visualized in a word cloud in Figure 11.7, and Figure 11.8 depicts the clinical NLP system distribution for information retrieval from 2006 to 2021.

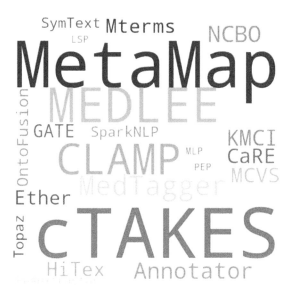

FIGURE 11.7   Word cloud visualization of the most frequently used clinical NLP system.

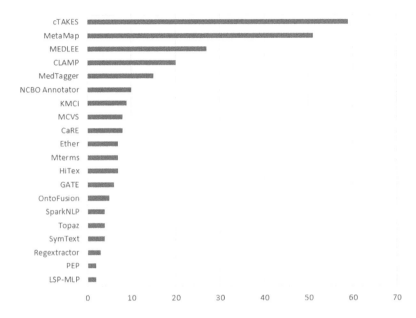

FIGURE 11.8   NLP system usage for information extraction in the biomedical domain from 2006 to 2021.

Each database has its own set of searchable fields and filtering capabilities, so slightly different search criteria were utilized based on the databases used (see Table 11.1). Aside from the parameters stated in Table 11.1, the language of

TABLE 11.1
Literature Search Criteria

Database	Search Term	Search Field	Source/ Document Type	Other Filters
BioKDE	"NLP system name"	Title or abstract	Scientific Articles & Journals	N/A
PubMed	("NLP system name") AND ((healthcare) OR (clinical NLP) OR (biomedical))	All Fields	PubMed Central (PMC) articles	Text Availability: "Full text" Year Span: "2006–2021"
Science Direct	"NLP system name," healthcare OR Clinical NLP OR biomedical	Journal or Book Title, abstract or author-specified keywords	Research Articles, Book Chapters, Journals	Year(s): "2006–2021"
Google Scholar	"NLP system name" AND "healthcare" OR "Biomedical"	General search option	Scholarly Journals, Research Articles, Conference Papers & Proceedings	Type: "include citations" Custom range: "2006–2021"

publications was also restricted to English in all four database searches. The search terms used include the relevant system name, "biomedical," "Healthcare," and "Clinical NLP." The publications were narrowed down for each NLP system in the Mendeley software, and the "Check for Duplicates" feature examined all fields for probable duplicates and deleted them. To get the final set of articles, a manual review of the titles and abstracts of the remaining papers was performed. The search time-frame was from January 2006 to December 2021 (Table 11.2).

TABLE 11.2
NLP Systems Employed in the Clinical Sector for Information Extraction from Medical Documents

Sl. No.	NLP System Name	Purpose	Reference
1	CaRE (Category/ Concept And Relationship Extractor)	The CaRE system focuses on patient-physician discussions; this technology produces structured data that accurately represents patients' medical circumstances. For instance, it records the conversation during a patient's clinical visit, locates clinically significant words in the recognized speech, and summarizes them into a draft of the interaction note. In addition to processing post-discharge reports and other clinical information, this system's only purpose is to assist physicians during consultations.	Klann and Szolovits (2009); Kocaballi et al. (2020); Quiroz et al. (2019); Willis and Jarrahi (2019); Schloss and Konam (2020); Molenaar et al. (2020); Islam et al. (2010); Y. Xu et al. (2012)

(Continued)

TABLE 11.2 (*Continued*)
NLP Systems Employed in the Clinical Sector for Information Extraction from Medical Documents

Sl. No.	NLP System Name	Purpose	Reference
2	cTAKES (Clinical Text Analysis Knowledge Extraction System)	cTAKES is a free and open-source system that uses the Unstructured Information Management Architecture (UIMA) architecture to retrieve clinical entities like prescription drugs, signs/symptoms, diseases/disorders, and treatment plans. Medical decision support systems and medical trials can benefit from this method's extensive linguistic and semantic labels. It is specifically used to extract clinical entities from breast cancer patients' chest CT scans, radiology reports, and other medical records.	Savova et al. (2010); Q. Li et al. (2015); Tianyong Hao (2015); S. Zheng, Wang, and Lu (2013); Cui et al. (2012); T. Cai et al. (2016); Alawieh et al. (2014); Piliouras et al. (2013); H. Xu et al. (2011); Savova et al. (2012); S. T. Wu et al. (2013); Saeed Hassanpoura (2016); Lin et al. (2015); Pathak et al. (2011, 2013); Susan Rea et al. (2012); Kersloot et al. (2019); Reátegui and Ratté (2018); Timothy Miller, Dmitriy Dligach, Steven Bethard, Chen Lin (2017); Cuzzola, Jovanović, and Bagheri (2017); C. Liu et al. (2019); Yan et al. (2016); Reátegui et al. (2019); Miller, Avillach, and Mandl (2020); Digan et al. (2021); Tseytlin et al. (2016); Collier, Oellrich, and Groza (2015); Fan et al. (2019); Griffis et al. (2016); Joshua et al. (2016); Weng et al. (2017); Khalifa and Meystre (2015); Peng et al. (2020); Wadia et al. (2018); Oellrich et al. (2015); K. Xu et al. (2018); Park et al. (2016); Zolnoori et al. (2019); Tulkens et al. (2019); Alfattni et al. (2020); Buchan et al. (2017); Castro et al. (2017); Hong et al. (2019); Koola et al. (2018); Hassanzadeh, Karimi, and Nguyen (2020); Scheurwegs et al. (2017); Segura-Bedmar et al. (2018); Badger et al. (2019); Y. Wu et al. (2012); Alfattni et al. (2021); Bompelli, Silverman, et al. (2020); Rahman et al. (2020); Redjdal et al. (2021a); Dreyfus et al. (2021); Tsuji et al. (2021); Sahoo et al. (2021); Abbas et al. (2021); Ganoe et al. (2021); Bai et al. (2021)

(Continued)

TABLE 11.2 (*Continued*)
NLP Systems Employed in the Clinical Sector for Information Extraction from Medical Documents

Sl. No.	NLP System Name	Purpose	Reference
3	GATE (General Architecture for Text Engineering)	GATE is a free, open-source software toolkit compatible with all modern operating systems and licensed under GNU open-source license. It provides a conceptual framework and a plethora of essential plugins for clinical NLP systems and can handle nearly any text processing challenges. It is mainly used to retrieve basic details from pharmacological patent documents and psychological state test scores and date information from mental health care data.	Cunningham et al. (2013); Klann and Szolovits (2009); Digan et al. (2021); Iqbal et al. (2015); Hernandez-Boussard et al. (2017, 2019)
4	LSP-MLP (Linguistic String Project- Medical Language Processor)	LSP is a medical language processing system with a rule-based interface that can handle input in several languages. The LSP-MLP is intended to assist doctors in extracting and summarizing sign/symptom details, and medicine doses and identifying probable pharmaceutical adverse reactions from Dutch medical reports like clinical records, x-ray reports, and discharge summaries and transform them into SNOMED (Systemized Nomenclature of Medicine) codes.	Alawieh et al. (2014); Baechle et al. (2017)

(Continued)

TABLE 11.2 (*Continued*)
NLP Systems Employed in the Clinical Sector for Information Extraction from Medical Documents

Sl. No.	NLP System Name	Purpose	Reference
5	MedLEE (Medical Language Extraction and Encoding System)	MedLEE is an open-source rule-based NLP system designed to transform the medical narrative text into structured information that may be utilized in a wide range of clinical research and applications. Clinical reports may now be structured and encoded with the help of MedLEE. It was initially developed to handle chest x-ray results, but it was later expanded to incorporate mammography and pathology reports. Recent research expands MedLEE's scope to extract medication information from discharge summaries.	Carol et al. (2006); Cui et al. (2012); T. Cai et al. (2016); Alawieh et al. (2014); H. Xu et al. (2011); Saeed Hassanpoura (2016); Johnson et al. (2008); E. S. Chen, Hripcsak, and Friedman (2006); Hripcsak et al. (2007, 2009); Hyun et al. (2009); L. Li et al. (2008); Morrison et al. (2009); Peissig et al. (2012); Salmasian et al. (2013); K. Yadav et al. (2013); K. Yadav et al. (2016); C. Liu et al. (2019); Chiang et al. (2010); Y. Wu et al. (2012); Haerian et al. (2012); Sevenster et al. (2012); Chase et al. (2017); Boyd et al. (2018); Y. Wu et al. (2018); Son et al. (2018); Posada et al. (2017)
6	MedTagger	MedTagger is an open-source platform for collaboratively annotating clinical datasets. It includes several applications, including dictionaries-based indexing, pattern-based information extraction, and ML-based named entity identification. It was designed to extract UMLS (Unified Medical Language System) term mentions (like symptom, treatment, drug name, etc.) from clinical narratives, radiology reports, and neuroimaging scans.	Moon et al. (2019); H. Liu et al. (2012); Y. Wang, Mehrabi, et al. (2019); Fu et al. (2019); Wagholikar et al. (2013); Zhu et al. (2015); Sheikhalishahi et al. (2019); Morid et al. (2016); Chaudhry et al. (2018); Hong et al. (2016); F. Shen et al. (2019); University, Utah, and Carolina (2015); Y. Wang et al. (2016); N. Afzal et al. (2017); Sahoo et al. (2021)

(*Continued*)

TABLE 11.2 (*Continued*)
NLP Systems Employed in the Clinical Sector for Information Extraction from Medical Documents

SI. No.	NLP System Name	Purpose	Reference
7	MetaMap	MetaMap is an open-source rule-based NLP system initially developed for data extraction from medical and biological literature manuscripts. It is now being used to retrieve and map biomedical content from patient records to the suitable UMLS Metathesaurus or detect Metathesaurus concepts mentioned in English text equivalently.	Aronson and Lang (2010); Venkataraman et al. (2020); Martinez et al. (2014); Lowe et al. (2009); T. Cai et al. (2016); Alawieh et al. (2014); Lam et al. (2016); H. Liu et al. (2012); Ly et al. (2018); Reátegui and Ratté (2018); Cuzzola, Jovanović, and Bagheri (2017); C. Liu et al. (2019); Peng et al. (2020); Oellrich et al. (2015); K. Xu et al. (2018); Y. Wu et al. (2012); Son et al. (2018); Dilthey et al. (2019); Simon et al. (2018); Justyna (2020); Xing, Luo, and Song (2020); Savery et al. (2020); Y. F. Luo, Sun, and Rumshisky (2019); Sabbir, Jimeno-Yepes, and Kavuluru (2017); Sung, Lin, and Hu (2020); Z. Zeng, Yao, et al. (2019); Hanauer et al. (2020); Z. H. Luo et al. (2020); Z. Zeng et al. (2018); Guo et al. (2020); J. Chen, Zheng, and Yu (2016); Abulaish, Parwez, and Jahiruddin (2019); Bompelli, Silverman, et al. (2020); Rahman et al. (2020); Redjdal et al. (2021b); Sahoo et al. (2021); Abbas et al. (2021); Shah-Mohammadi, Cui, and Finkelstein (2021b); Davoodijam et al. (2021); Buckland, Hogan, and Chen (2020); Karagounis, Sarkar, and Chen (2020); J. Wu et al. (2021); Havrilla et al. (2021); Shannon et al. (2021); Deng et al. (2021); X. Luo et al. (2021); Naseri et al. (2021); Bai et al. (2021)

(*Continued*)

TABLE 11.2 (*Continued*)

NLP Systems Employed in the Clinical Sector for Information Extraction from Medical Documents

Sl. No.	NLP System Name	Purpose	Reference
8	MCVS (Multithreaded Clinical Vocabulary Server)	MCVS focuses on using the Systematized Nomenclature of Medicine-Clinical Terms (SNOMED-CT) to capture health-related data's semantics and enable successful clinical data capture to enhance patient care. The MCVS system is a rule-based natural language processing (NLP) system designed to retrieve SNOMED-CT terms from chest radiography reports, CT scans, and other medical reports.	T. Cai et al. (2016); Henry et al. (2013); P. L. Elkin et al. (2009); L. Elkin (2012); Gobbel et al. (2014); A. P. L. Elkin et al. (2008); Garvin et al. (2013); Gaudet-Blavignac et al. (2021)
9	NCBO Annotator (National Center for Biomedical Ontology Annotator)	The NCBO Annotator (previously known as the Open Biomedical Annotator (OBA)) allows the biomedical sector to automatically annotate/ label raw data to ontology concepts (SNOMED-CT, UMLS, and RxNorm). It is an ontology-based Web service that uses text information to label publically available datasets with biomedical ontology terms. The NCBO Annotator links keywords relevant to medication and disease ontologies with medical concepts from UMLS and RxNorm in the patient records, pathology, and radiology reports.	Huang et al. (2014); Cole et al. (2013); Oellrich et al. (2015); Hassanzadeh, Karimi, and Nguyen (2020); Tchechmedjiev et al. (2018); Kelahan, Kalaria, and Filice (2017); Filice and Kahn (2019); Hu et al. (2018); Lobo, Lamurias, and Couto (2017); Hassanzadeh, Nguyen, and Verspoor (2019)

(*Continued*)

TABLE 11.2 (*Continued*)
NLP Systems Employed in the Clinical Sector for Information Extraction from Medical Documents

Sl. No.	NLP System Name	Purpose	Reference
10	Regextractor	Regextractor is an open-source rule-based NLP system to parse, abstract, and assemble structured data from textual metadata in electronic health records. It has its major implementation in retrieving numeric values from PFT (pulmonary function test) reports, cardiac catheterization, and echocardiography data, thereby allowing clinicians and bioinformatics researchers to perform research/ analysis.	Hinchcliff et al. (2012); Kim et al. (2020); Akgün et al. (2020)
11	CLAMP (Clinical Language Annotation, Modeling, and Processing)	CLAMP is an open-source NLP system that allows the automated detection and encoding of medical data in narrative healthcare reports. This system is available in two forms: CLAMP-CMD and CLAMP-GUI. The former is a command-line application that implements cutting-edge methodologies for obtaining biomedical concepts from the medical text. The latter presents a graphical user interface (GUI) for effectively constructing Clinical NLP pipelines for specific applications.	D. Van Le et al. (2018); Soysal et al. (2018); Cooley-Rieders and Zheng (2021); Digan et al. (2021); Peng et al. (2020); Soysal et al. (2019); Redman et al. (2017); Wei et al. (2019); Sulieman, Robinson, and Jackson (2020); Alfattni et al. (2021); Bompelli, Silverman, et al. (2020); Bompelli, Li, et al. (2020); Oliveira et al. (2020); Q. Chen et al. (2020); Rahman et al. (2020); Sahoo et al. (2021); J. M. Wang et al. (2020); Shah-Mohammadi, Cui, and Finkelstein (2021a); Bai et al. (2021); S. Chen et al. (2021)

(*Continued*)

TABLE 11.2 (*Continued*)
NLP Systems Employed in the Clinical Sector for Information Extraction from Medical Documents

Sl. No.	NLP System Name	Purpose	Reference
12	KMCI (Knowledge Map Concept Indexer)	The KMCI is the underlying NLP engine used in the Knowledge Map system. It was initially developed to improve the content delivery of medical education to staff and students but later expanded to accommodate a wide variety of clinical and genetic research investigations. The system retrieves biomedical terms from a range of clinical databases, comprising medical records, ECG findings, healthcare portals, and associates them with the UMLS concepts.	Y. Wu et al. (2018); Zhao et al. (2021b, 2021a); Denny et al. (2005); Denny, Bastarache, et al. (2009); Y. Chen et al. (2014); Denny, Miller, et al. (2009); Denny et al. (2010); Denny, Peterson, et al. (2009)
13	SymText/ Mplus (Symbolic Text Processor)	SPRUS was the initial system, and it progressed into SymText (Symbolic Text Processor), and the most recent version of the system is termed MPLUS (M++). SymText system defines a formal paradigm for encoding free clinical text data by integrating syntax and semantics. This system was created with the sole purpose of extracting key findings like disease and drug mentions from chest radiograph reports using Bayesian networks as a context model.	T. Cai et al. (2016); Alawieh et al. (2014); Saeed Hassanpoura (2016); E. S. Chen, Hripcsak, and Friedman (2006)

(*Continued*)

TABLE 11.2 *(Continued)*

NLP Systems Employed in the Clinical Sector for Information Extraction from Medical Documents

Sl. No.	NLP System Name	Purpose	Reference
14	HiTex (Health Information Text Extraction)	HITEx is an open-source NLP system based on GATE architecture. It includes a set of Gate plugins designed to handle challenges in the healthcare sector, like extraction of primary diagnoses, discharge prescriptions, and lifestyle factors. This system is designed to extract critical findings like diagnostic procedures and family medical history from discharge summaries and other clinical reports.	Alawieh et al. (2014); L Zhou et al. (2014); Liao et al. (2015); Q. T. Zeng et al. (2006); Murphy et al. (2009); Liao et al. (2010); Z. Zeng, Deng, et al. (2019)
15	TOPAZ	Topaz is a pipeline-based NLP system that utilizes deduction rules to retrieve domain-specific medical observations and their modifiers from patient records. The modifier includes whether the observation is missing or prevalent, current or historical, or perceived by the patient or a family member. Along with the rules, the Topaz system uses pattern matching techniques to capture and normalize symptoms like cough, sore throat, and fever from clinical text.	Ye et al. (2014); Ferraro et al. (2017); Chapman et al. (2010); López Pineda et al. (2015)

(Continued)

TABLE 11.2 (*Continued*)
NLP Systems Employed in the Clinical Sector for Information Extraction from Medical Documents

Sl. No.	NLP System Name	Purpose	Reference
16	MTERMS (Medical Text Extraction, Reasoning and Mapping System)	MTERMS is a rule-based NLP system that retrieves pharmaceutical knowledge from healthcare records to allow real-time medication management and supports a spectrum of medical informatics applications and programs. The core functionalities of the system include the extraction of various clinical entities(like diagnoses, prescription drugs, signs/ symptoms, and social-behavioral information) from unstructured medical reports, the encoding of derived data using conventional clinical terminology (like RxNorm, SNOMED-CT, and ICD-9/10), and producing standardized output (HL7 document format).	L. Zhou et al. (2014); Li Zhou et al. (2012, 2011); Goss et al. (2014); Li Zhou et al. (2015); Topaz et al. (2016); Blackley et al. (2020)
17	OntoFusion	OntoFusion is an ontology-based NLP system that is intended for information extraction and the integration of biomedical databases. It creates a logical data schema by inferring relationships between data and integrating them in clinical trial documentation and biomedical research.	M. Garcia-Remesal, V. Maojo, H. Billhardt (2010); Pérez-Rey et al. (2006); García-Remesal et al. (2007); Alonso-Calvo et al. (2007); Maojo et al. (2007)

(*Continued*)

TABLE 11.2 (*Continued*)

NLP Systems Employed in the Clinical Sector for Information Extraction from Medical Documents

Sl. No.	NLP System Name	Purpose	Reference
18	PEP (Pathology Extraction Pipeline)	PEP is an open-source rule-based NLP system for extracting information from pathology reports with the objective of storing the information in a research database. PEP is constructed on the UIMA paradigm (Unstructured Information Management Architecture), which accepts semi-structured textual pathology records as input, retrieves the relevant entities, and integrates the derived data into the database. This system is used to extract features from reports on lung, prostate, and breast cancer.	Ashish et al. (2014); J. Lee et al. (2018)
19	Spark NLP	Spark NLP toolkit is an extended version of Spark ML with a deep learning framework. The open-source version of Spark NLP provides rudimentary information extraction functionalities, but the licensed version handles real-world healthcare issues. Spark NLP for Healthcare is a commercial version of Spark NLP that allows you to mine medical and biological content. It also includes nearly 50 pre-trained healthcare models for Named Entity recognition that can detect clinical entities like medicines, risk factors, anatomical structures, demographic factors, and confidential information from medical documents.	Kocaman and Talby (2021b, 2021a); Mayer et al. (2018); Z. Shen, Wang, and Spruit (2019)

(*Continued*)

TABLE 11.2 (*Continued*)
NLP Systems Employed in the Clinical Sector for Information Extraction from Medical Documents

SI. No.	NLP System Name	Purpose	Reference
20	ETHER (Event-based Text-mining of Health Electronic Records)	ETHER is a complex rule-based NLP system that retrieves medical concepts and temporal relationships from adverse event narratives contained in Post Market Surveillance (PMS) report. The system primarily extracts clinical entities (like vaccination details, family medical history, preliminary diagnosis, or secondary diagnosis) from medical reports and maps them to MedDRA (Medical Dictionary for Regulatory Activities) terminology.	Ly et al. (2018); Ball et al. (2018); Spiker et al. (2020); Botsis et al. (2017); Kreimeyer et al. (2021); Pandey et al. (2019); Botsis et al. (2016)

11.5 CONCLUSION

The healthcare system contains a deluge of unstructured patient data such as physician case notes, written prescriptions, laboratory reports, discharge summaries, etc. This information is generally stored in varied formats across different platforms, making it difficult for systems to comprehend and make useful inferences. To alleviate the problem, the concept of EHR and Fast Healthcare Interoperability Resources (FHIR) compliance for structuring clinical information was introduced. Albeit several measures to structure the information, it is still difficult for automated or AI-based systems to grasp the key information's content at a glance or in minimal time. CNLP methods can analyze unstructured healthcare data, interpret their grammatical structure to identify the context of the data, and translate it so that the EHR systems can readily process it. At the same time, these approaches lower healthcare costs while still improving efficiency. For any clinical NLP research, background knowledge is essential, and the UMLS is a significant element for the same in most NLP systems. Several CNLP systems tend to be dominated by rule-based methods that leverage the UMLS. Traditionally, rule-based NLP systems have performed well in certain fields and document categories, including hospital discharge summaries and radiology reports. One of the significant benefits of applying a rule-based strategy to any clinical text is that rules are straightforward to modify. In light of this, this article conducts a systematic analysis of the components and stages of an NLP system, discusses NLP applications in the healthcare domain, and offers a synopsis of predominantly used CNLP systems. This article can be used as guidance for researchers in the field of clinical NLP.

Statements and Declarations

Conflict of Interest: The authors declare no competing interests.

REFERENCES

Abacha, Asma Ben, and Pierre Zweigenbaum. 2015. "MEANS: A Medical Question-Answering System Combining NLP Techniques and Semantic Web Technologies." *Information Processing and Management* 51 (5): 570–94. https://doi.org/10.1016/j.ipm.2015.04.006.

Abbas, Asim, Muhammad Afzal, Jamil Hussain, Taqdir Ali, Hafiz Syed Muhammad Bilal, Sungyoung Lee, and Seokhee Jeon. 2021. "Clinical Concept Extraction with Lexical Semantics to Support Automatic Annotation." *International Journal of Environmental Research and Public Health* 18 (20): 10564. https://doi.org/10.3390/IJERPH182010564.

Abed, Amira Hassan, Essam M Shaaban, Om Prakash Jena, and Ahmed A. Elngar. 2022. "A Comprehensive Survey on Breast Cancer Thermography Classification Using Deep Neural Network." *Machine Learning and Deep Learning in Medical Data Analytics and Healthcare Applications*, January, 169–82. https://doi.org/10.1201/9781003226147-9.

Abulaish, Muhammad, Md Aslam Parwez, and Jahiruddin. 2019. "DiseaSE: A Biomedical Text Analytics System for Disease Symptom Extraction and Characterization." *Journal of Biomedical Informatics* 100 (October): 103324. https://doi.org/10.1016/j.jbi.2019.103324.

Afzal, Muhammad, Fakhare Alam, Khalid Mahmood Malik, and Ghaus M Malik. 2020. "A Clinical Context-Aware Automated Summarization Using Deep Neural Network: Model Development and Validation." *Journal of Medical Internet Research* 22 (10). https://doi.org/10.2196/19810.

Afzal, Naveed, Sunghwan Sohn, Sara Abram, Christopher G. Scott, Rajeev Chaudhry, Hongfang Liu, Iftikhar J. Kullo, and Adelaide M. Arruda-Olson. 2017. "Identifying Peripheral Arterial Disease Cases Using Natural Language Processing of Clinical Notes." *Journal of Vascular Surgery* 65 (6): 1753–61. https://doi.org/10.1016/j.jvs.2016.11.031.

Akgün, Kathleen M., Keith Sigel, Kei Hoi Cheung, Farah Kidwai-Khan, Alex K. Bryant, Cynthia Brandt, Amy Justice, and Kristina Crothers. 2020. "Extracting Lung Function Measurements to Enhance Phenotyping of Chronic Obstructive Pulmonary Disease (COPD) In an Electronic Health Record Using Automated Tools." *PLoS ONE* 15 (1): 1–10. https://doi.org/10.1371/journal.pone.0227730.

Alawieh, Ali, Zahraa Sabra, Amaly Nokkari, Atlal El-assaad, Stefania Mondello, Fadi Zaraket, Bilal Fadlallah, and Firas H Kobeissy. 2014. "Natural Language Processing in Biomedicine : A Unifi Ed System Architecture Overview." *Clinical Bioinformatics* 1168 (1): 263–73. https://doi.org/10.1007/978-1-4939-0847-9.

Alfattni, Ghada, Maksim Belousov, Niels Peek, and Goran Nenadic. 2021. "Extracting Drug Names and Associated Attributes from Discharge Summaries: Text Mining Study." *JMIR Medical Informatics* 9 (5). https://doi.org/10.2196/24678.

Alfattni, Ghada, Niels Peek, and Goran Nenadic. 2020. "Extraction of Temporal Relations from Clinical Free Text: A Systematic Review of Current Approaches." *Journal of Biomedical Informatics* 108 (July): 103488. https://doi.org/10.1016/j.jbi.2020.103488.

Alonso-Calvo, R., V Maojo, H Billhardt, F. Martin-Sanchez, M. García-Remesal, and D. Pérez-Rey. 2007. "An Agent- and Ontology-Based System for Integrating Public Gene, Protein, and Disease Databases." *Journal of Biomedical Informatics* 40 (1): 17–29. https://doi.org/10.1016/j.jbi.2006.02.014.

Andrenucci, Andrea. 2008. "Automated Question-Answering Techniques and the Medical Domain." *HEALTHINF 2008-1st International Conference on Health Informatics, Proceedings*, 2: 207–12. https://doi.org/10.5220/0001044202070212.

Aronson, Alan R. 2001. "Effective Mapping of Biomedical Text to the UMLS Metathesaurus: The MetaMap Program." *Proceedings / AMIA... Annual Symposium. AMIA Symposium*: 17–21.

Aronson, Alan R, and François Michel Lang. 2010. "An Overview of MetaMap: Historical Perspective and Recent Advances." *Journal of the American Medical Informatics Association* 17 (3): 229–36. https://doi.org/10.1136/jamia.2009.002733.

Ashish, Naveen, Lisa Dahm, and Charles Boicey. 2014. "University of California, Irvine-Pathology Extraction Pipeline: The Pathology Extraction Pipeline for Information Extraction from Pathology Reports." *Health Informatics Journal* 20 (4): 288–305. https://doi.org/10.1177/1460458213494032.

Aswathy, K. P., R. Rathi, and Shyam Shankar E. P. 2019. "NLP Based Segmentation Protocol for Predicting Diseases and Finding Doctors." *International Research Journal of Engineering and Technology (IRJET)* 06 (02): 737–39.

Badger, Jonathan, Eric LaRose, John Mayer, Fereshteh Bashiri, David Page, and Peggy Peissig. 2019. "Machine Learning for Phenotyping Opioid Overdose Events." *Journal of Biomedical Informatics* 94 (July 2018): 103185. https://doi.org/10.1016/j.jbi.2019.103185.

Baechle, C., Agarwal, A. & Zhu, X. 2017. "Big Data Driven Co-Occurring Evidence Discovery in Chronic Obstructive Pulmonary Disease Patients." *Journal of Big Data* 4 (9). https://doi.org/10.1186/s40537-017-0067-6.

Bai, Lu, Maurice D. Mulvenna, Zhibao Wang, and Raymond Bond. 2021. "Clinical Entity Extraction: Comparison between MetaMap, CTAKES, CLAMP and Amazon Comprehend Medical." *2021 32nd Irish Signals and Systems Conference, ISSC 2021*, June. https://doi.org/10.1109/ISSC52156.2021.9467856.

Ball, Robert, Sengwee Toh, Jamie Nolan, Kevin Haynes, Richard Forshee, and Taxiarchis Botsis. 2018. "Evaluating Automated Approaches to Anaphylaxis Case Classification Using Unstructured Data from the FDA Sentinel System." *Pharmacoepidemiology and Drug Safety* 27 (10): 1077–84. https://doi.org/10.1002/pds.4645.

Basyal, Ganga Prasad, Bhaskar P Rimal, and David Zeng. 2020. "A Systematic Review of Natural Language Processing for Knowledge Management in Healthcare." *Computer Science & Information Technology (CS & IT)*, 275–85. https://doi.org/10.5121/csit.2020.100921.

Behera, Pitambar, and Om Prakash Jena. 2021. "Domain Adaptation of Parts of Speech Annotators in Hindi Biomedical Corpus: An NLP Approach." *Computational Intelligence and Healthcare Informatics*, October, 377–91. https://doi.org/10.1002/9781119818717.CH20.

Bennet Praba, M. S., Sagari Sen, Chailshi Chauhan, and Divya Singh. 2019. "Ai Healthcare Interactive Talking Agent Using Nlp." *International Journal of Innovative Technology and Exploring Engineering* 9 (1): 3470–73. https://doi.org/10.35940/ijitee.A4915.119119.

Bessmertny, I. A., A V Platonov, E A Poleschuk, and Ma Pengyu. 2017. "Syntactic Text Analysis without a Dictionary." *Application of Information and Communication Technologies, AICT 2016- Conference Proceedings*. https://doi.org/10.1109/ICAICT.2016.7991677.

Blackley, Suzanne V, Erin MacPhaul, Bianca Martin, Wenyu Song, Joji Suzuki, and Li Zhou. 2020. "Using Natural Language Processing and Machine Learning to Identify Hospitalized Patients with Opioid Use Disorder." *AMIA... Annual Symposium Proceedings. AMIA Symposium 2020*: 233–42.

Bompelli, Anusha, Jianfu Li, Yiqi Xu, Nan Wang, Yanshan Wang, Terrence Adam, Zhe He, and Rui Zhang. 2020a. "Deep Learning Approach to Parse Eligibility Criteria in Dietary Supplements Clinical Trials Following OMOP Common Data Model." *AMIA... Annual Symposium Proceedings. AMIA Symposium* 2020 (September): 243–52. https://doi.org/10.1101/2020.09.16.20196022.

Bompelli, Anusha, Greg Silverman, Raymond Finzel, Jake Vasilakes, Benjamin Knoll, Serguei Pakhomov, and Rui Zhang. 2020b. "Comparing NLP Systems to Extract Entities of Eligibility Criteria in Dietary Supplements Clinical Trials Using NLP-ADAPT." In *Lecture Notes in Computer Science (Including Subseries Lecture Notes in Artificial Intelligence and Lecture Notes in Bioinformatics)*, 12299 LNAI: 67–77. Springer International Publishing. https://doi.org/10.1007/978-3-030-59137-3_7.

Botsis, Taxiarchis, Matthew Foster, Nina Arya, Kory Kreimeyer, Abhishek Pandey, and Deepa Arya. 2017. "Application of Natural Language Processing and Network Analysis Techniques to Post-Market Reports for the Evaluation of Dose-Related Anti-Thymocyte Globulin Safety Patterns." *Applied Clinical Informatics* 8 (2): 396–411. https://doi.org/10.4338/ACI-2016-10-RA-0169.

Botsis, Taxiarchis, Christopher Jankosky, Deepa Arya, Kory Kreimeyer, Matthew Foster, Abhishek Pandey, Wei Wang, et al. 2016. "Decision Support Environment for Medical Product Safety Surveillance." *Journal of Biomedical Informatics* 64: 354–62. https://doi.org/10.1016/j.jbi.2016.07.023.

Boyd, Andrew D., Karen Dunn Lopez, Camillo Lugaresi, Tamara Macieira, Vanessa Sousa, Sabita Acharya, Abhinaya Balasubramanian, et al. 2018. "Physician Nurse Care: A New Use of UMLS to Measure Professional Contribution." *International Journal of Medical Informatics* 113 (1): 63–71. https://doi.org/10.1016/j.ijmedinf.2018.02.002.

Breuel, Thomas M., Adnan Ul-Hasan, Mayce Ali Al-Azawi, and Faisal Shafait. 2013. "High-Performance OCR for Printed English and Fraktur Using Lstm Networks." *Proceedings of the International Conference on Document Analysis and Recognition, ICDAR*: 683–87. https://doi.org/10.1109/ICDAR.2013.140.

Buchan, Kevin, Michele Filannino, and Özlem Uzuner. 2017. "Automatic Prediction of Coronary Artery Disease from Clinical Narratives." *Journal of Biomedical Informatics* 72: 23–32. https://doi.org/10.1016/j.jbi.2017.06.019.

Buckland, Ryan S, Joseph W Hogan, and Elizabeth S Chen. 2020. "Selection of Clinical Text Features for Classifying Suicide Attempts." *AMIA... Annual Symposium Proceedings. AMIA Symposium 2020*: 273–82. https://www.ncbi.nlm.nih.gov/pubmed/33936399.

Cai, Meng. 2021. "Natural Language Processing for Urban Research: A Systematic Review." *Heliyon*. Elsevier Ltd. https://doi.org/10.1016/j.heliyon.2021.e06322.

Cai, Tianrun, Andreas A. Giannopoulos, Sheng Yu, Tatiana Kelil, Beth Ripley, Kanako K. Kumamaru, Frank J. Rybicki, and Dimitrios Mitsouras. 2016. "Natural Language Processing Technologies in Radiology Research and Clinical Applications." *Radiographics* 36 (1): 176–91. https://doi.org/10.1148/rg.2016150080.

Cairns, Brian L, Rodney D Nielsen, James J Masanz, James H Martin, Martha S Palmer, Wayne H Ward, and Guergana K Savova. 2011. "The MiPACQ Clinical Question Answering System." *AMIA... Annual Symposium Proceedings / AMIA Symposium. AMIA Symposium 2011*: 171–80.

Carol, Friedman, Tara Borlawsky, Lyudmila Shagina, Hongmei R. Xing, and Yves A. Lussier. 2006. "Bio-Ontologies and Text: Bridging the Modeling Gap Between." *Bioinformatics* 22 (19): 2421–29. https://doi.org/10.1093/bioinformatics/btl405.Bio-Ontologies.

Castro, Sergio M., Eugene Tseytlin, Olga Medvedeva, Kevin Mitchell, Shyam Visweswaran, Tanja Bekhuis, and Rebecca S. Jacobson. 2017. "Automated Annotation and Classification of BI-RADS Assessment from Radiology Reports." *Journal of Biomedical Informatics* 69: 177–87. https://doi.org/10.1016/j.jbi.2017.04.011.

Chakravarthi, R. Ravi, and E. Chandra. 2017. "Digital Signature Representation Using SOM Method in OCR Technique." *International Journal of Latest Engineering and Management Research (IJLEMR)* 02 (08): 1–11.

Chan, Katherine Redfield, Xinghua Lou, Theofanis Karaletsos, Christopher Crosbie, Stuart Gardos, David Artz, and Gunnar Ratsch. 2013. "An Empirical Analysis of Topic Modeling for Mining Cancer Clinical Notes." In *Proceedings - IEEE 13th International Conference on Data Mining Workshops, ICDMW 2013:* 56–63. https://doi.org/10.1109/ICDMW.2013.91.

Chapman, W., M. Conway, J. Dowling, R. Tsui, Q. Li, L. M. Christensen, and H. Harkema. 2010. "Challenges in Adapting an NLP System for Real-Time Surveillance." *Conference of the International Society for Disease Surveillance.* https://doi.org/10.3134/ehtj.10.068.

Chase, Herbert S., Lindsey R. Mitrani, Gabriel G. Lu, and Dominick J. Fulgieri. 2017. "Early Recognition of Multiple Sclerosis Using Natural Language Processing of the Electronic Health Record." *BMC Medical Informatics and Decision Making* 17 (1): 24. https://doi.org/10.1186/s12911-017-0418-4.

Chatterjee, Riddhi, Ratula Ray, Satya Ranjan Dash, and Om Prakash Jena. 2021. "Conceptualizing Tomorrow's Healthcare Through Digitization." *Computational Intelligence and Healthcare Informatics*, October, 359–76. https://doi.org/10.1002/9781119818717.CH19.

Chaudhry, Alisha P., Naveed Afzal, Mohamed M. Abidian, Vishnu Priya Mallipeddi, Ravikumar K. Elayavilli, Christopher G. Scott, Iftikhar J. Kullo, et al. 2018. "Innovative Informatics Approaches for Peripheral Artery Disease: Current State and Provider Survey of Strategies for Improving Guideline-Based Care." *Mayo Clinic Proceedings: Innovations, Quality & Outcomes* 2 (2): 129–36. https://doi.org/10.1016/j.mayocpiqo.2018.02.001.

Chen, Elizabeth S, George Hripcsak, and Carol Friedman. 2006. "Disseminating Natural Language Processed Clinical Narratives." *AMIA... Annual Symposium Proceedings / AMIA Symposium. AMIA Symposium*: 126–30.

Chen, Jinying, Jiaping Zheng, and Hong Yu. 2016. "Finding Important Terms for Patients in Their Electronic Health Records: A Learning-to-Rank Approach Using Expert Annotations." *JMIR Medical Informatics* 4 (4). https://doi.org/10.2196/medinform.6373.

Chen, Qingyu, Jingcheng Du, Sun Kim, W John Wilbur, and Zhiyong Lu. 2020. "Deep Learning with Sentence Embeddings Pre-Trained on Biomedical Corpora Improves the Performance of Finding Similar Sentences in Electronic Medical Records." *BMC Medical Informatics and Decision Making* 20 (Suppl 1): 1–11. https://doi.org/10.1186/s12911-020-1044-0.

Chen, Suhao, Tuan Dung Le, Thanh Thieu, Zhuqi Miao, Phuong D. Nguyen, and Andrew Gin. 2021. "Computer-Assisted Medical Billing Information Extraction: Comparing Rule-Based and End-to-End Transfer Learning Approaches." *Proceedings -2021 IEEE/ACM Conference on Connected Health: Applications, Systems and Engineering Technologies, CHASE 2021*: 132–33. https://doi.org/10.1109/CHASE52844.2021.00031.

Chen, Yukun, Jesse Wrenn, Hua Xu, Anderson Spickard, Ralf Habermann, James Powers, and Joshua C Denny. 2014. "Automated Assessment of Medical Students' Clinical Exposures According to AAMC Geriatric Competencies." *AMIA... Annual Symposium Proceedings / AMIA Symposium. AMIA Symposium 2014*: 375–84.

Chiang, Jung Hsien, Jou Wei Lin, and Chen Wei Yang. 2010. "Automated Evaluation of Electronic Discharge Notes to Assess Quality of Care for Cardiovascular Diseases Using Medical Language Extraction And Encoding System (MedLEE)." *Journal of the American Medical Informatics Association* 17 (3): 245–52. https://doi.org/10.1136/jamia.2009.000182.

Chintalapudi, Nalini, Gopi Battineni, Marzio Di Canio, Getu Gamo Sagaro, and Francesco Amenta. 2021. "Text Mining with Sentiment Analysis on Seafarers' Medical Documents." *International Journal of Information Management Data Insights* 1 (1): 100005. https://doi.org/10.1016/j.jjimei.2020.100005.

Chiu, Chung Cheng, Anshuman Tripathi, Katherine Chou, Chris Co, Navdeep Jaitly, Diana Jaunzeikare, Anjuli Kannan, et al. 2018. "Speech Recognition for Medical Conversations." In *Proceedings of the Annual Conference of the International Speech Communication Association, INTERSPEECH*: 2972–76. https://doi.org/10.21437/Interspeech.2018-40.

Chiudinelli, Lorenzo, Arianna Dagliati, Valentina Tibollo, Sara Albasini, Nophar Geifman, Niels Peek, John H Holmes, et al. 2020. "Mining Post-Surgical Care Processes in Breast Cancer Patients." *Artificial Intelligence in Medicine* 105 (April): 101855. https://doi.org/10.1016/j.artmed.2020.101855.

Cole, Tyler S., Jennifer Frankovich, Srinivasan Iyer, Paea LePendu, Anna Bauer-Mehren, and Nigam H. Shah. 2013. "Profiling Risk Factors for Chronic Uveitis in Juvenile Idiopathic Arthritis: A New Model for EHR-Based Research." *Pediatric Rheumatology* 11 (1): 1–9. https://doi.org/10.1186/1546-0096-11-45.

Collier, Nigel, Anika Oellrich, and Tudor Groza. 2015. "Concept Selection for Phenotypes and Diseases Using Learn to Rank." *Journal of Biomedical Semantics* 6 (1): 1–12. https://doi.org/10.1186/s13326-015-0019-z.

Cooley-Rieders, Keaton, and Kai Zheng. 2021. "Physician Documentation Matters. Using Natural Language Processing to Predict Mortality in Sepsis." *Intelligence-Based Medicine* 5 (February): 100028. https://doi.org/10.1016/j.ibmed.2021.100028.

Coquet, Jean, Selen Bozkurt, Kathleen M. Kan, Michelle K. Ferrari, Douglas W. Blayney, James D. Brooks, and Tina Hernandez-Boussard. 2019. "Comparison of Orthogonal NLP Methods for Clinical Phenotyping and Assessment of Bone Scan Utilization among Prostate Cancer Patients." *Journal of Biomedical Informatics* 94 (November 2018). https://doi.org/10.1016/j.jbi.2019.103184.

Cui, Licong, Alireza Bozorgi, Samden D. Lhatoo, Guo Qiang Zhang, and Satya S. Sahoo. 2012. "EpiDEA: Extracting Structured Epilepsy and Seizure Information from Patient Discharge Summaries for Cohort Identification." *AMIA... Annual Symposium Proceedings / AMIA Symposium. AMIA Symposium*: 1191–1200.

Cunningham, Hamish, Valentin Tablan, Angus Roberts, and Kalina Bontcheva. 2013. "Getting More Out of Biomedical Documents with GATE's Full Lifecycle Open Source Text Analytics." *PLoS Computational Biology* 9 (2). https://doi.org/10.1371/journal.pcbi.1002854.

Cuzzola, John, Jelena Jovanović, and Ebrahim Bagheri. 2017. "RysannMD: A Biomedical Semantic Annotator Balancing Speed and Accuracy." *Journal of Biomedical Informatics* 71: 91–109. https://doi.org/10.1016/j.jbi.2017.05.016.

Dahiwade, Dhiraj, Gajanan Patle, and Ektaa Meshram. 2019. "Designing Disease Prediction Model Using Machine Learning Approach." *Proceedings of the 3rd International Conference on Computing Methodologies and Communication, ICCMC 2019*, no. ICCMC: 1211–15. https://doi.org/10.1109/ICCMC.2019.8819782.

Dai, Hong Jie, Chun Yu Chen, Chi Yang Wu, Po Ting Lai, Richard Tzong Han Tsai, and Wen Lian Hsu. 2012. "Coreference Resolution of Medical Concepts in Discharge Summaries by Exploiting Contextual Information." *Journal of the American Medical Informatics Association* 19 (5): 888–96. https://doi.org/10.1136/amiajnl-2012-000808.

Davoodijam, Ensieh, Nasser Ghadiri, Maryam Lotfi Shahreza, and Fabio Rinaldi. 2021. "MultiGBS: A Multi-Layer Graph Approach to Biomedical Summarization." *Journal of Biomedical Informatics* 116 (April). https://doi.org/10.1016/J.JBI.2021.103706.

Denecke, Kerstin. n.d. "Extracting Medical Concepts from Medical Social Media with Clinical NLP Tools: A Qualitative Study."

Denecke, Kerstin, and Yihan Deng. 2015. "Sentiment Analysis in Medical Settings: New Opportunities and Challenges." *Artificial Intelligence in Medicine* 64 (1): 17–27. https://doi.org/10.1016/j.artmed.2015.03.006.

Deng, Lizong, Luming Chen, Tao Yang, Mi Liu, Shicheng Li, and Taijiao Jiang. 2021. "Constructing High-Fidelity Phenotype Knowledge Graphs for Infectious Diseases With a Fine-Grained Semantic Information Model: Development and Usability Study." *Journal of Medical Internet Research* 23 (6). https://doi.org/10.2196/26892.

Denny, Joshua C., Lisa Bastarache, Elizabeth Ann Sastre, and Anderson Spickard. 2009. "Tracking Medical Students' Clinical Experiences Using Natural Language Processing." *Journal of Biomedical Informatics* 42 (5): 781–89. https://doi.org/10.1016/j.jbi.2009.02.004.

Denny, Joshua C., Randolph A. Miller, Lemuel Russell Waitman, Mark A. Arrieta, and Joshua F. Peterson. 2009. "Identifying QT Prolongation from ECG Impressions Using a General-Purpose Natural Language Processor." *International Journal of Medical Informatics* 78 (Suppl 1): S34–42. https://doi.org/10.1016/j.ijmedinf.2008.09.001.

Denny, Joshua C., Jeffrey D. Smithers, Randolph A. Miller, and Anderson Spickard. 2003. "'Understanding' Medical School Curriculum Content Using KnowledgeMap." *Journal of the American Medical Informatics Association* 10 (4): 351–62. https://doi.org/10.1197/jamia.M1176.

Denny, Joshua C, Plomarz R Irani, Firas H Wehbe, Jeffrey D Smithers, and Anderson Spickard. 2003. "The KnowledgeMap Project: Development of a Concept-Based Medical School Curriculum Database." *AMIA... Annual Symposium Proceedings / AMIA Symposium. AMIA Symposium*: 195–99.

Denny, Joshua C, Josh F. Peterson, Neesha N Choma, Hua Xu, Randolph A Miller, Lisa Bastarache, and Neeraja B Peterson. 2009. "Development of a Natural Language Processing System to Identify Timing and Status of Colonoscopy Testing in Electronic Medical Records." *AMIA... Annual Symposium Proceedings / AMIA Symposium. AMIA Symposium 2009* (2): 141.

—. 2010. "Extracting Timing and Status Descriptors for Colonoscopy Testing from Electronic Medical Records." *Journal of the American Medical Informatics Association* 17 (4): 383–88. https://doi.org/10.1136/jamia.2010.004804.

Denny, Joshua C, Anderson Spickard, Randolph A Miller, Jonathan Schildcrout, Dawood Darbar, S Trent Rosenbloom, and Josh F Peterson. 2005. "Identifying UMLS Concepts from ECG Impressions Using KnowledgeMap." *AMIA... Annual Symposium Proceedings / AMIA Symposium. AMIA Symposium*: 196–200.

Devi, N Vasunthira, and R Ponnusamy. 2018. "A Systematic Survey of Natural Language Processing (NLP) Approaches in Different Systems." *International Journal of Computer Sciences and Engineering*, no. January.

Digan, William, Aurélie Névéol, Antoine Neuraz, Maxime Wack, David Baudoin, Anita Burgun, and Bastien Rance. 2021. "Can Reproducibility Be Improved in Clinical Natural Language Processing? A Study of 7 Clinical NLP Suites." *Journal of the American Medical Informatics Association* 28 (3): 504–15. https://doi.org/10.1093/jamia/ocaa261.

Dilthey, Alexander T., Chirag Jain, Sergey Koren, and Adam M. Phillippy. 2019. "Strain-Level Metagenomic Assignment and Compositional Estimation for Long Reads with MetaMaps." *Nature Communications* 10 (1): 3066. https://doi.org/10.1038/s41467-019-10934-2.

Dinesh, Kumar G., K. Arumugaraj, Kumar D. Santhosh, and V. Mareeswari. 2018. "EFFECTIVE PREDICTION OF CARDIOVASCULAR Disease Using Cluster of Machine Learning Algorithms." *Proceedings of the 2018 International Conference on Current Trends towards Converging Technologies, ICCTCT 2018* 7 (18): 2192–2201. https://doi.org/10.1109/ICCTCT.2018.8550857.

Dodiya, Tripti, and Sonal Jain. 2016. "Speech Recognition System for Medical Domain." *International Journal of Computer Science and Information Technologies* 7 (1): 185–89.

Dreyfus, Brian, Anuj Chaudhary, Parth Bhardwaj, and V. Karthikhaa Shree. 2021. "Application of Natural Language Processing Techniques to Identify Off-Label Drug Usage from Various Online Health Communities." *Journal of the American Medical Informatics Association* 28 (10): 2147–54. https://doi.org/10.1093/JAMIA/OCAB124.

Elkin, Authors Peter L., David Froehling, Dietlind Wahner-roedler, Brett Trusko, Gail Welsh, Haobo Ma, Armen X Asatryan, I. Tokars, S. Trent Rosenbloom, and M. P. H. Steven H Brown. 2008. "NLP-Based Identification of Pneumonia Cases from Free-Text Radiological Reports Abstract : Introduction : AMIA 2008 Symposium Proceedings Page -172 AMIA 2008 Symposium Proceedings Page -173." *Symposium A Quarterly Journal In Modern Foreign Literatures:* 172–76.

Elkin, Peter L., Mark S. Tuttle, Brett E. Trusko, and Steven H. Brown. 2009. "BioProspecting: Novel Marker Discovery Obtained by Mining the Bibleome." *BMC Bioinformatics* 10 (S2): 1–8. https://doi.org/10.1186/1471-2105-10-s2-s9.

Fan, Yadan, Andrew Wen, Feichen Shen, Sunghwan Sohn, Hongfang Liu, and Liwei Wang. 2019. "Evaluating the Impact of Dictionary Updates on Automatic Annotations Based on Clinical NLP Systems." *AMIA Joint Summits on Translational Science Proceedings. AMIA Joint Summits on Translational Science 2019*: 714–21. https://www.ncbi.nlm. nih.gov/pubmed/31259028%0Ahttps://www.pubmedcentral.nih.gov/articlerender. fcgi?artid=PMC6568114.

Farhanaaz, and V. Sanju. 2016. "An Exploration on Lexical Analysis." In *International Conference on Electrical, Electronics, and Optimization Techniques, ICEEOT 2016*: 253–58. https://doi.org/10.1109/ICEEOT.2016.7755127.

Ferraro, Jeffrey P., Ye Ye, Per H. Gesteland, Peter J. Haug, Fuchiang Rich Tsui, Gregory F. Cooper, Rudn Van Bree, Thomas Ginter, Andrew J. Nowalk, and Michael Wagner. 2017. "The Effects of Natural Language Processing on Cross-Institutional Portability of Influenza Case Detection for Disease Surveillance." *Applied Clinical Informatics* 8 (2): 560–80. https://doi.org/10.4338/ACI-2016-12-RA-0211.

Filice, Ross W., and Charles E. Kahn. 2019. "Integrating an Ontology of Radiology Differential Diagnosis with ICD-10-CM, RadLex, and SNOMED CT." *Journal of Digital Imaging* 32 (2): 206–10. https://doi.org/10.1007/s10278-019-00186-3.

Friedman, Carol. 1997. "Towards a Comprehensive Medical Language Processing System: Methods and Issues." *Journal of the American Medical Informatics Association* 4 (SUPPL.): 595–99.

Friedman, Carol, and Stephen B. Johnson. 2006. "Natural Language and Text Processing in Biomedicine." In, 312–43. https://doi.org/10.1007/0-387-36278-9_8.

Friedman, Carol, Lyudmila Shagina, Yves Lussier, and George Hripcsak. 2004. "Automated Encoding of Clinical Documents Based on Natural Language Processing." *Journal of the American Medical Informatics Association* 11 (5): 392–402. https://doi.org/10.1197/ jamia.M1552.

Fu, Sunyang, Lester Y. Leung, Yanshan Wang, Anne Olivia Raulli, David F. Kallmes, Kristin A. Kinsman, Kristoff B. Nelson, et al. 2019. "Natural Language Processing for the Identification of Silent Brain Infarcts from Neuroimaging Reports." *JMIR Medical Informatics* 7 (2). https://doi.org/10.2196/12109.

Ganoe, Craig H., Weiyi Wu, Paul J. Barr, William Haslett, Michelle D. Dannenberg, Kyra L. Bonasia, James C. Finora, et al. 2021. "Natural Language Processing for Automated Annotation of Medication Mentions in Primary Care Visit Conversations." *JAMIA Open* 4 (3). https://doi.org/10.1093/JAMIAOPEN/OOAB071.

García-Remesal, Miguel, Victor Maojo, José Crespo, and Holger Billhardt. 2007. "Logical Schema Acquisition from Text-Based Sources for Structured and Non-Structured Biomedical Sources Integration." *AMIA... Annual Symposium Proceedings / AMIA Symposium. AMIA Symposium*: 259–63.

Garcia, Klaifer, and Lilian Berton. 2021. "Topic Detection and Sentiment Analysis in Twitter Content Related to COVID-19 from Brazil and the USA." *Applied Soft Computing* 101: 107057. https://doi.org/10.1016/j.asoc.2020.107057.

Garvin, Jennifer H., Peter L. Elkin, Shuying Shen, Steven Brown, Brett Trusko, Enlai Wang, Linda Hoke, et al. 2013. "Automated Quality Measurement in Department of the Veterans Affairs Discharge Instructions for Patients with Congestive Heart Failure." *Journal for Healthcare Quality : Official Publication of the National Association for Healthcare Quality* 35 (4): 16–24. https://doi.org/10.1111/j.1945-1474.2011.195.x.

Gaudet-Blavignac, Christophe, Vasiliki Foufi, Mina Bjelogrlic, and Christian Lovis. 2021. "Use of the Systematized Nomenclature of Medicine Clinical Terms (SNOMED CT) for Processing Free Text in Health Care: Systematic Scoping Review." *Journal of Medical Internet Research* 23 (1). https://doi.org/10.2196/24594.

Geletta, Simon, Lendie Follett, and Marcia Laugerman. 2019. "Latent Dirichlet Allocation in Predicting Clinical Trial Terminations." *BMC Medical Informatics and Decision Making* 19 (1): 1–12. https://doi.org/10.1186/s12911-019-0973-y.

Gobbel, Glenn T., Ruth Reeves, Shrimalini Jayaramaraja, Dario Giuse, Theodore Speroff, Steven H Brown, Peter L. Elkin, and Michael E. Matheny. 2014. "Development and Evaluation of RapTAT: A Machine Learning System for Concept Mapping of Phrases from Medical Narratives." *Journal of Biomedical Informatics* 48: 54–65. https://doi.org/10.1016/j.jbi.2013.11.008.

Goss, Foster R., Joseph M. Plasek, Jason J. Lau, Diane L. Seger, Frank Y. Chang, and Li Zhou. 2014. "An Evaluation of a Natural Language Processing Tool for Identifying and Encoding Allergy Information in Emergency Department Clinical Notes." *AMIA... Annual Symposium Proceedings / AMIA Symposium. AMIA Symposium* 2014: 580–88.

Griffis, Denis, Chaitanya Shivade, Eric Fosler-lussier, and Albert M. Lai. 2016. "A Quantitative and Qualitative Evaluation of Sentence Boundary Detection for the Clinical Domain Department of Computer Science and Engineering, Department of Biomedical Informatics, The Ohio State University, Columbus, OH. National Institutes of Hea." *AMIA Summits on Translational Science Proceedings 2016*: 88–97.

Guo, Donglin, Guihua Duan, Ying Yu, Yaohang Li, Fang Xiang Wu, and Min Li. 2020. "A Disease Inference Method Based on Symptom Extraction and Bidirectional Long Short Term Memory Networks." *Methods* 173 (February): 75-82. https://doi.org/10.1016/j.ymeth.2019.07.009.

Haerian, K, D Varn, S Vaidya, L Ena, H S Chase, and C Friedman. 2012. "Detection of Pharmacovigilance-Related Adverse Events Using Electronic Health Records and Automated Methods." *Clinical Pharmacology & Therapeutics* 92 (2): 228–34. https://doi.org/10.1038/clpt.2012.54.

Hanauer, David A, Jill S. Barnholtz-Sloan, Mark F Beno, Guilherme Del Fiol, Eric B. Durbin, Oksana Gologorskaya, Daniel Harris, et al. 2020. "Electronic Medical Record Search Engine (EMERSE): An Information Retrieval Tool for Supporting Cancer Research." *JCO Clinical Cancer Informatics*, no. 4: 454–63. https://doi.org/10.1200/cci.19.00134.

Hanumanthappa, M., S. Rashmi, and N. M. Jyothi. 2014. "Impact of Phonetics in Natural Language Processing : A Literature Survey." *IJISET-International Journal of Innovative Science, Engineering & Technology* 1 (3): 532–36. www.ijiset.com.

Hassanzadeh, Hamed, Sarvnaz Karimi, and Anthony Nguyen. 2020. "Matching Patients to Clinical Trials Using Semantically Enriched Document Representation." *Journal of Biomedical Informatics* 105 (January): 103406. https://doi.org/10.1016/j.jbi.2020.103406.

Hassanzadeh, Hamed, Anthony Nguyen, and Karin Verspoor. 2019. "Quantifying Semantic Similarity of Clinical Evidence in the Biomedical Literature to Facilitate Related Evidence Synthesis." *Journal of Biomedical Informatics* 100 (June): 103321. https://doi.org/10.1016/j.jbi.2019.103321.

Havrilla, James Margolin, Mengge Zhao, Cong Liu, Chunhua Weng, Ingo Helbig, Elizabeth Bhoj, and Kai Wang. 2021. "Clinical Phenotypic Spectrum of 4095 Individuals with Down Syndrome from Text Mining of Electronic Health Records." *Genes* 12 (8). https://doi.org/10.3390/GENES12081159.

Henry, Fern Fitz, Harvey J. Murff, Michael E. Matheny, Nancy Gentry, Elliot M. Fielstein, Steven H. Brown, Ruth M. Reeves, et al. 2013. "Exploring the Frontier of Electronic Health Record Surveillance the Case of Postoperative Complications." *Medical Care* 51 (6): 509–16. https://doi.org/10.1097/MLR.0b013e31828d1210.

Hernandez-Boussard, Tina, Panagiotis D. Kourdis, Tina Seto, Michelle Ferrari, Douglas W. Blayney, Daniel Rubin, and James D. Brooks. 2017. "Mining Electronic Health Records to Extract Patient-Centered Outcomes Following Prostate Cancer Treatment." *AMIA... Annual Symposium Proceedings. AMIA Symposium 2017*: 876–82.

Hernandez-Boussard, Tina, Keri L. Monda, Blai Coll Crespo, and Dan Riskin. 2019. "Real World Evidence in Cardiovascular Medicine: Ensuring Data Validity in Electronic Health Record-Based Studies." *Journal of the American Medical Informatics Association* 26 (11): 1189–94. https://doi.org/10.1093/jamia/ocz119.

Hinchcliff, Monique, Eric Just, Sofia Podlusky, John Varga, Rowland W. Chang, and Warren A. Kibbe. 2012. "Text Data Extraction for a Prospective, Research-Focused Data Mart: Implementation and Validation." *BMC Medical Informatics and Decision Making* 12 (1). https://doi.org/10.1186/1472-6947-12-106.

Hong, Na, Dingcheng Li, Yue Yu, Qiongying Xiu, Hongfang Liu, and Guoqian Jiang. 2016. "A Computational Framework for Converting Textual Clinical Diagnostic Criteria into the Quality Data Model." *Journal of Biomedical Informatics* 63: 11–21. https://doi.org/10.1016/j.jbi.2016.07.016.

Hong, Na, Andrew Wen, Daniel J. Stone, Shintaro Tsuji, Paul R. Kingsbury, Luke V. Rasmussen, Jennifer A. Pacheco, et al. 2019. "Developing a FHIR-Based EHR Phenotyping Framework: A Case Study for Identification of Patients with Obesity and Multiple Comorbidities from Discharge Summaries." *Journal of Biomedical Informatics* 99 (September): 103310. https://doi.org/10.1016/j.jbi.2019.103310.

Hripcsak, George, Charles Knirsch, Li Zhou, Adam Wilcox, and Genevieve B Melton. 2007. "Using Discordance to Improve Classification in Narrative Clinical Databases: An Application to Community-Acquired Pneumonia." *Computers in Biology and Medicine* 37 (3): 296–304. https://doi.org/10.1016/j.compbiomed.2006.02.001.

Hripcsak, George, Nicholas D. Soulakis, Li Li, Frances P. Morrison, Albert M. Lai, Carol Friedman, Neil S. Calman, and Farzad Mostashari. 2009. "Syndromic Surveillance Using Ambulatory Electronic Health Records." *Journal of the American Medical Informatics Association* 16 (3): 354–61. https://doi.org/10.1197/jamia.M2922.

Hu, Yang, Tianyi Zhao, Ningyi Zhang, Tianyi Zang, Jun Zhang, and Liang Cheng. 2018. "Identifying Diseases-Related Metabolites Using Random Walk." *BMC Bioinformatics* 19 (Suppl 5). https://doi.org/10.1186/s12859-018-2098-1.

Huang, Sandy H., Paea LePendu, Srinivasan V. Iyer, Ming Tai-Seale, David Carrell, and Nigam H. Shah. 2014. "Toward Personalizing Treatment for Depression: Predicting Diagnosis and Severity." *Journal of the American Medical Informatics Association* 21 (6): 1069–75. https://doi.org/10.1136/amiajnl-2014-002733.

Hughes, Mark, Irene Li, Spyros Kotoulas, and Toyotaro Suzumura. 2017. "Medical Text Classification Using Convolutional Neural Networks." *Studies in Health Technology and Informatics* 235 (April): 246–50. https://doi.org/10.3233/978-1-61499-753-5-246.

Hyun, Sookyung, Stephen B. Johnson, and Suzanne Bakken. 2009. "Exploring the Ability of Natural Language Processing to Extract Data From Nursing Narratives." *CIN: Computers, Informatics, Nursing* 27 (4): 215–23. https://doi.org/10.1097/NCN.0b013e3181a91b58.

Ikonomakis, M., Sotos Kotsiantis, and V Tampakas. 2005. "Text Classification Using Machine Learning Techniques." *WSEAS Transactions on Computers* 4 (8): 966–74.

Iqbal, Ehtesham, Robbie Mallah, Richard George Jackson, Michael Ball, Zina M. Ibrahim, Matthew Broadbent, Olubanke Dzahini, Robert Stewart, Caroline Johnston, and Richard J.B. Dobson. 2015. "Identification of Adverse Drug Events from Free Text Electronic Patient Records and Information in a Large Mental Health Case Register." *PLoS ONE* 10 (8): 1–14. https://doi.org/10.1371/journal.pone.0134208.

Iroju, Olaronke G., and Janet O. Olaleke. 2015. "A Systematic Review of Natural Language Processing in Healthcare." *International Journal of Information Technology and Computer Science* 7 (8): 44–50. https://doi.org/10.5815/ijitcs.2015.08.07.

Islam, Md Tawhidul, Mostafa Shaikh, Abhaya Nayak, and Shoba Ranganathan. 2010. "Extracting Biomarker Information Applying Natural Language Processing and Machine Learning." In *2010 4th International Conference on Bioinformatics and Biomedical Engineering, ICBBE 2010:* 8–11. https://doi.org/10.1109/ICBBE.2010.5514717.

Johnson, Stephen B., Suzanne Bakken, Daniel Dine, Sookyung Hyun, Eneida Mendonça, Frances Morrison, Tiffani Bright, Tielman Van Vleck, Jesse Wrenn, and Peter Stetson. 2008. "An Electronic Health Record Based on Structured Narrative." *Journal of the American Medical Informatics Association* 15 (1): 54–64. https://doi.org/10.1197/jamia. M2131.

Joshua Valdez, Michael Rueschman, Matthew Kim, Susan Redline, and Satya S. Sahoo. 2016. "An Ontology-Enabled Natural Language Processing Pipeline for Provenance Metadata Extraction from Biomedical Text." *On Move Meaningful Internet Systems*, 699–708. https://doi.org/10.1007/978-3-319-48472-3_43.

Justyna, Widomska. 2020. "How Have Experimental Cancer Interventions Evolved over Time?" *Studies in Health Technology and Informatics* 270: 252–56. https://doi. org/10.3233/SHTI200161.

K. Yadav, E. Sarioglu, H.A. Choi, W.B.t. Cartwright, P.S. Hinds, J.M., and Chamberlain. 2016. "Automated Outcome Classification of Computed Tomography Imaging Reports for Pediatric Traumatic Brain Injury." *Academic Emergency Medicine* 23: 171–78. https:// doi.org/10.1111/acem.12859.Automated.

K. Yadav, E. Sarioglu, M. Smith, and H.A. Choi. 2013. "Automated Outcome Classification of Emergency Department Computed Tomography Imaging Reports." *Academic Emergency Medicine* 20: 848–854. https://doi.org/10.1111/acem.12174.Automated.

Kandpal, Prathamesh, Kapil Jasnani, Ritesh Raut, and Siddharth Bhorge. 2020. "Contextual Chatbot for Healthcare Purposes (Using Deep Learning)." *Proceedings of the World Conference on Smart Trends in Systems, Security and Sustainability*, WS4 2020: 625–34. https://doi.org/10.1109/WorldS450073.2020.9210351.

Karagounis, Sotiris, Indra Neil Sarkar, and Elizabeth S. Chen. 2020. "Coding Free-Text Chief Complaints from a Health Information Exchange: A Preliminary Study." *AMIA Annual Symposium Proceedings* 2020: 638. /pmc/articles/PMC8075463/.

Kelahan, Linda C, Amit D Kalaria, and Ross W Filice. 2017. "PathBot: A Radiology-Pathology Correlation Dashboard." *Journal of Digital Imaging* 30 (6): 681–86. https:// doi.org/10.1007/s10278-017-9969-2.

Kersloot, Martijn G, Francis Lau, Ameen Abu-Hanna, Derk L Arts, and Ronald Cornet. 2019. "Automated SNOMED CT Concept and Attribute Relationship Detection through a Web-Based Implementation of CTAKES." *Journal of Biomedical Semantics* 10 (1): 1–13. https://doi.org/10.1186/s13326-019-0207-3.

Khaled, Dr. 2014. "Natural Language Processing and Its Use in Education." *International Journal of Advanced Computer Science and Applications* 5 (12): 72–76. https://doi. org/10.14569/ijacsa.2014.051210.

Khalifa, Abdulrahman, and Stéphane Meystre. 2015. "Adapting Existing Natural Language Processing Resources for Cardiovascular Risk Factors Identification in Clinical Notes." *Journal of Biomedical Informatics* 58 (December): S128–32. https://doi.org/10.1016/j. jbi.2015.08.002.

Kidwai, Bushra, and Nadesh Rk. 2020. "Design and Development of Diagnostic Chabot for Supporting Primary Health Care Systems." In *Procedia Computer Science*, 167:75–84. Elsevier B.V. https://doi.org/10.1016/j.procs.2020.03.184.

Kim, Tong Min, Seo Joon Lee, Hwa Young Lee, Dong Jin Chang, Chang Ii Yoon, In Young Choi, and Kun Ho Yoon. 2020. "CIMI: Classify and Itemize Medical Image System for PFT Big Data Based on Deep Learning." *Applied Sciences (Switzerland)* 10 (23): 1–13. https://doi.org/10.3390/app10238575.

Klann, Jeffrey G., and Peter Szolovits. 2009. "An Intelligent Listening Framework for Capturing Encounter Notes from a Doctor-Patient Dialog." *BMC Medical Informatics and Decision Making* 9 (SUPPL. 1): 1–10. https://doi.org/10.1186/1472-6947-9-S1-S3.

Kocaballi, A Baki, Juan C. Quiroz, Liliana Laranjo, Dana Rezazadegan, Rafal Kocielnik, Leigh Clark, Q. Vera Liao, Sun Young Park, Robert J. Moore, and Adam Miner. 2020. "Conversational Agents for Health and Wellbeing." In *Conference on Human Factors in Computing Systems - Proceedings*: 1–8. https://doi.org/10.1145/3334480.3375154.

Kocaman, Veysel, and David Talby. 2021a. "Improving Clinical Document Understanding on COVID-19 Research with Spark NLP." In *CEUR Workshop Proceedings*. Vol. 2831.

—. 2021b. "Spark NLP: Natural Language Understanding at Scale." *Software Impacts* 8 (January): 100058. https://doi.org/10.1016/j.simpa.2021.100058.

Koola, Jejo D., Sharon E. Davis, Omar Al-Nimri, Sharidan K. Parr, Daniel Fabbri, Bradley A. Malin, Samuel B. Ho, and Michael E. Matheny. 2018. "Development of an Automated Phenotyping Algorithm for Hepatorenal Syndrome." *Journal of Biomedical Informatics* 80 (March): 87–95. https://doi.org/10.1016/j.jbi.2018.03.001.

Kreimeyer, Kory, Oanh Dang, Jonathan Spiker, Monica A. Muñoz, Gary Rosner, Robert Ball, and Taxiarchis Botsis. 2021. "Feature Engineering and Machine Learning for Causality Assessment in Pharmacovigilance: Lessons Learned from Application to the FDA Adverse Event Reporting System." *Computers in Biology and Medicine* 135 (May). https://doi.org/10.1016/j.compbiomed.2021.104517.

Kreimeyer, Kory, Matthew Foster, Abhishek Pandey, Nina Arya, Gwendolyn Halford, Sandra F. Jones, Richard Forshee, Mark Walderhaug, and Taxiarchis Botsis. 2017. "Natural Language Processing Systems for Capturing and Standardizing Unstructured Clinical Information: A Systematic Review." *Journal of Biomedical Informatics* 73: 14–29. https://doi.org/10.1016/j.jbi.2017.07.012.

Kumah-Crystal, Yaa A., Claude J. Pirtle, Harrison M Whyte, Edward S Goode, Shilo H Anders, and Christoph U Lehmann. 2018. "Electronic Health Record Interactions through Voice: A Review." *Applied Clinical Informatics* 9 (3): 541–52. https://doi.org/10.1055/s-0038-1666844.

L. Elkin, Peter. 2012. "Bioprospecting the Bibleome: Adding Evidence to Support the Inflammatory Basis of Cancer." *Journal of Postgenomics: Drug & Biomarker Development* 02 (04): 319. https://doi.org/10.4172/2153-0769.1000112.

Lam, Calvin, Fu Chih Lai, Chia Hui Wang, Mei Hsin Lai, Nanly Hsu, and Min Huey Chung. 2016. "Text Mining of Journal Articles for Sleep Disorder Terminologies." *PLoS ONE* 11 (5): 1–14. https://doi.org/10.1371/journal.pone.0156031.

Latif, Siddique, Junaid Qadir, Adnan Qayyum, Muhammad Usama, and Shahzad Younis. 2021. "Speech Technology for Healthcare: Opportunities, Challenges, and State of the Art." *IEEE Reviews in Biomedical Engineering* 14 (c): 342–56. https://doi.org/10.1109/RBME.2020.3006860.

Le, Duy Van, James Montgomery, Kenneth C Kirkby, and Joel Scanlan. 2018. "Risk Prediction Using Natural Language Processing of Electronic Mental Health Records in an Inpatient Forensic Psychiatry Setting." *Journal of Biomedical Informatics* 86 (June): 49–58. https://doi.org/10.1016/j.jbi.2018.08.007.

Le, Nguyen Thinh, Frank Loll, and Niels Pinkwart. 2013. "Operationalizing the Continuum between Well-Defined and Ill-Defined Problems for Educational Technology." *IEEE Transactions on Learning Technologies* 6 (3): 258–70. https://doi.org/10.1109/TLT.2013.16.

Le, Nguyen Thinh, and Laura Wartschinski. 2018. "A Cognitive Assistant for Improving Human Reasoning Skills." *International Journal of Human Computer Studies* 117: 45–54. https://doi.org/10.1016/j.ijhcs.2018.02.005.

Lecun, Yann, Yoshua Bengio, and Geoffrey Hinton. 2015. "Deep Learning." *Nature* 521 (7553): 436–44. https://doi.org/10.1038/nature14539.

Lee, Jeongeun, Hyun Je Song, Eunsil Yoon, Seong Bae Park, Sung Hye Park, Jeong Wook Seo, Peom Park, and Jinwook Choi. 2018. "Automated Extraction of Biomarker Information from Pathology Reports." *BMC Medical Informatics and Decision Making* 18 (1): 1–12. https://doi.org/10.1186/s12911-018-0609-7.

Lee, Jong Koo. 2019. "Topic Modeling." *Osong Public Health and Research Perspectives.* https://doi.org/10.24171/J.PHRP.2021.12.1.01.

Lee, Kyung-eun, and Hyun-seok Park. 2014. "A Review of Three Different Studies on Hidden Markov Models for Epigenetic Problems: A Computational Perspective." *Genomics & Informatics* 12 (4): 145. https://doi.org/10.5808/gi.2014.12.4.145.

Li, Li, Herbert S Chase, Chintan O Patel, Carol Friedman, and Chunhua Weng. 2008. "Comparing ICD9-Encoded Diagnoses and NLP-Processed Discharge Summaries for Clinical Trials Pre-Screening: A Case Study." *AMIA... Annual Symposium Proceedings / AMIA Symposium. AMIA Symposium*: 404–8.

Li, Qi, Stephen Andrew Spooner, Megan Kaiser, Nataline Lingren, Jessica Robbins, Todd Lingren, Huaxiu Tang, Imre Solti, and Yizhao Ni. 2015. "An End-to-End Hybrid Algorithm for Automated Medication Discrepancy Detection." *BMC Medical Informatics and Decision Making* 15 (1): 1–12. https://doi.org/10.1186/s12911-015-0160-8.

Liao, Katherine P., Tianxi Cai, Vivian Gainer, Sergey Goryachev, Qing Zeng-treitler, Soumya Raychaudhuri, Peter Szolovits, et al. 2010. "Electronic Medical Records for Discovery Research in Rheumatoid Arthritis." *Arthritis Care & Research* 62 (8): 1120–27. https://doi.org/10.1002/acr.20184.

Liao, Katherine P, Ashwin N Ananthakrishnan, Vishesh Kumar, Zongqi Xia, Andrew Cagan, Vivian S Gainer, Sergey Goryachev, et al. 2015. "Methods to Develop an Electronic Medical Record Phenotype Algorithm to Compare the Risk of Coronary Artery Disease across 3 Chronic Disease Cohorts." *PLoS ONE* 10 (8): 1–11. https://doi.org/10.1371/journal.pone.0136651.

Lin, Chen, Elizabeth W. Karlson, Dmitriy Dligach, Monica P. Ramirez, Timothy A. Miller, Huan Mo, Natalie S. Braggs, et al. 2015. "Automatic Identification of Methotrexate-Induced Liver Toxicity in Patients with Rheumatoid Arthritis from the Electronic Medical Record." *Journal of the American Medical Informatics Association* 22 (e1): e151–61. https://doi.org/10.1136/amiajnl-2014-002642.

Liu, Cong, Casey N. Ta, James R. Rogers, Ziran Li, Junghwan Lee, Alex M. Butler, Ning Shang, et al. 2019. "Ensembles of Natural Language Processing Systems for Portable Phenotyping Solutions." *Journal of Biomedical Informatics* 100 (5): 103318. https://doi.org/10.1016/j.jbi.2019.103318.

Liu, Hongfang, Stephen T. Wu, Dingcheng Li, Siddhartha Jonnalagadda, Sunghwan Sohn, Kavishwar Wagholikar, Peter J. Haug, Stanley M. Huff, and Christopher G. Chute. 2012. "Towards a Semantic Lexicon for Clinical Natural Language Processing." *AMIA... Annual Symposium Proceedings/AMIA Symposium. AMIA Symposium 2012* (4): 568–76.

Liu, Zengjian, Ming Yang, Xiaolong Wang, Qingcai Chen, Buzhou Tang, Zhe Wang, and Hua Xu. 2017. "Entity Recognition from Clinical Texts via Recurrent Neural Network." *BMC Medical Informatics and Decision Making* 17 (Suppl 2). https://doi.org/10.1186/s12911-017-0468-7.

Lobo, Manuel, Andre Lamurias, and Francisco M Couto. 2017. "Identifying Human Phenotype Terms by Combining Machine Learning and Validation Rules." *BioMed Research International* 2017. https://doi.org/10.1155/2017/8565739.

López Pineda, Arturo, Ye Ye, Shyam Visweswaran, Gregory F Cooper, Michael M Wagner, and Fuchiang Rich Tsui. 2015. "Comparison of Machine Learning Classifiers for Influenza Detection from Emergency Department Free-Text Reports." *Journal of Biomedical Informatics* 58: 60–69. https://doi.org/10.1016/j.jbi.2015.08.019.

Lorigo, Liana M., and Venu Govindaraju. 2006. "Offline Arabic Handwriting Recognition: A Survey." *IEEE Transactions on Pattern Analysis and Machine Intelligence* 28 (5): 712–24. https://doi.org/10.1109/TPAMI.2006.102.

Lowe, Henry J., Yang Huang, and Donald P. Regula. 2009. "Using a Statistical Natural Language Parser Augmented with the UMLS Specialist Lexicon to Assign SNOMED CT Codes to Anatomic Sites and Pathologic Diagnoses in Full Text Pathology Reports." *AMIA... Annual Symposium Proceedings / AMIA Symposium. AMIA Symposium 2009*: 386–90.

Luo, Xiao, Susan Storey, Priyanka Gandhi, Zuoyi Zhang, Megan Metzger, and Kun Huang. 2021. "Analyzing the Symptoms in Colorectal and Breast Cancer Patients with or without Type 2 Diabetes Using EHR Data." *Health Informatics Journal* 27 (1). https://doi.org/10.1177/14604582211000785.

Luo, Yen Fu, Weiyi Sun, and Anna Rumshisky. 2019. "MCN: A Comprehensive Corpus for Medical Concept Normalization." *Journal of Biomedical Informatics* 92 (February): 103132. https://doi.org/10.1016/j.jbi.2019.103132.

Luo, Zhi Hui, Zhi Hui Luo, Meng Wei Shi, Meng Wei Shi, Zhuang Yang, Zhuang Yang, Hong Yu Zhang, Zhen Xia Chen, and Zhen Xia Chen. 2020. "PyMeSHSim: An Integrative Python Package for Biomedical Named Entity Recognition, Normalization, and Comparison of MeSH Terms." *BMC Bioinformatics* 21 (1): 1–14. https://doi.org/10.1186/s12859-020-03583-6.

Ly, Thomas, Carol Pamer, Oanh Dang, Sonja Brajovic, Shahrukh Haider, Taxiarchis Botsis, David Milward, Andrew Winter, Susan Lu, and Robert Ball. 2018. "Evaluation of Natural Language Processing (NLP) Systems to Annotate Drug Product Labeling with MedDRA Terminology." *Journal of Biomedical Informatics*. Elsevier. https://doi.org/10.1016/j.jbi.2018.05.019.

M. Garcia-Remesal, V. Maojo, H. Billhardt, and J. Crespo. 2010. "Integration of Relational and Textual Biomedical Sources. A Pilot Experiment Using a Semi-Automated Method for Logical Schema Acquisition." *Methods of Information in Medicine* 49: 337–348.

Mahajan, Papiya, Rinku Wankhade, Anup Jawade, Pragati Dange, and Aishwarya Bhoge. 2020. "Healthcare Chatbot Using Natural Language Processing." *International Research Journal of Engineering and Technology (IRJET)*, 7 (11): 1715–20.

Mani, Anirudh, Shruti Palaskar, and Sandeep Konam. 2020. "Towards Understanding ASR Error Correction for Medical Conversations." *Proceedings of the 1st Workshop on NLP for Medical Conversations*, 7–11. https://doi.org/10.18653/v1/2020.nlpmc-1.2.

Maojo, Victor, J Crespo, G. De La Calle, J Barreiro, and M. Garcia-Remesal. 2007. "Using Web Services for Linking Genomic Data to Medical Information Systems." In *Methods of Information in Medicine*, 46:484–92. https://doi.org/10.1160/ME9056.

Martinez, David, Graham Pitson, Andrew MacKinlay, and Lawrence Cavedon. 2014. "Cross-Hospital Portability of Information Extraction of Cancer Staging Information." *Artificial Intelligence in Medicine* 62 (1): 11–21. https://doi.org/10.1016/j.artmed.2014.06.002.

Massa Cereda, Paulo Roberto, Newton Kiyotaka Miura, and João José Neto. 2018. "Syntactic Analysis of Natural Language Sentences Based on Rewriting Systems and Adaptivity." In *Procedia Computer Science*, 130:1102–7. Elsevier B.V. https://doi.org/10.1016/j.procs.2018.04.164.

Mayer, Benjamin, Joshua Arnold, Edmon Begoli, Everett Rush, Michael Drewry, Kris Brown, Eduardo Ponce, and Sudarshan Srinivas. 2018. "Evaluating Text Analytic Frameworks for Mental Health Surveillance." In *Proceedings - IEEE 34th International Conference on Data Engineering Workshops, ICDEW 2018*, 39–47. https://doi.org/10.1109/ICDEW.2018.00014.

Miller, Timothy A., Paul Avillach, and Kenneth D. Mandl. 2020. "Experiences Implementing Scalable, Containerized, Cloud-Based NLP for Extracting Biobank Participant Phenotypes at Scale." *JAMIA Open* 3 (2): 185–89. https://doi.org/10.1093/jamiaopen/ooaa016.

Mishra, Rashmi, Jiantao Bian, Marcelo Fiszman, Charlene R. Weir, Siddhartha Jonnalagadda, Javed Mostafa, and Guilherme Del Fiol. 2014. "Text Summarization in the Biomedical Domain: A Systematic Review of Recent Research." *Journal of Biomedical Informatics* 52: 457–67. https://doi.org/10.1016/j.jbi.2014.06.009.

Moher, David, Alessandro Liberati, Jennifer Tetzlaff, Douglas G. Altman, Doug Altman, Gerd Antes, David Atkins, et al. 2009. "Preferred Reporting Items for Systematic Reviews and Meta-Analyses: The PRISMA Statement." *PLoS Medicine* 6 (7). https://doi.org/10.1371/journal.pmed.1000097.

Molenaar, Sabine, Lientje Maas, Verónica Burriel, Fabiano Dalpiaz, and Sjaak Brinkkemper. 2020. "Medical Dialogue Summarization for Automated Reporting in Healthcare." In *Lecture Notes in Business Information Processing*, 382 LNBIP:76–88. https://doi.org/10.1007/978-3-030-49165-9_7.

Moon, Sungrim, Sijia Liu, Christopher G Scott, Sujith Samudrala, Mohamed M Abidian, Jeffrey B Geske, Peter A Noseworthy, et al. 2019. "Automated Extraction of Sudden Cardiac Death Risk Factors in Hypertrophic Cardiomyopathy Patients by Natural Language Processing." *International Journal of Medical Informatics* 128 (May): 32–38. https://doi.org/10.1016/j.ijmedinf.2019.05.008.

Moradi, Milad, and Nasser Ghadiri. 2019. "Text Summarization in the Biomedical Domain," 1–12. https://arxiv.org/abs/1908.02285.

Morid, Mohammad Amin, Marcelo Fiszman, Kalpana Raja, Siddhartha R. Jonnalagadda, and Guilherme Del Fiol. 2016. "Classification of Clinically Useful Sentences in Clinical Evidence Resources." *Journal of Biomedical Informatics* 60: 14–22. https://doi.org/10.1016/j.jbi.2016.01.003.

Morrison, Frances P., Li Li, Albert M. Lai, and George Hripcsak. 2009. "Repurposing the Clinical Record: Can an Existing Natural Language Processing System De-Identify Clinical Notes?" *Journal of the American Medical Informatics Association* 16 (1): 37–39. https://doi.org/10.1197/jamia.M2862.

Murphy, Shawn, Susanne Churchill, Lynn Bry, Henry Chueh, Scott Weiss, Ross Lazarus, Qing Zeng, et al. 2009. "Instrumenting the Health Care Enterprise for Discovery Research in the Genomic Era." *Genome Research* 19 (9): 1675–81. https://doi.org/10.1101/gr.094615.109.

Naseri, Hossein, Kamran Kafi, Sonia Skamene, Marwan Tolba, Mame Daro Faye, Paul Ramia, Julia Khriguian, and John Kildea. 2021. "Development of a Generalizable Natural Language Processing Pipeline to Extract Physician-Reported Pain from Clinical Reports: Generated Using Publicly-Available Datasets and Tested on Institutional Clinical Reports for Cancer Patients with Bone Metastases." *Journal of Biomedical Informatics* 120 (August). https://doi.org/10.1016/J.JBI.2021.103864.

Névéol, Aurélie, Hercules Dalianis, Sumithra Velupillai, Guergana Savova, and Pierre Zweigenbaum. 2018. "Clinical Natural Language Processing in Languages Other than English: Opportunities and Challenges." *Journal of Biomedical Semantics*. https://doi.org/10.1186/s13326-018-0179-8.

Oellrich, Anika, Nigel Collier, Damian Smedley, and Tudor Groza. 2015. "Generation of Silver Standard Concept Annotations from Biomedical Texts with Special Relevance to Phenotypes." *PLoS ONE* 10 (1): 1–17. https://doi.org/10.1371/journal.pone.0116040.

Oliveira, Carlos R, Patrick Niccolai, Anette Michelle Ortiz, Sangini S Sheth, Eugene D. Shapiro, Linda M Niccolai, and Cynthia A Brandt. 2020. "Natural Language Processing for Surveillance of Cervical and Anal Cancer and Precancer: Algorithm Development and Split-Validation Study." *JMIR Medical Informatics* 8 (11): 1–8. https://doi.org/10.2196/20826.

Omoregbe, Nicholas A.I., Israel O Ndaman, Sanjay Misra, Olusola O. Abayomi-Alli, and Robertas Damaševičius. 2020. "Text Messaging-Based Medical Diagnosis Using Natural Language Processing and Fuzzy Logic." *Journal of Healthcare Engineering* 2020. https://doi.org/10.1155/2020/8839524.

Pai T., Vaikunth, and P. S. Aithal. 2020. "A Systematic Literature Review of Lexical Analyzer Implementation Techniques in Compiler Design." *International Journal of Applied Engineering and Management Letters (IJAEML)* 4 (2): 285–301.

Pakhomov, Sergey, Michael Schonwetter, and Joan Bachenko. 2001. "Generating Training Data for Medical Dictations." In *2nd Meeting of the North American Chapter of the Association for Computational Linguistics, NAACL 2001*. https://doi.org/10.3115/1073336.1073353.

Pampari, Anusri, Preethi Raghavan, Jennifer Liang, and Jian Peng. 2018. "EMRQA: A Large Corpus for Question Answering on Electronic Medical Records." In *Proceedings of the 2018 Conference on Empirical Methods in Natural Language Processing, EMNLP 2018:* 2357–68. https://doi.org/10.18653/v1/d18-1258.

Pandey, Abhishek, Kory Kreimeyer, Matthew Foster, Oanh Dang, Thomas Ly, Wei Wang, Richard Forshee, and Taxiarchis Botsis. 2019. "Adverse Event Extraction from Structured Product Labels Using the Event-Based Text-Mining of Health Electronic Records (ETHER) System." *Health Informatics Journal* 25 (4): 1232–43. https://doi.org/10.1177/1460458217749883.

Park, Min Sook, Zhe He, Zhiwei Chen, Sanghee Oh, and Jiang Bian. 2016. "Consumers' Use of Umls Concepts on Social Media: Diabetes-Related Textual Data Analysis in Blog and Social Q&A Sites." *JMIR Medical Informatics* 4 (4). https://doi.org/10.2196/medinform.5748.

Pasha, Syed Javeed, and E. Syed Mohamed. 2020. "Novel Feature Reduction (NFR) Model with Machine Learning and Data Mining Algorithms for Effective Disease Risk Prediction." *IEEE Access* 8: 184087–108. https://doi.org/10.1109/ACCESS.2020.3028714.

Pathak, Jyotishman, Kent R. Bailey, Calvin E. Beebe, Steven Bethard, David S. Carrell, Pei J. Chen, Dmitriy Dligach, et al. 2013. "Normalization and Standardization of Electronic Health Records for High-Throughput Phenotyping: The Sharpn Consortium." *Journal of the American Medical Informatics Association* 20 (E2): 341–48. https://doi.org/10.1136/amiajnl-2013-001939.

Pathak, Jyotishman, Sean P. Murphy, Brian N. Willaert, Hilal M. Kremers, Barbara P. Yawn, Walter A. Rocca, and Christopher G. Chute. 2011. "Using RxNorm and NDF-RT to Classify Medication Data Extracted from Electronic Health Records: Experiences from the Rochester Epidemiology Project." *AMIA... Annual Symposium Proceedings / AMIA Symposium. AMIA Symposium* 2011: 1089–98.

Patra, Sudhansu Shekhar, Om Praksah Jena, Gaurav Kumar, Sreyashi Pramanik, Chinmaya Misra, and Kamakhya Narain Singh. 2021. "Random Forest Algorithm in Imbalance Genomics Classification." *Data Analytics in Bioinformatics: A Machine Learning Perspective*, January, 173–90. https://doi.org/10.1002/9781119785620.CH7.

Patra, Sudhansu Shekhar, Mamta Mittal, and Om Prakash Jena. 2022. "Multiobjective Evolutionary Algorithm Based on Decomposition for Feature Selection in Medical Diagnosis." *Predictive Modeling in Biomedical Data Mining and Analysis*, 253–93. https://doi.org/10.1016/B978-0-323-99864-2.00005-6.

Pattnayak, Parthasarathi, and Om Prakash Jena. 2021. "Innovation on Machine Learning in Healthcare Services-An Introduction." *Machine Learning for Healthcare Applications*, January, 1–15. https://doi.org/10.1002/9781119792611.CH1.

Peissig, Peggy L., Luke V. Rasmussen, Richard L. Berg, James G. Linneman, Catherine A. McCarty, Carol Waudby, Lin Chen, et al. 2012. "Importance of Multi-Modal Approaches to Effectively Identify Cataract Cases from Electronic Health Records." *Journal of the American Medical Informatics Association* 19 (2): 225–34. https://doi.org/10.1136/amiajnl-2011-000456.

Peng, Jacqueline, Mengge Zhao, James Havrilla, Cong Liu, Chunhua Weng, Whitney Guthrie, Robert Schultz, Kai Wang, and Yunyun Zhou. 2020. "Natural Language Processing (NLP) Tools in Extracting Biomedical Concepts from Research Articles: A Case Study on Autism Spectrum Disorder." *BMC Medical Informatics and Decision Making* 20 (11): 1–9. https://doi.org/10.1186/s12911-020-01352-2.

Pérez-Rey, D., V Maojo, M. García-Remesal, R. Alonso-Calvo, H Billhardt, F. Martin-Sánchez, and A. Sousa. 2006. "ONTOFUSION: Ontology-Based Integration of Genomic and Clinical Databases." *Computers in Biology and Medicine* 36 (7-8): 712–30. https://doi.org/10.1016/j.compbiomed.2005.02.004.

Piliouras, Dimitrios, Ioannis Korkontzelos, Andrew Dowsey, and Sophia Ananiadou. 2013. "Dealing with Data Sparsity in Drug Named Entity Recognition." *Proceedings -2013 IEEE International Conference on Healthcare Informatics, ICHI 2013:* 14–21. https://doi.org/10.1109/ICHI.2013.9.

Posada, Jose D., Amie J. Barda, Lingyun Shi, Diyang Xue, Victor Ruiz, Pei Han Kuan, Neal D. Ryan, and Fuchiang (Rich) Tsui. 2017. "Predictive Modeling for Classification of Positive Valence System Symptom Severity from Initial Psychiatric Evaluation Records." *Journal of Biomedical Informatics* 75: S94–104. https://doi.org/10.1016/j.jbi.2017.05.019.

Prasad, Jayashree Rajesh, and Rajesh Prasad. 2008. "A Decision Support System for Agriculture Using Natural Language Processing (ADSS)." *Lecture Notes in Engineering and Computer Science* 2168 (1): 365–69.

Preum, Sarah Masud, Sirajum Munir, Meiyi Ma, Mohammad Samin Yasar, David J. Stone, Ronald Williams, Homa Alemzadeh, and John A. Stankovic. 2021. "A Review of Cognitive Assistants for Healthcare: Trends, Prospects, and Future Directions." *ACM Computing Surveys* 53 (6). https://doi.org/10.1145/3419368.

Qadri, Muhammad Tahir, and Muhammad Asif. 2009. "Automatic Number Plate Recognition System for Vehicle Identification Using Optical Character Recognition." In *2009 International Conference on Education Technology and Computer, ICETC 2009:* 335–38. https://doi.org/10.1109/ICETC.2009.54.

Quiroz, Juan C, Liliana Laranjo, Ahmet Baki Kocaballi, Shlomo Berkovsky, Dana Rezazadegan, and Enrico Coiera. 2019. "Challenges of Developing a Digital Scribe to Reduce Clinical Documentation Burden." *Npj Digital Medicine* 2 (1). https://doi.org/10.1038/s41746-019-0190-1.

Rahman, M Arif, Sarah M Preum, Ronald Williams, Homa Alemzadeh, and John A Stankovic. 2020. "Grace: Generating Summary Reports Automatically for Cognitive Assistance in Emergency Response." In *AAAI 2020-34th AAAI Conference on Artificial Intelligence:* 13356–62. https://doi.org/10.1609/aaai.v34i08.7049.

Rajani S, M. Hanumanthappa, and Computer. 2016. "Techniques of Semantic Analysis for Natural Language Processing - A Detailed Survey." *International Journal of Advanced Research in Computer and Communication Engineering ISO* 5 (2): 146–49. https://doi.org/10.17148/IJARCCE.

Randhawa, Gurdeeshpal, Mariella Ferreyra, Rukhsana Ahmed, Omar Ezzat, and Kevin Pottie. 2013. "Using Machine Translation in Clinical Practice." *Canadian Family Physician* 59 (4): 382–83.

Reátegui, Ruth, and Sylvie Ratté. 2018. "Comparison of MetaMap and CTAKES for Entity Extraction in Clinical Notes." *BMC Medical Informatics and Decision Making* 18 (Suppl 3). https://doi.org/10.1186/s12911-018-0654-2.

Reátegui, Ruth, Sylvie Ratté, Estefanía Bautista-Valarezo, and Víctor Duque. 2019. "Cluster Analysis of Obesity Disease Based on Comorbidities Extracted from Clinical Notes." *Journal of Medical Systems* 43 (3). https://doi.org/10.1007/s10916-019-1172-1.

Redjdal, Akram, Jacques Bouaud, Joseph Gligorov, and Brigitte Séroussi. 2021a. "Are Semantic Annotators Able to Extract Relevant Complexity-Related Concepts from Clinical Notes?" *Studies in Health Technology and Informatics* 287 (November): 153–57. https://doi.org/10.3233/SHTI210836.

---. 2021b. "Are Semantic Annotators Able to Extract Relevant Complexity-Related Concepts from Clinical Notes?" *Studies in Health Technology and Informatics* 287 (November): 153–57. https://doi.org/10.3233/SHTI210836.

Redman, Joseph S, Yamini Natarajan, Jason K Hou, Jingqi Wang, Muzammil Hanif, Hua Feng, Jennifer R Kramer, et al. 2017. "Accurate Identification of Fatty Liver Disease in Data Warehouse Utilizing Natural Language Processing." *Digestive Diseases and Sciences* 62 (10): 2713–18. https://doi.org/10.1007/s10620-017-4721-9.

Sabbir, Akm, Antonio Jimeno-Yepes, and Ramakanth Kavuluru. 2017. "Knowledge-Based Biomedical Word Sense Disambiguation with Neural Concept Embeddings." *Proceedings -2017 IEEE 17th International Conference on Bioinformatics and Bioengineering, BIBE 2017* 2018-January: 163–70. https://doi.org/10.1109/BIBE.2017.00-61.

Saeed Hassanpoura, Curtis P. Langlotz. 2016. "Information Extraction from Multi-Institutional Radiology Reports." *Artif Intell Med.* 66: 29–39. https://doi.org/10.1016/j.artmed.2015.09.007.

Sahoo, Himanshu S., Greg M. Silverman, Nicholas E. Ingraham, Monica I. Lupei, Michael A. Puskarich, Raymond L. Finzel, John Sartori, et al. 2021. "A Fast, Resource Efficient, and Reliable Rule-Based System for COVID-19 Symptom Identification." *JAMIA Open* 4 (3). https://doi.org/10.1093/JAMIAOPEN/OOAB070.

Salmasian, Hojjat, Daniel E. Freedberg, and Carol Friedman. 2013. "Deriving Comorbidities from Medical Records Using Natural Language Processing." *Journal of the American Medical Informatics Association* 20 (E2): 239–42. https://doi.org/10.1136/amiajnl-2013-001889.

Sangwan, Meetu, and Daulat Sihag. 2015. "Handwritten Signature Recognition, Verification and Dynamic Updation Using Neural Network." *International Journal of Advanced Research in Computer and Communication Engineering* 4 (8): 218–21. https://doi.org/10.17148/IJARCCE.2015.4846.

Sarioglu, Efsun, Kabir Yadav, and Hyeong-Ah Choi. 2013. "Topic Modeling Based Classification of Clinical Reports." *Proceedings of the ACL Student Research Workshop*, 67–73.

Savery, Max E, Willie J Rogers, Malvika Pillai, James G Mork, and Dina Demner-Fushman. 2020. "Chemical Entity Recognition for MEDLINE Indexing." *AMIA Joint Summits on Translational Science Proceedings. AMIA Joint Summits on Translational Science 2020*: 561–68.

Savova, Guergana K., Janet E. Olson, Sean P. Murphy, Victoria L. Cafourek, Fergus J. Couch, Matthew P. Goetz, James N. Ingle, Vera J. Suman, Christopher G. Chute, and Richard M. Weinshilboum. 2012. "Automated Discovery of Drug Treatment Patterns for Endocrine Therapy of Breast Cancer within an Electronic Medical Record." *Journal of the American Medical Informatics Association* 19 (E1): 83–89. https://doi.org/10.1136/amiajnl-2011-000295.

Savova, Guergana K, James J Masanz, Philip V Ogren, Jiaping Zheng, Sunghwan Sohn, Karin C. Kipper-Schuler, and Christopher G Chute. 2010. "Mayo Clinical Text Analysis and Knowledge Extraction System (CTAKES): Architecture, Component Evaluation and Applications." *Journal of the American Medical Informatics Association* 17 (5): 507–13. https://doi.org/10.1136/jamia.2009.001560.

Scheurwegs, Elyne, Madhumita Sushil, Stéphan Tulkens, Walter Daelemans, and Kim Luyckx. 2017. "Counting Trees in Random Forests: Predicting Symptom Severity in Psychiatric Intake Reports." *Journal of Biomedical Informatics* 75 (2017): S112–19. https://doi.org/10.1016/j.jbi.2017.06.007.

Schloss, Benjamin, and Sandeep Konam. 2020. "Towards an Automated SOAP Note: Classifying Utterances from Medical Conversations." *Proceedings of Machine Learning Research*: 1–21. https://arxiv.org/abs/2007.08749.

Segura-Bedmar, Isabel, Cristobal Colón-Ruíz, Miguél Ángel Tejedor-Alonso, and Mar Moro-Moro. 2018. "Predicting of Anaphylaxis in Big Data EMR by Exploring Machine Learning Approaches." *Journal of Biomedical Informatics* 87 (September): 50–59. https://doi.org/10.1016/j.jbi.2018.09.012.

Sevenster, Merlijn, Rob Van Ommering, and Yuechen Qian. 2012. "Automatically Correlating Clinical Findings and Body Locations in Radiology Reports Using MedLEE." *Journal of Digital Imaging* 25 (2): 240–49. https://doi.org/10.1007/s10278-011-9411-0.

Shah-Mohammadi, Fatemeh, Wanting Cui, and Joseph Finkelstein. 2021a. "Comparison of ACM and CLAMP for Entity Extraction in Clinical Notes." *Annual International Conference of the IEEE Engineering in Medicine and Biology Society. IEEE Engineering in Medicine and Biology Society. Annual International Conference 2021*: 1989–92. https://doi.org/10.1109/EMBC46164.2021.9630611.

---. 2021b. "Entity Extraction for Clinical Notes, a Comparison Between MetaMap and Amazon Comprehend Medical." *Studies in Health Technology and Informatics* 281 (July): 258–62. https://doi.org/10.3233/SHTI210160.

Shahane, P.R., A.S. Choukade, and A.N. Diyewar. 2015. "Online Signature Recognition Using Matlab." *IJIREEICE* 3 (2): 107–12. https://doi.org/10.17148/ijireeice.2015.3222.

Shannon, George J., Naga Rayapati, Steven M. Corns, and Donald C. Wunsch. 2021. "Comparative Study Using Inverse Ontology Cogency and Alternatives for Concept Recognition in the Annotated National Library of Medicine Database." *Neural Networks : The Official Journal of the International Neural Network Society* 139 (July): 86–104. https://doi.org/10.1016/J.NEUNET.2021.01.018.

Sheikhalishahi, Seyedmostafa, Riccardo Miotto, Joel T. Dudley, Alberto Lavelli, Fabio Rinaldi, and Venet Osmani. 2019. "Natural Language Processing of Clinical Notes on Chronic Diseases: Systematic Review." *JMIR Medical Informatics* 7 (2): 1–18. https://doi.org/10.2196/12239.

Shen, Feichen, David W. Larson, James M. Naessens, Elizabeth B. Habermann, Hongfang Liu, and Sunghwan Sohn. 2019. "Detection of Surgical Site Infection Utilizing Automated Feature Generation in Clinical Notes." *Journal of Healthcare Informatics Research* 3 (3): 267–82. https://doi.org/10.1007/s41666-018-0042-9.

Shen, Huiying, and James M. Coughlan. 2012. "Towards a Real-Time System for Finding and Reading Signs for Visually Impaired Users." In *Lecture Notes in Computer Science (Including Subseries Lecture Notes in Artificial Intelligence and Lecture Notes in Bioinformatics)*, 7383 LNCS:41–47. https://doi.org/10.1007/978-3-642-31534-3_7.

Shen, Zhengru, Xi Wang, and Marco Spruit. 2019. "Big Data Framework for Scalable and Efficient Biomedical Literature Mining in the Cloud." In *ACM International Conference Proceeding Series:* 80–86. https://doi.org/10.1145/3342827.3342843.

Simon, L. M., S. Karg, A. J. Westermann, M. Engel, A. H.A. Elbehery, B. Hense, M. Heinig, L. Deng, and F. J. Theis. 2018. "MetaMap: An Atlas of Metatranscriptomic Reads in Human Disease-Related RNA-Seq Data." *GigaScience* 7 (6): 1–8. https://doi.org/10.1093/gigascience/giy070.

Son, Jung Hoon, Gangcai Xie, Chi Yuan, Lyudmila Ena, Ziran Li, Andrew Goldstein, Lulin Huang, et al. 2018. "Deep Phenotyping on Electronic Health Records Facilitates Genetic Diagnosis by Clinical Exomes." *American Journal of Human Genetics* 103 (1): 58–73. https://doi.org/10.1016/j.ajhg.2018.05.010.

Soysal, Ergin, Jingqi Wang, Min Jiang, Yonghui Wu, Serguei Pakhomov, Hongfang Liu, and Hua Xu. 2018. "CLAMP – a Toolkit for Efficiently Building Customized Clinical Natural Language Processing Pipelines." *Journal of the American Medical Informatics Association* 25 (3): 331–36. https://doi.org/10.1093/jamia/ocx132.

Soysal, Ergin, Jeremy L. Warner, Jingqi Wang, Min Jiang, Krysten Harvey, Sandeep Kumar Jain, Xiao Dong, et al. 2019. "Developing Customizable Cancer Information Extraction Modules for Pathology Reports Using Clamp." In *Studies in Health Technology and Informatics*, 264:1041–45. https://doi.org/10.3233/SHTI190383.

Spiker, Jonathan, Kory Kreimeyer, Oanh Dang, Debra Boxwell, Vicky Chan, Connie Cheng, Paula Gish, et al. 2020. "Information Visualization Platform for Postmarket Surveillance Decision Support." *Drug Safety* 43 (9): 905–15. https://doi.org/10.1007/s40264-020-00945-0.

Stevenson, Mark, and Yikun Guo. 2010. "Disambiguation of Ambiguous Biomedical Terms Using Examples Generated from the UMLS Metathesaurus." *Journal of Biomedical Informatics* 43 (5): 762–73. https://doi.org/10.1016/j.jbi.2010.06.001.

Sulieman, Lina, Jamie R Robinson, and Gretchen P Jackson. 2020. "Automating the Classification of Complexity of Medical Decision-Making in Patient-Provider Messaging in a Patient Portal." *Journal of Surgical Research* 255: 224–32. https://doi.org/10.1016/j.jss.2020.05.039.

Sung, Sheng Feng, Chia Yi Lin, and Ya Han Hu. 2020. "EMR-Based Phenotyping of Ischemic Stroke Using Supervised Machine Learning and Text Mining Techniques." *IEEE Journal of Biomedical and Health Informatics* 24 (10): 2922–31. https://doi.org/10.1109/JBHI.2020.2976931.

Susan Rea, Jyotishman Pathak, Guergana Savova, Thomas A. Oniki, Les Westberg, Calvin E. Beebe, Cui Tao, Craig G. Parker, Peter J. Haug, Stanley M. Huff, and Christopher G. Chute. 2012. "Building a Robust, Scalable and Standards-Driven Infrastructure for Secondary Use of EHR Data: The SHARPn Project." *Journal of Biomedical Informatics* 45: 763–771. https://doi.org/10.1016/j.jbi.2012.01.009.Building.

Tang, Buzhou, Hongxin Cao, Yonghui Wu, Min Jiang, and Hua Xu. 2013. "Recognizing Clinical Entities in Hospital Discharge Summaries Using Structural Support Vector Machines with Word Representation Features." *BMC Medical Informatics and Decision Making* 13 (SUPPL1): S1. https://doi.org/10.1186/1472-6947-13-S1-S1.

Tchechmedjiev, Andon, Amine Abdaoui, Vincent Emonet, Soumia Melzi, Jitendra Jonnagaddala, and Clement Jonquet. 2018. "Enhanced Functionalities for Annotating and Indexing Clinical Text with the NCBO Annotator+." *Bioinformatics* 34 (11): 1962–65. https://doi.org/10.1093/bioinformatics/bty009.

Tianyong Hao, Chunhua Weng. 2015. "Adaptive Semantic Tag Mining from Heterogeneous Clinical Research Texts." *Methods of Information in Medicine* 2 (4): 164–70. https://doi.org/10.3414/ME13-01-0130.

Timothy Miller, Dmitriy Dligach, Steven Bethard, Chen Lin, and Guergana Savova. 2017. "Towards Generalizable Entity-Centric Clinical Coreference Resolution." *Journal of Biomedical Informatics* 69: 251–58. https://doi.org/10.1016/j.jbi.2017.04.015. Towards.

Topaz, Maxim, Kenneth Lai, Dawn Dowding, Victor J Lei, Anna Zisberg, Kathryn H Bowles, and Li Zhou. 2016. "Automated Identification of Wound Information in Clinical Notes of Patients with Heart Diseases: Developing and Validating a Natural Language Processing Application." *International Journal of Nursing Studies* 64: 25–31. https://doi.org/10.1016/j.ijnurstu.2016.09.013.

Trenkle, J., A. Gillies, S. Erlanson, S. Schlosser, and S. Cavin. 2001. "Advances In Arabic Text Recognition." *Symposium on Document Image Understanding Technology (SDIUT 2001)*, no. May 2001: 159–68.

Trivedi, Vishal. 2018. "Lexical and Syntax Analysis in Compiler Design." *International Journal of Creative Research Thoughts (IJCRT)* 6 (1): 634–38.

Tseytlin, Eugene, Kevin Mitchell, Elizabeth Legowski, Julia Corrigan, Girish Chavan, and Rebecca S. Jacobson. 2016. "NOBLE - Flexible Concept Recognition for Large-Scale Biomedical Natural Language Processing." *BMC Bioinformatics* 17 (1): 1–15. https://doi.org/10.1186/s12859-015-0871-y.

Tsuji, Shintaro, Andrew Wen, Naoki Takahashi, Hongjian Zhang, Katsuhiko Ogasawara, and Gouqian Jiang. 2021. "Developing a RadLex-Based Named Entity Recognition Tool for Mining Textual Radiology Reports: Development and Performance Evaluation Study." *Journal of Medical Internet Research* 23 (10). https://doi.org/10.2196/25378.

Tulkens, Stéphan, Simon Šuster, and Walter Daelemans. 2019. "Unsupervised Concept Extraction from Clinical Text through Semantic Composition." *Journal of Biomedical Informatics* 91 (February): 103120. https://doi.org/10.1016/j.jbi.2019.103120.

University, Northwestern, University of Utah, and University or North Carolina. 2015. "Concept-Based Information Retrieval for Clinical Case Summaries." *Trec.Nist. Gov.* https://trec.nist.gov/pubs/trec24/papers/NU_UU_UNC-CL.pdf%5Cnpapers3://publication/uuid/446B8AB8-D87E-4576-8D50-6E024AD7692E.

Vasudeven, Karthy, and Ajay James. 2015. "A Survey on Optical Character Recognition System." *Journal of Information & Communication Technology-JICT* 10 (December): 16–23. https://doi.org/10.3850/978-981-09-5346-1_cse-024.

Venkataraman, Guhan Ram, Arturo Lopez Pineda, Oliver J. Bear Don't Walk, Ashley M. Zehnder, Sandeep Ayyar, Rodney L. Page, Carlos D. Bustamante, and Manuel A. Rivas. 2020. "FastTag: Automatic Text Classification of Unstructured Medical Narratives." *PLoS ONE* 15 (6 June): 1–18. https://doi.org/10.1371/journal.pone.0234647.

Vij, Anneketh, and Jyotika Pruthi. 2018. "An Automated Psychometric Analyzer Based on Sentiment Analysis and Emotion Recognition for Healthcare." In *Procedia Computer Science*, 132:1184–91. Elsevier B.V. https://doi.org/10.1016/j.procs.2018.05.033.

Vogel, Markus, Wolfgang Kaisers, Ralf Wassmuth, and Ertan Mayatepek. 2015. "Analysis of Documentation Speed Using Web-Based Medical Speech Recognition Technology: Randomized Controlled Trial." *Journal of Medical Internet Research* 17 (11): 1–12. https://doi.org/10.2196/jmir.5072.

Wadia, Roxanne, Kathleen Akgun, Cynthia Brandt, Brenda T. Fenton, Woody Levin, Andrew H. Marple, Vijay Garla, Michal G. Rose, Tamar Taddei, and Caroline Taylor. 2018. "Comparison of Natural Language Processing and Manual Coding for the Identification of Cross-Sectional Imaging Reports Suspicious for Lung Cancer." *JCO Clinical Cancer Informatics*, no. 2: 1–7. https://doi.org/10.1200/cci.17.00069.

Wagholikar, Kavishwar B., Manabu Torii, Siddhartha R. Jonnalagadda, and Hongfang Liu. 2013. "Pooling Annotated Corpora for Clinical Concept Extraction." *Journal of Biomedical Semantics* 4 (1): 3. https://doi.org/10.1186/2041-1480-4-3.

Wang, Jingqi MS, Huy BS Anh Pham, Frank Manion, Masoud Rouhizadeh, and Yaoyun Zhang. 2020. "COVID-19 SignSym – A Fast Adaptation of General Clinical NLP Tools to Identify and Normalize COVID-19 Signs and Symptoms to OMOP Common Data Model." *ArXiv*, July. /pmc/articles/PMC7480086/.

Wang, Yanshan, Saeed Mehrabi, Sunghwan Sohn, Elizabeth J. Atkinson, Shreyasee Amin, and Hongfang Liu. 2019. "Natural Language Processing of Radiology Reports for Identification of Skeletal Site-Specific Fractures." *BMC Medical Informatics and Decision Making* 19 (S3): 73. https://doi.org/10.1186/s12911-019-0780-5.

Wang, Yanshan, Majid Rastegar-mojarad, Ravikumar Komandur-elayavilli, Sijia Liu, and Hongfang Liu. 2016. "An Ensemble Model of Clinical Information Extraction and Information Retrieval for Clinical Decision Support." *Proceedings of The Twenty-Fifth Text REtrieval Conference, TREC 2016.*

Wang, Yanshan, Sunghwan Sohn, Sijia Liu, Feichen Shen, Liwei Wang, Elizabeth J Atkinson, Shreyasee Amin, and Hongfang Liu. 2019. "A Clinical Text Classification Paradigm Using Weak Supervision and Deep Representation 08 Information and Computing Sciences 0801 Artificial Intelligence and Image Processing 17 Psychology and Cognitive Sciences 1702 Cognitive Sciences." *BMC Medical Informatics and Decision Making* 19 (1): 1–13. https://doi.org/10.1186/s12911-018-0723-6.

Wei, Qiang, Zongcheng Ji, Yuqi Si, Jingcheng Du, Jingqi Wang, Firat Tiryaki, Stephen Wu, Cui Tao, Kirk Roberts, and Hua Xu. 2019. "Relation Extraction from Clinical Narratives Using Pre-Trained Language Models." *AMIA... Annual Symposium Proceedings.* AMIA Symposium *2019* (April): 1236–45.

Weng, Wei Hung, Kavishwar B. Wagholikar, Alexa T. McCray, Peter Szolovits, and Henry C. Chueh. 2017. "Medical Subdomain Classification of Clinical Notes Using a Machine Learning-Based Natural Language Processing Approach." *BMC Medical Informatics and Decision Making* 17 (1): 1–13. https://doi.org/10.1186/s12911-017-0556-8.

Willis, Matt, and Mohammad Hossein Jarrahi. 2019. "Automating Documentation: A Critical Perspective into the Role of Artificial Intelligence in Clinical Documentation." In *Lecture Notes in Computer Science (Including Subseries Lecture Notes in Artificial Intelligence and Lecture Notes in Bioinformatics)*, 11420 LNCS:200–209. https://doi.org/10.1007/978-3-030-15742-5_19.

Wołk, Krzysztof, and Krzysztof Marasek. 2015. "Neural-Based Machine Translation for Medical Text Domain. Based on European Medicines Agency Leaflet Texts." In *Procedia Computer Science*, 64:2–9. Elsevier Masson SAS. https://doi.org/10.1016/j.procs.2015.08.456.

Wu, Julia, Venkatesh Sivaraman, Dheekshita Kumar, Juan M. Banda, and David Sontag. 2021. "Pulse of the Pandemic: Iterative Topic Filtering for Clinical Information Extraction from Social Media." *Journal of Biomedical Informatics* 120 (February). https://doi.org/10.48550/arxiv.2102.06836.

Wu, Stephen T., Vinod C. Kaggal, Dmitriy Dligach, James J. Masanz, Pei Chen, Lee Becker, Wendy W. Chapman, Guergana K. Savova, Hongfang Liu, and Christopher G. Chute. 2013. "A Common Type System for Clinical Natural Language Processing." *Journal of Biomedical Semantics* 4 (1): 1–12. https://doi.org/10.1186/2041-1480-4-1.

Wu, Yonghui, Joshua C. Denny, S. Trent Rosenbloom, Randolph A. Miller, Dario A. Giuse, and Hua Xu. 2012. "A Comparative Study of Current Clinical Natural Language Processing Systems on Handling Abbreviations in Discharge Summaries." *AMIA... Annual Symposium Proceedings / AMIA Symposium. AMIA Symposium 2012*: 997–1003.

Wu, Yonghui, Min Jiang, Jun Xu, Degui Zhi, and Hua Xu. 2017. "Clinical Named Entity Recognition Using Deep Learning Models." *AMIA... Annual Symposium Proceedings. AMIA Symposium 2017*: 1812–19.

Wu, Yonghui, Xi Yang, Jiang Bian, Yi Guo, Hua Xu, and William Hogan. 2018. "Combine Factual Medical Knowledge and Distributed Word Representation to Improve Clinical Named Entity Recognition." *AMIA... Annual Symposium Proceedings. AMIA Symposium 2018*: 1110–17.

Xing, Rui, Jie Luo, and Tengwei Song. 2020. "BioRel: Towards Large-Scale Biomedical Relation Extraction." *BMC Bioinformatics* 21 (16): 1–13. https://doi.org/10.1186/s12859-020-03889-5.

Xu, Hua, Zhenming Fu, Anushi Shah, Yukun Chen, Neeraja B. Peterson, Qingxia Chen, Subramani Mani, Mia A. Levy, Q. Dai, and Josh C. Denny. 2011. "Extracting and Integrating Data from Entire Electronic Health Records for Detecting Colorectal Cancer Cases." *AMIA... Annual Symposium Proceedings / AMIA Symposium. AMIA Symposium 2011*: 1564–72.

Xu, Kai, Zhanfan Zhou, Tao Gong, Tianyong Hao, and Wenyin Liu. 2018. "SBLC: A Hybrid Model for Disease Named Entity Recognition Based on Semantic Bidirectional LSTMs and Conditional Random Fields." *BMC Medical Informatics and Decision Making* 18 (Suppl 5). https://doi.org/10.1186/s12911-018-0690-y.

Xu, Yan, Kai Hong, Junichi Tsujii, and Eric I-chao Chang. 2012. "Feature Engineering Combined with Machine Learning and Rule-Based Methods for Structured Information Extraction from Narrative Clinical Discharge Summaries." *Journal of the American Medical Informatics Association* 19 (5): 824–32. https://doi.org/10.1136/amiajnl-2011-000776.

Yadav, Shweta, Asif Ekbal, Sriparna Saha, and Pushpak Bhattacharyya. 2019. "Medical Sentiment Analysis Using Social Media: Towards Building a Patient Assisted System." In *LREC 2018-11th International Conference on Language Resources and Evaluation*: 2790–97.

Yan, Zihao, Ronilda Lacson, Ivan Ip, Vladimir Valtchinov, Ali Raja, David Osterbur, and Ramin Khorasani. 2016. "Evaluating Terminologies to Enable Imaging-Related Decision Rule Sharing." *AMIA... Annual Symposium Proceedings. AMIA Symposium* 2016 (9): 2082–89. https://www.ncbi.nlm.nih.gov/pubmed/28269968.

Yao, Liang, Chengsheng Mao, and Yuan Luo. 2019. "Clinical Text Classification with Rule-Based Features and Knowledge-Guided Convolutional Neural Networks." *BMC Medical Informatics and Decision Making* 19 (Suppl 3). https://doi.org/10.1186/s12911-019-0781-4.

Ye, Ye, Fuchiang Rich Tsui, Michael Wagner, Jeremy U Espino, and Qi Li. 2014. "Influenza Detection from Emergency Department Reports Using Natural Language Processing and Bayesian Network Classifiers." *Journal of the American Medical Informatics Association* 21 (5): 815–23. https://doi.org/10.1136/amiajnl-2013-001934.

Zahid, M. A. H., Ankush Mittal, R. C. Joshi, and G. Atluri. 2018. "CLINIQA: A Machine Intelligence Based Clinical Question Answering System," no. 1: 1–30. https://arxiv.org/abs/1805.05927.

Zeng, Qing T., Sergey Goryachev, Scott Weiss, Margarita Sordo, Shawn N. Murphy, and Ross Lazarus. 2006. "Extracting Principal Diagnosis, Co-Morbidity and Smoking Status for Asthma Research: Evaluation of a Natural Language Processing System." *BMC Medical Informatics and Decision Making* 6: 1–9. https://doi.org/10.1186/1472-6947-6-30.

Zeng, Zexian, Yu Deng, Xiaoyu Li, Tristan Naumann, and Yuan Luo. 2019. "Natural Language Processing for EHR-Based Computational Phenotyping." *IEEE/ACM Transactions on Computational Biology and Bioinformatics* 16 (1): 139–53. https://doi.org/10.1109/TCBB.2018.2849968.

Zeng, Zexian, Sasa Espino, Ankita Roy, Xiaoyu Li, Seema A Khan, Susan E Clare, Xia Jiang, Richard Neapolitan, and Yuan Luo. 2018. "Using Natural Language Processing and Machine Learning to Identify Breast Cancer Local Recurrence." *BMC Bioinformatics* 19 (Suppl 17). https://doi.org/10.1186/s12859-018-2466-x.

Zeng, Zexian, Liang Yao, Ankita Roy, Xiaoyu Li, Sasa Espino, Susan E Clare, Seema A Khan, and Yuan Luo. 2019. "Identifying Breast Cancer Distant Recurrences from Electronic Health Records Using Machine Learning." *Journal of Healthcare Informatics Research* 3 (3): 283–99. https://doi.org/10.1007/s41666-019-00046-3.

Zhang, Xingyu, Joyce Kim, Rachel E. Patzer, Stephen R Pitts, Aaron Patzer, and Justin D. Schrager. 2017. "Prediction of Emergency Department Hospital Admission Based on Natural Language Processing and Neural Networks." *Methods of Information in Medicine* 56 (5): 377–89. https://doi.org/10.3414/ME17-01-0024.

Zhao, Juan, Monika E. Grabowska, Vern Eric Kerchberger, Joshua C. Smith, H. Nur Eken, Qi Ping Feng, Josh F. Peterson, S. Trent Rosenbloom, Kevin B. Johnson, and Wei Qi Wei. 2021a. "ConceptWAS: A High-Throughput Method for Early Identification of COVID-19 Presenting Symptoms and Characteristics from Clinical Notes." *Journal of Biomedical Informatics*. https://doi.org/10.1016/j.jbi.2021.103748.

Zhao, Juan, Monika E Grabowska, Vern Eric Kerchberger, Joshua C Smith, H Nur Eken, Qi Ping Feng, Josh F Peterson, S. Trent Rosenbloom, Kevin B Johnson, and Wei Qi Wei. 2021b. "ConceptWAS: A High-Throughput Method for Early Identification of COVID-19 Presenting Symptoms and Characteristics from Clinical Notes." *Journal of Biomedical Informatics*. https://doi.org/10.1016/j.jbi.2021.103748.

Zheng, Jiaping, Wendy W Chapman, Rebecca S Crowley, and Guergana K Savova. 2011. "Coreference Resolution: A Review of General Methodologies and Applications in the Clinical Domain." *Journal of Biomedical Informatics*. Elsevier Inc. https://doi.org/10.1016/j.jbi.2011.08.006.

Zheng, Jiaping, Wendy W Chapman, Timothy A Miller, Chen Lin, Rebecca S Crowley, and Guergana K Savova. 2012. "A System for Coreference Resolution for the Clinical Narrative." *Journal of the American Medical Informatics Association* 19 (4): 660–67. https://doi.org/10.1136/amiajnl-2011-000599.

Zheng, Shuai, Fusheng Wang, and James J. Lu. 2013. "ASLForm: An Adaptive Self Learning Medical Form Generating System." *AMIA... Annual Symposium Proceedings / AMIA Symposium. AMIA Symposium 2013*: 1590–99.

Zhou, L, Y Lu, C J Vitale, P L Mar, F Chang, N Dhopeshwarkar, and R A Rocha. 2014. "Representation of Information about Family Relatives as Structured Data in Electronic Health Records." *Applied Clinical Informatics* 5 (2): 349–67. https://doi.org/10.4338/ACI-2013-10-RA-0080.

Zhou, Li, Amy W. Baughman, Victor J Lei, Kenneth H. Lai, Amol S Navathe, Frank Chang, Margarita Sordo, et al. 2015. "Identifying Patients with Depression Using Free-Text Clinical Documents." In *Studies in Health Technology and Informatics*, 216:629–33. https://doi.org/10.3233/978-1-61499-564-7-629.

Zhou, Li, Joseph M Plasek, Lisa M Mahoney, Frank Y Chang, Dana DiMaggio, and Roberto A Rocha. 2012. "Mapping Partners Master Drug Dictionary to RxNorm Using an NLP-Based Approach." *Journal of Biomedical Informatics* 45 (4): 626–33. https://doi.org/10.1016/j.jbi.2011.11.006.

Zhou, Li, Joseph M Plasek, Lisa M Mahoney, Neelima Karipineni, Frank Chang, Xuemin Yan, Fenny Chang, Dana Dimaggio, Debora S Goldman, and Roberto A Rocha. 2011. "Using Medical Text Extraction, *Reasoning and Mapping System (MTERMS) to Process Medication Information in Outpatient Clinical Notes*." *AMIA... Annual Symposium Proceedings / AMIA Symposium. AMIA Symposium 2011*: 1639–48.

Zhu, Qian, Hongfang Liu, Christopher G. Chute, and Matthew Ferber. 2015. "EHR Based Genetic Testing Knowledge Base (IGTKB) Development." *BMC Medical Informatics and Decision Making* 15 (4): S3. https://doi.org/10.1186/1472-6947-15-S4-S3.

Zolnoori, Maryam, Kin Wah Fung, Timothy B. Patrick, Paul Fontelo, Hadi Kharrazi, Anthony Faiola, Yi Shuan Shirley Wu, et al. 2019. "A Systematic Approach for Developing a Corpus of Patient Reported Adverse Drug Events: A Case Study for SSRI and SNRI Medications." *Journal of Biomedical Informatics* 90 (December 2018): 103091. https://doi.org/10.1016/j.jbi.2018.12.005.

Index